INTERMEDIATE
STATISTICS
A Modern Approach
Second Edition

INTERMEDIATE STATISTICS
A Modern Approach
Second Edition

James P. Stevens
University of Cincinnati

LAWRENCE ERLBAUM ASSOCIATES, PUBLISHERS
1999   Mahwah, New Jersey   London

Lawrence Erlbaum Associates, Inc., Publishers
10 Industrial Avenue
Mahwah, New Jersey 07430

Library of Congress Cataloging-in-Publication Data

Stevens, James.
   Intermediate statistics : a modern approach / James P. Stevens. --
2nd ed.
    p. cm.
   Includes bibliographical references and index.
   ISBN 0-8058-2960-1 (cloth : alk. paper). --ISBN 0-8058-2961-X
(pbk. : alk. paper)
   1. Statistics. I. Title.
QA276.S828 1999
519.5--dc21   99-32699
                                          CIP

Books published by Lawrence Erlbaum Associates are printed
on acid-free paper, and their bindings are chosen
for strength and durability.

Printed in the United States of America

10 9 8 7 6 5 4 3 2 1

To my wife, Florence,
and my three sons—Mark, Jerry, and Jimmy

Contents

Preface

This book is written for applied social science researchers at the advanced undergraduate or beginning graduate level. The text emphasizes conceptual understanding of the statistical techniques (definitional formulas along with considerable narrative discussion are employed), the effective use of statistical software to run the analyses, and the correct interpretation of the printout that results from such runs. The two remaining major statistical software packages, SPSS and SAS, are an integral part of each chapter, as the cover design suggests. Incidentally, since the first edition of this text, SPSS has bought out BMDP and SYSTAT.

There are three major changes in the second edition of this text:

1. Perhaps the most fundamental change for the entire book is the advent of "windows," and running analyses by simply clicking a series of buttons. I have illustrated this approach in some detail, using the SPSS package. A lot has changed in the computer world since the first edition of this text, and one major change is the increasing use of the World Wide Web. SAS and SPSS are located on the Web and their addresses are: WWW.SAS.COM and WWW.SPSS.COM. In this regard, it is of interest to note that the SPSS newsletter (KEYWORDS) is no longer printed, but is available on the Web.

2. I have added a chapter on multiple regression. Much of the material in this chapter is taken from my multivariate text (Stevens, 1996), but I have eliminated the matrix algebra and toned the material down to a more readable level.

3. Power analysis was an important feature of the first edition of this text. Since the first edition, I have become aware of, and have on my notebook computer, a very nice and fast program that does power analysis for a variety

of designs. It is called PASS 6.0, and was written by Dr. Jerry Ilintze. This program does power analysis for *t* tests, one way ANOVA, and factorial ANOVA (up to a three way design). This program is very nice for trying out different sample sizes, alpha levels and effect sizes in experimental planning.

I am still firmly committed to several principles that I stated in the preface to the first edition of this text, and I reiterate them below:

1. The running of all analyses with both of the major statistical packages continues to be a theme. I still firmly believe that any modern statistics book should feature at least one of the packages. Again, I have included both SPSS and SAS to give the instructor some flexibility.

2. Selected, annotated printout is given from at least one of the packages for each analysis. It is important to have the explanation right on the printout, or on the same page. As I stated in the first edition, for students to have to flip back and forth from printout to explanation in the body of the text is awkward and reduces learning efficiency.

3. The assumptions underlying each analysis are given special attention, and the reader is shown how to test the critical assumption(s) using SPSS and SAS.

4. Power analysis is an integral part of the book. In addition to Cohen's tables in the back, there is now the very nice PASS program for quickly obtaining power results for differing sample sizes and alpha levels simultaneously.

5. There are no computational formulas in this text. I took the position that they are not needed about ten years ago, and it is even more true today.

The instructional mix of strategies that is employed to illustrate each statistical technique consists of two parts: (a) First, I use definitional formulas on small data sets. These formulas are useful in conveying conceptual insight into what is being measured or quantified; (b) Then I proceed directly to the use of the packages to indicate how to efficiently process data. I feel very strongly about using the above strategies for teaching statistics, and have employed this approach for 25 years.

Although familiarity with the packages is essential, because they are most likely to be used in practice, merely presenting printout is not sufficient. Students need guidance as to what numbers to zero in on from the printout, and what those numbers mean. Also, the order of examining the printout becomes important, such as first looking at printout related to data screening (checking for outliers), then looking at printout related to a check of any crucial assumption(s), and finally, looking at printout pertaining to the main hypothesis or hypotheses being tested. Jumping right to the main hypothesis being tested can be very misleading if an outlier is present, or if a certain critical assumption is violated, and this needs to be stressed.

The reader should have a background of a one quarter course in statistics that has covered at least the t tests for independent and dependent samples. The mathematics has been deliberately toned down, although there are a few proofs sprinkled throughout the text.

The exercises involve a mixture of numerical, conceptual, and computer-related problems. I have de-emphasized purely numerical exercises, for I agree entirely with Cobb (1987, p. 323) that "computing rules are just the skin of our subject; it is focus that reveals the skeleton of fundamental concepts and connections that hold the body of knowledge together." Answers are provided to half the exercises in the book. The answers to the remaining exercises are available for instructors from the publisher.

On the quarter system I have been able to cover one, two, and three way ANOVA and ANCOVA (although some of the original chapter from my multivariate book is omitted). It seems possible to me that on a semester system all of these could be covered in addition to an abbreviated treatment of repeated measures and an introduction to multiple regression.

There are many people to thank. The three reviewers for this second edition provided many pages of constructive criticism. Listed alphabetically, they are George Cobb (Mt. Holyoke College), Lynne Edwards and Joseph Wisenbaker (University of Georgia). I am very indebted to them for their thoughtful comments and insights. Three individuals at Lawrence Erlbaum Associates were also quite helpful. Larry Erlbaum continues to be very supportive and helpful. Judy Amsel was instrumental in motivating me to write this second edition. Art Lizza again did an excellent job in getting the book out.

James P. Stevens

1 Introduction

1.1 FOCUS AND OVERVIEW OF TOPICS

This book has been written for applied social science researchers at the advanced undergraduate or beginning graduate level. It is assumed that you have had a one quarter course in beginning statistics that covered measures of central tendency, measures of variability, standard scores (z, T, stanines, etc.), correlation, and inferential statistics, including at least the t tests for independent and dependent samples. In the next four sections of this chapter, we review briefly some descriptive statistics, summation notation, and testing for a "significant"

1

difference. These sections are not intended to thoroughly teach this material again, but to refresh your memory.

The emphasis in the book is on conceptual understanding of the statistical techniques, learning how to effectively use statistical software to run the analyses, and learning how to interpret the computer printout that results from such runs. The two major statistical packages, SAS (Statistical Analysis System) and SPSS (Statistical Package for the Social Sciences), are an integral part of this book. Details on SAS and SPSS are given in Section 1.7. I have attempted to make the text as practical as possible. To accent the practical emphasis, eight real data sets have been provided in Appendix A in the back of the book. For convenience, these data sets are also available on a 3.5-inch disk. Some of the exercises in the chapters involve running these data sets, or a part of a real data set. Singer and Willett (1988) have provided an excellent annotated bibliography, indicating where numerous other real data sets may be found.

The instructional mix of strategies adopted to illustrate each statistical technique involves two parts:

1. First, we illustrate each technique using *definitional* formulas on small data sets. These formulas are useful in yielding conceptual insight into what is being measured or quantified. As a simple example, the definitional formula for sample variance is

$$s^2 = [(x_1 - \bar{x})^2 + (x_2 - \bar{x})^2 + \cdots + (x_n - \bar{x})^2]/(n - 1)$$

This formula shows very clearly that variance is measuring how much the scores for the subjects scatter or disperse about the mean.

2. Then we move directly to the computer, that is, to the statistical packages, to show how to efficiently process data. And more importantly, how to interpret the printout from the packages. In practice, analyses will very likely be run on one or more of these packages, and thus it is important to become familiar with them.

Now we give an overview of the topics in the book. The reader may recall that the t test for independent samples is appropriate for comparing two groups to determine whether they differ on the average on a dependent variable. But what if we wish to compare more than two groups *simultaneously* on a dependent variable? For example, we wish to compare the effect of four counseling methods on attitude toward education. Then a statistical procedure called analysis of variance is needed. This technique is covered in Chapter 2. Suppose that for this example there was reason to believe that the sex of the subjects might moderate the effect of the counseling methods, and we wanted to check this possibility. This would lead us to a more complicated analysis of variance design, since we are examining the effect of two independent variables (sex and counseling method) on attitude toward education. It is an example of a factorial design. These designs are covered in Chapter 4.

Chapter 3 deals with power analysis. The power of a statistical test is the probability of rejecting the null hypothesis when it is false. Although it may seem obvious that we would want to achieve this, many researchers in the literature have failed to do so, as Cohen (1969) and others have pointed out. The reason is that power is generally inadequate with small group sizes (especially with 20 or less subjects per group), and in some areas of research such sample sizes are quite common for pragmatic or other reasons. Chapter 3 provides a detailed and practical approach to estimating the power of completed studies and also for estimating sample size required for adequate power in an upcoming study—a very nice feature, since the first edition of this text is the PASS 6.0 program, which is inexpensive, fast, and easy to use. It enables one to try out different sample sizes for different alpha levels quite easily.

In Chapter 5 we treat the class of situations in which the same subjects are measured more than twice on a dependent variable. For example, suppose a dietitian wishes to assess the immediate and long term effects of a behavior modification approach on weight loss for a group of overweight men. She measures the weight loss immediately following treatment and then 7 additional times (in three month intervals) over a two year period. The appropriate statistical analysis here is a different type of analysis of variance from that in Chapter 2, called repeated measures analysis. The simplest case of a repeated measures design measures the subjects just twice, e.g., pretest–treatment–posttest. The investigator is interested in testing for a significant gain or change on the dependent variable, and the appropriate test is the t test for correlated (dependent) samples that you studied in beginning statistics.

Chapter 6, which is a new addition to my intermediate text, deals with multiple regression. Much of the material is taken from my multivariate text (Stevens, 1996). Multiple regression is a much used and abused technique. One of the problems is that many researchers use multiple regression without validating their results on an independent sample of data. I have made validating the model a major theme in this chapter.

Analysis of covariance is now found in Chapter 7. This technique combines analysis of variance and regression analysis. Because of this, and because of the suggestions of two reviewers of this edition, I have covariance after regression and ANOVA. A covariate is a variable that is significantly correlated with the dependent variable. Analysis of covariance can be quite helpful in randomized studies, that is, studies where the subjects have been randomly assigned to the treatments, in increasing the sensitivity (power) of an experiment.

Analysis of variance procedures and multiple regression are used very often in the literature. Thus it is important to learn this material in order to be able to intelligently and critically read the literature.

1.2   SOME BASIC DESCRIPTIVE STATISTICS

The measure of central tendency that is used most frequently is the mean or average for a set of scores. It is defined as

$$\bar{x} = (x_1 + x_2 + \cdots + x_n)/n,$$

where n is the number of subjects and x_1 is the score for subject 1 on variable x, x_2 is the score for subject 2, etc. The mean is an example of a summary statistic—it summarizes an important or salient feature of a set of data. For example, if you are told that the average weight for a pro football lineman is 280 pounds, or that the average income of people living in a certain community is $80,000, each of these numbers packs a message. The average weight of 280 pounds indicates that the weights of most linemen tend to cluster around that value, and the income of $80,000 means that the incomes of most people in that community cluster around $80,000. These statements are accurate provided that there are no extreme values or outliers (see Section 1.6).

Although the mean is useful in characterizing one important feature of a set of data, it can be misleading just by itself. To see this consider the following scores for three groups of 10 children each on a 20 item pretest in mathematics:

Group 1	Group 2	Group 3
10	10	10
13	11	18
7	11	2
12	10	13
13	12	17
11	11	3
8	11	8
14	10	15
9	12	19
12	11	4
$\bar{x}_1 = 10.9$	$\bar{x}_2 = 10.9$	$\bar{x}_3 = 10.9$

On the average there is no difference between these three groups of children. However, there *is* a major difference among the groups in terms of variability of the scores about the mean. One can see intuitively that there is the least variability for group 2 (since the scores cluster very tightly about the mean of 10.9), while variability is greatest for group 3. This differential amount of variability would have definite instructional implications, if you had to teach one of these three groups mathematics. Other things being equal, group 2 would be easier to teach since they are all at about the same level of ability.

To quantify the amount of variability in a set of scores we use the sample variance s_2, the *definitional* formula of which is

$$s^2 = \frac{(x_1 - \bar{x})^2 + (x_2 - \bar{x})^2 + \cdots + (x_n - \bar{x})^2}{n - 1}$$

Notice that variance simply measures how much the scores vary about the mean. Now we find the variances for the three groups of children. Although the emphasis in this book is on using the computer for doing statistical analysis, there is a wide array of very inexpensive calculators that are conveniently used for calculating the mean and variance for a set of data. In Appendix 1 at the end of this chapter we give the details for the TI-30Xa and CASIO fx-300SA for the children in group 1. The variances for the three groups are: $s_1^2 = 5.43$, $s_2^2 = .54$, and $s_3^2 = 41.43$.

Summary statistics like the mean and variance are especially useful in comparing different data sets (groups of subjects) on the same variable. Consider the following two sets of scores, which represent the age of 25 automobile salesmen in the United States and 25 automobile salesmen in Western Europe:

United States					Western Europe				
23	63	25	22	32	43	26	30	27	40
56	30	34	56	30	35	48	36	47	41
25	48	44	27	26	34	45	30	38	33
38	26	30	39	30	35	44	24	33	40
36	32	36	38	33	31	23	29	37	28

It is far from obvious by just looking at these sets how the ages for the two groups differ, if at all. Computation of the mean and variance for the groups yields: U.S. ($\bar{x} = 35.16$, $s^2 = 117.22$) and Western Europe ($\bar{x} = 35.08$, $s^2 = 51.16$). These statistics indicate that the average age is about the same for the groups and that the variability in age for the U.S. salesmen is over twice that for the Western Europeans.

1.3 SUMMATION NOTATION

The reader probably was exposed to the summation operator in an introductory statistics course. Nevertheless, a brief review of some basic properties of Σ (sigma) will be helpful. The symbol Σ means "take the sum of." Suppose we had measured 50 subjects on anxiety. The sum of their scores is

$$x_1 + x_2 + x_3 \cdots + x_{50}$$

This sum can be expressed concisely using Σ as follows:

$$\sum_{i=1}^{50} x_i$$

The first term (x_1) is obtained by setting $i = 1$, the second term (x_2) by setting $i = 2$, on down to the last term (x_{50}) for $i = 50$. The quantity i is called the index of summation; it is what we are summing on. Let us consider a few more examples to illustrate. Suppose we have measured 75 subjects on a variable y and wish to represent the sum of those scores using Σ. Then it would look like this:

$$y_1 + y_2 + \cdots + y_{75} = \sum_{i=1}^{75} y_i$$

Or if we had 100 subjects measured on variable z and wish the sum of the scores for subjects 3 through 100, then we have

$$z_3 + z_4 + \cdots + z_{100} = \sum_{i=3}^{100} z_i$$

If the limits are understood, then they are dropped, and we would just write Σz_i. Note that the mean for a set of n scores can be written using Σ:

$$\bar{x} = (x_1 + x_2 + \cdots + x_n)/n = \sum x_i/n$$

Often we may wish to concisely represent a sum of squares of some type. Suppose we have n subject scores $(x_1, x_2, \ldots x_n)$ and wish to denote the sum of the squared scores. This is

$$x_1^2 + x_2^2 + \cdots + x_n^2 = \sum x_i^2$$

The sample variance for a set of scores involves a sum of squares (squared deviations):

$$s^2 = [(x_1 - \bar{x})^2 + (x_2 - \bar{x})^2 + \cdots + (x_n - \bar{x})^2]/(n - 1)$$
$$= \sum_{i=1}^{n} (x_i - \bar{x})^2/(n - 1)$$

or as $s^2 = \Sigma (x - \bar{x})^2/(n - 1)$ if the limits are understood.

Example

Evaluate $\sum x_i^2$, where $x_1 = 10$, $x_2 = 8$, $x_3 = 13$, and $x_4 = 5$.

$$\sum x_i^2 = x_1^2 + x_2^2 + x_3^2 + x_4^2 = 10^2 + 8^2 + 13^2 + 5^2 = 358$$

The following four properties of the summation operator are useful to know:

1. $\sum (x+y) = \sum x + \sum y$

   summation   sum
   of sum   of summations

2. $\sum (x-y) = \sum x - \sum y$

   summation of   difference
   difference   in summations

3. $\sum cx_i = c \sum x_i$ (a constant c can be moved across the summation)

To show that property 3 holds note that

$$\sum cx_i = cx_1 + cx_2 + \cdots + cx_n = c(x_1 + x_2 + \cdots + x_n) = c \sum x_i$$

4. $\sum c = nc$ (summing over n subjects)

The constant c mentioned in properties 3 and 4 can appear in many different subtle ways. To illustrate that and also to show how to apply several of the above properties, we will prove that the mean of a set of z scores is 0.

Denote the z scores by $z_1, z_2, \ldots, z_n$. Then by definition of a mean we have

$$\bar{z} = \sum z_i / n$$

To show that $\bar{z} = 0$ it suffices to show that $\sum z = 0$.

By definition $z_i = (x_i - \bar{x})/s$. Therefore by substitution:

$$\sum z_i = \sum (x_i - \bar{x})/s$$

Note that $1/s$ is a constant here; that is, it does not depend on i (index of summation). By property 3 we can move it across the summation and write

$$\sum z_i = (1/s) \sum (x_i - \bar{x})$$

Now by property 2 we can further rewrite this as

$$\sum z_i = (1/s)[\sum x_i - \sum \bar{x}]$$

Next, $\bar{x}$ is a constant and thus by property 4 we have that $\sum \bar{x} = n\bar{x}$. Also, since $\bar{x} = \sum x/n$ (by definition), this implies that $\sum x = n\bar{x}$. Plugging these values in we obtain

$$\sum z_i = (1/s)[n\bar{x} - n\bar{x}] = (1/s) \cdot 0 = 0$$

1.4 t TEST FOR INDEPENDENT SAMPLES

As an example we consider a study by air force psychologists conducting research into the relative effectiveness of training pilots. The first method makes use of computer simulated flight while the second uses traditional flight instruction. The 18 subjects were randomly assigned to the two methods and the following performance test scores were obtained:

Computer Simulation	Flight
2	1
5	1
5	2
6	3
6	3
7	4
8	5
9	7
	7
	8

We wish to test at the $\alpha = .05$ level of significance whether the average performance for the two groups is different. Recall that we wish to test the null hypothesis (H_0) that the population means are equal:

$$H_0: \mu_1 = \mu_2$$

It is called the null hypothesis because saying the population means are equal is equivalent to saying that the difference in the means is 0, i.e., $\mu_1 - \mu_2 = 0$, or that the difference is null.

Remember that level of significance is our probability of making a type I error. *Type I error is the probability of rejecting the null hypothesis when it is true, or saying the groups differ when they don't.* This type of error can not be eliminated; however, we can and do control the risk by setting $\alpha = .05$ or $.01$. Then there is only a 5% or 1% chance of making this type of error.

It should be recalled that the t test is based on the following three assumptions:

1. Normality—the scores on the dependent variable are normally distributed in each group.
2. Homogeneity of variance—the population variances are equal for the two groups.
3. Independence of the observations—each subject's score on the dependent variable is not affected by other subjects in the same treatment group.

Briefly, considerable research has shown that a violation of the normality assumption is of little consequence. Unequal variances will distort the type I error rate appreciably *only if* the group sizes are sharply unequal (largest/smallest > 1.5). Finally, dependent observations have a very serious effect on type I error rate. We discuss violations of assumptions in considerable detail in Chapter 2.

To test H_0 we use the following t statistic:

$$t = \frac{\bar{x}_1 - \bar{x}_2}{\sqrt{s_p^2(1/n_1 + 1/n_2)}}, \text{ with } (n_1 + n_2 - 2)\ df \tag{1}$$

where $s_p^2 = [(n_1 - 1)s_1^2 + (n_2 - 1)s_2^2]/(n_1 + n_2 - 2)$ is the pooled estimate of the assumed common population variance for the groups (the homogeneity of variance assumption). Now, s_1^2 and s_2^2 are the sample variances for groups 1 and 2, while n_1 and n_2 are the respective group sizes. This test statistic can be calculated relatively easily by obtaining the mean and variance for each group with the TI-30Xa or some other calculator. With the variances obtained, we find that

$$s_p^2 = [(8 - 1)\ 4.57 + (10 - 1)\ 6.54]/(10 + 8 - 2) = 5.68$$

Using Equation 1 we calculate

$$t = \frac{6 - 4.1}{\sqrt{5.68\ (1/8 + 1/10)}} = \frac{1.9}{1.13} = 1.68$$

Recall that we decided to reject H_0 only if the value of t obtained was *very unlikely* (would occur only 5% of the time) under the assumption of equal population means. The sampling distribution of t values (under the null hypothesis of equal population means) for this case is shown below:

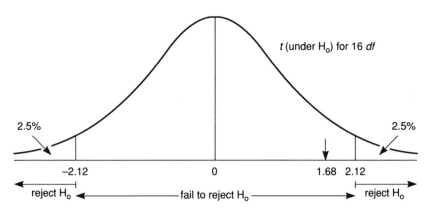

From the figure we can see that only 2.5% of the time will we obtain a t value greater than 2.12 or less than −2.12 *if the null hypothesis is true.* The 2.12 and −2.12 are called critical values because they are critical or pivotal points for our decision on H_0. Note that the critical values define the critical regions, where rejection of H_0 occurs. In general, if the value of t is greater than (in absolute value) the critical value, we will reject H_0; otherwise, we fail to reject. In this case since $t = 1.68$ is not in the critical region, we fail to reject H_0.

The null hypothesis could have also been tested using a *confidence interval.* Confidence intervals are an important part of inferential statistics. The confidence interval will give us a range of values within which the population mean difference lies with a certain probability (or confidence). For the above t test for independent samples the confidence interval is given by:

$$(\bar{x}_1 - \bar{x}_2) - t\,.05;\mathrm{df}\, s_{\bar{x}_1 - \bar{x}_2} < \mu_1 - \mu_2 < (\bar{x}_1 - \bar{x}_2) + t\,.05;\mathrm{df}\, s_{\bar{x}_1 - \bar{x}_2}$$

where $t\,.05;\mathrm{df}$ denotes the two tailed critical value at .05 with $(n_1 + n_2 - 2)$ degrees of freedom and $s_{\bar{x}_1 - \bar{x}_2}$ is the denominator of the t statistic. Thus, the 95% confidence interval for the above problem is given by

$$1.9 - 2.12\,(1.13) < \mu_1 - \mu_2 < 1.9 + 2.12\,(1.13)$$
$$-.496 < \mu_1 - \mu_2 < 4.296$$

Since this interval covers (crosses) 0, this means 0 is a likely value for $\mu_1 - \mu_2$, which means it is likely that $\mu_1 - \mu_2 = 0$ or that $\mu_1 = \mu_2$. Since it is likely that the population means are equal we would not reject the null hypothesis. On the other hand, if the confidence interval does *not cross* 0 then we conclude there is a significant difference between the groups, because this would mean 0 is not a likely value for the population mean difference. *Confidence intervals are more informative than a test of significance because they not only test the null hy-*

pothesis but also give us a range of values that is useful in judging the practical significance of results. We discuss the practical significance of results more in Chapter 2 on one way analysis of variance.

1.5 *t* TEST FOR DEPENDENT SAMPLES

The *t* test for dependent samples is appropriate in a variety of situations, of which the following three are common:

a. Pretest–treatment–posttest.
b. Two groups of matched or paired subjects are compared on some dependent variable. For example, 16 girl beginners are matched on SES, I.Q., number of children in the family, and general health. Eight of the girls had attended kindergarten; the other 8 had not. We wish to determine whether they differ on a test of first grade readiness.
c. We are comparing naturally occurring correlated pairs, such as twins, husband and wife, parent and child, etc.

Our numerical example does *not* fit into the above three categories.

Example

A political candidate wishes to determine if endorsing increased social spending is likely to affect her standing in the polls. She has access to data on the popularity of several other candidates who have endorsed social spending. The data were available both before and after the candidates announced their positions on the issue, as follows:

	Popularity		
Candidate	*Before*	*After*	d_i
1	42	43	1
2	41	45	4
3	50	56	6
4	52	54	2
5	58	65	7
6	32	29	−3
7	39	46	7
8	42	48	6
9	48	47	−1
10	47	53	6

The d_i are the difference scores in popularity and are fundamental in defining the test statistic for correlated samples:

$$t = \frac{\bar{d}}{s_d/\sqrt{n}} \text{ , with } (n-1) \; df \qquad (2)$$

where $\bar{d}$ is the average difference score, s_d is the standard deviation for the difference scores and n is the number of subjects or matched pairs. By using the TI-30Xa calculator on the difference scores above one obtains $\bar{d} = 3.5$ and $s_d = 3.57$. Therefore, t is calculated as $t = \dfrac{3.5}{3.57\sqrt{10}} = 3.097$. *The critical value at the .05 level is* $t_{.05;9} = 2.262$. Since the value of the test statistic is greater than the critical value, we reject and conclude that mean popularity after endorsement is greater than the mean popularity before endorsement.

Note that the mean difference is equal to the difference in the means, as we show below, where x_a and x_b denote the scores after and before:

$$\bar{d} = \sum d_i/n = \sum (x_a - x_b)/n = \sum x_a/n - \sum x_b/n = \bar{x}_a - \bar{x}_b$$

If we rewrite the equation for the t test for independent samples as

$$t = \frac{\bar{x}_1 - \bar{x}_2}{s_p\sqrt{1/n_1 + 1/n_2}}$$

then by placing this side by side with the t test for dependent samples we can see that they are structurally identical:

Independent t	*Dependent* t
$t = \dfrac{\bar{x}_1 - \bar{x}_2}{s_p\sqrt{1/n_1 + 1/n_2}}$	$t = \dfrac{\bar{x}_a - \bar{x}_b}{s_d\sqrt{1/n}}$

The numerator in each case involves an estimate of the difference in the means; in the first case for the two groups and in the second case for the matched pairs or subjects on two different occasions. In the denominators, s_p and s_d provide estimates of the amount of sampling error for each mean difference.

1.6.   OUTLIERS

An outlier is a data point which splits off or is very different from the rest of the data. Specific examples of outliers would be an I.Q. of 160 (among normal subjects), or a weight of 350 lbs. in a normal population of subjects. It is very important to detect outliers because they can have a dramatic effect on the results of *any* statistical analysis.

Outliers can occur because of two fundamental reasons:

1. a data recording or entry error was made, or
2. the subjects are different from the rest.

The first type of outlier can be identified by *always* listing the data and checking to make sure the data has been read in accurately. Consider the following small data set with two variables:

	X1	X2	Zscore(X1)	Zscore(X2)
1	101.00	68.00	−.25078	.53882
2	92.00	46.00	−.77566	−.94293
3	90.00	50.00	−.89230	−.67352
4	107.00	59.00	.09914	−.06735
5	98.00	50.00	−.42574	−.67352
6	150.00	66.00	2.60691	.40411
7	108.00	54.00	.15746	−.40411
8	110.00	51.00	.27410	−.60617
9	103.00	59.00	−.13414	−.06735
10	94.00	97.00	−.65902	2.49202
Total N	10	10	10	10

Do you see any outlier(s) for x_1 or x_2? Subject 6 is an outlier for x_1; notice how 150 splits off dramatically from the rest of the scores, which fall in the range from 90 to 110. Subject 10 is an outlier for x_2, since the score of 97 splits off sharply from the rest of the scores, which fall mostly in the range from about 50 to the mid 60s.

The z scores make the outliers quite apparent, and the z scores are very high since Shiffler (1988) has shown that the *largest possible z* score in a sample of size 10 is 2.846. We elaborate on this later on in the section.

You actually encountered the notion of an outlier in a beginning statistics course, although it may not have been called that by the instructor. In discussing measures of central tendency, your instructor probably indicated that whenever you have extreme scores in a set of data, the median should be used to characterize the data, rather than the mean. Extreme scores are called outliers here. The reason you were told to use the median is that it is essentially unaffected by extreme scores whereas the mean is drastically affected. Consider the following set of data: 2, 3, 5, 6, 44. The last number is an outlier. If we were to use the mean

(12), it would be quite misleading in characterizing the data set, as there are no scores around 12. The median, on the other hand, is 5 and does indicate where most of the scores lie (although there are only 5 of them).

To show the dramatic effect an outlier can have on a correlation, consider the two scatterplots in Figure 1.1. Notice how inclusion of the outlier in each case *drastically* changes the interpretation of the results. For Case A there is no relationship without the outlier but there is a strong relationship with the outlier, while for Case B the relationship changes from strong (without outlier) to weak.

From the above it should be clear that *it is very important to identify outliers and then decide what to do about them.* Why? Because we want our analysis results reflecting most of the data, and not being unduly influenced by just 1 or 2 errant points.

Detecting Outliers

If the variable is approximately normally distributed, then z scores around 3 in absolute value should be considered as potential outliers. Why? Because in an approximate normal distribution about 99% of the scores should lie within three standard deviations of the mean. Therefore, any z value > 3 indicates a value very unlikely to occur. Of course, if n is large (say > 100), then simply by chance we might expect a few subjects to have z scores > 3 and this should be kept in mind. However, even for *any type of distribution* the above rule is reasonable, although we might consider extending the rule to $z > 4$. It was shown many years ago that regardless of how the data are distributed the percentage of observations that are, contained within k standard deviations of the mean must be at *least* $(1 - 1/k^2) \cdot 100\%$. The above holds only for $k > 1$ and yields the following percentages for $k = 2$ through 5:

Number of standard deviations	*Percentage of observations*
2	at least 75%
3	at least 88.89%
4	at least 93.75%
5	at least 96%

Shiffler (1988) has shown that the largest possible value z value in a data set of size n is bounded by $(n - 1)/\sqrt{n}$. This means for $n = 10$ the largest possible z is 2.846 and for $n = 11$ the largest possible z is 3.015. Thus, for small sample size any data point with a z around 2.5 should be seriously considered as a possible outlier.

When comparing group differences, as with the t test for independent samples, we want the z scores computed separately for each group. In Appendix 2 we show how using the SPLIT FILE feature of SPSS and the DESCRIPTIVES

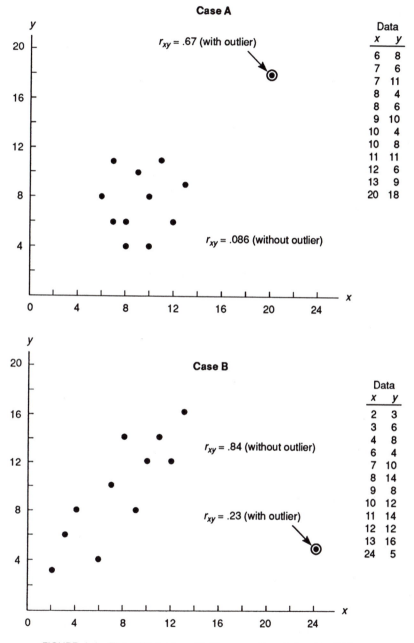

Case A

Data

x	y
6	8
7	6
7	11
8	4
8	6
9	10
10	4
10	8
11	11
12	6
13	9
20	18

$r_{xy} = .67$ (with outlier)

$r_{xy} = .086$ (without outlier)

Case B

Data

x	y
2	3
3	6
4	8
6	4
7	10
8	14
9	8
10	12
11	14
12	12
13	16
24	5

$r_{xy} = .84$ (without outlier)

$r_{xy} = .23$ (with outlier)

FIGURE 1.1 The Effect of an Outlier on a Correlation Coefficient.

procedure we can obtain and save both the raw and z scores for each variable. Then, using the CASE SUMMARIES feature we can get these printed out for each group. After the outliers are identified, what should be done with them? The action to be taken is not to automatically drop the outlier(s) from the analysis. If one finds after further investigation of the outlying points that an outlier was due to a recording or entry error, then of course one would correct the data value and redo the analysis. Or if it is found that the errant data value is due to an instrumentation error or that the process that generated the data for that subject was different, then it is legitimate to drop the outlier. If, however, none of these appears to be the case, then one should *not* drop the outlier, but perhaps report two analyses (one including the outlier and the other excluding it). Outliers should not necessarily be regarded as "bad." As a matter of fact, it has been argued that outliers can provide some of the most interesting cases for further study.

1.7   SPSS AND SAS STATISTICAL PACKAGES

The Statistical Analysis System (SAS) and the Statistical Package for the Social Sciences (SPSS) were selected for use in this text for several reasons.

1. They are very widely distributed.
2. They are easy to use.
3. They do a very wide range of analyses—from simple descriptive statistics to various analysis of variance designs to complex multivariate analyses.
4. They are well documented, having been in development for over two decades.

The control language that is used by both packages is quite natural, and you will see that with a little practice complex analyses are run quite easily, and with a small set of control line instructions. A major change from the previous edition of this text is the advent of Windows and running analyses by simply clicking a series of buttons. It is assumed that the reader will be either running a Windows version of one or both of these packages on a desktop computer, or perhaps a notebook computer, or running the analyses from the program editor (called this in SAS, or from the syntax editor, as called by SPSS). We illustrate the SPSS for Windows Releases 7.5 and 8.0 in some detail. Examples are considered where the data is part of the control lines. We will not be concerned with getting data from either a floppy disk or from the hard disk.

Structurally, an SAS program is composed of three fundamental blocks:

1. Statements setting up the data.
2. The data lines.

3. Procedure (PROC) statements—procedures are SAS computer programs which read the data and do various statistical analyses.

To illustrate how to set up the control lines, suppose we wish to compute the correlations between locus of control, achievement motivation, and achievement in language for a hypothetical set of 9 subjects. First we create a data set and give it a name. The name *must* begin with a letter and be 8 or less characters. Let us call the data set LOCUS. Now, each SAS statement *must* end with a semicolon. So our first SAS line looks like this

```
DATA LOCUS;
```

The next statement needed is called an INPUT statement. This is where we give names for our variables and indicate the format of the data (i.e., how the data is arranged on each line). We will use what is called free format. With this format the scores for each variable do not have to be in specific columns. However, at least one blank column must separate the score for each variable from the next variable. Furthermore, we will put in our INPUT statement the following symbols @ @. In SAS this set of symbols allows you to put the data for more than one subject on the same line.

In SAS, as with the other packages, there are certain rules for variable names. Each variable name must begin with a letter and be 8 or less characters. The variable name can contain numbers, but *not* special characters or an imbedded blank(s). For example, I.Q., $x1 + x2$, and SOC CLAS, are not valid variable names. We have special characters in the first two names (periods in I.Q. and the $+$ in $x1 + x2$) and there is an embedded blank in the abbreviation for social class.

Our INPUT statement is as follows:

```
INPUT LOCUS ACHMOT ACHLANG @@;
```

Following the INPUT statement there is a LINES statement, which tells SAS that the data is to follow. Thus, the first three statements here setting up the data look like this:

```
DATA LOCUS;
INPUT LOCUS ACHMOT ACHLANG @@;
LINES;
```

Recall that the next structural part of a SAS program is the set of data lines. Remember there are dime variables, so we have three scores for each subject. We will put the scores for three subjects on each data line. Adding the data lines to the above three statements, we now have the following part of the SAS program:

```
DATA LOCUS;
INPUT LOCUS ACHMOT ACHLANG @@;
LINES;
11 23 31   13 25 38   21 28 29
21 34 28   14 36 37   29 20 37
17 24 39   19 30 39   23 28 41
```

The first 3 scores (11, 23, and 31) are the scores on locus of control, achievement motivation, and achievement in language for the first subject; the next 3 numbers (13, 25, and 38) are the scores on these variables for subject 2; etc.

Now we come to the last structural part of a SAS program, calling up some SAS procedure(s) to do whatever statistical analysis(es) we desire. In this case we want correlations, and the SAS procedure for that is called CORR. Also, as mentioned earlier, we should always print the data. For this we use PROC PRINT. Adding these lines we get our complete SAS program:

```
DATA LOCUS;
INPUT LOCUS ACHMOT ACHLANG @@;
LINES;
11 23 31   13 25 38   21 28 29
21 34 28   14 36 37   29 20 37
17 24 39   19 30 39   23 28 41
PROC CORR;
PROC PRINT;
```

Note that there is a semicolon at the end of each statement, but *not* for the data lines.

In Table 1.1 we present some of the basic rules of the control language for SAS, and in Table 1.2 give the complete SAS control lines for obtaining descriptive statistics, for obtaining a set of correlations (this is the example we just went over in detail), and for obtaining both the independent and dependent samples *t* tests. Although the rules are basic, they are important. For example, failing to end a statement in SAS with a semicolon or using a variable name longer than 8 characters will cause the program to terminate. The four sets of control lines in Table 1.2 show the structural similarity of the control line flow for different types of analyses. Notice in each case we start with the DATA statement, then an INPUT statement (naming the variables being read in and describing the format of the data), and then the LINES statement preceding the data. Then, after the data, one or more PROC statements are used to perform the wanted statistical analysis, or to print the data (PROC PRINT).

These 4 sets of control lines serve as useful models for running analyses of the same type, where only the variable names change and/or the names and number of

TABLE 1.1
Some Basic Elements of the SAS Control Language

Non-columned oriented. Columns only become relevant when using column input for the data.

SAS statements give instructions. Each statement *must* end with a semicolon.

Structurally a SAS program is composed of three fundamental blocks: (1) statements setting up the data, (2) the data lines and (3) procedure (PROC) statements—procedures are SAS computer programs which read the data and do various statistical analyses.

DATA SETUP

First there is the DATA statement, where you are creating a data set. The name for the data set must begin with a letter and be 8 or less characters.

Then there is the INPUT statement, where the variables are named and the format of the data is specified.

Variable names must be 8 or less characters, must begin with a letter, and cannot contain special characters.

We can use *column* input, where we indicate what column(s) the score for a variable is. If the variable is non-numeric then we need to put a $ after the variable name.

Example

Suppose we have a group of subjects measured on IQ, attitude toward education and grade point average (GPA), and will label them as M for male and F for female.
SEX $ 1 IQ 3–5 ATTITUDE 7–8 GPA 10–12.2

This tells SAS that sex (M or F) is in column 1, IQ is in columns 3 through 5, attitude in columns 7 to 8, and grade point average in columns 10 to 12. The .2 is to insert a decimal point *before* the last two digits.

If we are using free format then the scores for the variables do *not* have to be in specific columns, they simply need to be separated from each other by at least one blank.

The LINES statement follows the DATA and INPUT statements and precedes the data lines

More than one statement can go on the same line, although for readability we recommend putting statements on separate lines. If we wish to do analysis on only some of the variables in the INPUT statement, then this is indicated in a VAR (abbreviation for variable) statement. For example, if we had 6 variables on the INPUT statement (X1 X2 X3 X4 X5 X6) and only wished to compute correlations for the first 3, then we would insert VAR X1 X2 X3; after the PROC CORR statement.

Statistics for subgroups of subjects are obtained with the BY statement. Suppose we want the correlations for males and females on variables X, Y and Z. If the subjects have not been sorted on sex, then we sort them first using PROC SORT, and the control lines are

PROC CORR;
PROC SORT;
BY SEX;

TABLE 1.2
SAS Control Lines for Obtaining Set of Correlations, Descriptive Statistics, and Independent and Dependent T Tests

CORRELATIONS	T TEST

① DATA LOCUS;
② INPUT LOCUS ACHMOT ACHLANG @@;
③ LINES;
    11 23 31 13 25 38 21 28 29
    21 34 28 14 36 37 29 20 27
    17 24 39 19 30 39 23 28 41
    PROC CORR;
④ PROC PRINT;

    DATA ATTITUDE;
⑤ INPUT TREAT $ ATT @@;
    LINES;
    C 82 C 95 C 89 99 C 87
    C 79 C 98 C 86
    T 94 T 97 T 98 T 93 T 96
    T 99 T 88 T 92 T 94 T 95
    T 92 T 97 T 96 T 90 T 89
    PROC TTEST;
⑥ CLASS TREAT;
    PROC PRINT;

MEANS AND STANDARD DEVIATIONS

DATA MEANS;
INPUT DRINK $ TACTUAL @@;
LINES;
A 34 A 26 A 18 A 26 A 9
A 28 A 14 A 33 A 43 A 50
NA 15 NA 2 NA 23 NA 7 NA 18
NA 13 NA 9 NA 23 NA 8 NA 16
PROC MEANS;
⑦ BY DRINK;

DEPENDENT SAMPLES T TEST

DATA COFFEE;
INPUT PRODWCB PRODWITH @@;
⑧ DIFF=PRODWITH−PRODWCB;
    LINES;
    23 28   35 38   29 29
    33 37   43 42   32 30
⑨ PROC MEANS N MEAN T PRT;
    VAR DIFF;

①Here we are giving a name to the data set. Remember it must be eight or less letters and must begin with a letter. Note that there is a semicolon at the end of the line, and at the end of *every* line for all 4 examples (except for the data lines).

②Note that the names for the variables all begin with a letter and are less than or equal to 8 characters. The double @@ is needed in order to put the data for more than one subject on the same data line; here we have data for 3 subjects on each line.

③When the data is part of the control lines, as here, then this LINES command always precedes the data.

④PROC (short for procedure) CORR yields the correlations, and PROC PRINT gives a listing of the data.

⑤The $ after TREAT is used to denote a non-numeric variable; note in the data lines that TREAT is either *C*(control) or *T*(treatment).

⑥We call up the t test procedure and tell it that TREAT is the grouping variable.

⑦This BY statement yields means and standard deviations for each of the sub-groups defined by DRINK (alcoholics & non-alcoholics)

⑧We create the difference variable (DIFF) on which the analysis is done.

⑨Procedure MEANS is used, with MEAN, *T*, and PRT yielding the mean on the difference variable, *t* is test statistic and PRT is the tail probability.

variables change. For example, suppose you want all correlations on 5 attitudinal variables (call them $x1$, $x2$, $x3$, $x4$, and $x5$). Then the control lines are:

```
DATA ATTITUDE;
INPUT X1 X2 X3 X4 X5 @@;
LINES;


        DATA LINES


PROC CORR;
PROC PRINT;
```

where the data lines have just been indicated schematically.

In Table 1.3 we present some of the basic elements of the SPSS control language, and in Table 1.4 give the complete SPSS control lines for descriptive statistics, correlations, and the t tests for independent and dependent samples. Some of the common errors committed in running SPSS programs are (1) using invalid variable names, (2) failing to indent for a subcommand, and (3) not starting a command in column 1.

TABLE 1.3
Some Basic Elements of the SPSS Control Language

SPSS operates on commands and subcommands

It is column oriented to the extent that each command begins in column 1 and continues for as many lines as needed. All continuation lines are indented at least one column.
Examples of Commands: TITLE, DATA LIST, BEGIN DATA
The title can be put in apostrophes, and can be up to 60 characters.
All subcommands begin with a keyword followed by an equals sign, then the specifications, and are terminated by a slash.
Each subcommand is indented at least one column.
The subcommands are further specifications for the commands.
For example, if the command is DATA LIST, then
DATA LIST FREE involves the subcommand FREE which indicates the data will be in free format.
Names for variables must be eight or less characters.
They must begin with a letter, or one of the following characters: @, # or $.
FREE format—the variables must be in the same order for each case but do not have to be in the same location. Also, multiple cases can go on the same line, with the values for the variables separated by blanks or commas.
When the data is part of the command file, then the BEGIN DATA command precedes the data and the END DATA follows the last line of data.
The LIST command can be used to list the data.
We can use the keyword TO in specifying a set of consecutive variables, rather than listing all the variables. For example, if we had the six variables X1,X2,X3,X4,X5,X6, the following subcommand are equivalent:
VARIABLES=X1,X2,X3,X4,X5,X6/ or VARIABLES=X1 TO X6/

TABLE 1.4
SPSS Control Lines for Obtaining a Set of Correlations
Descriptive Statistics, and Independent and Dependent *T* Tests

---

CORRELATIONS	T TEST

CORRELATIONS

```
   TITLE 'CORRELATIONS FOR 3 VARIABLES'.
①  DATA LIST FREE/LOCUS ACHMOT ACHLANG.
②  BEGIN DATA.
   11 23 31   13 25 38   21 28 29
   11 34 28   14 36 37   29 20 37
   17 24 39   19 30 39   23 28 41
   END DATA.
③  CORRELATIONS VARIABLES=LOCUS ACHMOT
   ACHLANG/
   PRINT=TWOTAIL/
④    STATISTICS=DESCRIPTIVES/.
```

T TEST

```
   TITLE 'T TEST'.
   DATA LIST FREE/TREAT ATT.
   BEGIN DATA.
⑥  1 82   1 95   1 89   1 99
   1 87   1 79   1 98   1 86
   2 94   2 97   2 98   2 93
   2 96   2 99   2 88   2 92
   2 94   2 95   2 92   2 97
   2 96   2 90   2 89
   END DATA.
⑤  LIST.
⑦  T-TEST GROUPS=TREAT(1,2)/
   VARIABLES=ATT/.
```

MEANS AND STANDARD DEVIATIONS

```
   TITLE 'DESCRIPTIVE STATISTICS'.
   DATA LIST FREE/DRINK TACTUAL.
   VALUE LABELS DRINK 1 'ALCOHOLIC'
   2 'NON ALCOHOLIC'.
   BEGIN DATA.
   1 34   1 26   1 18   1 26   1 9
   1 28   1 14   1 33   1 43   1 50
   2 15   2 2   2 23   2 7    2 18
   2 13   2 9   2 23   2  8 2 16
   END DATA.
⑧  MEANS TABLES=TACTUAL BY DRINK/.
```

DEPENDENT SAMPLES T TEST

```
   TITLE 'COFFEE BREAK'
   DATA LIST FREE/PWO PWITH.
   BEGIN DATA.
   23 28   35 38   29 29
   33 37   43 42   32 30
   END DATA.
⑨  T-TEST PAIRS=PWO PWITH/.
```

①The FREE on this DATA LIST command is a further specification, indicating that the data will be in free format.

②When the data is part of the command file, it is preceded by BEGIN DATA and terminated by END DATA.

③This VARIABLES subcommand specifies the variables to be analyzed.

④This yields the means and standard deviations for all variables.

⑤This LIST command gives a listing of the data.

⑥The first number for each pair is the group identification and the second is the score for the dependent variable. Thus, 82 is the score for the first subject in group 1 and 97 is the score for the second subject in group 2.

⑦The t test procedure is called and the number of levels for the grouping variables is put in parentheses.

⑧The MEANS procedure calculates means and variances for a dependent variable(s) over subgroups defined by one or more classification variables. The TABLES subcommand is used to indicates for which variables the means and variances are desired.

⑨The PAIRS subcommand names the variables being compared.

It should be understood that although we give some important basic elements of the packages in Tables 1.1 and 1.3, and present *complete* control lines for various types of analyses in this text, our treatment is in no sense a substitute for the SAS and SPSS manuals. All the contingencies one might encounter in a practical problem can't be covered in this text. One final important point before we leave the packages: The examples in this book were run on SPSS for Windows 7.5 or 8.0 or SAS 6.12. It is possible if you are running a different release of SPSS or SAS that things may change a bit. Your instructor can help you with this.

1.8   SPSS FOR WINDOWS—RELEASES 7.5 AND 8.0

Since the introduction of SPSS for Windows in 1993, data analysis has changed considerably. As noted in the *SPSS for Windows Base Guide (Release 6)*, "SPSS for Windows Release 6 brings the full power of the mainframe version of SPSS to the personal computer environment. . . . *SPSS for Windows provides a user interface that makes statistical analysis more accessible for the casual user and more convenient for the experienced user.* Simple menus and dialog box selections make it possible to perform complex analyses without typing a single line of command syntax. The Data Editor offers a simple and efficient spreadsheet-like facility for entering data and browsing the working data file."

The introduction of SPSS for Windows (Release 7.0) in 1996 brought further enhancements. One of the very nice enhancements was the introduction of the Output Navigator. This divides the output into two panes: the left pane, having the analysis(ses) that was run in outline (icon) form, and the statistical content in the right pane. One can do all kinds of things with the output, including printing all or just some of the output. We discuss this very nice feature in more detail shortly. SPSS for Windows Release 7.5 (1997) and Release 8.0 (1998) are both available on a compact disk.

A fantastic bargain, in my opinion, is the SPSS Graduate Pack for Windows 7.5 or SPSS Graduate Pack for Windows 8.0, both of which come on compact disk and sell at a university for students for only $160. It is important to note that you are getting the full package here, not a student version. The hard disk requirement has gone up considerably from Release 7.0 to Release 8.0 (25.9 megabytes for 7.0, 35.8 megabytes for 7.5, and 49.9 megabytes for 8.0).

For Releases 7.0 and 7.5 the Windows 95 operating system or Windows NT 3.51 is required. For Release 8.0 the Windows 95 operating system or Windows NT 4.0 is required. You also should have at least 16 MB of RAM. Although some of the simpler analyses and ANOVAs will run on 8 MB of RAM, to run more complicated analyses and use the full power of SPSS you need 16 MB of RAM. If you have purchased a computer within the last 2 years these requirements should not be a problem.

Statistical analysis is done on data, so getting data into SPSS for Windows is crucial. I discuss how one can do this from a word processing program such as MS Word or WordPerfect, or from a spreadsheet such as Excel or Lotus 1-2-3. A key point here, especially with spreadsheet data, is to *save the file as an ASCII (text) file.* I also discuss how one can get data from a floppy disk (either in free or fixed format) into SPSS for Windows. Finally, I discuss entering and editing data in the SPSS spreadsheet like Data Editor.

One change in SPSS for Windows versus running SPSS on the mainframe or on a minicomputer such as the VAX is that each COMMAND *must* end with a period.

1.9   DATA FILES

As noted in the *SPSS Base 8.0 Users Guide* (1998, p. 23), "Data files come in a variety of formats, and SPSS is designed to handle many of them," including:

Spreadsheet files created with Lotus 1-2-3 and Excel.

Database files created with dBase and various SQL formats.

Tab-delimited and other types of ASCII text files.

SPSS data files created on other systems.

Chapter 3 of this guide describes how SPSS reads spreadsheet data, how it reads dBase files, how it reads text files, etc. We do not wish to duplicate what is in the guide, but rather focus on one common type of data file that is often available either on a hard drive or on a 3.5-inch disk, that is, a text file. We will illustrate how one can transfer a data text file, either in freefield or fixed format, into a SPSS data file. The file may have been created in a spreadsheet such as Excel or Lotus 1-2-3, or in a word processing program such as MS Word or WordPerfect.

Creating an SPSS Data File From a Freefield ASCII File (File on Hard Drive (C) or in Word Processing Subdirectory) — Small Data Set

Suppose we have typed in the following data file in MS Word:

12	13	19
23	29	72
29	38	111
36	16	28
44	40	104
21	14	28
40	44	16
42	60	57
24	16	18
30	37	41

We save the above file as a text file named FREFIELD.TXT. Now, working within SPSS (8.0), click on FILE and then scroll down to READ ASCII DATA FILE and scroll across to FREEFIELD and then click. The DEFINE FREEFIELD VARIABLES box appears. Click on BROWSE, and the following screen appears:

Click on the down arrow opposite SPSSWIN8 and double click on C from the dropdown menu, and the screen appears as follows:

Now double click on Msoff and double click on WINWORD from the drop-down menu. The reason for all this clicking is to get to the directory (folder) where the file is located. Click within the FILE NAME box and type in FREFIELD.TXT. At this point the box is as follows:

When you click on OPEN the following screen appears:

Type each variable name in and then click on ADD. There are various rules for variable names. Among them are that the name must begin with a letter, must be 8 or less characters, and must not end with a period. A safe variable naming procedure is to use 8 or less continuous letters, which is what we have done. The 3 variable names are QUALITY, NFACULTY, and NGRADS. When you are done with all 3 variables click on OK. Click on FILE, and then click on SAVE AS from the dropdown menu. Use the down arrow key to change to the C drive, then select SPSSWIN8 (which is where we wish to save the file).

Type in FREFIELD for the file name. The file is saved as FREFIELD.SAV.

Creating an SPSS Data File From a Spreadsheet File

Suppose the data file had been created in Excel or Lotus 1-2-3, two of the most popular spreadsheets. The key point here in each case is to *save the file as an ASCII (text) file.* Many will have Excel as part of a suite called Microsoft Office. I will illustrate how a file created and saved in Excel as a text file can be transferred to SPSS for Windows for data analysis. To illustrate we shall use the following four group data set:

Group 1	Group 2	Group 3	Group 4
2	7	4	8
3	9	4	4
5	11	5	7
6		8	7
		3	

I have Microsoft Office installed on my notebook computer in a subdirectory called Msoff. Working within SPSS 8.0, as before I click on FILE and scroll down to READ ASCII DATA and scroll across to FREEFIELD, and then click. Click on BROWSE, then click on the down arrow key and double click on C. Double click on MSOFF and then double click on EXCEL. Click within the FILE NAME box and type in ANOVA47.TXT. This tells SPSS exactly where the file is and what it is called. The screen appears as follows:

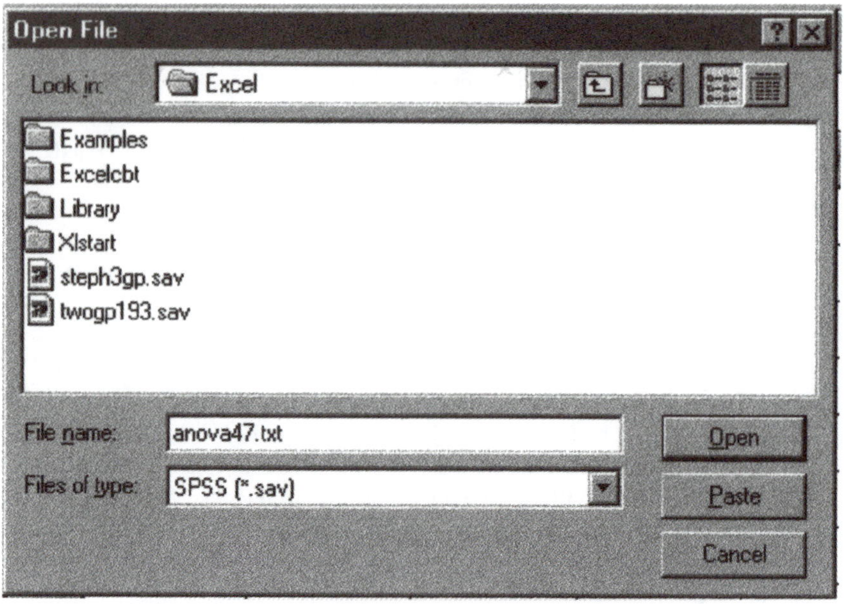

Now, click on OPEN and the following screen appears:

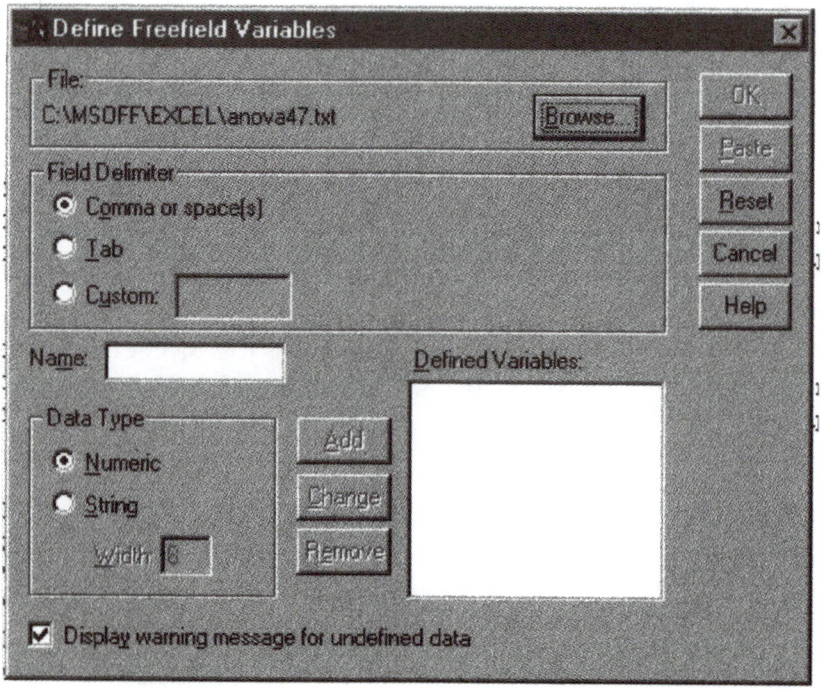

Click within the NAME box and type in GPID for the first variable. The ADD box will light up; click on it to add this variable in the VARIABLES DEFINED box. Do the same for y. At this point the DEFINE VARIABLES box will look as follows:

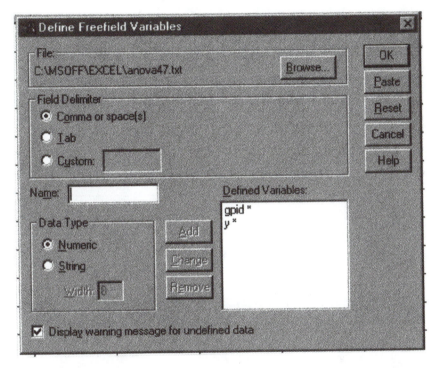

When you now click on OK, the data file will appear in the SPSS editor. To save it click on FILE and click on SAVE AS from the dropdown menu. Use the down arrow key to change to the C drive and then select SPSSWIN8. Click within the file name box and type in TXT193 and click on SAVE. The file is saved as TXT193.SAV.

Now we turn to an example using Lotus 1-2-3 (1997 edition). When this edition of Lotus is first opened, the following screen appears:

Click on CREATE A BLANK WORKBOOK, and the following screen appears:

We use for illustrative purposes the two way ANOVA data set on page 104 of the first edition of this book. Type that data set in the above blank spreadsheet, and save it as a text file. To do that you need to scroll on the SAVE AS TYPE window until you come to TEXT. Type the following in the file name box

TWOWAY.TXT, and click on SAVE. The file will be saved as an ASCII (text) file. Before clicking on SAVE, the SAVE AS window looks as follows:

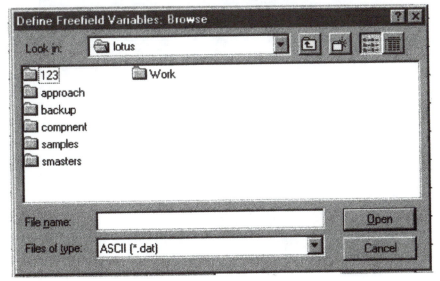

Now, working within SPSS 8.0, click on FILE and scroll down to READ ASCII DATA and then across to FREEFIELD, then click and click on BROWSE from the next screen. Click on the down arrow key and double click on C and then double click on LOTUS. This will take you to the following screen.

Double click on WORK and then double click on 123. Then click within the FILE NAME box and type in the file name. At this point, the screen looks as follows:

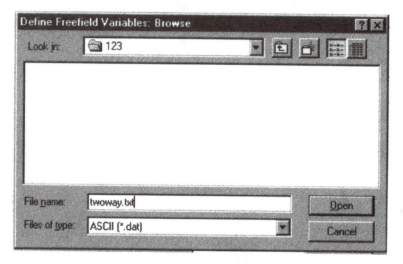

Click on OPEN and the DEFINE FREEFIELD VARIABLES screen appears. Click within the NAME box and type in SEX. The ADD box will light up. Click on it, and SEX will appear in the DEFINED VARIABLES box. Do the same for TREAT and DEP. At this point the screen looks as follows:

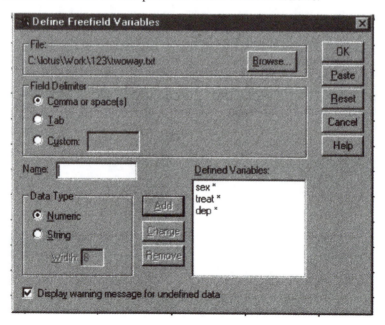

When you click on OK, the file will appear in the SPSS Data Editor. To save it, click on FILE and go down to SAVE AS and type TWOWAY for the file name. The file will be saved as TWOWAY.SAV. Recall that SPSS adds the appendage SAV to each saved file.

Creating an SPSS Data File From a Freefield ASCII File
(Data File on Floppy Disk—Large Data Set)

As before, click on FILE and then scroll down to READ ASCII DATA and across to FREEFIELD. When you now click on OK, a screen will come up where you click on BROWSE, then the down arrow to the A drive. Click within the FILE NAME box and type in SESAM596.TXT. At this point the screen looks as follows:

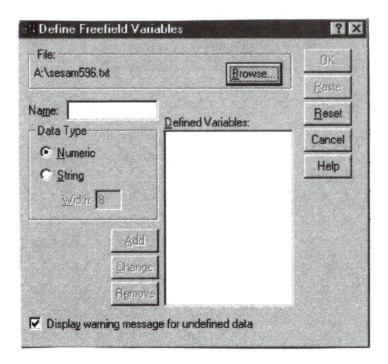

Click within the NAME box and type in the variable names, clicking on ADD after each name to add the variable to the DEFINED VARIABLES box. At this point the screen looks as follows:

We are going to transfer the Sesame Street data in Appendix B from the floppy disk to an SPSS data file. This is a large data set, with 240 subjects measured on 20 variables. As in the previous example, we type in each variable name and then click on ADD. When done entering all 20 variables click on OK. Click on FILE and click on SAVE AS from the dropdown menu. Change back to the C drive, and then select SPSSWIN8. Type in SESAM596 for the file name and then click SAVE. The file, partially shown below, is saved as an SPSS data file called SESAM596.SAV. The reader might think this transfer process would take a while, but it only took about 20 seconds on my COMPAQ CONTURA, which at 25 MHz is very slow by today's standards. It took about 7 seconds on my TOSHIBA 205CDS with 100 MHz Pentium processor.

SESAME STREET DATA

ID	SITE	SEX	AGE	VIEWCAT	SETTING	VIEWENC	PREBODY	PRELET	PREFORM	PRENUMB	PRERELAT	PRECLASF	POSTBODY	POSTLET	POSTFORM	POSTNUMB	POSTREL	POSTCLAS	PEABODY
1	1	1	66	1	2	1	16	23	12	40	14	20	18	30	14	44	14	23	62
2	1	2	67	3	2	1	30	26	9	39	16	22	30	37	17	39	14	22	80
3	1	1	56	3	2	2	22	14	9	9	9	8	21	46	15	40	9	19	32
4	1	1	49	1	2	2	23	11	10	14	9	13	21	14	13	19	8	15	27
5	1	1	69	4	2	2	32	47	15	51	17	22	32	53	18	54	14	21	71
6	1	2	54	3	2	2	29	26	10	33	14	14	27	36	14	39	16	24	32

Creating an SPSS Data File
From a Fixed Format ASCII File
(Data File on Floppy Disk—A Drive)

To illustrate the process we consider a very small data set which has no spaces between variables, and furthermore we wish to deal with an implied decimal point. There are five variables. The variable names and the columns they occupy are

VARIABLE	COLUMN(S)
LIKERT	1
ATTIT	2-3
GPA	4-6
ACH	7-8
SOC	9

The data set is:

```
243267598
356213678
578324435
465243567
679143324
```

As in the other previous cases, click on FILE, scroll down to READ ASCII DATA and across to FIXED. Click, and then click on BROWSE in the next screen. Click on the down arrow and double click on the A drive from the dropdown menu. Click within the FILE NAME box, and type in MASHED.TXT. At this point, the screen is as follows:

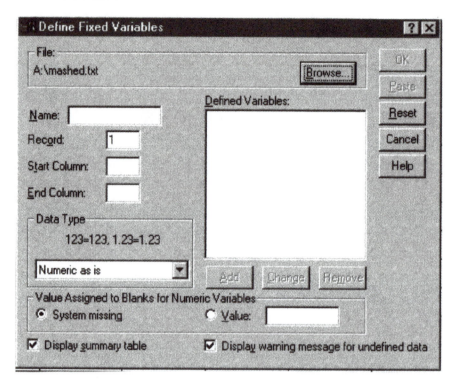

Type in the name LIKERT for the first variable, and since it is a single digit integer, indicate 1 for the START COLUMN and 1 for the END COLUMN. Click on ADD, and the variable name will appear in the DEFINED VARIABLES box. The next variable name is ATTIT, which is in columns 2–3. So, type in the name and START COLUMN as 2 and END COLUMN as 3. Click on ADD and the second variable name will appear in the DEFINED VARIABLES box. The situation for GPA is a little more complex because there is an implied decimal. GPA appears in columns 4–6. Proceed as before, except now select under DATA TYPE the following: NUMERIC 2 DECIMAL(2). Thus, 267 will become 2.67, etc. Before adding the remaining 2 variable names (ACH and SOC), make sure you switch back under DATA TYPE to NUMERIC AS IS. Then click on OK.

At this point, the screen is as follows:

When you click on OK the data will appear in the SPSS Data Editor. To save it, click on FILE and then on SAVE AS from the dropdown menu, and the following screen appears:

Use the down arrow key to change to the C drive and then select SPSSWIN8. Click within the FILE NAME box and type MASHED5, and click on SAVE. The file will be saved in the SPSS 8.0 directory (folder).

1.10   DATA EDITING

As noted in the *SPSS Base for Windows User's Guide* (1998, p. 51), the Data Editor provides a convenient, spreadsheet-like method for creating and editing SPSS data files. The Data Editor window, shown below, opens automatically when you start an SPSS session:

Rows are cases and columns are variables. For illustrative purposes, let us reconsider the data set on 10 subjects for 3 variables (QUALITY, NFACULTY, NGRADS) that was saved previously in SPSS 8.0 as FREFIELD.SAV.

Opening a Data File

Click on FILE, and then click on OPEN in the dropdown menu. Scroll over to FREFIELD.SAV and click on it. This file name appears in the file name box. Note that SPSS adds the extension .SAV to every saved file. The OPEN FILE dialog box looks as shown below:

Open File   ? ✕

| Look in: | 📁 spsswin8 | ▼ | 🔼 | 📷 | ▦ | ▤ |

📁 Looks	📄 ancova3gp.sav
📁 Scripts	📄 anocv156.sav
📄 1b2wrep.sav	📄 ANOVA48.sav
📄 AML survival.sav	📄 anovout.sav
📄 AN3WY129.sav	📄 anscomb.sav
📄 ancov3gp.sav	📄 Anxiety 2.sav

File name:	frefield.sav		Open
Files of type:	SPSS (*.sav)	▼	Paste
			Cancel

Click on OPEN to bring this file up into the Data Editor. That SPSS data set in the editor looks like this:

	quality	nfaculty	ngrads
1	12.00	13.00	19.00
2	23.00	29.00	72.00
3	29.00	38.00	111.00
4	36.00	16.00	28.00
5	44.00	40.00	104.00
6	21.00	14.00	28.00
7	40.00	44.00	16.00
8	42.00	60.00	57.00
9	24.00	16.00	18.00
10	30.00	37.00	41.00
11			

Changing a Cell Value

Suppose we wished to change the circled value to 23. Move to that cell. Enter the 23 and press ENTER. The new value appears in the cell. It is as simple as that.

Inserting a Case

Suppose we wished to insert a case after the 7th subject. How would we do it? As the guide points out:

1. Select any cell in the case (row) *below* the position where you want to insert the new case.
2. From the menus choose:
      DATA
         INSERT CASE

A new row is inserted for the case and all variables receive the system-missing value. It would look as follows:

	quality	nfaculty	ngrads
1	12.00	13.00	19.00
2	23.00	29.00	72.00
3	29.00	38.00	111.00
4	36.00	16.00	28.00
5	44.00	40.00	104.00
6	21.00	14.00	28.00
7	40.00	44.00	16.00
8			
9	42.00	60.00	57.00
10	24.00	16.00	18.00
11	30.00	37.00	41.00

Suppose the new case we typed in was 35 17 63.

Inserting a Variable

Now we wish to add a variable after NFACULTY. How would we do it?

1. Select any cell in the variable (column) to the *right* of the position where you want to insert the new variable.
2. From the menus choose:
   DATA
      INSERT A VARIABLE

When this is done, the data file in the editor looks as follows:

	quality	nfaculty	var00001	ngrads
1	12.00	13.00		19.00
2	23.00	29.00		72.00
3	29.00	38.00		111.00
4	36.00	16.00		28.00
5	44.00	40.00		104.00
6	21.00	14.00		28.00
7	40.00	44.00		16.00
8	35.00	17.00		63.00
9	42.00	60.00		57.00
10	24.00	16.00		18.00
11	30.00	37.00		41.00
12				

Deleting a Case

To delete a case is also simple. Click on the row (case) you wish to delete. The entire row is highlighted. From the menus choose:

EDIT
   CLEAR

The selected row (case) is deleted and the cases below it move it up. To illustrate, suppose for the above data set we wished to delete case 4 (row 4).

Click on 4 and choose EDIT and CLEAR. The case is deleted, and we are back to 10 cases, as shown below:

	quality	nfaculty	var00001	ngrads
1	12.00	13.00		19.00
2	23.00	29.00		72.00
3	29.00	38.00		111.00
4	44.00	40.00		104.00
5	21.00	14.00		28.00
6	40.00	44.00		16.00
7	35.00	17.00		63.00
8	42.00	60.00		57.00
9	24.00	16.00		18.00
10	30.00	37.00		41.00
11				

Splitting and Merging Files

Split file analysis (*SPSS Base 7.5 for Windows User's Guide,* pp. 103–104) splits the data file into separate groups for analysis, based on the values of the grouping variable (there can be more than one). We will find this useful in Chapter 2 on assumptions when we wish to obtain the z scores *within* each group. To obtain a split file analysis, click on DATA and then on SPLIT FILE from the dropdown menu. Select the variable on which you wish to divide into groups and then select ORGANIZE OUTPUT BY GROUPS.

Merging data files can be done in two different ways: (1) merging files with the same variables and different cases, and (2) merging files with the same cases but different variables (*SPSS Base for Windows User's Guide,* p. 95). SPSS gives the following marketing example for the first case. For example, you might record the same information for customers in two different sales regions and maintain the data for each region in separate files. We will give an example to illustrate how one would merge files with the same variable and different cases. As the guide notes (p. 96), open one of the data files. Then, from the menus choose:

DATA
    MERGE FILES
        ADD CASES

Then select the data file to merge with the open data file.

Example

To illustrate the process of merging files, we consider two small, artificial data sets. We denote these data sets by MERGE1 and MERGE2, respectively, and they are shown below:

caseid	y1	y2	y3
1.00	23.00	45.00	56.00
2.00	26.00	38.00	63.00
3.00	32.00	48.00	59.00
4.00	41.00	31.00	51.00

caseid	y1	y2	y3
1.00	23.00	34.00	67.00
2.00	34.00	45.00	76.00
3.00	21.00	42.00	63.00
4.00	27.00	41.00	65.00
5.00	31.00	48.00	72.00
6.00	34.00	49.00	68.00

As indicated above, we open MERGE1 and then select DATA and MERGE FILES and ADD CASES from the dropdown menus. When we open MERGE2 the ADD CASES window appears:

When you click on the OK the merged file appears, as given below:

	caseid	y1	y2	y3
1	1.00	23.00	45.00	56.00
2	2.00	26.00	38.00	63.00
3	3.00	32.00	48.00	59.00
4	4.00	41.00	31.00	51.00
5	1.00	23.00	34.00	67.00
6	2.00	34.00	45.00	76.00
7	3.00	21.00	42.00	63.00
8	4.00	27.00	41.00	65.00
9	5.00	31.00	48.00	72.00
10	6.00	34.00	49.00	68.00

1.11   SPSS OUTPUT NAVIGATOR

The Output Navigator was introduced in SPSS for Windows (7.0) in 1996. It is very nice. A survey researcher is conducting a pilot study on a 12 item scale to check out possible ambiguous wording, whether any items are sensitive, whether they discriminate, etc. She administers the scale to 16 subjects. The items are scaled from 1 to 5, with 1 representing strongly agree and 5 representing strongly disagree. The first 8 subjects are male and the last 8 are female. There is some missing data, which is coded as a 0. She wishes to compare males and females on 3 subtests (SUBTEST1, SUBTEST2, SUBTEST3), and also to determine the internal consistency of these subtests. We will illustrate only *some* of the things that can be done with output for the above survey example. First, the entire command syntax for running the analysis is presented below:

```
TITLE 'SURVEY RESEARCH WITH MISSING DATA'.
DATA LIST FREE/ID I1 I2 I3 I4 I5 I6 I7 I8 I9 I10 I11 I12 SEX.
BEGIN DATA.
1 1 2 2 3 3 1 1 2 2 1 2 2 1
2 1 2 2 3 3 3 1 2 2 1 1 1 1
3 1 2 1 3 3 2 3 3 2 1 2 3 1
4 2 2 4 2 3 3 2 2 3 3 2 3 1
5 2 3 2 4 2 1 2 3 0 3 4 0 1
6 2 3 2 3 3 2 3 4 3 2 4 2 1
7 3 4 4 3 5 2 2 1 2 3 3 4 1
8 3 2 3 4 4 3 4 3 3 3 4 2 1
9 3 3 4 2 4 3 3 4 5 3 5 3 2
10 4 4 5 5 3 3 5 4 4 4 5 3 2
11 4 4 0 5 5 5 4 3 0 5 4 4 2
12 4 4 4 5 5 4 3 3 5 4 4 5 2
13 4 4 0 4 3 2 5 1 3 3 0 4 2
14 5 5 3 4 4 4 4 5 3 5 5 3 2
15 5 5 4 5 3 5 5 4 4 5 3 5 2
16 5 4 3 4 3 5 4 4 3 2 2 3 2
END DATA.
LIST.
MISSING VALUES ALL (0).
COMPUTE SUBTEST1 = I1+I2+I3+I4+I5.
COMPUTE SUBTEST2 = I6+I7+I8+I9.
COMPUTE SUBTEST3 = I10+I11+I12.
RELIABILITY VARIABLES=I1 TO I12/
   SCALE(SUBTEST1) = I1 TO I5/
   SCALE(SUBTEST2) = I6 TO I9/
   SCALE(SUBTEST3) = I10 I11 I12/
   STATISTICS = CORR/.
T-TEST GROUPS = SEX(1,2)/
   VARIABLES = SUBTEST1 SUBTEST2 SUBTEST3/.
```

This is run from the command syntax window by clicking on RUN and then on ALL. The first thing you want to do is save the output. To do that click on FILE and then click on SAVE AS from the dropdown menu. Type in a name for the output (we will use MISSING), and then click on OK. The output, in the navigator, appears as follows:

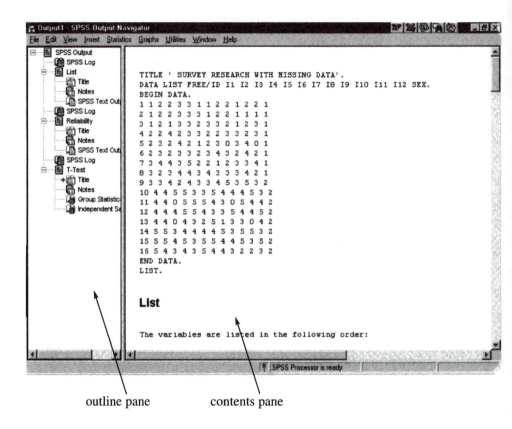

outline pane   contents pane

As shown above, the output is divided into two panes. The left pane gives in outline form the analysis(ses) that have been run, and the right pane has the statistical contents. To print the entire output, simply click on FILE and then click on PRINT from the dropdown menu. Select how many copies you want and click on OK. It is also possible to print only part of the output. I will illustrate. Suppose we wished to print only the reliability part of the output. Click on that in the left part of the pane; it is highlighted (as shown in the figure below). Click on FILE and PRINT from the dropdown menu. Now, when the print window appears click on SELECTION and then OK. Only the reliability part of the output will be printed.

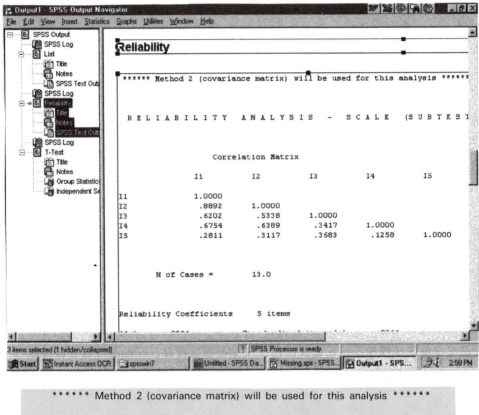

****** Method 2 (covariance matrix) will be used for this analysis ******

R E L I A B I L I T Y   A N A L Y S I S - S C A L E   (S U B T E S T 1)

Correlation Matrix

	I1	I2	I3	I4	I5
I1	1.0000				
I2	.8892	1.0000			
I3	.6202	.5338	1.0000		
I4	.6754	.6389	.3417	1.0000	
I5	.2811	.3117	.3683	.1258	1.0000

N of Cases =   13.0

Reliability Coefficients   5 items

Alpha = .8331   Standardized item alpha = .8211

R E L I A B I L I T Y   A N A L Y S I S - S C A L E   (S U B T E S T 2)

Correlation Matrix

	I6	I7	I8	I9
I6	1.0000			
I7	.6336	1.0000		
I8	.5428	.7641	1.0000	
I9	.5154	.5226	.5248	1.0000

N of Cases =   13.0

Reliability Coefficients   4 items

Alpha = .8494   Standardized item alpha = .8488

R E L I A B I L I T Y   A N A L Y S I S - S C A L E   (S U B T E S T 3)

Correlation Matrix

	I10	I11	I12
I10	1.0000		
I11	.6725	1.0000	
I12	.6677	.2647	1.0000

N of Cases =   13.0

Reliability Coefficients   3 items

Alpha = .7786   Standardized item alpha = .7753

It is also easy to move and delete output in the output navigator. Suppose for the missing data example we wished to move the corresponding to LIST to just above the *t* Test. We simply click on the LIST in the outline pane and drag it (holding the mouse down) to just above the *t* Test and then release.

To delete output is also easy. Suppose we wish to delete the LIST output. Click on LIST. To delete the output one can either hit DEL (delete) key on the keyboard, or click on EDIT and then click on DELETE from the dropdown menu.

As mentioned at the beginning of this section, there are many, many other things one can do with output. See *SPSS Base 8.0 for Windows User's Guide* (Chapter 7) and *SPSS Base 7.5 for Windows User's Guide* (Chapter 7).

1.12 SAS AND SPSS OUTPUT FOR CORRELATIONS, DESCRIPTIVES, AND t TESTS

In Table 1.5 we present SPSS Windows 8.0 printout for the correlations and SAS 6.12 printout for the descriptives statistics. Table 1.6 presents SPSS for Windows 8.0 screens for the t test for independent samples. Table 1.7 has the SPSS for Windows 8.0 printout for the independent samples t test and the SAS 6.12 printout for the dependent samples t test. In Appendix 2 we present appropriate SPSS Windows screens for splitting a file and obtaining z scores for each subject in each group.

TABLE 1.5
Correlations and Descriptive Statistics From
SPSS for Windows 8.0 and SAS 6.12

Correlations

		ACHLANG	ACHMOT	LOCUS
ACHLANG	Pearson Correlation	1.000	–.187	.386
	Sig. (2-tailed)	.	.631	.305
	N	9	9	9
ACHMOT	Pearson Correlation	–.187	1.000	–.427
	Sig. (2-tailed)	.631	.	.251
	N	9	9	9
LOCUS	Pearson Correlation	.386	–.427	1.000
	Sig. (2-tailed)	.305	.251	.
	N	9	9	9

The SAS System

Analysis Variable : TACTUAL
------------------------------- DRINK=A -------------------------------

N	Mean	Std Dev	Minimum	Maximum
10	28.1000000	12.6266913	9.0000000	50.0000000

------------------------------- DRINK=NA -------------------------------

N	Mean	Std Dev	Minimum	Maximum
10	13.4000000	6.9474216	2.0000000	23.0000000

TABLE 1.6
SPSS Windows 8.0 Screens for
Running *t* Test for Independent Samples

TABLE 1.7
t Test for Independent Samples From SPSS Windows 8.0
and t Test for Correlated Samples From SAS 6.12

T-Test

Group Statistics

	GPID	N	Mean	Std. Deviation	Std. Error Mean
ATT	1.00	8	89.3750	7.3473	2.5976
	2.00	15	94.0000	3.3166	.8563

		Levene's Test for Equality of Variances	
		F	Sig.
ATT	Equal variances assumed	8.521	.008
	Equal variances not assumed		

Independent Samples Test

		t-test for Equality of Means			
		t	df	Sig. (2-tailed)	Mean Difference
ATT	Equal variances assumed	-2.099	21	.048	-4.6250
	Equal variances not assumed	-1.691	8.554	.127	-4.6250

The SAS System

Analysis Variable : DIFF

N	Mean	T	Prob>|T|
6	1.5000000	1.2753455	0.2582

51

APPENDIX 1: OBTAINING THE MEAN AND VARIANCE
ON THE TI-30Xa AND CASIO fx-300SA CALCULATORS

We consider the data for the children in group 1 (example in Section 1.2), which is as follows:

10, 13, 7, 12, 13, 11, 8, 14, 9, 12

TI-30Xa

STEP   DISPLAY

1. Enter 10 and press Σ+   n=1 (indicates 1 data point has been entered)
2. Enter 13 and press Σ+   n=2 (indicates 2 data points entered)
3. Enter 7 and press Σ+   n=3
4. Enter the remaining 7 data points, and at that point the display will show n=10, indicating that 10 data points have been entered.
5. Press 2ND and then X^2 10.9 (this is the mean)
6. Press 2ND and then $\sqrt{X}$ 2.33095 (standard deviation)
7. Press X^2 5.4333 (variance)

CASIO fx - 300SA

1. Press SHIFT and AC   0 (clears all statistical registers)
2. Press MODE and 2   0 and DEG AND SD underneath
3. Press 10 and M+   10 and DATA in the upper left corner
4. Press 13 and M+   13 and DATA in the upper left corner
5. Press 7 and M+   7 and DATA in the upper left corner
6. Enter the remaining data points; after the last data point has been entered there will be a 12 in the display.
7. Press shift and 1   10.9 (mean)
8. Press shift and 3   2.33095 (standard deviation)
9. Press X^2 5.4333 (variance)

APPENDIX 2: OBTAINING THE *z* SCORES WITHIN EACH GROUP FOR A VARIABLE USING SPLIT FILE, DESCRIPTIVES PROCEDURE, AND CASE SUMMARIES IN SPSS

SPLIT FILE SCREEN

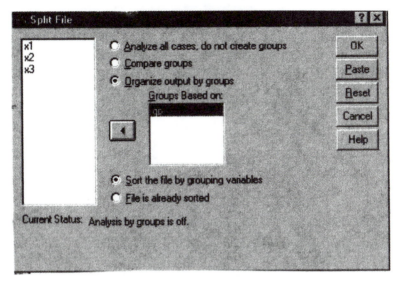

STATISTICS SCREEN

DESCRIPTIVES SCREEN

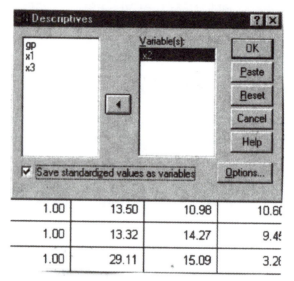

CASE SUMMARIES SCREEN

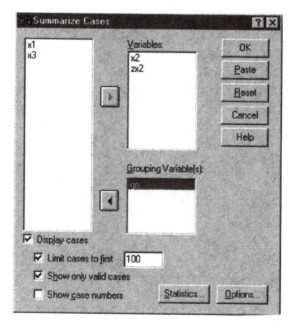

Case Summaries[a]

			X2	Zscore(X2)
GP	1.00	1	12.43	1.03078
		2	2.70	-1.29221
		3	1.35	-1.61451
		4	5.78	-.55687
		5	5.05	-.73116
		6	5.78	-.55687
		7	10.98	.68460
		8	14.27	1.47007
		9	15.09	1.66584
		10	7.61	-.11997
		11	5.80	-.55210
		12	3.63	-1.07017
		13	5.07	-.72638
		14	6.15	-.46854
		15	14.26	1.46769
		16	2.59	-1.31847
		17	6.05	-.49241
		18	2.70	-1.29221
		19	7.73	-.09132
		20	14.02	1.41039
		21	17.44	2.22689
		22	8.24	.03044
		23	13.37	1.25520
		24	10.78	.63685
		25	5.16	-.70489
		26	4.49	-.86485
		27	11.59	.83024
		28	8.63	.12355
		29	2.16	-1.42113
		30	7.95	-.03880
		31	11.22	.74190
		32	9.85	.41482
		33	11.42	.78965
		34	9.18	.25486
		35	4.67	-.82188
		36	6.86	-.29903
		Total N	36	36
	Total N		36	36

a. Limited to first 100 cases.

Case Summaries[a]

			X2	Zscore(X2)
GP	2.00	1	12.26	.29459
		2	5.13	-1.10773
		3	3.32	-1.46372
		4	8.89	-.36822
		5	9.95	-.15974
		6	2.94	-1.53846
		7	14.72	.77842
		8	4.17	-1.29655
		9	12.72	.38506
		10	5.06	-1.12150
		11	17.86	1.39600
		12	11.75	.19429
		13	13.25	.48930
		14	10.14	-.12237
		15	6.22	-.89335
		16	12.90	.42047
		17	5.69	-.99759
		18	16.77	1.18162
		19	17.65	1.35469
		20	21.52	2.11585
		21	13.22	.48340
		22	12.18	.27886
		23	9.22	-.30331
		Total N	23	23
	Total	N	23	23

a. Limited to first 100 cases.

Milk Data for Problem in Appendix 2

Group 1

x1	x2	x3	x1	x2	x3	x1	x2	x3
16.44	12.43	11.23	11.11	6.15	7.61	9.70	11.59	6.83
7.19	2.70	3.92	12.17	14.26	14.39	12.72	8.63	5.59
9.92	1.35	9.75	10.24	2.59	6.09	9.49	2.16	6.23
4.24	5.78	7.78	10.18	6.05	12.14	8.22	7.95	6.72
11.20	5.05	10.67	8.88	2.70	12.23	13.70	11.22	4.91
14.25	5.78	9.88	12.34	7.73	11.68	8.21	9.85	8.17
13.50	10.98	10.60	8.51	14.02	12.01	15.86	11.42	13.06
13.32	14.27	9.45	26.16	17.44	16.89	9.18	9.18	9.49
29.11	15.09	3.28	12.95	8.24	7.18	12.49	4.67	11.94
12.68	7.61	10.23	16.93	13.37	17.59	17.32	6.86	4.44
7.51	5.80	8.13	14.70	10.78	14.58			
9.90	3.63	9.13	10.32	5.16	17.00			
10.25	5.07	10.17	8.98	4.49	4.26			

Group 2

x1	x2	x3	x1	x2	x3	x1	x2	x3
8.50	12.26	9.11	9.60	12.72	11.00	11.94	5.69	14.77
7.42	5.13	17.15	9.70	5.06	20.84	9.54	16.77	22.66
10.28	3.32	11.23	9.77	17.86	35.18	10.43	17.65	10.66
6.47	8.89	19.00	11.61	11.75	17.00	10.87	21.52	28.47
11.35	9.95	14.53	9.09	13.25	20.66	7.13	13.22	19.44
9.15	2.94	13.68	8.53	10.14	17.45	11.88	12.18	21.20
10.16	14.72	5.99	8.29	6.22	16.38	12.03	9.22	23.09
12.79	4.17	29.28	15.90	12.90	19.09			

Tests of Normality

	GP	Kolmogorov-Smirnov[a]			Shapiro-Wilk		
		Statistic	df	Sig.	Statistic	df	Sig.
X2	1.00	.125	36	.171	.958	36	.304

a. Lilliefors Significance Correction

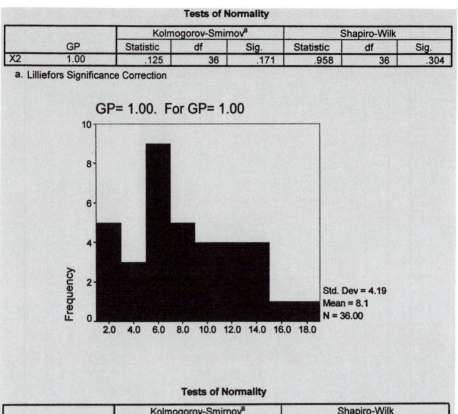

GP= 1.00. For GP= 1.00

Std. Dev = 4.19
Mean = 8.1
N = 36.00

Tests of Normality

	GP	Kolmogorov-Smirnov[a]			Shapiro-Wilk		
		Statistic	df	Sig.	Statistic	df	Sig.
X2	2.00	.119	23	.200*	.962	23	.500

*. This is a lower bound of the true significance.

a. Lilliefors Significance Correction

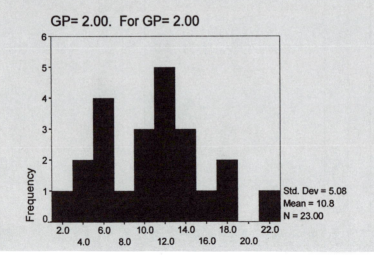

GP= 2.00. For GP= 2.00

Std. Dev = 5.08
Mean = 10.8
N = 23.00

EXERCISES

1. (a) An advertisement in the paper claims that the average pay at Smith Industries, a small factory, is $22,000. You are currently making $15,000 and decide to apply for a job there. Subsequently you find out that most people at Smith also make $15,000, and you are upset about the ad. You later determine that the salary structure at Smith Industries is as follows:

50 workers	$15,000 each
Managers of the two divisions at Smith	$35,000 each
Two executives	$70,000 each
Owner	$250,000

(a) Why was the $22,000 figure in the paper so misleading?
(b) Which measure(s) of central tendency should have been used to convey a more accurate picture of the salaries at Smith?

2. Suppose Mr. Jones had administered the same math test to each of his two eighth grade classes, with the results shown below:

	Class 1	Class 2
Size	20	40
Mean	60	80

Mr. Jones then naively computed the average for all students by taking the average of the above two means, yielding 70.
(a) Intuitively, why is this not correct?
(b) The correct formula for finding the combined mean is to use a weighted average:

$$\bar{x}_c = (n_1\bar{x}_1 + n_2\bar{x}_2)/(n_1 + n_2)$$

where n_1 and n_2 are the respective group sizes and $\bar{x}_1$ and $\bar{x}_2$ are the group means. Plugging the above numbers into this formula yields the correct overall mean of 73.33.

Now, let $x_1, x_2, \ldots, x_{n1}$ represent the subjects scores in group 1 and let $x_1, x_2, \ldots, x_{n2}$ represent the subjects scores in group 2. Prove that the formula for the combined mean is as given above.

HINT: Start with the definition for the mean for all subjects combined:

$$\bar{x}_c = \frac{(x_1 + x_2 + \cdots + x_{n1}) + (x_1 + x_2 + \cdots + x_{n2})}{n_1 + n_2}$$

3. An investigator runs a t test for independent samples on two groups of subjects (45 subjects in group 1 and 35 in group 2). She notes that the distributions of scores are quite positively skewed in both groups. Should she be concerned about this?

4. (a) Suppose that in a hospital each patient's pulse is taken in the morning, at noon, and in the evening. For two patients, on a given day, the average pulse readings are both 74. The records for that day show the following:

	Morning	Noon	Evening	Mean
Patient A	72	76	74	74
Patient B	72	91	59	74

Are the clinical implications for these two patients the same? Explain.

(b) You are a scout for the Boston Celtics professional basketball team and are looking for a guard. From scouting reports you focus in on two guards from Duke and UCLA, schools that play on a similar level of competition. It is noted that each guard averaged 20 points over all games in his senior year, so you decide to examine their performance game by game:

UCLA guard: 21, 18, 19, 23, 25, 20, 22, 17, 23, 24 etc.
Duke guard: 13, 35, 28, 11, 8, 40, 22, 31, 15, 29 etc.

Which guard might you prefer, and why?
What is the main point that each of the two parts of this exercise illustrates?

5. (a) Suppose that $c = 3$, $x_1 = 5$, $x_2 = 8$, $x_3 = 1$, and $x_4 = 7$. Evaluate the following:

$$\sum_{i=1}^{4} cx_i$$

(b) Prove that the variance of a constant times a variable x is equal to C^2 times the variance of x; that is, prove that

$$s_{cx}^2 = c^2 s_x^2$$

Hint: The scores on cx may be represented as: $cx_1, cx_2, \ldots, cx_n$. Apply the definitional formula for variance to this set of scores and mathematically rearrange.

(c) Suppose there are 10 subjects in each of three groups. The means for the groups are $\bar{x}_1 = 4.1$, $\bar{x}_2 = 6.3$ and $\bar{x}_3 = 8.5$. Evaluate the following:

$$\sum_{i=1}^{3} 10(\bar{x}_i - \bar{x})^2, \text{ where } \bar{x} \text{ is the grand mean for all the subjects.}$$

6. A team of researchers is comparing two diets, a behavior modification approach and the Beverly Hills diet, in their effect on weight loss for a group of overweight women. Suppose that the data for the 10 subjects in each diet is as follows:

Behavioral Modification		Beverly Hills	
10	14	8	12
15	17	16	10
11	32	13	7
22	15	4	15
8	9	10	11

Label the independent variable here DIET and the dependent variable WGTLOSS. Use column format, with group identification (1 or 2) in column 1 and weight loss in columns 3 and 4. Show the complete SAS control lines for running the t test for independent samples on this data.

7. A researcher has the following heights and weights on 14 men:

						Subject								
	1	2	3	4	5	6	7	8	9	10	11	12	13	14
Height	67	66	63	61	68	69	69	70	71	73	75	74	77	71
Weight	148	161	152	145	169	162	170	183	174	115	205	186	233	158

The heights are given in inches.
(a) Compute the correlation between height and weight. What conclusion would you draw?
(b) Check the data to see if there is an outlier.
(c) Compute the correlation without the outlier. Now, what do you conclude?

8. A worker in a neighborhood clinic wishes to asses the impact of showing an educational film on patient compliance in taking an antihypertension medication. The diastolic blood pressure is the dependent variable here. During the study the medication dosage is kept constant. Blood pressure was measured one week prior to the film, then the film was shown, and the blood pressure was measured again three weeks later. The data are:

					Patient					
	1	2	3	4	5	6	7	8	9	10
Before	110	105	98	100	89	82	113	102	101	118
After	100	95	88	92	83	86	100	101	96	112

(a) Denote the diastolic blood pressure by DIASTOL and the treatment (independent variable) by FILM. Show the complete set of control lines for running the t test for dependent samples on SPSSX to determine whether there was a significant change in the blood pressure.

9. Two school psychologists have conducted two group studies comparing two types of interventions in reducing the number of disruptive behaviors for learning disabled children. The first school psychologist has 10 children for each of the interventions while the second psychologist has 100 children for each intervention. Suppose that to demonstrate clinical (practical) significance the difference in the average number of disruptive behaviors must be at least 2. Now, t tests for independent samples are run in both studies: $t = 2.3 = 4/1.74$ for the first study and $t = 7.02 = 4/.57$ for the second study.

(a) Compute the 95% confidence intervals for each study. Is the null hypothesis of equal population means rejected in both cases?

(b) Can we be confident of clinical significance in the first study? in the second study? Explain.

2 One Way Analysis of Variance

CONTENTS

2.1   INTRODUCTION

One of the statistical tests encountered in introductory statistics courses is the t test for independent samples. This test is appropriate when comparing two groups

63

of subjects on a single dependent variable. Three classical applications of this test are given below:

1. Comparing a treatment group against a control group.
2. Comparing the relative efficacy of treatment 1 vs. treatment 2
3. Comparing two intact groups (such as males and females or two social classes) on some dependent variable.

However, in many situations we may wish to compare more than two groups simultaneously on a dependent variable. In these cases a different statistical technique, called analysis of variance (ANOVA), is needed. We consider 7 examples below:

1. A counselor wishes to compare the effectiveness of two types of counseling* (Rogerian and Adlerian) on changing the attitude of low achieving high school students toward school. She also has a control group in her study. Thus, there are 3 groups being compared on the dependent variable of attitude toward school.

2. A psychologist wants to determine if five drugs have a differential effect on reaction time (dependent variable) for 100 subjects, 20 of which have been randomly assigned to each drug.

3. A dietician wishes to discover whether four diets produce differential weight loss (the dependent variable) for 80 overweight women. Here diets are the treatments, and we have four groups being compared.

4. A researcher for a school district wishes to determine whether the reading achievement on a standardized test differs on the average for six elementary schools in similar socioeconomic areas. Here we have six groups (the schools) being compared on reading achievement (the dependent variable).

5. A marketing researcher wishes to determine if shelf location has an effect on volume of sales of a product. If there are 4 shelf locations (from high to low), then we have a 4 group ANOVA, with sales as the dependent variable.

6. We wish to determine whether violent crime varies in different regions of the country. If there are 7 different regions being compared, then we have a 7 group ANOVA.

7. Doughnuts absorb fat in various amounts when they are cooked. Suppose an experiment is set up involving three types of fat: peanut oil, corn oil, and lard. We would have a 3 group ANOVA, with amount of fat absorbed as the dependent variable.

---

*This chapter deals with what is called *fixed effects* ANOVA, since counseling methods, teaching methods, diets, etc. are generally not randomly sampled from some population of methods or diets. Thus, our inferences are fixed to the counseling methods, teaching methods or diets under consideration. Further elaboration of this point is given in Section 4.7, where we distinguish between fixed and random effects ANOVA.

Let us review some of the basic terminology concerned with hypothesis testing before considering how to do an ANOVA. Recall that with the t test we talked about testing a null hypothesis versus some alternative hypothesis, which looked like this:

$$H_0: \mu_1 = \mu_2 \text{ (population means are equal)}$$
$$H_1: \mu_1 \neq \mu_2$$

Why is it called the *null* hypothesis? Because to say that the population means are equal is equivalent to saying that their difference is null, i.e., that $\mu_1 - \mu_2 = 0$. Also, in testing the null hypothesis the notion of testing at some level of significance was encountered. What does it mean to do a t test at the $\alpha = .05$ level of significance? This means we are taking a 5% chance of rejecting the null hypothesis when it is true, that is, saying the groups differ when in fact they do not. Level of significance is also called the probability of making a type I error.

Notice that the alternative hypothesis (H_1) for the t test is very simple, since either the two groups are equal or they differ. In analysis of variance (for k groups) the alternative is much more complex. What is the null hypothesis for a one way analysis of variance with k groups? It is that the k population means are equal:

$$H_0: \mu_1 = \mu_2 = \mu_3 = \cdots = \mu_k$$

The alternative hypothesis here is more complicated than that for the t test. Let us consider the four group case to illustrate. If we reject the null hypothesis it could be for various reasons. It might be because only two groups are different, or it might be because only 3 groups are different, or because group 1 differs only from groups 3 and 4, or because all 4 groups are different, etc. How can we characterize all these possibilities into an alternative hypothesis? Notice that in all the above cases *at least two* of the groups differed. Thus, a way of stating the alternative hypothesis is as follows:

$$H_1: \text{At least two of the } \mu_i \text{ are different.}$$

2.2 RATIONALE FOR ANOVA

Now that we know what the null hypothesis is that is being tested in a one way ANOVA, we might ask the following questions, "Why bother doing an ANOVA when comparing k groups? Why not simply do several t tests?" To see why the latter is problematic, let us consider the four group case ($T_1 \ T_2 \ T_3 \ T_4$). There are six paired comparisons here (12, 13, 14, 23, 24, 34). We could do six t tests, each at the .05 level, to determine which of these pairs are significantly different. Now, for just one of these t tests the α level is under control at .05. But, for the *set of 6* tests the α level gets out of control, since there is a 5% risk of false rejection for each test. We define the *overall α level* for a set of tests as the probability of at least one type I error (false rejection) when H_0 is true. Now, it can be shown that if α is small, then overall $\alpha \approx r\alpha$, where r is the number of tests being done. Actually, $r\alpha$ is an *upper bound* on the overall α level. Let us use this to see how rapidly the overall α inflates as the number of groups increases:

Number of groups	Number of t tests	Approximate overall α
3	3	.15
4	6	.30
5	10	.50
6	15	.75

This table shows that if we were to compare five groups with 10 t tests, each at the .05 level, then we have an approximate 50% chance of at least one false rejection. Thus, the probability of a few false rejections here is uncomfortably high. For six groups and 15 t tests, the probability of 2 or 3 false rejections is *very likely* (approximately .75)! Thus, it should be clear that using multiple t tests in a k group situation is not the way to proceed. We see later on in the chapter (Section 2.15) that a much tighter upper bound than $r\alpha$ can be put on overall α, especially when each test is done at the $\alpha = .05$ level.

2.3   NUMERICAL EXAMPLE

The analysis of variance procedure, which is appropriate, was developed by R. A. Fisher in an agricultural context back in the 1920s. ANOVA is based on the following three assumptions:

1. The observations are normally distributed on the dependent variable in each group.
2. The population variances for the groups are equal.
3. The observations in each group are independent.

We consider the effect of violations of these assumptions in detail in Section 2.7.

For our example, suppose a consumer organization wants to compare the price of a particular toy in three types of stores in a suburban county: variety stores, department stores, and discount toy stores. A random sample of 3 variety stores, 4 department stores, and 5 discount toy stores is selected and the following prices (in dollars) are recorded. We wish to test whether there is a difference in the average prices on this toy for the populations of stores from which these stores were selected.

The null hypothesis that is being tested here is

$$H_0: \mu_1 = \mu_2 = \mu_3$$

The sample means above are estimating the population means:

$$\bar{x}_1 = \hat{\mu}_1, \bar{x}_2 = \hat{\mu}_2, \bar{x}_3 = \hat{\mu}_3$$

Variety	Dept.	Discount
3	4	4
6	7	5
8	9	2
	8	3
		5
$\bar{x}_1 = 5.67$	$\bar{x}_2 = 7$	$\bar{x}_3 = 3.8$

We wish to determine whether the sample means differ sufficiently, given sampling error, to suggest that the underlying population means differ. To determine this the ANOVA computes and compares two basic sources of variation:

1. Between group variation—determines how much the group means vary about the grand (overall) mean.
2. Within group variation—determines how much the subjects scores vary who are in the same group. Variation here is primarily due to individual differences.

Between Group Variation

The general formula here is given by

$$SS_b = \sum_{i=1}^{k} n_i(\bar{x}_i - \bar{x})^2$$
$$SS_b = n_1(\bar{x}_1 - \bar{x})^2 + n_2(\bar{x}_2 - \bar{x})^2 + \cdots + n_k(\bar{x}_k - \bar{x})^2 \qquad (1)$$

where Σ is the summation symbol, n_i denotes the number of subjects in the ith group, $\bar{x}$ denotes the grand mean, and SS_b stands for sum of squares between. It is a weighted sum of squares, where each deviation is weighted by the number of subjects in that group.

For the above data this becomes

$$SS_b = \sum n_i(\bar{x}_i - 5.33)^2$$
$$= n_1(\bar{x}_1 - 5.33)^2 + n_2(\bar{x}_2 - 5.33)^2 + n_3(\bar{x}_3 - 5.33)^2$$
$$= 3(5.67 - 5.33)^2 + 4(7 - 5.33)^2 + 5(3.8 - 5.33)^2$$
$$= .3468 + 11.1556 + 11.7045 = 23.2069$$

In calculating the grand (overall) mean above it is simplest to add up all the scores and divide by total number of subjects. Thus, in the above case this yields $\bar{x} = 64/12 = 5.33$. One can also obtain the grand mean from the individual means with the following formula:

$$\bar{x}_c = (n_1 \bar{x}_1 + n_2 \bar{x}_2 + \cdots + n_k \bar{x}_k)/N$$

where n_1 is the number of subjects in group 1, n_2 is the number of subjects in group 2, etc., and N represents total number of subjects. Note that this is a *weighted* average and that means based on
a larger number of subjects receive greater weight in determining the grand mean. Because of this it is not appropriate to find the grand mean with unequal group sizes by simply taking the average of the means—a mistake frequently made.

We need the mean sum of square between (MS_b), since this represents a variance (we see why in Section 2.5). MS_b is simply sum of squares between (SS_b) divided by degrees of freedom, i.e.,

$$MS_b = SS_b / (k - 1) = 23.2069 / (3 - 1) = 11.6035 \qquad (2)$$

Within Group Variation

Verbally, within group variability is calculated by deviating each score in group 1 about the mean in group 1, and squaring and summing these deviations. We then square the deviations of all scores of group 2 about the mean for group 2 and sum them, and so forth on to the kth group. We then pool (add) these squared deviations to obtain the sum of squares within, denoted by SS_w. Symbolically then, it looks like

$$SS_w = \sum_1 (x_{i1} - \bar{x}_1)^2 + \sum_2 (x_{i2} - \bar{x}_2)^2 + \cdots + \sum_k (x_{ik} - \bar{x}_k)^2 \qquad (3)$$

where x_{i1} is the score of the ith subject in group 1, x_{i2} is the score of the ith subject in group 2, and x_{ik} is the score of the ith subject in group k. Now we calculate SS_w for the above data:

$SS_w = (3 - 5.67)^2 + (6 - 5.67)^2 + (8 - 5.67)^2$ (variability within gp 1)

$+ (4 - 7)^2 + (9 - 7)^2 + (8 - 7)^2$ (variability within gp 2)

$+ (4 - 3.8)^2 + (5 - 3.8)^2 + (2 - 3.8)^2 + (3 - 3.8)^2 + (5 - 3.8)^2$

(variability within gp 3)

$SS_w = 33.4667$ pooled within group variability. Once again we need MS_w (mean sum of squares within), which represents a variance, rather than SS_w. The formula for MS_w is

$$MS_w = SS_w/(N - k) = 33.4667/(12 - 3) = 3.7185 \qquad (4)$$

where N denotes the total number of subjects.

The F Test

To test the tenability of the null hypothesis the following F statistic is used: $F = MS_b/MS_w$. Thus, for our data this is

$$F = MS_b/MS_w = 11.6035/3.7185 = 3.12 \qquad (5)$$

To determine whether this is large enough to reject H_0 we must ascertain if this is a very unlikely value to occur if indeed the null hypothesis is true. To get at this we need to refer to the *sampling distribution of F under H_0 (assuming the population means are equal)*. Here we must think conceptually as follows. If we were to draw samples of sizes 3, 4, and 5 repeatedly from populations with equal means, and compute an F ratio for each draw, what would the distribution of F's look like? This is the sampling distribution of F under H_0. Statisticians have determined that the distribution will be positively skewed, with a modal value of approximately 1. We will sketch the distribution shortly.

Now, suppose we are testing H_0 at $\alpha = .05$. The above sampling distribution will have the following pair of degrees of freedom:

$df_b = k - 1$ (degrees of freedom between) and

$df_w = N - k$ (degrees of freedom within)

Thus, for our data $df_b = 3 - 1 = 2$ and $df_w = 12 - 3 = 9$. For an F distribution with 2 and 9 degrees of freedom it has been determined that the 95th percentile point is 4.26 (the point corresponding to testing at .05 level). That is, if the null hypothesis is true, then only 5% of the time would we expect to obtain an F greater than 4.26. Thus, 4.26 is our critical value, and if the value of the test statistic is greater than 4.26 we will reject H_0. For our case $F = 3.12$, so we fail to reject H_o and conclude that it is possible that the population means are equal. The sampling distribution is sketched below:

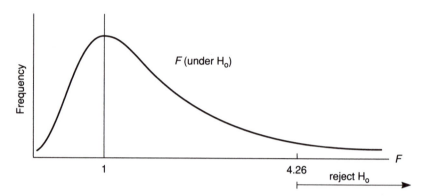

The results of an ANOVA are typically summarized in a table as follows:

Source	SS	df	MS	F
Between	$\Sigma\, n_i(\bar{x}_i - \bar{x})^2$	$k - 1$	$SS_b/(k - 1)$	MS_b/MS_w
Within	$\Sigma(x_{i1} - \bar{x}_1)^2 +$	$N - k$	$SS_w/(N - k)$	
	$\Sigma(x_{i2} - \bar{x}_2)^2 +$			
	$\cdots + \Sigma(x_{ik} - \bar{x}_k)^2$			

For the above example this table would be:

Source	SS	df	MS	F
Between	23.2069	2	11.6035	3.12
Within	33.4667	9	3.7185	

The critical values for ANOVAs with varying sample size and different α levels have been tabled, and are found in Table B.1 at the end of this book. To give the reader practice in using these tables we consider two examples.

Example 1

An experimenter runs a 3 group ANOVA with 10 subjects per group, testing at $\alpha = .10$. He obtains $F = 2.16$. Does he reject the null hypothesis? First we find degrees of freedom between and within: $df_b = 3 - 1 = 2$ and $df_w = 30 - 3 = 27$. Reference to Table B.1 then shows that the critical value $= F_{.10;2,27} = 2.51$, and thus he would fail to reject the null hypothesis.

Example 2

An investigator runs a 4 group ANOVA with following sample sizes: $n_1 = 15$, $n_2 = 20$, $n_3 = 10$, and $n_4 = 25$. She will test at $\alpha = .01$. Will she reject H_0 if she obtains $F = 5.26$? The degrees of freedom are $df_b = 3$ and $df_w = 70 - 4 = 66$. Reference to Table B.1 shows that critical value for 3 and 66 degrees of freedom is not in the table. What do we do here? Note that the tabled values for error degrees of freedom are given from 1 to 30 and then jump to 40, 60, 120, and infinity. The reason is that the critical values change very little once the degrees of freedom gets beyond 30. We could interpolate in our case between 60 and 90, but since the values change so little our recommendation is simply to use the critical value for the closest error degrees of freedom, which here is 60. Thus, the critical value is $F_{.01;3,60} = 4.13$. Since the value of $F = 5.26$, which is greater than 4.13, we reject the null hypothesis.

When we reject the null hypothesis at some α level all we know is that there is an *overall difference* among the groups. To locate where the differences lie (e.g., which pairs of groups are significantly different) we need some post hoc (after this—from the Latin) procedure. Many such post hoc procedures have been developed, and we consider these in Section 2.10.

2.4 EXPECTED MEAN SQUARES

Earlier we stated that the modal value of F in the sampling distribution under H_0 was about 1; i.e., this is the value we would *expect* to obtain most frequently *if* indeed the population means are equal. In other words, we were saying that the expected value of F is about 1, or in symbols $E(F) \approx 1$. The reason this is true is because of the expected values for MS_b and MS_w under the null hypothesis.

The reader can think of expected value as the long term average. As a simple example, consider flipping a coin 1,000 times. Then, if it is a fair coin, we would expect about 500 heads and 500 tails, that is, $E(H) = E(T) = .5$. In the ANOVA context we think of repeating the experiment thousands of times, and computing a MS_b and MS_w each time. Now, it can be shown that if we were to average the thousands of MS_w's, then the average would be σ^2. Recall that σ^2 was the assumed common population variance for the groups. That is, σ^2 involved one of the assumptions underlying the analysis of variance. Thus we have

$$E(MS_w) = \sigma^2 \text{ (when } H_0 \text{ is true)} \qquad (6)$$

Also, it is important to note that the size of MS_w does *not* depend on whether the population means differ or not. However, we will see that the $E(MS_b)$ does depend on differences in population means. It can be shown that

$$E(MS_b) = \sigma^2 + n_i \sum (\mu_i - \mu)^2/(k-1) \tag{7}$$

If the population means are equal (H_0 is true), then this means $\mu_1 = \mu_2 = \cdots = \mu_k = \mu$ and the second term in the above expression will be 0, or in other words,

$$E(MS_b) = \sigma^2 \text{ (when } H_0 \text{ is true)} \tag{8}$$

Thus, when the null hypothesis is true, the expected values for numerator and denominator of the F ratio are equal and the expected value of F statistic is equal to about 1. The reason that $E(F)$ is not exactly equal to 1 is because the expected value of a quotient is not equal to the quotient of expected values.

Thus, evidence in favor of rejecting H_0 will be reflected in an F ratio greater than 1. How much greater than 1 the F must be to reject H_0 depends a great deal on sample size. The next chapter on power deals with this issue in detail.

2.5 MS_w AND MS_b AS VARIANCES

We mentioned earlier that MS_w and MS_b actually represent variances. Now we show this algebraically. This is easiest to see for equal n per group and so that is demonstrated. Using Equations 3 and 4, we can write MS_w as

$$MS_w = \left[\sum (x_{i1} - \bar{x}_1)^2 + \sum (x_{i2} - \bar{x}_2)^2 + \cdots + \sum (x_{ik} - \bar{x}_k)^2 \right]/(N-k)$$

For equal n per group, we have $N = nk$ and therefore we have $N - k = nk - k = k(n-1)$. Thus, we can rewrite the above equation as

$$MS_w = 1/k(n-1) \left[\sum (x_{i1} - \bar{x}_1)^2 + \sum (x_{i2} - \bar{x}_2)^2 + \cdots + \sum (x_{ik} - \bar{x}_k)^2 \right]$$

or

$$MS_w = 1/k \left[\underbrace{\frac{\Sigma(x_{ik} - \bar{x}_1)^2}{n-1}}_{\substack{\text{variance} \\ \text{for gp 1}}} + \underbrace{\frac{\Sigma(x_{i2} - \bar{x}_2)^2}{n-1}}_{\substack{\text{variance} \\ \text{for gp 2}}} + \cdots + \underbrace{\frac{\Sigma(x_{ik} - \bar{x}_k)^2}{n-1}}_{\substack{\text{variance} \\ \text{for gp } k}} \right]$$

Recall from beginning statistics that each is in the *form* of a variance, since variance for a single group of subjects is $s^2 = \Sigma(x_i - \bar{x})^2/(n-1)$.

Thus, for equal group size, MS_w *is just the average of the sample variances for the groups.*

Using Equations 1 and 2, we can write MS_b as follows:

$$MS_b = \left[n(\bar{x}_1 - \bar{x})^2 + n(\bar{x}_2 - \bar{x})^2 + \cdots + n(\bar{x}_k - \bar{x})^2 \right] / (k - 1)$$

or

$$MS_b = n \underbrace{\sum (\bar{x}_i - \bar{x})^2 / (k - 1)}$$

variance for k group means
about the grand mean

Thus, MS_b *is a weighted variance of the group means about the grand mean.* This is somewhat more subtle, but note that except for the n we have the *form of a variance*, where the group means are playing the role of individual observations and the grand mean is playing the role of the mean for a single group.

2.6   A LINEAR MODEL FOR THE DATA

We now state the *linear* model for each subject's score on which the one way ANOVA is based. The model for the score of the ith subject in group j (y_{ij}) is given by:

$$y_{ij} = \mu + \alpha_j + e_{ij} \tag{9}$$

where μ is the grand mean for all subjects, $\alpha_j = \mu_j - \mu$ is the treatment effect for the jth treatment, and e_{ij} is the random error for the ith subject in the jth treatment.

Thus, we are postulating that a subject's score is composed of three parts: (1) a general effect—the grand mean, (2) an effect unique and constant within a given treatment (α_j), and (3) an effect that is unpredictable, that is, e_{ij}. It is assumed that the e_{ij} are independent, normally distributed within each treatment, and have the *same* variance for each treatment. Note that these assumptions for the e_{ij} imply exactly the same assumptions for the y_{ij} (the subjects' scores), since e_{ij} is the only random part of the model on the right side of Equation 9.

To gain some feeling for the above linear model, consider three treatments with 4 subjects in each treatment. Suppose there is just a general effect (i.e., no treatment effect or random error). Then the data would look like this:

MODEL: $y_{ij} = \mu$

T_1	T_2	T_3
20	20	20
20	20	20
20	20	20
20	20	20

Next, suppose there is in addition a treatment effect but no random error. Then the data might look like this:

MODEL: $y_{ij} = \mu + \alpha_j$

T_1	T_2	T_3
19	17	24
19	17	24
19	17	24
19	17	24

In the above we have $\alpha_1 = -1$, $\alpha_2 = -3$, and $\alpha_3 = 4$.

But both of the above situations are too simple for real data, since subjects' scores will essentially always vary within each treatment group. The main reason they will differ is because of individual differences (they come to the treatments with different capabilities, backgrounds, motivation, etc.). Measurement error also contributes to within treatment variability. Since the y_{ij} will vary, this implies the random error components will vary. If we now add an error component to each subject's score we might obtain a realistic data set like this:

MODEL: $y_{ij} = \mu + \alpha_j + e_{ij}$

T_1	T_2	T_3
18	18	23
24	19	22
21	11	27
17	16	28

Here we have added an error component of $e_{11} = -1$ for the first subject's score in treatment 1, an $e_{21} = 5$ for the second subject in treatment 1, an $e_{31} = 2$ for the third subject, etc.

2.7   ASSUMPTIONS IN ANOVA

We mentioned earlier that the analysis of variance is based on the following three assumptions:

1. The observations are normally distributed on the dependent variable in *each* group.
2. The population variances for the groups are equal. This is the so-called *homogeneity of variance* assumption. In symbols this would be $\sigma_1^2 = \sigma_2^2 = \cdots = \sigma_k^2 = \sigma^2$.
3. The observations are independent.

Why is it important to study the assumptions underlying ANOVA? Because in ANOVA we set up a mathematical model based on the assumptions, and all mathematical models are approximations to reality. Therefore, violations of the assumptions are inevitable. The salient question becomes, "How radically must a given assumption be violated before it has a serious effect on type I and type II error rates?" Thus, we may set our $\alpha = .05$ and think we are rejecting falsely 5% of the time, but if a given assumption is violated we may be rejecting falsely 40% of the time. For these kind of situations we would certainly want to be able to detect such violations and take some corrective action. But all violations of assumptions are not serious, and hence it is crucial to know *which* assumptions to be particularly concerned about, and under what conditions. Before we begin our review of a considerable literature on violations of assumptions in ANOVA, it is helpful to cover some basic terminology that is needed in discussing the results of Monte Carlo (i.e., simulation) studies.

The nominal α (level of significance) is the level set by the experimenter, and is the percent of time one is rejecting falsely when the null hypothesis is true *and all* assumptions are met. The actual α is the percent of time one is rejecting falsely if one or more of the assumptions is violated. We say a test statistic is *robust* if the actual α is very close to the nominal α.

Numerous studies have examined the effect of violations of assumptions in ANOVA, and an excellent summary of this literature has been provided by Glass, Peckham, and Sanders (1972). Their review indicates that non-normality has only a slight effect on the type I error rate, even for very skewed or kurtotic distributions. For example, the actual α's for some very non-normal populations were only .055 or .06: very minor deviations from the nominal level of .05. We say the F statistic is robust with respect to the normality assumption.

The reader may be puzzled as to how this can be. The basic reason is the *Central Limit Theorem,* which states that the sum of independent observations having any distribution whatsoever approaches a normal distribution as the number of observations increases. To be somewhat more specific, Bock (1975) notes, "even for distributions which depart markedly from normality, sums of 50 or more observations approximate to normality. For moderately non-normal distributions the approximation is good with as few as 10 to 20 observations" (p. 111). Now, since the sums of independent observations approach normality rapidly, so do the means, and the sampling distribution of F is based on means. Thus, the sampling distribution of F is only slightly affected, and therefore the critical values when sampling from normal and non-normal distributions will not differ by much.

Lack of normality due to skewness also has only a slight effect on power (a few hundredths). Platykurtosis (a flattened out distribution relative to the normal) does affect power, and the effect can be substantial for small n.

Now, we deal with the second assumption, homogeneity of the population variances. If the group sizes are equal or approximately equal (largest/smallest

< 1.5), then the F statistic is robust for unequal variances. That is, the actual α stays close to the nominal α (level of significance). The only time one need worry is when the group sizes are sharply unequal (largest/smallest > 1.5) *and* a statistical test shows that the population variances are unequal. For this class of situations the studies have found that if the large variances are associated with the small group sizes, then F is *liberal*. A statistic being liberal means we are rejecting falsely too often, i.e., the actual α > nominal α. Thus, an experimenter may think he or she is rejecting falsely 5% of the time (nominal α), but in fact the true rejection rate may be 11% (actual α). On the other hand, when the large variances are associated with the large group sizes, then the F statistic is *conservative*. This means the actual α < nominal α. Many researchers would not consider this serious; however, note that the smaller α will cause a decrease in power.

There are many statistical tests for homogeneity of variance (e.g., Bartlett's, Cochran's, Hartley's F_{max}), but these all suffer from being very sensitive to non-normality. That is, one may reject with these tests and conclude that the population variances are different when in fact the rejection may have been due to non-normality in the underlying populations. Fortunately there is a test, due to Levene, which is somewhat more robust against non-normality, and it is available on SAS and SPSS.

Examples

Consider the three data situations below. In which (if any) of the cases would you be concerned?

	Case 1 GROUPS			Case 2 GROUPS			Case 3 GROUPS			
	1	2	3	1	2	3	1	2	3	4
n_i	18	20	17	20	50	30	10	30	15	25
s_i^2	15	90	42	80	10	35	50	100	70	140

In Case 1 there is no need to be concerned since the group cases are approximately equal (20/17 < 1.5), and therefore F is robust. In Case 2 the group sizes are sharply unequal (50/20 > 1.5), so there will be a problem if a statistical test shows the population variances to be different. We use Hartley's F_{max} = largest variance/smallest variance, assuming normality is not a problem, and find that $F_{max} = 80/10 = 8$. Referring to Table B.4, and using the average group size (35) to enter the table, we find that the critical value at .05 is about 2.4. Thus, we conclude the population variances are different. In this case the large sample variances are associated with the smaller group sizes, so that F will be liberal. What is to be done here? There are at least 3 possibilities. One is to do an

ANOVA which does not assume equal variances. Another choice is to simply test at a more stringent α level (say .01), realizing that the actual α will probably be in the vicinity of .05. A third choice is to seek help from a statistician on a variance stabilizing transformation (such as square root or log). I would recommend either of the first two choices for applied researchers.

In Case 3 we again have a potential problem because the group sizes are sharply unequal (30/10 > 1.5). Using Table B.4 and an average group size of 20 to enter the table, we find $F_{max} = 140/50 = 2.8$. This is not significant since the critical value $= 3.29$. Therefore there is no problem here since the assumption is tenable.

So far we have treated heterogeneity of variance as a nuisance, something we wish will not happen so that the analysis on the means can proceed accurately. However, unequal variances, or a focus on dispersion, in some situations may be an interesting and important finding. Raudenbusch and Bryk (1987) cite a study by Bryk (1977) in which a compensatory program that increased mean achievement also increased dispersion in achievement. As they note, such a program might increase the number of children failing to attain some minimum standard even though it raised mean achievement. Also, occasionally variance reduction is an explicit goal of educational programs, as in some mastery learning programs (Bloom, 1984).

2.8   THE INDEPENDENCE ASSUMPTION

Although we have listed the independence assumption last, it is *by far the most important assumption, for even a small violation of it produces a substantial effect on both the level of significance and the power of the F statistic.* Just a small amount of dependence among the observations causes the actual α to be several times greater than the nominal α. Dependence among the observations is measured by the intraclass correlation R, where:

$$R = (MS_b - MS_w)/(MS_b + (n - 1)MS_w) \qquad (10)$$

MS_b and MS_w are the numerator and denominator of the F statistic and n is the number of subjects per group.

Table 2.1, from Scariano and Davenport (1987), shows precisely how dramatic of an effect dependence has on type I error. For example, for the 3 group case with 10 subjects per group and moderate dependence (intraclass correlation = .30) the actual α is .5379! Also, for 3 groups with 30 subjects per group and small dependence (intraclass correlation = .10) the actual α is .4917, almost 10 times the nominal α of .05! Notice, also from the table that for a fixed value of the intraclass correlation the situation does not improve with larger sample size, but gets far worse.

Now let us consider some situations in social science research where dependence among the observations will be present. Teaching methods studies constitute

TABLE 2.1
Actual Type I Error Rates for Correlated Observations in a One Way
ANOVA (Nominal $\alpha = .05$)

m	n	.00	.01	.10	.30	.50	.70	.90	.95	.99
						ϱ				
2	3	.0500	.0522	.0740	.1402	.2374	.3819	.6275	.7339	.8800
	10	.0500	.0606	.1654	.3729	.5344	.6752	.8282	.8809	.9475
	30	.0500	.0848	.3402	.5928	.7205	.8131	.9036	.9335	.9708
	100	.0500	.1658	.5716	.7662	.8446	.8976	.9477	.9640	.9842
3	3	.0500	.0529	.0837	.1866	.3430	.5585	.8367	.9163	.9829
	10	.0500	.0641	.2227	.5379	.7397	.8718	.9639	.9826	.9966
	30	.0500	.0985	.4917	.7999	.9049	.9573	.9886	.9946	.9990
	100	.0500	.2236	.7791	.9333	.9705	.9872	.9966	.9984	.9997
5	3	.0500	.0540	.0997	.2684	.5149	.7808	.9704	.9923	.9997
	10	.0500	.0692	.3151	.7446	.9175	.9798	.9984	.9996	1.0000
	30	.0500	.1192	.6908	.9506	.9888	.9977	.9998	1.0000	1.0000
	100	.0500	.3147	.9397	.9945	.9989	.9998	1.0000	1.0000	1.0000
10	3	.0500	.0560	.1323	.4396	.7837	.9664	.9997	1.0000	1.0000
	10	.0500	.0783	.4945	.9439	.9957	.9998	1.0000	1.0000	1.0000
	30	.0500	.1594	.9119	.9986	1.0000	1.0000	1.0000	1.0000	1.0000
	100	.0500	.4892	.9978	1.0000	1.0000	1.0000	1.0000	1.0000	1.0000

m—number of groups
n—number of observations per group
ϱ—intraclass correlation

a broad class of situations where dependence is undoubtedly present. For example, a few troublemakers in a classroom would have a detrimental effect on the achievement of many children in the classroom. Thus, their posttest achievement would be at least partially dependent on the disruptive classroom atmosphere. On the other hand, even in a good classroom atmosphere, dependence is introduced, for the achievement of many of the children will be enhanced by the positive learning situation. Therefore, in either case (positive or negative classroom atmosphere), the achievement of the children is not independent of the other children in the classroom.

Another situation I came across recently in which dependence among the observations was present involved a study comparing the achievement of students working in pairs at microcomputers vs. students working in groups of three at the micros. Here, if Bill and John are working at the same microcomputer, then obviously Bill's achievement is partially influenced by John. The proper unit of analysis in this study is the *mean* achievement for each pair and triplet of students, as it is plausible to assume that the achievement of students on one micro is independent of the students working at the other micros.

Glass and Hopkins (1984) make the following statement concerning situations where independence may or may not be tenable: "Whenever the treatment is individually administered, observations are independent. But where treatments involve interaction among persons, such as 'discussion' method or group counseling, the observations may influence each other" (p. 353).

What Should Be Done With Correlated Observations?

Given the results in Table 2.1 for a positive intraclass correlation, one route investigators should seriously consider if they suspect that the nature of their study will lead to correlated observations is to test at a more stringent level of significance. For the 3 and 5 group cases in Table 2.1 with 10 observations per group and intraclass correlation = .10, the error rates are 5 to 6 times greater than the assumed level of significance of .05. Thus, for this type of situation it would be wise to test at $\alpha = .01$, realizing that your actual error rate will be about .05 or somewhat greater. For the 3 and 5 group cases in Table 2.1 with 30 observations per group and intraclass correlation = .10, the error rates are about *10 times* greater than .05. Here, it would be advisable to either test at $\alpha = .01$, realizing that actual α will be about .10, or test at an even more stringent level than .01.

If several small groups (counseling, social interaction, etc.) are involved in each treatment, and there is clear reason to suspect that subjects' observations will be correlated within groups, but that observations will not be correlated across the groups, then consider using the *group mean as the unit of analysis.* Of course this will reduce the effective sample size considerably; however, this will not cause as drastic a drop in power as some have feared. The reason is that the means are much more stable than individual observations and hence the within variability will be far less.

Table 2.2, from Barcikowski (1981), shows that if the effect size is medium or large, then the number of groups needed per treatment for power > .80 doesn't have to be that large. For example, at $\alpha = .10$, intraclass correlation = .10, and medium effect size, 10 groups (of 10 subjects each) are needed per treatment. For power > .70 (which I consider adequate) at $\alpha = .15$ one probably could get by with about 5 or 6 groups of 10 per treatment. This is a rough estimate, since it involves double extrapolation.

Before we leave the topic of correlated observations, we wish to mention an interesting paper by Kenny and Judd (1986), who discuss how non-independent observations can arise because of several factors, grouping being one of them. The following quote from their paper is important to keep in mind for applied researchers:

> Throughout this article we have treated nonindependence as a statistical nuisance, to be avoided because of the bias that it introduces. . . . There are, however, many occasions when nonindependence is the substantive problem that we are trying to understand in psychological research. For instance, in developmental psychology, a frequently asked question concerns the development of social interaction. Developmental researchers study the content and rate of vocalization from infants

TABLE 2.2
Number of Groups per Treatment Necessary for Power > .80 in a Two
Treatment Level Design

		Intraclass Correlation					
			.10			.20	
	Effect Size	.20	.50	.80	.20	.50	.80[a]
α level	Number per group						
	10	73	13	6	107	18	8
	15	62	11	5	97	17	8
	20	56	10	5	92	16	7
.05	25	53	10	5	89	16	7
	30	51	9	5	87	15	7
	35	49	9	5	86	15	7
	40	48	9	5	85	15	7
	10	57	10	5	83	14	7
	15	48	9	4	76	13	6
	20	44	8	4	72	13	6
.10	25	41	8	4	69	12	6
	30	39	7	4	68	12	6
	35	38	7	4	67	12	5
	40	37	7	4	66	12	5

[a] .20—small effect size
.50—medium effect size
.80—large effect size

for cues about the onset of interaction. Social interaction implies nonindependence between the vocalizations of interacting individuals. To study interaction developmentally, then, we should be interested in nonindependence not solely as a statistical problem but also a substantive focus in itself. . . . In social psychology, one of the fundamental questions concerns how individual behavior is modified by group contexts. (p. 431)

2.9   ANOVA ON SPSS AND SAS

Now we consider how to run a one way ANOVA on SPSS and SAS, and how to interpret the printout. To illustrate we shall use the following 4 group data set:

Group 1	Group 2	Group 3	Group 4
2	7	4	8
3	9	4	4
5	11	5	7
6		8	7
		3	

TABLE 2.3
SAS Control Lines for One Way ANOVA and
Tukey Procedure on Sample Problem

```
      DATA INTERM;
  ①  INPUT GPID Y @@;
      LINES;
  ②  1 2   1 3   1 5   1 6
      2 7   2 9   2 11
      3 4   3 4   3 5   3 8   3 3
      4 8   4 4   4 7   4 7
  ③  PROC MEANS;
      BY GPID;
      PROC ANOVA;
  ④  CLASS GPID;
      MODEL Y=GPID;
      MEANS GPID/TUKEY;
  ⑤  PROC PRINT;
```

①There is a semicolon at the end of every SAS command, except for the data lines. The @@ is needed in order to put data for more than one subject on the same line.

②The first number of each pair is the group identification of the subject and the second number is the score on the dependent variable.

③This PROC MEANS is necessary to obtain the means on the dependent variable in each group.

④The ANOVA procedure is called and GPID is identified as the grouping (independent) variable through this CLASS statement.

⑤This procedure provides a listing of the data.

The complete SAS control lines for obtaining the ANOVA and Tukey procedure are presented in Table 2.3, and the annotated SAS printout is given in Table 2.4. We also ran the above data on SPSS for Windows 8.0, and appropriate screens are given in Table 2.5. First click on STATISTICS, then scroll down to COMPARE MEANS and over to ONE WAY ANOVA. When you click on ONE WAY ANOVA and select Y as the dependent variable and GPID as the factor, the screen appears as in the middle of Table 2.5. When you select POST HOC and select TUKEY, the screen appears as in the bottom of Table 2.5. Selected ANOVA and Tukey printout from SPSS for Windows 8.0 appears in Table 2.6.

p Values (Tail Probabilities)

In Tables 2.4 and 2.6 the reader will note to the right of the F statistic for the ANOVA the following for SAS (PR > F) and for SPSS (SIG), with a numerical value of .0196 in both cases. Although labeled somewhat differently by the packages, these are p values, or tail probabilities. It is the probability of obtaining an F larger than 4.857 when the null hypothesis is true (population means are equal). If we had set $\alpha = .05$ a priori, then we would reject H_0 here since we

TABLE 2.4
Selected Printout from SAS ANOVA for a One Way ANOVA

DEPENDENT VARIABLE: Y

SOURCE	DF	SUM OF SQUARES	MEAN SQUARE	F VALUE
MODEL	3	50.6375000	16.87916667	4.85
ERROR	12	41.80000000	3.48333333	
CORRECTED TOTAL	15	92.43750000		

SOURCE	DF	ANOVA SS	F VALUE	PR > F
GPID	3	50.63750000	4.85	0.0196

TUKEY'S STUDENTIZED RANGE (HSD) TEST FOR VARIABLE: Y
NOTE: THIS TEST CONTROLS THE TYPE I EXPERIMENTWISE ERROR RATE

ALPHA=0.05 CONFIDENCE=0.95 DF=12 MSE=3.48333 ①
CRITICAL VALUE OF STUDENTIZED RANGE=4.199 ②

COMPARISONS SIGNIFICANT AT THE 0.05 LEVEL ARE INDICATED BY '***'

	GPID COMPARISON		SIMULTANEOUS LOWER CONFIDENCE LIMIT	DIFFERENCE BETWEEN MEANS	SIMULTANEOUS UPPER CONFIDENCE LIMIT	
	2	−4	−1.732	2.500	6.732	
	2	−3	0.153	4.200	8.247	***
	2	−1	0.768	5.000	9.232	***
	4	−2	−6.732	−2.500	1.732	
③	4	−3	−2.017	1.700	5.417	
	4	−1	−1.418	2.500	6.418	
	3	−2	−8.247	−4.200	−0.153	***
	3	−4	−5.417	−1.700	2.017	
	3	−1	−2.917	0.800	4.517	
	1	−2	−9.232	−5.000	−0.768	***
	1	−4	−6.418	−2.500	1.418	
	1	−3	−4.517	−0.800	2.917	

①This is the pooled within error term which we denoted by MS_w.
②This is just a tabled value, found in Table B.2.
③There are only six paired comparison. SAS prints out 12, considering the difference between each pair of means in both order (i.e., $\bar{x}_2 - \bar{x}_4$ and $\bar{x}_4 - \bar{x}_2$). This can be confusing at first. Because of this redundancy note that there are only two significant differences: group 2 differs from group 3 and group 2 differs from group 1.

TABLE 2.5
SPSS for Windows 8.0 Screens for One Way ANOVA
and Tukey Procedure on Sample Problem

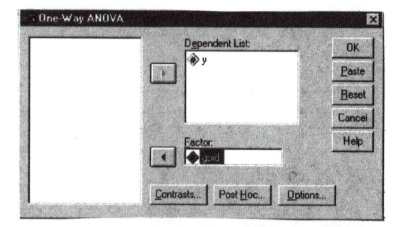

TABLE 2.6
Selected ANOVA and Tukey Procedure Printout From SPSS for Windows 8.0

Oneway

ANOVA

Y

	Sum of Squares	df	Mean Square	F	Sig.
Between Groups	50.638	3	16.879	4.846	.020
Within Groups	41.800	12	3.483		
Total	92.438	15			

Post Hoc Tests

Multiple Comparisons

Dependent Variable: Y
Tukey HSD

		Mean Difference (I-J)	Std. Error	Sig.	95% Confidence Interval	
(I) GPID	(J) GPID				Lower Bound	Upper Bound
1.00	2.00	-5.0000*	1.425	.020	-9.2321	-.7679
	3.00	-.8000	1.252	.917	-4.5171	2.9171
	4.00	-2.5000	1.320	.281	-6.4182	1.4182
2.00	1.00	5.0000*	1.425	.020	.7679	9.2321
	3.00	4.2000*	1.363	.041	.1533	8.2467
	4.00	2.5000	1.425	.340	-1.7321	6.7321
3.00	1.00	.8000	1.252	.917	-2.9171	4.5171
	2.00	-4.2000*	1.363	.041	-8.2467	-.1533
	4.00	-1.7000	1.252	.547	-5.4171	2.0171
4.00	1.00	2.5000	1.320	.281	-1.4182	6.4182
	2.00	-2.5000	1.425	.340	-6.7321	1.7321
	3.00	1.7000	1.252	.547	-2.0171	5.4171

*. The mean difference is significant at the .05 level.

Homogeneous Subsets

Y

Tukey HSD[a,b]

GPID	N	Subset for alpha = .05	
		1	2
1.00	4	4.0000	
3.00	5	4.8000	
4.00	4	6.5000	6.5000
2.00	3		9.0000
Sig.		.293	.293

Means for groups in homogeneous subsets are displayed.
a. Uses harmonic mean sample size = 3.871.
b. The group sizes are unequal. The harmonic mean of the group sizes is used. Type I error levels are not guaranteed.

are willing to take a 5% chance of rejecting falsely, and the tail probability indicates there is only about a 2% chance. These tail probabilities, which are printed out on all the major statistical packages, eliminate the need to look up critical values. We can adopt the following rules:

tail prob. < α level $\Rightarrow$ reject at that α level

tail prob. > α level $\Rightarrow$ fail to reject at that α level

Students often get confused when told to reject if the tail probability is *less* than the α level, since they may have been told repeatedly in an introductory statistics course to reject if the value of the test statistic is *greater* than the critical value. The connection that needs to be made here is to see that if the tail probability is < α level, then the value of the test statistic must be in the critical region. To illustrate this, suppose that in the computer problem we had tested F for significance by using the critical value at the .05 level, which is 3.49. It is very important to note that the critical value cuts off a tail probability of .05, i.e., only 5% of F values will be greater than 3.49 if H_0 is true (this area is shaded in the diagram below). Now, any value of F greater than 3.49 (in the critical region) must have a tail probability *less than .05*. Why? Because any $F > 3.49$ will have a smaller area under the F distribution, and this area represents the tail probability. For example, $F = 4.49$ has a tail probability = .025; the lined area, while $F = 5.95$ has a tail probability = .01. Notice that both of these F's (4.49 and 5.95) are in the critical region.

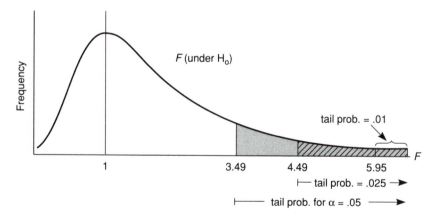

Huberty (1987) has written an interesting article in which he discusses p values and notes:

The lack of discussion in textbooks written for behavioral science researchers is somewhat puzzling in light of the common practice of reporting P-values (the lowercase p is often used) in journal articles, and in light of attention paid to them in publication manuals (e.g., American Psychological Association). (p. 5)

2.10 POST HOC PROCEDURES

As mentioned earlier, there are numerous post hoc procedures available for determining where the differences lie after the F statistic has indicated there is a significant overall difference. Among the post hoc procedures are the Tukey, Scheffé, Newman-Keuls, Duncan, and Fisher's LSD (the so-called protected t test). All these procedures have two fundamental purposes:

1. To enable us to ferret out where the differences lie, and
2. To maintain the overall α level (or experimentwise error rate) at some predetermined level, usually set at .05. In other words, keep a lid on the probability of false rejections for all the tests being done.

Unfortunately, the Newman-Keuls, Duncan, and Fisher's LSD do not control overall α as claimed. That is, they tend to be liberal. On the other hand, the Scheffé procedure tends to be quite conservative (since it allows for a wide range of comparisons to be done). We discuss and illustrate the Scheffé procedure in Section 2.12. For paired comparisons we favor and present the Tukey procedure for 3 reasons:

1. The Tukey *does* control the overall α as claimed (Hayter, 1984).
2. The Tukey procedure examines a focused, meaningful, and easily interpreted set of comparisons, that is, all paired comparisons.
3. The Tukey is a fairly powerful procedure for detecting differences.

Thus the Tukey provides a nice balance in terms of controlling on both type I and type II errors, while focusing on meaningful, easily interpreted comparisons.

However, if you are *only* interested in comparing each of several treatment groups against a control group, then the Dunnett (1955) procedure is most powerful and should be used (see Exercise 16).

2.11 TUKEY PROCEDURE

The Tukey procedure, which is sometimes called the HSD (honestly significant difference) test, enables us to examine *all pairwise* group comparisons with the experimentwise (overall) α level held in check. The studentized range statistic (which we denote by q) is used in the procedure, and the critical values for it are given in Table B.2 in the back of the book. The procedure establishes a set of *simultaneous confidence intervals* for each pair of population means. The intervals are given by:

$$(\bar{x}_i - \bar{x}_j) \pm q_{\alpha;k,N-k} \sqrt{MS_w/n} \qquad (11)$$

or

$$(\bar{x}_i - \bar{x}_j) - q_{\alpha;k,N-k} \sqrt{MS_w/n} < \mu_i - \mu_j < (\bar{x}_i - \bar{x}_j) + q_{\alpha;k,N-k} \sqrt{MS_w/n}$$

where $\bar{x}_i$ and $\bar{x}_j$ represent the means for any two groups, q is just a tabled value, MS_w is the denominator of the F statistic, and n is the assumed common group size.

In deriving the procedure, Tukey assumed equal group sizes. In practice, however, often the group sizes are not equal. Does this severely limit the utility of the procedure? No, since various studies (Dunnett, 1980; Kesselman, Murray, & Rogan, 1976) indicate that the Tukey still controls overall α *provided that the population variances are equal and that n is replaced by the harmonic mean* $2n_1n_2/(n_1 + n_2)$ *for each pair of groups.* The harmonic mean for each pair of groups is what is used by default for both SAS and SPSS. Thus, for unequal group sizes the n in Equation 11 is replaced by $2n_in_j/(n_i + n_j)$ when comparing groups i and j. When this replacement is made, it is called the Tukey–Kramer procedure. Now let us consider a numerical example to illustrate how to calculate and interpret the intervals.

Example

Consider the following 4 group problem with unequal group sizes. The reader may check with Hartley's F_{max} that homogeneity of variance is tenable here.

	1	2	3	4
n_i	20	17	14	18
$\bar{x}_i$	7	8	10	13
s_i	4	5	6	4

A one way ANOVA on this data yields $F = 129.02/22.22 = 5.81$ ($p < .05$). Therefore we know there is a significant overall difference among the groups. To locate the pairs that are significantly different we use the Tukey procedure, with overall $\alpha = .05$. First, we need the harmonic means for each pair of groups:

Groups	Harmonic mean
1 and 2	2(20)(17)/37 = 18.38
1 and 3	2(20)(14)/34 = 16.47
1 and 4	2(20)(18)/38 = 18.95
2 and 3	2(17)(14)/31 = 15.35
2 and 4	2(17)(18)/35 = 17.49
3 and 4	2(14)(18)/32 = 15.75

The tabled value is $q_{.05;4,65} = 3.74$. Now we set up the intervals:

Differences	Critical value	Confidence intervals
$\bar{x}_1 - \bar{x}_2 = -1$	$3.74\sqrt{22.22/18.38} = 4.11$	$(-5.11, 3.11)$
$\bar{x}_1 - \bar{x}_3 = -3$	$3.74\sqrt{22.22/16.47} = 4.34$	$(-7.34, 1.34)$
$\bar{x}_1 - \bar{x}_4 = -6$	$3.74\sqrt{22.22/18.95} = 4.05$	$(-10.05, -1.95)$
$\bar{x}_2 - \bar{x}_3 = -2$	$3.74\sqrt{22.22/15.35} = 4.50$	$(-6.5, 2.5)$
$\bar{x}_2 - \bar{x}_4 = -5$	$3.74\sqrt{22.22/17.49} = 4.22$	$(-9.22, -.78)$
$\bar{x}_3 - \bar{x}_4 = -3$	$3.74\sqrt{22.22/15.75} = 4.44$	$(-7.44, 1.44)$

Note that the lower limit for the first interval is obtained by subtracting the critical value (4.11) from the difference in the means (−1) and the upper limit is found by adding the critical value to −1. Therefore

$$-1 - 4.11 < \mu_1 - \mu_2 < -1 + 4.11 \text{ or } -5.11 < \mu_1 - \mu_2 < 3.11$$

How do we interpret these intervals? First, if the confidence interval *includes 0* we conclude the population means are not different. Why? Because if the interval includes 0 it means 0 is a likely value for $\mu_i - \mu_j$, which is to say it is likely that $\mu_i = \mu_j$. Thus, in comparing groups 1 and 2 above, we see that the interval for $\mu_1 - \mu_2$ is given by

$$-5.11 < \mu_1 - \mu_2 < 3.11$$

Therefore, 0 is a likely value for $\mu_1 - \mu_2$, since 0 is in the interval. Thus, groups 1 and 2 are not significantly different. On the other hand, if the interval does not include 0, then the groups are significantly different, since 0 is not a likely value for the population mean difference. Examining the above intervals, we find that only groups 1 and 4, and groups 2 and 4 are significantly different.

Confidence intervals are more informative than tests of significance because they both indicate significance *and* give a range of values within which the population mean difference probably lies. Thus, confidence intervals are one way of judging the practical significance of results. Consider groups 1 and 4. Suppose a researcher had decided a priori that the population mean difference had to be at least 4 units to be of any practical significance. Now, the confidence interval for groups 1 and 4 is:

$$-10.05 < \mu_1 - \mu_4 < -1.95$$

and the result would not be practically significant because the difference could be as small as −1.95.

2.12   THE SCHEFFÉ PROCEDURE

The big advantage of the Scheffé procedure is its flexibility. For a k group problem one can examine *all possible simple (pairwise) and complex* contrasts (this is defined very shortly) among the group means with the assurance that the overall α will be less than some preassigned value (say .05). Thus in exploratory research this procedure provides the ultimate in data snooping potential. However, in order to keep overall $\alpha = .05$, while doing all the statistical tests for the very large number of comparisons possible, the critical value necessary for significance will be large relative to what it would be for other multiple comparison procedures. This means power will suffer, which will not be of concern if sample size in your study is large (say about 100 subjects per group). If your group sizes are small (about 20 subjects per group), however, then on power considerations it would be wise to set overall α at .10, or even at .15.

In general, for k groups with population means $\mu_1, \mu_2, \ldots, \mu_k$, a *contrast* among the population means is given by

$$L = c_1\mu_1 + c_2\mu_2 + \cdots + c_k\mu_k$$

where the sum of the coefficients (c_i) must equal 0. Note, first of all, that all the paired comparisons tested by the Tukey procedure are contrasts. Why? The general form for a paired comparison is $\mu_i - \mu_j$, for the ith and jth groups. The coefficient for μ_i is 1, while the coefficient for μ_j is −1. But the sum of these coefficients is 0 and therefore we have a contrast.

To illustrate the wide variety of contrasts possible with the Scheffé, consider a 4 group problem, with population means $\mu_1, \mu_2, \mu_3,$ and μ_4. First, we can test all paired contrasts for significance (as with the Tukey). Recall that there are 6 paired comparisons (1 vs. 2, 1 vs. 3, 1 vs. 4, 2 vs. 3, 2 vs. 4, and 3 vs. 4). But, in addition, we can test all kinds of complex *contrasts* involving more than two groups for significance. Below we list just four possible complex contrasts:

$$L_1 = \mu_1 - (\mu_2 + \mu_3)/2 \qquad L_2 = (\mu_1 + \mu_2) - (\mu_3 + \mu_4)$$
$$L_3 = \mu_1 - (\mu_2 + \mu_3 + \mu_4)/3 \qquad L_4 = \mu_2 - (\mu_3 + \mu_4)/2$$

Remember that for each of the above to be a contrast the sum of the coefficients must be 0. We show this below for the first two and leave as an exercise for the reader to show that L_3 and L_4 are contrasts.

For L_1 the coefficients are $c_1 = 1, c_2 = c_3 = -.5$. Therefore, $c_1 + c_2 + c_3 = 1 + (-.5) + (-.5) = 0$, and L_1 is a contrast. For L_2 the coefficients are $c_1 = c_2 = 1$ and $c_3 = c_4 = -1$. Again, $c_1 + c_2 + c_3 + c_4 = 1 + 1 + (-1) + (-1) = 0$, and L_2 is a contrast.

As with the Tukey procedure, the Scheffé method establishes a set of simultaneous confidence intervals for all population mean contrasts. The lower and upper limits for the intervals are:

$$\hat{L} - \hat{\sigma}_{\hat{L}} \sqrt{(k-1)\, F_{\alpha;k-1;N-k}} \ \text{and}\, \hat{L} + \hat{\sigma}_{\hat{L}} \sqrt{(k-1)\, F_{\alpha;k-1;N-k}} \qquad (12)$$

where $\hat{L}$ is the estimate of the contrast and $\hat{\sigma}_{\hat{L}}$ is the estimated standard error of the contrast. Now, the estimate for a general contrast is obtained by replacing the population means by sample means, that is, $L = c_1\bar{x}_1 + c_2\bar{x}_2 + \cdots + c_k\bar{x}_k$. In the Appendix of this chapter we show that the estimated variance for a contrast is given by

$$\hat{\sigma}_{\hat{L}}^2 = MS_w \left(\sum c_i^2/n_i\right) \qquad (13)$$

where MS_w is the denominator of the F test and the n_i represents the number of subjects in the ith group. The standard error of the contrast is simply the square root of Equation 13. To illustrate calculation of a few Scheffé intervals we reconsider the data example used for the Tukey procedure in Section 2.11. There were 4 groups with differing group sizes and $MS_w = 22.22$.

	1	2	3	4
n_i	20	17	14	18
$\bar{x}_i$	7	8	10	13

We test the following contrasts for significance at an experimentwise error rate = .10, i.e., we will obtain the 90% simultaneous confidence intervals:

$$L_1 = \mu_1 - (\mu_2 + \mu_3)/2 \ \text{and}\ L_2 = \mu_1 - (\mu_2 + \mu_3 + \mu_4)/3$$

The estimates for contrasts L_1 and L_2 are given by

$$\hat{L}_1 = 7 - (8 + 10)/2 = -2 \ \text{and}\, \hat{L}_2 = 7 - (8 + 10 + 13)/3 = -3.33$$

The standard error for $\hat{L}_1$ is:

$$\hat{\sigma}_{\hat{L}_1} = \sqrt{22.22\,[(1^2)/20 + (-.5)^2/17 + (-.5)^2/14]} = 1.355$$

and the standard error for $\hat{L}_2$ is:

$$\hat{\sigma}_{\hat{L}_2} = \sqrt{22.22\,[(1^2)/20 + (-.33)^2/17 + (-.33)^2/14 + (-.33)^2/18]} = 1.25$$

Also, $\sqrt{(4-1)\,F_{.10;3,65}} = \sqrt{3(2.18)} = 2.56$.
The confidence interval for L_1 is given by

$$(-2 - 1.355(2.56), -2 + 1.355(2.56)) \text{ or } (-5.469, 1.469)$$

while the confidence interval for L_2 is given by

$$(-3.33 - 1.25(2.56), -3.33 + 1.25(2.56)) \text{ or } (-6.53, -.13)$$

Recall that if a confidence interval covers 0 it means the contrast is *not* significant. Therefore, L_1 is not significant. However, L_2 is significant since that interval does not cover 0.

2.13   HETEROGENEOUS VARIANCES AND UNEQUAL GROUP SIZES

As previously indicated, the analysis of variance is robust against unequal population variances provided that the group sizes are equal or approximately equal. When heterogeneous variances are present various procedures have been recommended: Welch (1951), Brown and Forsythe (1974) and the Kruskal–Wallis nonparametric test. A Monte Carlo study by Tomarkin and Serlin (1986) examined the above three procedures and found that the Welch test was superior in most cases studied in terms of better control on type I error and greater power.

In terms of post hoc procedures, recall that the Tukey maintained an honest experimentwise error rate with unequal group sizes *only* if the homogeneity of variance assumption is tenable *and* the assumed common n in the Tukey test statistic is replaced by the harmonic mean for each pair of groups. Fortunately, there is also a Welch t statistic which does *not* assume equal variances. Games and Howell (1976), in a Monte Carlo study on the Tukey procedure, found that the Welch approximate t statistic kept the experimentwise error rate under control when heterogeneous variances and unequal group sizes are both present. The Welch approximate t, which we denote by t_w, is given by

$$t_w = (\bar{x}_i - \bar{x}_j)/\sqrt{s_i^2/n_i + s_j^2/n_j}$$

where s_i^2 and s_j^2 are the sample variances for the ith and jth groups and n_i and n_j are the respective group sizes. Note that since the homogeneity of variance of assumption is not tenable the Welch statistic uses only those variances for the pair of groups being compared. A pooled error term would be inappropriate since the sample variances are estimating different population values. The degrees of freedom (v) for each Welch statistic will in general be different and is given by

$$v = \frac{(s_i^2/n_i + s_j^2/n_j)^2}{\dfrac{(s_i^2/n_i)^2}{n_i - 1} + \dfrac{(s_j^2/n_j)^2}{n_j - 1}}$$

A pair of means was declared to be significantly different in the Games and Howell study if

$$|t_w| > q_{\alpha,k,v}/\sqrt{2}$$

Note that with the above approach several different critical values from the studentized range table will be needed, since v will tend to be different for the various paired comparisons.

Below are a few selected results from their study comparing the Welch statistic against a pooled error term (MS_w) approach for a 4 group situation:

Group Sizes	MS_w	Welch
16, 14, 10, 6		
Population Variances		
1, 3, 5, 7	.122	.060
1, 1, 7, 7	.115	.064
1, 1, 1, 13	.122	.064

These error rates are to be compared against a significance level of .05. The above situations all represent positively biased situations, i.e., where the large variances are associated with the small group sizes. Recall that for ANOVA these are the situations where it was liberal, with the error rate greater than level of significance. The above results showed that use of a pooled error term caused the Tukey approach to be quite liberal, i.e., the actual error rate was over twice the significance level, while use of the Welch statistic kept the actual α quite close to the significance level of .05.

Example

To illustrate with an example, consider the following four group data set:

Group 1	Group 2	Group 3	Group 4
14	20	36	26
21	25	29	35
37	18	31	46
18	30	22	18
20	26	45	30
29	22	43	33
42	31	27	49
12	26	33	15
27	28	35	27
30	24	28	
33	19	36	
	17	40	
	21	38	
	23	29	
	27	22	
	32		
	19		
	29		
	28		
	23		

These data were run on SPSS for Windows 8.0, and a selected printout from that run is given in Table 2.7.

2.14 MEASURES OF ASSOCIATION (VARIANCE ACCOUNTED FOR)

One of the facts of "statistical life" is that whether we obtain significance with *any* statistical test is *heavily* dependent on sample size. With large enough sample sizes even very small differences among the group means will be declared statistically significant. Why is this so? To shed some light on this it is helpful to first recall from Section 2.5 that the numerator of the F statistic, for equal group sizes, can be written as

$$MS_b = n \sum (\bar{x}_i - \bar{x})^2 / (k - 1)$$

Thus, the F ratio can be written as

$$F = \frac{n \sum (\bar{x}_i - \bar{x})^2 / (k - 1)}{MS_w}$$

Assuming the null hypothesis is false, the numerator can be made arbitrarily large by increasing the group sample size n. Now, increasing the sample sizes should not have any systematic effect on MS_w, and we assume for the sake of simplicity that MS_w remains the same. But, given the above two statements, we see that F can be made arbitrarily large by increasing sample size. We now consider a numerical example to illustrate the above. Suppose two studies are done, each with 3 groups, and the group means in both cases are 10, 14, and 18. Assume $MS_w = 100$ in both cases. One study has 16 subjects per group while the other has 100 subjects per group. The grand mean = 14, and the F for the first study is

$$F = 16/2 \, [(10 - 14)^2 + (18 - 14)^2] / 100 = 2.56$$

The critical value for significance at .05 is 3.15, and therefore this result would not be significant.

The other study, *with the same mean differences,* has an F of

$$F = 100/2 \, [(10 - 14)^2 + (18 - 14)^2] / 100 = 16$$

TABLE 2.7
Selected Printout From SPSS for Windows 8.0 for Unequal Variances
Example With Tamhane and Games–Howell Post Hoc Procedures

Descriptives

			Minimum	Maximum
DEP	GP	1.00	12.00	42.00
		2.00	17.00	32.00
		3.00	22.00	45.00
		4.00	15.00	49.00
		Total	12.00	49.00

Test of Homogeneity of Variances

	Levene Statistic	df1	df2	Sig.
DEP	3.935	3	51	.013

ANOVA

		Sum of Squares	df	Mean Square	F	Sig.
DEP	Between Groups	761.794	3	253.931	4.291	.009
	Within Groups	3017.915	51	59.175		
	Total	3779.709	54			

(Continued)

TABLE 2.7
(Continued)

Post Hoc Tests

Multiple Comparisons

Dependent Variable: DEP

	(I) GP	(J) GP	Mean Difference (I-J)	Std. Error	Sig.	95% Confidence Interval Lower Bound	Upper Bound
Tamhane	1.00	2.00	1.3273	2.888	.999	-8.2045	10.8591
		3.00	-7.2061	3.054	.259	-17.2890	2.8769
		4.00	-5.2727	3.458	.867	-19.5971	9.0516
	2.00	1.00	-1.3273	2.888	.999	-10.8591	8.2045
		3.00	-8.5333*	2.627	.002	-14.4761	-2.5906
		4.00	-6.6000	3.088	.556	-19.6948	6.4948
	3.00	1.00	7.2061	3.054	.259	-2.8769	17.2890
		2.00	8.5333*	2.627	.002	2.5906	14.4761
		4.00	1.9333	3.243	.998	-11.3258	15.1924
	4.00	1.00	5.2727	3.458	.867	-9.0516	19.5971
		2.00	6.6000	3.088	.556	-6.4948	19.6948
		3.00	-1.9333	3.243	.998	-15.1924	11.3258
Games-Howell	1.00	2.00	1.3273	2.888	.971	-7.6961	10.3506
		3.00	-7.2061	3.054	.186	-16.8489	2.4368
		4.00	-5.2727	3.458	.691	-18.9356	8.3902
	2.00	1.00	-1.3273	2.888	.971	-10.3506	7.6961
		3.00	-8.5333*	2.627	.002	-14.2475	-2.8192
		4.00	-6.6000	3.088	.385	-18.8123	5.6123
	3.00	1.00	7.2061	3.054	.186	-2.4368	16.8489
		2.00	8.5333*	2.627	.002	2.8192	14.2475
		4.00	1.9333	3.243	.966	-10.5838	14.4504
	4.00	1.00	5.2727	3.458	.691	-8.3902	18.9356
		2.00	6.6000	3.088	.385	-5.6123	18.8123
		3.00	-1.9333	3.243	.966	-14.4504	10.5838

*. The mean difference is significant at the .05 level.

and this would be significant well beyond the .001 level!

Now, we illustrate the other point. That is, even very small differences will be declared significant if n is large enough. Suppose again 3 groups with MS_w = 100, but now there are 400 subjects per group. The means for the groups are 10, 11 and 12. The F ratio here will be $F = 200[(10 - 11)^2 + (12 - 11)^2]/100 = 4$, which is significant at the .05 level, even though the mean differences are very small. To use a domestic analogy, this is like using a sledgehammer to pound out significance.

Because of this kind of situation it has been argued for some time (perhaps popularized most by Hays in his influential text *Statistics for Psychologists,* 1963) that we need some way of determining whether a statistically significant result is practically significant. Hays (1963) introduced his $\hat{\omega}^2$ as a measure of association (strength of relationship) to get at practical significance, and such measures have subsequently been recommended by various textbook authors (Cohen & Cohen, 1975; Kerlinger & Pedhazur, 1973; Kirk, 1982). The two most commonly used measures of this type are η^2 and Hays $\hat{\omega}^2$. The formulas for each of them for a one way ANOVA are given below:

$$\eta^2 = SS_b / SS_t \tag{14}$$

where $SS_t = SS_b + SS_w$ (total sum of squares), and

$$\hat{\omega}^2 = (SS_b - (k-1)MS_w) / (SS_t + MS_w) \tag{15}$$

Usually the numerical values for these two will not differ a great deal, although Hays' measure is generally regarded as preferable because he used unbiased estimates in deriving his measure (but the measure itself is *not* unbiased).

Such measures can be useful after the test of significance, since they are essentially independent of sample size. Nevertheless, there are limitations associated with these measures, as O'Grady (1982) has pointed out in an excellent review on measures of explained variance. He cites 3 basic reasons why such measures should be interpreted with caution (measurement, methodological, and theoretical). With respect to measurement he notes that the reliability of the variables somewhat restricts how large a measure of association can be, since these measures are correlational in nature. Several methodological factors are mentioned; we discuss just two of them. One is the homogeneity of the population sampled. Since measures of association are correlational measures, the more homogeneous the population, the smaller the correlation will tend to be, and therefore the smaller the percent of variance that can be potentially accounted for. This is simply the *restriction of range* phenomenon you encountered in beginning statistics when studying the Pearson correlation. A second factor that can have a substantial effect on the magnitude of a measure of association is the number of levels chosen, and how they are chosen, for a fixed effects ANOVA (which is what we are dealing with). To illustrate he uses the following example. Suppose there are 3 researchers that wish to examine the relationship between a hypothesized carcinogen and the incidence of cancer. The first researcher chooses to contrast a control condition (0 exposure) with a 2% exposure to the carcinogen. The second researcher chooses to maximize the changes of a relationship and contrasts 0% exposure with 20% exposure. Finally, the third researcher is interested in determining the shape of the relationship across various levels of the supposed carcinogen. Below we present the descriptive statistics, F ratios, and eta squares for the 3 studies:

		Exposure Group					
Study		0%	2%	5%	10%	20%	
1	$\bar{x}$	10	12				
	s	2	2				$F = 5,\ \eta^2 = .22$
2	$\bar{x}$	10				18	
	s	2				2	$F = 80,\ \eta^2 = .82$
3	$\bar{x}$	10	12	14	16	18	
	s	2	2	2	2	2	$F = 25,\ \eta^2 = .69$

Ten subjects are assumed in each group in each study. Notice how the measure of association is drastically affected by the number of levels and how the levels are chosen, even though the means and standard deviations are the same.

A theoretical point O'Grady mentions which should be kept in mind before casting asperations on a "low" amount of variance accounted for is that most behaviors have *multiple causes,* and hence it will be difficult in these cases to account for a large amount of variance with just a single cause (say treatments).

Anyone planning on using measures of association in their research should read and think carefully about O'Grady's paper. To enforce the point that a "small" amount of variance accounted for may indeed be practically significant we consider an example from Rosenthal and Rosnow (1984). They consider the comparison of a treatment and control group where the dependent variable is dichotomous, whether the subjects live or die. The following table is presented:

	Treatment Outcome		
	Alive	Dead	
Treatment	66	34	100
Control	34	66	100
	100	100	

Since both variables are dichotomous, the phi coefficient ϕ, a special case of the Pearson correlation for dichotomous variables (Glass & Hopkins, 1984), measures the relationship between them:

$$\phi = (34^2 - 66^2) \,/\, \sqrt{100(100)(100)(100)} = -.32$$

Squaring ϕ (since it is a correlation) yields variance accounted for, which is $(-.32)^2 = .10$. Thus, the treatment-control distinction accounts for "only" 10% of the variance in the outcome. However, this is enough to increase the survival rate from 34% to 66%, far from trivial! The same type of interpretation would hold if we were to consider some less dramatic type of outcome like improvement vs. no improvement, where treatment was, say, a type of psychotherapy. Also, the interpretation is *not* confined to just a dichotomous measure.

2.15   PLANNED COMPARISONS

One approach to the analysis of data is to first demonstrate overall significance, and then follow up to assess the significant subsources of variation (i.e., which particular groups differed). This approach is appropriate in *exploratory* studies where it is necessary to first establish that an effect exists. There may be a weak literature base, or none on which to base specific hypotheses. This type of study is somewhat unfocused and some have even referred to these studies as "fishing expeditions."

Now we consider a more focused type of study, where there either is a fairly strong theoretical and/or literature base, or the investigator has specific questions to ask of the data. These questions will be in the form of hypotheses involving group comparisons. This is more of a *confirmatory* type study. Here, a priori, the investigator sets up planned comparisons among the group means. It is important to use planned comparisons when the situation justifies them, since performing a small number of statistical tests cuts down on the probability of spurious results (type I errors).

Hays (1981) has shown that planned comparisons are a more powerful approach statistically. If we set up a small number of comparisons, then power will be enhanced and overall α can be controlled through the *Bonferroni Inequality*. This is a very important inequality. It states that if k hypotheses, k planned comparisons here, are tested separately with type I error rates of $\alpha_1, \alpha_2, \ldots, \alpha_k$, then

$$\text{overall } \alpha \leq \alpha_1 + \alpha_2 + \cdots + \alpha_k \tag{16}$$

If the hypotheses are each tested at the same alpha level, say α', then the Bonferroni upper bound becomes

$$\text{overall } \alpha \leq k\alpha' \tag{17}$$

If the comparisons are independent (this is defined shortly), then an *exact* calculation for overall α is available. First, $(1 - \alpha_1)$ is the probability of no type I error for the first comparison. Similarly, $(1 - \alpha_2)$ is the probability of no type I error for the second, $(1 - \alpha_3)$ the probability of no type I error for the third, etc. If the tests are independent, then we can multiply probabilities. Therefore, $(1 - \alpha_1) (1 - \alpha_2) \cdots (1 - \alpha_k)$ is the probability of *no* type I errors for all k tests. Thus,

$$\text{overall } \alpha = 1 - (1 - \alpha_1)(1 - \alpha_2) \cdots (1 - \alpha_k) \tag{18}$$

is the probability of at least one type I error. If the tests are not independent, then overall α will still be *less* than given in Equation 18 although it is very difficult to calculate. If we set the alpha levels equal, say to α', for each test, then Equation 18 becomes overall $\alpha = 1 - (1 - \alpha')(1 - \alpha') \cdots (1 - \alpha') = 1 - (1 - \alpha')^k$. This expression, $1 - (1 - \alpha')^k$, is approximately equal to $k\alpha'$ for small α'. The table below compares the two for $\alpha' = .05, .01,$ and $.001$ for number of tests ranging from 5 to 100.

	$\alpha' = .05$		$\alpha' = .01$		$\alpha' = .001$	
	$1 - (1 - \alpha')^k$	$k\alpha'$	$1 - (1 - \alpha')^k$	$k\alpha'$	$1 - (1 - \alpha')^k$	$k\alpha'$
No. of Tests						
5	.226	.25	.049	.05	.00499	.005
10	.401	.50	.096	.10	.00990	.010
15	.537	.75	.140	.15	.0149	.015
30	.785	1.5	.260	.30	.0296	.030
50	.923	2.5	.395	.50	.0488	.050
100	.994	5.0	.634	1	.0952	.100

First, the numbers in the table greater than 1 don't represent probabilities, since a probability can't be greater than 1. Second, note that if we are testing each of a large number of hypotheses at the .001 level, the difference between $1 - (1 - \alpha')^k$ and the Bonferroni upper bound of $k\alpha'$ is very small and of no practical consequence. Also, the differences between $1 - (1 - \alpha')^k$ and $k\alpha'$ when testing at $\alpha' = .01$ are also small for up to about 30 tests. For more than about 30 tests $1 - (1 - \alpha')^k$ provides a tighter bound and should be used. When testing at the $\alpha' = .05$ level, $k\alpha'$ is okay for up to about 10 tests, but beyond that $1 - (1 - \alpha')^k$ is much tighter and should be used.

Example 1

We have a 4 group problem with 3 planned comparisons and want overall $\alpha <$ .10. This can be achieved by simply dividing the overall α by the number of tests done, i.e., $.10/3 = .033$. Thus, if each comparison is tested at the $\alpha = .033$ level, we are assured by the Bonferroni inequality that

$$\text{overall } \alpha \leq .033 + .033 + .033 = .10$$

Example 2

Suppose there are 5 planned comparisons in a 6 group problem. If we test the first two at the .05 level (i.e., $\alpha_1 = .05$ and $\alpha_2 = .05$), and the remaining three comparisons at the .01 level ($\alpha_3 = \alpha_4 = \alpha_5 = .01$), then we are assured by the inequality that

$$\text{overall } \alpha \leq .05 + .05 + .01 + .01 + .01 = 13$$

Now let us consider a couple of research examples of setting up planned comparisons. The next sample has treatments of a structure that could be useful in a variety of fields.

Example 3

Consider a four group situation involving a comparison of two treatments, a combination of the two treatments, and a control group on some dependent measure. Schematically, we have

T_1 (control)	T_2	T_3	T_4 (T_2 and T_3 combined)
μ_1	μ_2	μ_3	μ_4

The two treatments might be two reading methods, two types of counseling, two diets, etc. Of course, the two treatments would have to be such that combining them made sense. Now there are three very meaningful, focused questions to ask of the data.

1. Is something better than nothing? Here we are comparing the control group vs. the treatment groups.
2. Do the two individual treatments differ in effectiveness?
3. Is the combination of treatments more effective than either treatment individually?

These comparisons will be set up as *contrasts* among the population means for the groups. In general, for k groups with population means $\mu_1, \mu_2, \ldots, \mu_k$, a contrast among the population means is given by

$$L = c_1\mu_1 + c_2\mu_2 + \cdots + c_k\mu_k$$

where the sum of the coefficients (c_i) must equal 0.

Let us set up the comparisons for the 3 questions above, and we will see that each is a contrast:

$$L_1 = \mu_1 - (\mu_2 + \mu_3 + \mu_4)/3$$

The coefficients here are $c_1 = 1$, $c_2 = c_3 = c_4 = -1/3$. The sum of these coefficients $= 0$, so L_1 is a contrast.

$$L_2 = \mu_2 - \mu_3$$

The coefficients are $c_2 = 1$ and $c_3 = -1$, so that $c_2 + c_3 = 0$ and L_2 is a contrast.

$$L_3 = \mu_4 - (\mu_2 + \mu_3)/2$$

Here $c_4 = 1$, $c_2 = c_3 = -.5$, so that $\Sigma c_i = 0$, and L_3 is a contrast. The formula for the sum of squares of a contrast is given by

$$SS_L = \hat{L}^2 / \sum c_i^2/n_i$$

where $\hat{L}$ is the estimate of the contrast and the n_i are the group sizes.

For *equal* group size the above set of three contrasts represent *orthogonal* comparisons. The sums of squares associated with the contrasts (denote them by SS_L) are independent, and it can be shown that:

$$SS_b = SS_{L_1} + SS_{L_2} + SS_{L_3} \tag{19}$$

That is, the overall between groups variation is additively partitioned into three independent pieces of variation. For equal group size the condition that needs to be met for a pair of contrasts to be independent is that the sum of the products of the coefficients equal 0. We now show that this condition is met for all three pairs of contrasts. We present the contrasts below in schematic form, just using the coefficients that define each contrast:

	T_1	T_2	T_3	T_4
L_1	1	$-1/3$	$-1/3$	$-1/3$
L_2	0	1	-1	0
L_3	0	$-1/2$	$-1/2$	1

The sum of the products of the coefficients for each pair are:

L_1 and L_2: $1(0) + (-1/3)(1) + (-1/3)(-1) + (-1/3)(0) = 0$

L_1 and L_3: $1(0) + (-1/3)(-1/2) + (-1/3)(-1/2) + (-1/3)(0) = 0$

L_2 and L_3: $0(0) + 1(-1/2) + (-1)(-1/2) + 0(1) = 0$

There are other sets of three orthogonal comparisons for this problem, and *any* such set will also provide for an additive partitioning of the SS_b. The nice feature about orthogonal contrasts is that significance on one contrast implies nothing about potential significance on another contrast. That is, we do *not* have a confounding of the sources of variation. With correlated contrasts the sources of variation are confounded; however, the unique sum of squares associated with each contrast can be obtained by using the SPSS MANOVA program, which since Release 2.2 has the unique sum of squares as the default option. *Although it is desirable to have orthogonal contrasts, the set of contrasts to impose in a given situation should be dictated by the research questions of the investigator.*

Now we express the condition for independence of two contrasts for equal group size in general form. Consider two general contrasts for k groups:

$$L_1 = c_{11}\mu_1 + c_{12}\mu_2 + \cdots + c_{1k}\mu_k$$
$$L_2 = c_{21}\mu_1 + c_{22}\mu_2 + \cdots + c_{2k}\mu_k$$

The condition for independence is

$$c_{11}c_{21} + c_{12}c_{22} + \cdots + c_{1k}c_{2k} = 0$$

If the group sizes are not equal, then the condition for independence is more complicated and becomes:

$$(c_{11}c_{21})/n_1 + (c_{12}c_{22})/n_2 + \cdots + (c_{1k}c_{2k})/n_k = 0$$

Example 4

A medical researcher wishes to evaluate the effectiveness of 4 drugs on reaction time. Schematically, the design is

	One Generic Type		Other Generic Type	
Control	Drug A	Drug B	Drug C	Drug D
μ_1	μ_2	μ_3	μ_4	μ_5

A set of 4 focused and relevant questions to ask here are:

1. Are drugs more effective than no drugs?

$$L_1 = \mu_1 - (\mu_2 + \mu_3 + \mu_4 + \mu_5)/4$$

2. Is one generic type of drug more effective than the other generic type?

$$L_2 = (\mu_2 + \mu_3)/2 - (\mu_4 + \mu_5)/2$$

3. Are the two drugs of the first generic type different in effectiveness?

$$L_3 = \mu_2 - \mu_3$$

4. Are the two drugs of the other generic type different in effectiveness?

$$L_4 = \mu_4 - \mu_5$$

The reader should verify that each of these comparisons is indeed a contrast.

2.16   TEST STATISTIC FOR PLANNED COMPARISONS

Recall that for k groups with population means μ_1, μ_2, . . . , μ_k, a contrast (L) among the population means is given by

$$L = c_1\mu_1 + c_2\mu_2 + \cdots + c_k\mu_k,$$

where $\Sigma c_i = 0$.

This contrast is estimated by replacing the population means by the sample means, yielding

$$\hat{L} = c_1\bar{x}_1 + c_2\bar{x}_2 + \cdots + c_k\bar{x}_k$$

To test whether a given contrast is significantly different from 0, i.e., to test

$$H_0: L = 0 \text{ vs. } H_1: L \neq 0$$

we need an expression for the variance of a contrast. We show in the Appendix at the end of this chapter that the variance for a contrast is given by

$$\hat{\sigma}_{\hat{L}}^2 = MS_w \left(\sum c_i^2/n_i \right)$$

where MS_w is the error term from all the groups (the denominator of the F test) and the n_i are the group sizes.

Therefore, the following F statistic can be used to test a contrast for significance,

$$F = \hat{L}^2 \; / \; (MS_w \sum c_i^2/n_i) = \frac{\hat{L}^2/\sum c_i^2/n_i}{MS_w} \tag{20}$$

with 1 and $(N - k)$ degrees of freedom. Note here that each contrast has just *one* degree of freedom. As Hays and others have indicated, the $(k - 1)$ between group degrees of freedom can be partitioned into $(k - 1)$ non-redundant single degree of freedom contrasts.

Note that if the group sizes are equal ($n_1 = n_2 = \cdots = n_k = n$), then Equation 20 can be written in somewhat simpler form as:

$$F = \frac{n\hat{L}^2 \; / \; \Sigma c_i^2}{MS_w}$$

Also, some authors present the test statistic for planned comparisons as a t statistic:

$$t = \frac{\hat{L}}{\sqrt{MS_w \, \Sigma c_i^2/n_i}} \tag{21}$$

Since it can be shown that $F = t^2$, the F test is equivalent to a two tailed t test at the same level of significance. SPSS, as shown in Table 2.10, uses the t statistic for contrasts. The probabilities given are for a *two tailed* test, so that if you are testing a directional hypothesis with your contrast the probability value should be divided by two.

Numerical Example

Suppose an investigator has a 4 group problem and wishes to examine the following planned comparisons:

	Groups				
	1	2	3	4	(in population means)
L_1	1	−.5	−.5	0	$L_1 = \mu_1 - (\mu_2 + \mu_3)/2$
L_2	.5	.5	−.5	−.5	$L_2 = (\mu_1 + \mu_2)/2 - (\mu_3 + \mu_4)/2$
L_3	0	0	1	−1	$L_3 = \mu_3 - \mu_4$

Notice that on the left the contrasts are indicated schematically by simply using the coefficients for the population means. This is the way contrasts are input for SPSS, and SAS.

Suppose we have the following descriptive information for the groups:

	1	2	3	4
n_i	10	8	11	13
$\bar{x}_i$	5.6	7.3	8.1	4.2

and it is known that the pooled error term for the groups is $MS_w = 8.7$.

We now show how to calculate the test statistic given in Equation 20 for testing contrasts 1 and 3, and leave the calculation of contrast 2 as an exercise for the reader.

Contrast 1

First we obtain the estimate of the contrast using the sample means:

$$\hat{L}_1 = 5.6 - (7.3 + 8.1)/2 = 5.6 - 7.7 = -2.1$$

Also, we have

$$\sum c_i^2/n_i = 1^2/10 + (-.5)^2/8 + (-.5)^2/11 = .154$$

$$F = \frac{(-2.1)^2/.154}{8.7} = 3.29$$

The critical value at .05 for this contrast is $F_{.05;1,38} = 4.08$. Therefore, this contrast would not be significant. Note that from the above critical value the between degrees of freedom for the contrast is 1.

Contrast 3

The estimate of the contrast is given by

$$\hat{L}_3 = 8.1 - 4.2 = 3.9$$

Also, we have

$$\sum c_i^2/n_i = 1^2/11 + (-1)^2/13 = .168$$

Thus,

$$F = \frac{(3.9)^2/.168}{8.7} = 10.406$$

The critical value for this contrast at the .05 level is the *same* as for contrast 1, i.e., 4.08. Thus, contrast 3 is significant.

2.17   PLANNED COMPARISONS ON SPSS AND SAS

To illustrate how to set up planned comparisons on the statistical packages, and how to interpret the output, we ran the data for Example 4 (Section 2.15) involving the effect of different generic type drugs on reaction time. The complete SAS control lines are given in Table 2.8. To obtain the planned comparisons on SPSS we used the Windows 8.0 version.

To obtain planned comparisons on SPSS with windows is a simple matter. One first goes to and clicks on STATISTICS, then on COMPARE MEANS, and finally click on ONE WAY ANOVA. When all of this is done the first screen displayed in Table 2.9 appears. Make REACTIME the dependent variable and DRUG the factor (grouping variable), and then click on CONTRASTS. When this is done the middle screen in Table 2.9 appears. Recall that for this example we have 5 groups, so we can have at most 4 contrasts. As noted in the *SPSS Base 8.0 User's Guide* (p. 236), "Enter a coefficient for each group (category) of the factor variable and click **ADD** after each entry. Each new value is added to the bottom of the coefficient list. To specify additional contrasts, click **NEXT**." For the current example, when the last contrast is entered the bottom screen appears. Click on CONTINUE and then click on OK to run the contrasts.

TABLE 2.8
SAS Control Lines for Planned Comparisons on Drug Data*

```
DATA CONTRAST;
INPUT DRUG REACTIME @@;
LINES;
1 5 1 8 1 8 1 11 1 1 1 9
1 5 1 9
2 16 2 18 2 5 2 12 2 11 2 12
2 23 2 19
3 16 3 7 3 10 3 4 3 7 3 23
3 12 3 13
4 2 4 10 4 9 4 13 4 11 4 9
4 13 4 9
5 7 5 11 5 12 5 9 5 14 5 16
5 24 5 19
PROC PRINT;
PROC MEANS;
  BY DRUG;
PROC GLM;
CLASS DRUG;
MODEL REACTIME=DRUG;
CONTRAST 'DRUG VS NO DRUG' DRUG 1 -.25 -.25 -.25 -.25;
CONTRAST 'GENTYPE1 VS GENTYPE2' DRUG 0 .5 .5 -.5 -.5;
CONTRAST 'DRUG A VS DRUG B' DRUG 0 1 -1 0 0;
CONTRAST 'DRUG C VS DRUG D' DRUG 0 0 0 1 -1;
```

*Recall that the design was

	One Generic Type		Other Generic Type	
Control	Drug A	Drug B	Drug C	Drug D
μ_1	μ_2	μ_3	μ_4	μ_5

Selected annotated printout from the SPSS and SAS runs is presented in Table 2.10.

2.18   THE EFFECT OF AN OUTLIER ON AN ANOVA

In Chapter 1 we indicated the importance of outliers and showed that they can have a dramatic effect on the results of a statistical analysis. Here we illustrate that effect for a one way analysis of variance.

Example

An investigator has collected the following data:

Gp 1	Gp 2	Gp 3
15	17	6
18	22	9
12	15	12
12	12	11
9	20	11
10	14	8
12	15	13
20	20	30
	21	7

The score of 30 in group 3 is an outlier. With that case in the ANOVA we do not find significance ($F = 2.61$, $p < .095$) at the .05 level, while with the case *deleted* we do find significance well beyond the .01 level ($F = 11.18$, $p < .0004$). Deleting the case has the effect of producing greater separation among the means, since the means with the case included are (13.5, 17.33, 11.89), while the means with the case deleted are (13.5, 17.33, 9.63). It also has the effect of reducing the within group variability in group 3 substantially, and hence the pooled within group variability (the error term for ANOVA) will be much smaller.

2.19 MULTIVARIATE ANALYSIS OF VARIANCE

In this chapter we have considered what is called *univariate* analysis of variance, since there is just one dependent variable in the analysis. In many studies, however, the subjects are measured on several variables. The appropriate statistical analysis for comparing the k groups on the p dependent variables *simultaneously* is called multivariate analysis of variance (MANOVA). This type of analysis is to be distinguished from doing a separate univariate ANOVA on each dependent variable. Four reasons why a MANOVA is preferable to such separate univariate analyses are:

1. The univariate analyses, especially for a moderate or large number of dependent variables, allow the overall type I error rate to go completely out of control. The situation here is analogous to what happened when doing several t tests for the k group problem.

2. The univariate ANOVAs ignore important information, such as the correlations among the dependent measures, whereas the multivariate tests incorporate these correlations into the test statistics.

3. The univariate tests may not show the groups to be significantly different on any of the variables, because of small unreliable differences on each of the variables. However, if measures are considered *jointly* (as in MANOVA) there

TABLE 2.9
SPSS for Windows 8.0 Screens for Obtaining Planned Comparisons

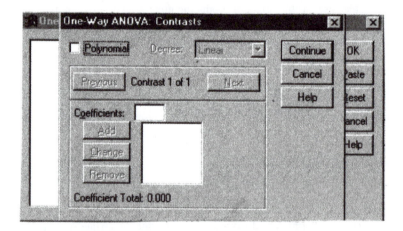

Contrast Coefficients

Contrast	DRUG				
	1.00	2.00	3.00	4.00	5.00
1	1	-.25	-.25	-.25	-.25
2	0	.5	.5	-.5	-.5
3	0	1	-1	0	0
4	0	0	0	1	-1

Contrast Tests

		Contrast	Value of Contrast	Std. Error	t	df	Sig. (2-tailed)
REACTIME	Assume equal variances	1	-5.3750	1.9434	-2.766	35	.009
		2	1.2500	1.7382	.719	35	.477
		3	3.0000	2.4582	1.220	35	.230
		4	-4.5000	2.4582	-1.831	35	.076
	Does not assume equal variances	1	-5.3750	1.4547	-3.695	17.697	.002
		2	1.2500	1.8613	.672	25.164	.508
		3	3.0000	2.9155	1.029	13.937	.321
		4	-4.5000	2.3146	-1.944	11.729	.076

SOURCE	DF	TYPE I SS	F VALUE	PR > F
DRUG	4	314.400000	3.25	0.0228

CONTRAST				
DRUG VS NODRUG	1	184.900000	7.65	0.0090
GENTYP1 VS GENTYP2	1	12.500000	③ ① 0.52	② 0.4768
DRUG A VS DRUG B	1	36.000000	1.49	0.2305
DRUG C VS DRUG D	1	81.000000	3.35	0.0757

①As indicated in 2.16, one can use a two tailed t test or an F test to check the contrast for significance. SPSS chooses to use the t test whereas SAS reports the F. The two are equivalent, as an examination of the tail probabilities shows.

It can be shown that $t^2 = F$, and note here that $(-2.766)^2 = 7.65$, $(.719)^2 = .52$, etc.

Suppose a priori we wished overall $\alpha \leq .05$ for the set of 4 statistical tests (contrasts). By doing each test at the .05/4 level of significance we are assured by the Bonferroni inequality that

$$\text{overall } \alpha \leq .0125 + .0125 + .0125 + .0125$$

②Using $\alpha = .0125$, we find by examining the tail probabilities that only contrast 1 is significant.

③Since the contrasts are orthogonal, the sums of squares (184.9 + 12.5 + 36 + 81) add up to between sum of squares, i.e., 314.4.

may be a significant difference. That is, small differences on each of the variables may combine to produce a reliable overall difference.

4. If treatments affect the dependent variables in different ways, and the dependent variables are at least moderately correlated within groups, the multivariate approach will be quite powerful and can detect differences that the univariate tests cannot. One of the exercises illustrates this situation.

2.20   SUMMARY

1. The analysis of variance (ANOVA) is appropriate for comparing k independent groups on a single dependent variable. It is the generalization of the t test, which is used to compare two groups.

2. It was shown how the use of multiple t tests for the k group problem allows the overall α level to get out of control, hence the need for ANOVA.

3. In testing the null hypothesis of equal population means, the ANOVA computes and compares two basic sources of variation (between and within). Between group variability measures variability of the group mean about the grand mean, while within group variability measures how much subjects vary who are treated alike.

4. It was shown that MS_w and MS_b both represent variances.

5. Analysis of variance rests on three assumptions: normality of scores in each group, equal population variances, and independence of the observations. Considerable research on violations of assumptions suggests that ANOVA is robust with respect to a violation of the normality assumption. It is robust against unequal variances provided that the group sizes are equal or approximately equal (largest/smallest < 1.5). ANOVA is severely affected by correlated observations. Two methods are suggested for dealing with correlated observations. One is to simply test at a more stringent α level. The other, if dealing with several small groups within each treatment, is to use the group mean as the unit of analysis.

6. After a significant F, several post hoc procedures are mentioned for locating where the differences lie. For most situations the Tukey procedure is preferred because of 3 reasons: (a) it does control the overall α, (b) it is fairly powerful for detecting differences, and (c) it examines a meaningful and easily interpreted set of comparisons (pairwise comparisons). For more extensive data-snooping, the Scheffé procedure should be used. This procedure is quite conservative, however, so for more adequate power one will either need to have a large number of subjects or set overall α at .10 or .15. The Dunnett procedure should be used if you are only interested in comparing each treatment group against the control group.

7. For situations where the homogeneity of variance assumption is not tenable and there are sharply unequal group sizes, an ANOVA and post hoc procedure that do not assume equal variances should be used. In Section 2.13 we illustrated two post hoc procedures (Tamhane and Games–Howell), which do not assume equal variances.

8. Confidence intervals and measures of associations (variance accounted for) are mentioned as two ways of determining the practical significance of a study. Several cautions to be observed in using measures of association are mentioned, and an example is given to illustrate that a "small" amount of variance accounted for could indeed be practically significant.

9. Planned comparisons are presented as an alternative way to analyze the k group problem. Here the researcher a priori is setting up comparisons among the group means corresponding to his or her hypotheses. An overall F test is *not* required in this approach. Planned comparisons are a more powerful approach, and overall α can be controlled through use of the Bonferroni Inequality.

APPENDIX

Theorem. The estimated variance for a contrast $\hat{L}$ is given by

$$\hat{\sigma}^2{}_{\hat{L}} = MS_w \sum (c_i^2/n_i),$$

where the n_i are the groups sizes for the k groups.

Proof. The estimated contrast is

$$\hat{L} = c_1\bar{x}_1 + c_2\bar{x}_2 + \cdots c_k\bar{x}_k$$

Now we take the variance for both sides

$$\mathrm{var}(\hat{L}) = \mathrm{var}(c_1\bar{x}_1 + c_2\bar{x}_2 + \cdots + c_k\bar{x}_k)$$

Since the means are sampled from independent groups, the random variables $c_1\bar{x}_1$, $\ldots$, $c_k\bar{x}_k$ are uncorrelated. But for uncorrelated variables the variance of a sum is equal to the sum of the variances (since all the covariance terms are 0), Thus,

$$\mathrm{var}(\hat{L}) = \mathrm{var}(c_1\bar{x}_1) + \mathrm{var}(c_2\bar{x}_2) + \cdots + \mathrm{var}(c_k\bar{x}_k)$$

Now recall from introductory statistics that if c is a constant, then the variance of cx is $\mathrm{var}(cx) = c^2\mathrm{var}(x)$.

Using this result the above may be rewritten as

$$\mathrm{var}(\hat{L}) = c_1^2 \, \mathrm{var}(\bar{x}_1) + c_2^2 \, \mathrm{var}(\bar{x}_2) + \cdots + c_k^2 \, \mathrm{var}(\bar{x}_k)$$

Now, it is well known that the variance of a sample mean based on a sample of size n is given by $\mathrm{var}(\bar{x}) = \sigma^2/n$, where σ^2 is the variance of the population. (See Glass & Hopkins, 1984, pp. 188–190, for a proof.) Applying this result to $\bar{x}_1$, $\bar{x}_2$, etc., we obtain:

$$\mathrm{var}(\hat{L}) = c_1^2 \; \sigma^2/n_1 + c_2^2 \, \sigma^2/n_2 + \cdots + c_k^2 \, \sigma^2/n_k$$

In obtaining the above we assumed the population variance was the same in each of the k groups, which is the homogeneity of variance assumption for ANOVA. Now, factoring out the common term σ^2 we have

$$\text{var}(\hat{L}) = \sigma^2(c_1^2/n_1 + c_2^2/n_2 + \cdots + c_k^2/n_k)$$

In practice σ^2 has to be estimated, and recall from the chapter that $MS_w = \hat{\sigma}^2$. Thus, replacing σ^2 by MS_w and writing the sum of the terms in parentheses using the summation operator, we obtain the result stated in the theorem:

$$\text{var}(\hat{L}) = MS_w \sum c_i^2/n_i$$

EXERCISES

1. For a 7 group problem there would be 21 t tests for the 21 paired comparisons. Using this approach, rather than the proper one way ANOVA, what would overall α be approximately (if each t test is done at .05 level)?

2. (a) If $k = 4$ and $n_1 = n_2 = n_3 = n_4 = 20$, then $df_b = ?$, $df_w = ?$
   (b) If $k = 3$ and $n_1 = 12$, $n_2 = 25$, and $n_3 = 20$, then $df_b = ?$ $df_w = ?$

3. (a) Find the critical value at the .05 level for a 3 group problem with 10 subjects per group.
   (b) Find the critical value at the .10 level for a 4 group problem with 20 subjects per group.
   (c) Find the critical value at the .01 level for a 5 group problem with 8 subjects per group.

4. (a) Do a one way analysis of variance on the following data, testing for significance at the .10 level.

Treat 1	Treat 2	Treat 3
11	10	15
14	8	14
13	12	10
17	7	11
18	13	16

   (b) Obtain MS_w by computing the variances for each group using your TI30Xa STAT calculator, or some other calculator that yields means and variances.

5. Do a one way ANOVA on this data; test for significance at .05:

Group 1	Group 2	Group 3	Group 4
2	7	4	8
3	9	4	4
5	11	5	7
6		8	7
		3	

In obtaining MS_w with your calculator, note that

$$SS_w = (n_1 - 1) s_1^2 + (n_2 - 1) s_2^2 + \cdots + (n_k - 1) s_k^2$$

where $s_1^2, s_2^2, \ldots, s_k^2$ are sample variances for groups.

6. As part of a study by Sarachen-Deily (1985), deaf high school students were classified as good readers, average readers or poor readers on the basis of scores on the Stanford Achievement Test, Special Edition for Hearing Impaired Students. The following table resulted:

Category	n	Mean	Stand. Deviation
Good reader	7	6.90	.49
Aver. reader	9	5.04	.56
Poor reader	4	3.38	.10

An ANOVA on this data yielded a significant overall difference at the .01 level.

(a) Are the sample variances for the groups sharply unequal?

(b) Would you be worried about the significant ANOVA result being spurious? Why, or why not?

7. A 4 group ANOVA is run on the following data:

	Gp1	Gp2	Gp3	Gp4
n_i	15	15	15	15
$\bar{x}_i$	5.6	7.3	4.1	8.7

The F statistic is $F = 63.73/22.35 = 2.85$, $p < .10$.

Apply the Tukey procedure at the .10 level to determine which pairs of groups are significantly different.

8. A study by Smith, Jones, and Waugh (1986) evaluated the effect of interactive computer assisted videodisc laboratory simulations in enhancing achievement in a freshmen college chemistry course. A group of 103 students were randomly assigned to one of three groups: (a) the first group was required to complete a series of interactive videodisc lessons on chemical equilibrium in place of labo-

ratory work (the VDISC group), (b) the second group was required to complete only a traditional laboratory experiment on the same content material (the LAB group) and (3) the third group was required to complete the interactive videodisc lessons *before* the traditional laboratory experiment (VDISC+LAB group). Following these treatments all students took a seven item multiple choice quiz that required them to apply knowledge of chemical equilibrium to solve both familiar and unfamiliar systems, with the following results:

	VDISC	VDISC+LAB	LAB
n	21	17	49
$\bar{x}$	5.810	5.588	4.163
sd	1.167	1.121	1.519

A one way ANOVA on these data yielded $F = 13.84$, $p < .00005$.
(a) The group sizes are sharply unequal. Would you be worried about the homogeneity of variance assumption? Why, or why not?
(b) Apply the Tukey procedure with overall $\alpha = .05$ to determine which pairs of groups differ significantly.
(c) Does there appear to be practical significance? In answering this, calculate the effect size(s) for the pair(s) that are significantly different.

9. One of the planned comparisons involved in the numerical example in 2.16 was

$$L_2 = (\mu_1 + \mu_2)/2 - (\mu_3 + \mu_4)/2$$

Test this contrast for significance at the .05 level.

10. For example 3 in Section 2.15 the following three contrasts were defined: $L_1 = \mu_1 - (\mu_2 + \mu_3 + \mu_4)/3$, $L_2 = \mu_2 - \mu_3$, and $L_3 = \mu_4 - (\mu_2 + \mu_3)/2$. Label the treatment variable TREAT and the dependent variable DEP. Show the complete control lines for running the above three contrasts on SPSS and on SAS. For the data lines element just put DATA.

11. O'Grady in his paper on measures of association, states

For instance, examining the relationship between the five different types of fitness programs and subsequent efficiency of the heart would, I suspect, produce quite different measures of explained variance for a population of runners in comparison with a population of sedentary individuals (which, in turn, would no doubt produce a quite different value than would be found for a random sample of the American adult population). (p. 773)

What does this relate to that was discussed in the chapter on measures of association?

12. Consider the following data for three groups of subjects on two dependent variables y_1 and y_2:

Group 1		Group 2		Group 3	
y_1	y_2	y_1	y_2	y_1	y_2
3	7	4	5	5	5
4	7	4	6	6	5
5	8	5	7	6	6
5	9	6	7	7	7
6	10	6	8	7	8

(a) Run a one way ANOVA for y_1 and for y_2 on SAS and a one way multivariate analysis of variance on SAS. All three analyses are obtained in one run. Simply put this in the MODEL statement:

```
MODEL Y1 Y2=GPID;
```

(b) Is there a significant difference for y_1 at the .05 level? for y_2 at the .05 level?
(c) Are the multivariate tests significant at the .05 level?
(d) In discussing the results from (b) and (c), first look at the pattern of means for y_1 and y_2 over the three groups. Are the patterns different? Another factor that is important is the within group correlation for y_1 and y_2, as this has a strong influence on the magnitude of the error term for the multivariate tests (see Stevens, 1986, Chapter 4).

13. An auditor from the Internal Revenue Service wishes to compare the efficiency of four regional tax processing centers. A random sample of 10 returns is selected from each center, and the number of days between receipt of the tax returns and final processing is determined. The results (in days) are as follows:

East	Midwest	South	West
49	47	39	52
54	56	55	42
40	40	48	57
60	51	43	46
43	55	50	50
65	36	63	34
59	38	48	40
70	52	57	51
61	41	49	39
48	43	65	36

There is a sig. difference b/w the 4 regions in their return time of IRS forms $(F(3,36) = 3.382, p = .029)$.

(a) Run this data on SAS to determine whether there is difference in average processing time among the 4 centers at the .05 level.

(b) Are there any significant pairwise differences at the .05 level with the Scheffé procedure? With the Tukey procedure?

(c) Explain the difference between the results found in (b) for the two parts of the problem.

14. An investigator randomly assigns 20 subjects to each of four groups (two control and two treatment) and is interested in the effect of treatments on sociability. She wishes to determine whether treatments differ from no treatment, whether the treatment groups do better than the Hawthorne control group, and whether there is a difference in the efficacy of the treatments. Schematically then we have the following contrasts:

	Control	Hawthrone Control	Treat 1	Treat 2
L_1	1	1	-1	-1
L_2	0	1	$-.5$	$-.5$
L_3	0	0	1	-1

Is this a set of orthogonal contrasts?

15. Levin, McCormick, Miller, Berry, and Presley (1982) had fourth grade students learn a list of relatively complex English vocabulary words in two experiments. In Experiment 1, pupils used either a mnemonic (keyword) contextual or a verbal contextual procedure. In Experiment 2, three other conditions were compared to the keyword context condition. In Experiment 2 the 64 fourth graders were randomly assigned, 16 to each group, with the following summary statistics resulting:

	Keyword Context	Experiential Context	Picture Context	Control
Mean	72.3	36.2	42.4	48.7
Stand. Dev.	22.9	27.0	23.1	25.6

Levin et al. state in their *Results* section,

Performance differences among conditions were assessed in terms of five planned non-orthogonal comparisons, each based on $\alpha = .01$. . . . Statistical analysis revealed that students in the keyword context condition substantially outperformed those in the control condition, $t = 2.71$, $p < .01$, and the picture context condition, $t = 3.42$, $p < .005$, as well as those in the experiential context condition, $t = 4.14$, $p < .001$. Neither picture context nor experiential context differed significantly from controls. (p. 130)

(a) What are the 5 planned comparisons?

(b) Show that they are non-orthogonal.

(c) Show how the three t values indicated above are obtained.

16. As mentioned in Section 2.10, if your interest in a study is confined to testing each of several treatment groups against a control group, then the Dunnett procedure is the most powerful. Let $t(d)$ represent the modified t value from Dunnett's table (Appendix B.3), n the number of subjects in each group, and MS_w the error term. Then the critical value that must be exceeded for a difference to be significant at some alpha level is given by $t(d)\sqrt{2(MS_w)/n}$. If the group sizes are not equal and the homogeneity of variance assumption is tenable, the use of the harmonic mean for each pair of groups is suggested.

Suppose a study has been run with 17 subjects per group. The error term is 67.24, and the means are as follows:

Control	Treat. 1	Treat. 2	Treat. 3
26.1	29.3	34.2	31.6

Use Dunnett's procedure at the .05 level to determine which of the treatment means is significantly different from the control group mean.

17. The following is an approximate 40% random sample of the CLINICAL data (in Appendix A in back of book), where we present data on only the FREEDIST variable:

GROUP 1	GROUP 2	GROUP 3
9.00	11.00	5.33
9.00	7.67	14.00
7.67	12.00	10.00
8.67	9.00	8.67
14.67	7.33	9.33
6.33	7.33	9.00
7.67	7.33	9.00
7.00	8.33	9.67
7.33	5.33	16.33
8.67	11.00	10.33
8.67	7.67	9.67
7.67	12.00	10.33
8.00	6.00	11.33
12.00	9.67	
7.00	9.33	
5.33	10.00	
8.00	9.67	
9.33		
5.00		
8.33		
9.00		

(a) Do a one way ANOVA on this data using either SAS or SPSS. What is the null hypothesis? Do you reject at the .10 level?
(b) Since the group sizes are sharply unequal, test the assumption of equal population variances with the Levene test. Is it significant at the .05 level?
(c) Apply the Tukey procedure at the .10 level. Which pairs of groups are significantly different?

18. The following is a sampling of 60 (all of site 1 - three to five year old disadvantaged children from inner city areas in various parts of the country) from the SESAME STREET data base. The grouping variable is VIEWCAT (coded as 1 if the children rarely watched the show to 4 if the children watched the show on average of more than 5 times a week). The dependent variable is POSTLET-PRELET, that is, a measure of how much the children have gained in their knowledge about letters.

VIEWCAT1	VIEWCAT2	VIEWCAT3	VIEWCAT4
n=9 7	n=17 −1	n=20 7	n=14 6
3	4	7	6
8	17	28	4
0	6	16	4
4	9	32	24
−1	6	8	27
2	4	−1	21
−1	10	10	−15
−1	9	26	4
	11	−22	24
	1	11	35
	−2	32	5
	6	10	8
	−10	33	7
	21	14	
	5	33	
	7	30	
		31	
		14	
		5	

(a) Do a one way ANOVA on this data at the .05 level of significance using either SAS or SPSS. What is the null hypothesis? Do you reject it?
(b) Since the group sizes are sharply unequal, test the assumption of equal population variances with the Levene test. Is it significant at the .05 level? Should we be concerned about the result in (a) being spurious? Explain.

(c) Apply the Tukey procedure at the .05 level. Which pairs of groups are significantly different?

19. It was mentioned in the chapter that $1 - (1 - \alpha')^k$ is approximately equal to $k\alpha'$ for small α'.

(a) Let $k = 3$. Expand $1 - (1 - \alpha')^3$, and show that it equals $3\alpha' - 3\alpha'^2 + \alpha'^3$.

(b) Let $\alpha' = .01$. Calculate $k\alpha'$ and $3\alpha' - 3\alpha'^2 + \alpha'^3$. What have we shown?

3

Power Analysis

3.1 INTRODUCTION

Recall from Chapter 2 that type I error, or the level of significance (α), is the probability of rejecting the null hypothesis when it is true, in effect saying the groups differ when they do not. The α level set by the experimenter is a *subjective* decision, but it is usually set at .05 or .01 by most researchers. The reason for setting α so low, of course, is to minimize the probability of making this error. In statistical inference we can never be sure we have made the correct decision; however, by setting α very low we can control quite effectively the risk of this type of error occurring. As we shall see shortly, though, it is not always wise to set α as low as .05 or .01, especially when the group sizes are less than 20.

There is another type of error that one can make in conducting a statistical test, and this is called a type II error. Type II error (denoted by β) is the probability of accepting H_0 when it is false, i.e., saying the groups don't differ when they

121

do. Note that only one of these errors can occur in a given study. Either we falsely reject H_0 or we falsely accept H_0. Now, not only can either of these errors occur, but in addition they are inversely related. That is, as we control on type I error, type II error increases. We illustrate the below for a two group problem with 15 subjects per group and a difference between the means of one half a standard deviation. Notice that as we control on α more severely (from .10 to .01), type II error increases fairly sharply (from .37 to .78).

α	β	$1 - \beta$
.10	.37	.63
.05	.52	.48
.01	.78	.22

The quantity in the last column is the *power* of a statistical test, and is the probability of rejecting H_0 when it is false. Thus, power is the probability of making a correct decision. In the above example, if we are willing to take a 10% chance of rejecting H_0 falsely, then we have a 63% chance of finding a difference of a specified magnitude in the population (more specifics on this later in the chapter). On the other hand, if we insist on only a 1% chance of rejecting H_0 falsely, then there are only about 2 chances out of 10 of finding the difference (i.e., power = .22). This example with small sample size suggests that in this case it might be prudent to abandon the traditional α levels of .01 or .05 (and especially .01) to a more liberal α level to improve power sharply. Of course, one does not get something for nothing. We are taking a greater risk of rejecting falsely, but that increased risk is *more than balanced* by the increase in power.

Cast in a broad context, power is dependent on many factors: (1) α level, (2) sample size, (3) effect size, (4) the statistical test used, and (5) the research design. For example, the t test for dependent samples is more powerful than the t test for independent samples, and a repeated measures design (discussed in Chapter 5) is more powerful than a one way ANOVA design. However, the power of a specific statistical test is dependent on these 3 factors:

1. The α level set by the experimenter.
2. Sample size.
3. Effect size—How much of a difference the treatments make, or the extent to which the groups differ in the population on the dependent variable.

We have already indicated that power may be increased substantially by adopting a somewhat more liberal α level, say .10 or .15. There are limits on this, however; no one would take α = .40 to gain still greater power, for this is taking far too great a risk of rejecting H_0 falsely.

Power is *heavily* dependent on sample size. Consider a two tailed test at the .05 level for the t test for independent samples. Suppose we have an effect size of .5 standard deviations in the population, i.e., the difference in the means divided by the standard deviation is .5. The table below shows how power changes dramatically as sample size increases from small (10) to large (100):

n (subjects per group)	power
10	.18
20	.33
50	.70
100	.94

With only 10 subjects per group we have only about a 20% chance of detecting this effect size, whereas with 100 subjects per group we are almost certain of detecting the effect (i.e., rejecting the null hypothesis).

As the above example suggests, when sample size is large (say more than 100 subjects per group) power will generally not be an issue. In these cases power will tend to be adequate (> .70) to excellent (> .90). It is when one is conducting a study where the group sizes are small ($n < 20$), or when one is evaluating a study that had small group size, that it is imperative to be very sensitive to the possibility of a type II error.

The third factor that affects power is effect size. If the effect size is small or medium, then we will see shortly that large group size is needed to detect these effects, i.e., to have adequate power. On the other hand, if the effect size is large (about one standard deviation or greater), then only about 15 subjects per group will be needed for adequate power.

In this chapter, and in Chapter 4 on factorial designs, we will make considerable use of a very nice and inexpensive program called PASS 6.0 by Dr. Jerry Hintze (1996). It does various types of power analysis very quickly: t tests, ANOVA, factorial ANOVA (up to a 3 way), and simple repeated measures designs. One of the features that is very nice is that one can obtain power values for various sample sizes and alpha levels in one run, and in a matter of seconds.

Most statistics books do not do a good job of discussing the *consequences* of making a type I or a type II error. Let me attempt to remedy this deplorable situation. Suppose you are comparing a treatment group vs. a control group on some dependent (outcome) variable. Treatment here is generic and could refer to teaching method, counseling method, diet, drug, etc. Schematically:

TREAT   CONTROL

μ_1 μ_2

The null and alternative hypotheses are as follows:

$$H_0: \mu_1 = \mu_2 \qquad H_a: \mu_1 \neq \mu_2$$

If a type I error is made (rejecting H_0 when it is true) we are saying that the treatment is effective when in fact it is not. This is false optimism. A school district, for example, may invest in a program heavily. If a statistical test is done and a type I error is made, the program is not effective and yet much money has been spent.

Now consider the other side of the coin, that is, a type II error. A type II error is accepting the null hypothesis when it is false. If a type II error is made, we may have "the greatest thing since sliced bread" and not know it. This is false negativism. In a medical sense a type II error could be dangerous or deadly. It would be like telling someone they don't have a disease when in fact they do. In this case, someone may die before it is realized that a type II error was made.

3.2   t TEST FOR INDEPENDENT SAMPLES

Cohen (1977) has defined the population effect size as

$$d = (\mu_1 - \mu_2)/\sigma \tag{1}$$

where σ is the assumed common population standard deviation. This population effect size is estimated by

$$\hat{d} = (\bar{x}_1 - \bar{x}_2)/s$$

where

$$\hat{\sigma}^2 = \frac{(n_1 - 1)s_1^2 + (n_2 - 1)s_2^2}{n_1 + n_2 - 2} = s^2$$

is the estimate of the assumed common population variance.

It is necessary to divide by σ in obtaining the effect size measure to adjust for scaling differences on variables which can be quite arbitrary in social science research. Note that Equation 1 expresses the difference between the groups in standard deviation units. For example, if the means for the groups were $\bar{x}_1 = 10$ and $\bar{x}_2 = 4$, with the estimated standard deviation $s = 15$, then $\hat{d} = (10 - 4)/15 = .4$, or the groups differ by .4 of a standard deviation.

An effect size around .20 is considered small, an effect size around .50, medium, and an effect size >.80 is large. A medium effect size is one that would be apparent to a researcher. For example, .5 standard deviations is the difference in mean I.Q. between semiskilled workers and professionals and managers. The difference in mean I.Q.'s between Ph.D.'s and typical college freshmen is an example of a large effect size, that is, about .8 standard deviations.

The following power values for the t test (α = .05, two tailed test) from Cohen's text illustrate precisely how poor power is with small group size and/or small effect size:

1. $n_1 = n_2 = 15$, $d = .50$, power = .26
2. $n_1 = n_2 = 35$, $d = .30$, power = .23

Power can be adequate with small group size, but only if the effect size is *large*. For example, with $n_1 = n_2 = 15$ and $d = 1$, then power = .75 at α = .05 for a two tailed test.

Cohen and many others have noted that *small and medium effect sizes are very common in social science research.* Light and Pillimer (1984) in *Summing Up* comment on the fact that most evaluations find small effects in reviews of the literature on programs of various types (social, educational, etc.): "Review after review confirms it and drives it home. Its importance comes from having managers understand that they should not expect large, positive findings to emerge routinely from a single study of a new program. Indeed *any* positive findings are good news" (pp. 153–154). To further document the fact that small and medium effect sizes are common, we present in Table 3.1 the effect sizes for three sets of studies in quite different areas. Note that there are *only 3 large effect sizes out of 40.*

How does one estimate power if the group sizes are unequal? Cohen has suggested using the harmonic mean. Recall from Chapter 2 that the harmonic mean for two groups is given by $2n_1n_2/(n_1 + n_2)$. Thus, if we had group sizes of 10 and 20, we compute the harmonic mean as $2(10)(20)/30 = 13.3$, and use 13 as the n with which to enter Cohen's power tables. Note that use of the harmonic mean weights the estimate of power down toward the *smaller* group size. The difference between the ordinary mean and harmonic mean is relatively small when group sizes are approximately equal, but when the group sizes are sharply unequal the difference can be considerable, as the following table shows:

Group 1	Group 2	Mean	Harmonic mean
10	15	12.5	12
10	20	15.0	13.3
10	30	20.0	15.0
10	40	25.0	16.0

Researchers not sufficiently sensitive to the power problem may interpret nonsignificant results from studies as demonstrating that "treatments" made no difference. In fact, however, it may be that treatments did make a difference, but

TABLE 3.1
Effect Sizes for Three Sets of Studies: Teacher Expectancy, ,
Desegregation and Gender Influenceability (Data from Becker, 1987)

	Teacher Expectancy Sample Size		
Study	n_e*	n_c	Effect Size
1	79	339	.03
2	60	189	.12
3	72	72	−.14
4	11	22	1.18
5	11	22	.26
6	129	348	−.06
7	110	636	−.02
8	26	99	−.32
9	75	74	.27
10	32	32	.80
11	22	22	.54
12	43	38	.18
13	24	24	−.02
14	19	32	.23
15	80	79	−.18
16	72	72	−.06
17	65	255	.30
18	233	224	.07
19	65	67	−.07

	Desegregation				Gender Influenceability		
Study	Des**	Seg	Effect	Study	M	F	Effect
1	27	32	.32	1	70	71	−.22
2	39	36	.37	2	60	59	.04
3	28	38	.49	3	118	136	.35
4	29	35	.12	4	77	114	−.30
5	36	35	.22	5	32	32	.63
6	42	35	.29	6	10	10	.81
7	25	48	.59	7	45	45	.39
8	24	48	−.32	8	30	30	.46
9	38	42	−.20	9	40	40	.36
10	131	78	.19	10	61	64	−.06
11	37	101	.24				

*n_e and n_c - numbers of subjects in experimental and control gps
**Des-no. of desegregated schools, Seg- no. of segregated schools

that the researchers had poor power for detecting the difference. The poor power may result from small sample size (e.g., < 20 S's per group) and/or from small effect size. *The danger of low power studies is that they may stifle or cut off further research in an area where effects do exist, but perhaps are more subtle* (as in personality, social, or clinical psychology).

In introductory statistics courses one vs. two tailed tests, or directional vs. non-directional alternative hypotheses, were discussed. It was indicated that one should do a one tail test if there is empirical evidence (previous studies) and/or theory to suggest a difference in a specified direction. The statistical advantage of a one tail test over a two tail test is that it is more powerful. In one of the exercises you are asked to explain why this is so. To further dramatize the considerable difference it can make in power if one adopts a somewhat more liberal α level *and* is able to do a one tail test, consider the table below:

Power of t test for independent samples

$(n_1 = n_2 = 20)$

α level & nature of test	moderate effect size $(d = .6)$	large effect size $(d = .8)$
$\alpha = .01$, two tail	.22	.44
$\alpha = .05$, one tail	.59	.80
$\alpha = .10$, one tail	.72	.89

At the traditional α level of .01 with a two tail test, power is poor in both cases, while at the .10 level, with the added advantage of a one tail test, power is good in both cases.

3.3   A PRIORI AND POST HOC ESTIMATION OF POWER

If a researcher is going to invest a great amount of time and money in carrying out a study, then he or she would certainly want to have a 70 or 80% chance (i.e., power = .70 or .80) of finding a difference if one is there. Thus, the a priori estimation of power alerts the researcher as to how many subjects per group are needed to have adequate power. This is an important part of experimental planning. More on this shortly.

The post hoc estimation of power is important in terms of how one interprets the results of completed studies. The following example shows how important an awareness of power can be. Cronbach and Snow (1969) had written a report on aptitude-treatment interaction research, not being fully cognizant of the importance of power. By the publication of their text, *Aptitude and Instructional Methods* (1977), on the same topic they acknowledged the importance of power, stating in the preface, "(We) ... became aware of the critical relevance of statistical power, and consequently changed our interpretations of individual studies and sometimes of whole bodies of literature." Why would they change their interpretation of a whole body of literature? Because, prior to being sensitive to power, when they found most studies in a given body of literature had nonsignificant results, they concluded no effect existed. However, *after* being sensitized to power they took into account the sample sizes in the studies, and also the magnitude of the effect sizes. If the sample sizes were small in most of the studies with nonsignificant results, then lack of significance is due to poor power. Or, in other words, *several low power studies that report nonsignificant results of the same character are evidence for an effect.* By the same character we mean that the test statistic is "leaning" in the same direction in all cases.

Incidentally, the effect size $(\hat{d})$ for the t test can be expressed in terms of the t statistic as follows:

$$\hat{d} = t\sqrt{1/n_1 + 1/n_2} \qquad (2)$$

where n_1 and n_2 are the respective group sizes. This equation is very helpful in estimating the power of completed studies, since from Equation 2, $\hat{d}$ is quickly computed and then Cohen's power tables are entered.

3.4   POWER ANALYSIS WITH PASS 6.0 FOR t TEST

The PASS 6.0 program, written by Dr. Jerry Hintze, is easy to use, relatively inexpensive, and very nice for trying out different samples and alpha levels in experimental planning. We illustrate the program in this chapter and use it again in Chapter 4 on factorial designs. As Hintze points out (*PASS 6.0 User's Guide*, p. 1), PASS can run on any system that runs either Windows 3.1, Windows 95, or Windows NT, and takes up about 5 MB of disk space. All PASS procedures are controlled by a template. A template is a window containing all of the settings, options, and parameters that control a particular procedure. When you open PASS the Navigator window appears and lets you select the procedure you wish to use.

Since we have been talking about the t test for independent samples, let us use the PASS program for different practical sample sizes ($n = 10$, 20, and 40) and alpha levels (.10, .05, and .01) for a medium and large effect size. It is obvious that more subjects per group will increase power and that we will obtain greater power with a larger effect size. What is not so obvious is how large n must be to have adequate power for a medium effect size and for a large effect size. We have opened the PASS program and selected the two sample t test. When you click on two sample t test, the screen at the bottom of Table 3.2 appears. We have clicked within each appropriate box and made changes for the results presented in Table 3.3.

Table 3.3, from PASS 6.0, shows that for a medium effect size we need 40 subjects per group at the .10 level just to have adequate power (.72286). On the other hand, if we wish to detect a large effect size, we have excellent power

TABLE 3.2

Screen for PASS 6.0 With *t* Test Selected, Template Screen
for *t* Test, and Screen for Run Results Given in Table 3.3

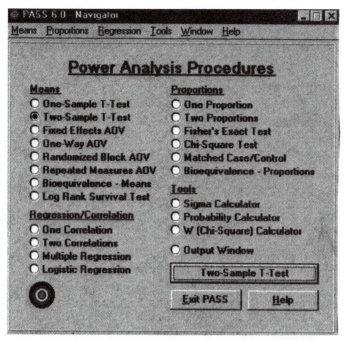

129

TABLE 3.2
(Continued)

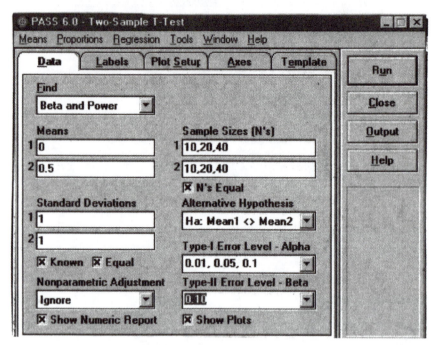

(.88538) with only 20 subjects per group at the .05 level. This is illustrated in Figure 3.1.

3.5 ESTIMATION OF POWER FOR ONE WAY ANALYSIS OF VARIANCE

To define the population effect size for a one way ANOVA we first define a measure of variability of the group means about the grand mean *which is independent of sample size*:

$$\hat{\sigma}_m^2 = \frac{\Sigma\, n_i(\bar{x}_i - \bar{x})^2}{N}$$

where $\bar{x}$ is the grand mean and N is total sample size. Dividing by N makes the measure independent of sample size. Notice that the numerator is just SS_b. To make our effect measure scale free, we again divide by σ as was done for the t test effect measure:

TABLE 3.3
Power Values From PASS 6.0 for *n* = 10, 20, and 40 and
α = .01, .05, and .10 for Medium and Large Effect Sizes for *t* Test

MEDIUM EFFECT SIZE

Numeric Results for Two-Sample T-Test
Null Hypothesis: Mean1=Mean2   Alternative Hypothesis: Mean1<>Mean2
The sigmas were assumed to be known and equal. The N's were forced to be equal.

Power	N1	N2	Alpha	Beta	Mean1	Mean2	Sigma1	Sigma2
0.07256	10	10	0.01000	0.92744	0.00	0.50	1.00	1.00
0.15996	20	20	0.01000	0.84004	0.00	0.50	1.00	1.00
0.36702	40	40	0.01000	0.63298	0.00	0.50	1.00	1.00
0.20096	10	10	0.05000	0.79904	0.00	0.50	1.00	1.00
0.35261	20	20	0.05000	0.64739	0.00	0.50	1.00	1.00
0.60878	40	40	0.05000	0.39122	0.00	0.50	1.00	1.00
0.30202	10	10	0.10000	0.69798	0.00	0.50	1.00	1.00
0.47523	20	20	0.10000	0.52477	0.00	0.50	1.00	1.00
0.72286	40	40	0.10000	0.27714	0.00	0.50	1.00	1.00

Plot Section

LARGE EFFECT SIZE

Numeric Results for Two-Sample T-Test
Null Hypothesis: Mean1=Mean2   Alternative Hypothesis: Mean1<>Mean2
The sigmas were assumed to be known and equal. The N's were forced to be equal.

Power	N1	N2	Alpha	Beta	Mean1	Mean2	Sigma1	Sigma2
0.36702	10	10	0.01000	0.63298	0.00	1.00	1.00	1.00
0.72121	20	20	0.01000	0.27879	0.00	1.00	1.00	1.00
0.97104	40	40	0.01000	0.02896	0.00	1.00	1.00	1.00
0.60878	10	10	0.05000	0.39122	0.00	1.00	1.00	1.00
0.88538	20	20	0.05000	0.11462	0.00	1.00	1.00	1.00
0.99400	40	40	0.05000	0.00600	0.00	1.00	1.00	1.00
0.72286	10	10	0.10000	0.27714	0.00	1.00	1.00	1.00
0.93542	20	20	0.10000	0.06458	0.00	1.00	1.00	1.00
0.99765	40	40	0.10000	0.00235	0.00	1.00	1.00	1.00

Plot Section

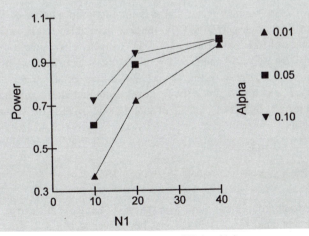

FIGURE 3.1   Power vs. N1 by Alpha

$$f = \sigma_m/\sigma \tag{3}$$

This measure represents the standard deviation of the standardized means, i.e., variability of z score group means about the grand mean. Now, it can be shown (this is one of the exercises) that the estimated effect size can be expressed in terms of the F statistic as follows:

$$\hat{f} = \sqrt{(k-1)F/N} \tag{4}$$

Cohen (1977) characterizes an f around .1 as a small effect size, an f around .25 as medium, and an $f > .4$ as a large effect size. The above equation is quite useful for post hoc estimation of power, since all one needs is the F statistic from the study to obtain the corresponding effect size. With the effect size and the common group size (or the *average* group size if the group sizes are unequal), the power for the study is easily determined using Cohen's power tables. We give two examples to illustrate.

Example 1

A three group study was done by Harrington (1968) on the efficacy of advance organizers in mathematics. He had 10 subjects per group and obtained $F = 4.38$. What was his power at $\alpha = .05$? First, we obtain the estimated effect size using Equation 2:

$$\hat{f} = \sqrt{(k-1)F/N} = \sqrt{2(4.38)/30} = .54 \text{ (large effect size)}$$

In using Cohen's tables recall that n is the common number of subjects per group. Also, for a one way ANOVA, the u in the tables refers to the between groups degrees of freedom, which is $(k-1)$. Thus, here we have $u = 2$. We find that power = .64 at $f = .50$ and power = .81 at $f = .60$ (cf. Table C.2). Therefore, by interpolation, power is estimated as .73, which is adequate. Incidentally, Harrington's F was significant at the .05 level. Note that Harrington had adequate power to reject H_0 in spite of his small sample size because his treatment effect was very large.

Example 2

Consider a four group study with $n_1 = 15$, $n_2 = 13$, $n_3 = 20$, and $n_4 = 17$. The investigator obtained $F = 1.4$. What was her power at $\alpha = .05$? at $\alpha = .10$?
First we obtain the effect size:

$$\hat{f} = \sqrt{3(1.4)/65} = .254 \quad \text{(medium effect size)}$$

Next, the average group size is 16.25 (we use 16), and $u = k - 1 = 3$. Therefore, at $\alpha = .05$, power $= .34$ (Table C.3), whereas at $\alpha = .10$, power $= .48$ (Table C.7). In both cases the power is inadequate.

If a post hoc power analysis is done on a study where significance is not found and the effect size is quite small ($< .10$), then one must decide whether such an effect has any practical significance. On the other hand, when significance is not found and a post hoc power analysis reveals a large or medium effect size, then it is essential to replicate the study with more adequate sample size.

3.6   A PRIORI ESTIMATION OF SUBJECTS NEEDED FOR A GIVEN POWER

Here we need an *expected* effect size in order to enter the power tables to determine how many subjects per group are necessary for a specified power at some α level. One could use the average of the estimated effect sizes from studies similar to yours; that is, similar in nature of treatments, duration of treatments, type of subjects, dependent variable used, instrument used to measure the dependent variable, etc. When a study is similar in enough of the above respects to qualify as an estimator of your expected effect size is of course a subjective judgement. But even if an estimate is fairly rough, as long as we can obtain at least two such estimates, the average of these will probably be reasonably accurate. Furthermore, it is surely better to have some estimate and hence be able to determine approximately how many subjects are needed, rather than to have no idea at all.

Example 3

Suppose investigator X has found two studies similar to his.

Study 1:   3 groups, $N = 42$, $F = 2.16$
Study 2:   3 groups, $N = 81$, $F = 1.42$

Now, by using Equation 2 relating F and effect size we find:

$$\hat{f_1} = \sqrt{2(2.16)/42} = .32 \text{ and } \hat{f_2} = \sqrt{2(1.42)/81} = .187$$

Thus, the expected effect size for investigator X's study is $(.32 + .187)/2 = .25$. Now, the investigator wishes to know how many subjects per group are necessary to have power $= .70$ at $\alpha = .05$ and at $\alpha = .10$. Referring to Table C.3

and reading down the column under $f = .25$ until we reach a power value of at least .70, we see that 42 subjects *per group* will be needed at .05 level. Now, using Table C.6 for the .10 level, we see that 32 subjects per group are needed.

In the above example the effect sizes were weighted evenly in determining the expected effect size. However, if one of the studies were much more similar to the study being conducted, then the investigator should weight that effect size more heavily, perhaps giving it double the weight.

3.7 POWER ANALYSIS FOR ONE WAY ANOVA WITH PASS 6.0

To obtain power analysis for one way ANOVA from PASS we simply click on ONE-WAY AOV (see Table 3.2) and then click again on ONE-WAY AOV. We have clicked within each appropriate box and changed the number of groups to 3 and 4, sample size to 10, 20, and 40, and effect size to medium. The resulting screen is presented in Table 3.4.

TABLE 3.4
PASS 6.0 One Way ANOVA Screen for Medium
Effect Size for Three and Four Groups

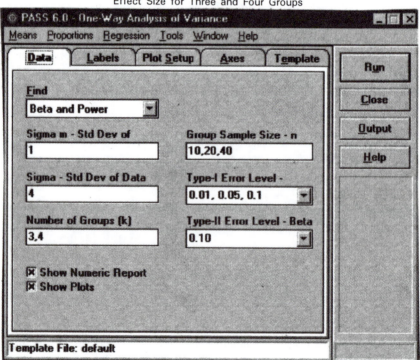

The PASS results for 3 and 4 groups with $n = 10$, 20, and 40, $\alpha = .10$, .05, and .01 for detecting a medium and a large effect size (which entails another run) are given in Table 3.5. Table 3.5 shows that for detecting a medium effect size we need 40 subjects per group (for 3 groups) just to have close to adequate power (.67567). On the other hand, if we wish to detect a large effect size, we need only 15 subjects per group to have good power (.883361).

3.8 WAYS OF IMPROVING POWER

Given how poor power is generally with less than 20 subjects per group, the investigator should consider the following four ways of improving power:

1. Adopt a more lenient α level, perhaps $\alpha = .10$ or $\alpha = .15$.

2. Use one tailed tests where the literature supports a directional hypothesis.

3. Consider ways of reducing within group variability, so that a more sensitive design results. One way is through sample selection; more homogeneous subjects will tend to vary less on the dependent variable. For example, use just males, rather than males and females, or just use 6 and 7 year old children rather than using 6 through 9 year old children. Another way is through the use of factorial designs, which will be considered in Chapter 4. A third way to reduce within group variability is through the use of analysis of covariance, to be covered in Chapter 7. Covariates that have low correlations with each other are particularly helpful because each is removing a somewhat different part of the within group variance. A fourth way is through the use of repeated measures designs. These designs are very helpful because individual differences due to the average response of subjects are removed from the error term, and such differences are the main reason for within group variability.

4. Make sure there is a strong linkage between the treatments and the dependent variable, and that the treatments extend over a long enough period of time to produce a large or at least a fairly large effect size.

It needs to be mentioned that how far one "pushes" the power issue depends on the *consequences* of making a type I error. One of the reviewers of this text noted that discussing power versus risk reduction (type I error) is most meaningfully considered within a given context and gave the following examples: "If I am testing two teaching methods which cost the same, I go for power. If one method is 10 times more dollars, I go for risk reduction. If I'm comparing drugs A and B and one has some potent side effects, I go for risk reduction."

In the teaching methods example, if a type I error is made in concluding that the method that is 10 times more expensive is more effective, this will be a very costly mistake for a school district. If a type I error is made in the drug example in concluding drug A (with potent side effects) is better when it is not, this will have serious health consequences for future subjects receiving drug A.

TABLE 3.5
Power Values from PASS 6.0 for One Way ANOVA (3 and 4 Groups) for *n* = 10,
20, and 40 for Medium Effect Size and *n* = 5, 10, and 15 for Large Effect Size

MEDIUM EFFECT SIZE

Numeric Results for One-Way Analysis of Variance

Power	n	k	Alpha	Beta	Sigma m	Sigma	Effect Size
0.06462	10.00	3	0.01000	0.93538	1.00	4.00	0.25000
0.19514	10.00	3	0.05000	0.80486	1.00	4.00	0.25000
0.30249	10.00	3	0.10000	0.69751	1.00	4.00	0.25000
0.16848	20.00	3	0.01000	0.83152	1.00	4.00	0.25000
0.37443	20.00	3	0.05000	0.62557	1.00	4.00	0.25000
0.50447	20.00	3	0.10000	0.49553	1.00	4.00	0.25000
0.43214	40.00	3	0.01000	0.56786	1.00	4.00	0.25000
0.67567	40.00	3	0.05000	0.32433	1.00	4.00	0.25000
0.78211	40.00	3	0.10000	0.21789	1.00	4.00	0.25000
0.07289	10.00	4	0.01000	0.92711	1.00	4.00	0.25000
0.21224	10.00	4	0.05000	0.78776	1.00	4.00	0.25000
0.32425	10.00	4	0.10000	0.67575	1.00	4.00	0.25000
0.20111	20.00	4	0.01000	0.79889	1.00	4.00	0.25000
0.42039	20.00	4	0.05000	0.57961	1.00	4.00	0.25000
0.55204	20.00	4	0.10000	0.44796	1.00	4.00	0.25000
0.52041	40.00	4	0.01000	0.47959	1.00	4.00	0.25000
0.74940	40.00	4	0.05000	0.25060	1.00	4.00	0.25000
0.84026	40.00	4	0.10000	0.15974	1.00	4.00	0.25000

LARGE EFFECT SIZE

Numeric Results for One-Way Analysis of Variance

Power	n	k	Alpha	Beta	Sigma m	Sigma	Effect Size
0.11490	5.00	3	0.01000	0.88510	1.00	2.00	0.50000
0.31419	5.00	3	0.05000	0.68581	1.00	2.00	0.50000
0.45357	5.00	3	0.10000	0.54643	1.00	2.00	0.50000
0.36797	10.00	3	0.01000	0.63203	1.00	2.00	0.50000
0.63524	10.00	3	0.05000	0.36476	1.00	2.00	0.50000
0.75633	10.00	3	0.10000	0.24367	1.00	2.00	0.50000
0.61866	15.00	3	0.01000	0.38134	1.00	2.00	0.50000
0.83361	15.00	3	0.05000	0.16639	1.00	2.00	0.50000
0.90473	15.00	3	0.10000	0.09527	1.00	2.00	0.50000
0.13930	5.00	4	0.01000	0.86070	1.00	2.00	0.50000
0.35356	5.00	4	0.05000	0.64644	1.00	2.00	0.50000
0.49583	5.00	4	0.10000	0.50417	1.00	2.00	0.50000
0.45163	10.00	4	0.01000	0.54837	1.00	2.00	0.50000
0.70969	10.00	4	0.05000	0.29031	1.00	2.00	0.50000
0.81574	10.00	4	0.10000	0.18426	1.00	2.00	0.50000
0.72580	15.00	4	0.01000	0.27420	1.00	2.00	0.50000
0.89572	15.00	4	0.05000	0.10428	1.00	2.00	0.50000
0.94472	15.00	4	0.10000	0.05528	1.00	2.00	0.50000

If the group sizes are not equal, which is often the case in practice, then use the
average group size as the *n* (following Cohen) to enter the program.

The point the reviewer was making, which is well taken, is that using alpha = .10 or .15 to improve power in some cases may not be a wise choice.

3.9   POWER ESTIMATION ON SPSS MANOVA

Starting with Release 2.2, you can obtain power estimates for various statistical tests using the SPSS MANOVA program with the POWER subcommand. To quote from the *SPSS User's Guide* (1988, 3rd edition), "The POWER subcommand requests power valued based on fixed-effects assumptions for all univariate and multivariate F and T tests" (p. 601). Power can be obtained for any α level between 0 and 1, with .05 being the default value. If we wish power at the .05 level for a one way ANOVA, we simply insert the following subcommand: POWER=F(.05)/, or if we wish to know the power at the .15 level: POWER=F(.15)/. We give two examples to illustrate use of the POWER subcommand. The first is the *t* test for independent samples example from Chapter 1 (Section 1.2), and the second is the one way ANOVA example from Chapter 2 (Section 2.9). The command lines for both and selected printout showing the power values are given in Table 3.6.

The effect size measure in each case in Table 3.6 is partial eta-squared (η_p^2), which is given by

$$\eta_p^2 = (df \cdot F)/(df_h \cdot F + df_e) \tag{5}$$

where df_h denotes degrees of freedom for hypothesis and df_e denotes degrees of freedom for error (Cohen, 1973). As the *SPSS User's Guide* (1988, p. 602) notes, "partial eta squared is an overestimate of the actual effect size. However, it is a consistent measure of effect size and is applicable to all *F* and *t* tests."

Cohen (1977, p. 281), in discussing power in one way ANOVA, notes the following relationship between η^2 and the effect size *f*:

$$\eta^2 = f/(1 + f^2) \tag{6}$$

By squaring Equation 4 we find that $\hat{f}^2 = (k - 1)F/N$. Plugging this into Equation 6, and with some algebraic simplification, we find that

$$\eta^2 = \frac{(k - 1) \cdot F}{(k - 1) \cdot F + N} \tag{7}$$

Now, let us compare this with what partial η^2 will be for a one way ANOVA. For one way ANOVA, $df_h = (k - 1)$ and $df = (N - k)$. Plugging these into Equation 5 we obtain

TABLE 3.6
Power Analysis Runs on SPSS MANOVA for t test for
Independent Samples and for a One Way ANOVA

t test	One Way ANOVA

```
TITLE 'T TEST FROM CHAP. 1'.
DATA LIST FREE/TREAT PERFORM.
BEGIN DATA.
1 2 1 5 1 5 1 6 1 6 1 7 1 8
1 9 2 1 2 1 2 2 2 3 2 3 2 4
2 5 2 7 2 7 2 8
END DATA.
MANOVA PERFORM BY TREAT(1,2)/
  POWER=F(.05)/
  PRINT=CELLINFO(MEANS)
  SIGNIF(EFSIZE)/.
```

```
TITLE 'ONE WAY ANOVA FROM 2.8'.
DATA LIST FREE/GPID Y.
BEGIN DATA.
1 2 1 3 1 5 1 6
2 7 2 9 2 11
3 4 3 4 3 5 3 8 3 3
4 8 4 4 4 7 4 7
END DATA.
MANOVA Y BY GPID(1,4)/
① POWER=F(.05)/
  PRINT=CELLINFO(MEANS)
② SIGNIF(EFSIZE)/.
```

Selected t test Printout

TESTS OF SIGNIFICANCE FOR PERFORM USING UNIQUE SUMS OF SQUARES (CONT.)

SOURCE OF VARIATION	SS	DF	MS	F	SIG OF F
WITHIN CELLS	90.90	16	5.68		
TREAT	16.04	1	16.04	2.82	.112

OBSERVED POWER AT THE .0500 LEVEL

SOURCE OF VARIATION	PARTIAL ETA SQD	NONCEN-TRALITY	POWER	
TREAT	.15000	2.82410	.352	③

Selected One Way ANOVA Printout

TESTS OF SIGNIFICANCE FOR Y USING UNIQUE SUMS OF SQUARES (CONT.)

SOURCE OF VARIATION	SS	DF	MS	F	SIG OF F
WITHIN CELLS	41.80	12	3.48		
GPID	50.64	3	16.88	4.85	.020

OBSERVED POWER AT THE .0500 LEVEL

SOURCE OF VARIATION		PARTIAL ETA SQD	NONCEN-TRALITY	POWER
GPID	④	.54780	14.53708	.781

①This is the POWER subcommand to obtain estimated power at the .05 level.
②This subcommand is needed to obtain the effect size measure partial η^2.
③Note that power is poor here. This was the example with large effect size but small sample size.
④Partial $\eta^2 = df_h \cdot F/(df_h \cdot F + df_e) = 3(4.85)/[3(4.85) + 12] = .5478$.

$$\text{partial } \eta^2 = (k - 1) \cdot F/[(k - 1) \cdot F + (N - k)] \tag{8}$$

Thus the only difference between η^2 and partial η^2 for one way ANOVA is N vs. $(N - k)$ in the denominator. Since the denominator for Equation 8 will always be smaller than for Equation 7, partial will be an overestimate of effect size; however, for moderately large N (say > 50) the difference between the two is small.

In discussing η^2 for one way ANOVA, Cohen (1977) characterizes $\eta^2 = .01$ as corresponding to a small effect size, $\eta^2 = .06$ to a medium effect size, and $\eta^2 = .14$ to a large effect size.

3.10 SUMMARY

1. Power is the probability of rejecting the null hypothesis when it is false.

2. Power for a specific statistical test is dependent on (a) level of significance, (b) sample size, and (c) effect size. It is important to realize that power is *heavily* dependent on sample size.

3. Small and medium effect sizes are very common in social science research.

4. Cohen has provided the following rough, but useful, guidelines for small, medium, and large effect sizes for the t test and for one way analysis of variance:

$$t \text{ test: } \hat{d} = .20 \text{ (small)}, \hat{d} = .50 \text{ (medium)}, \hat{d} > .80 \text{ (large)}$$
$$F \text{ test: } \hat{f} = .10 \text{ (small)}, \hat{f} = .25 \text{ (medium)}, \hat{f} > .40 \text{ (large)}$$

5. Post hoc estimation of power for completed studies is important in properly interpreting results. In particular, lack of significance in small sample studies *may* be simply due to inadequate power.

6. The following relationships exist between the t and F statistics and their corresponding effect size measures:

$$\hat{d} = t\sqrt{1/n_1 + 1/n_2}, \hat{f} = \sqrt{(k - 1) \cdot F/N}$$

Using these relationships, the corresponding effect size can be easily computed for any study in the literature and then Cohen's power tables entered to determine power.

7. A priori determination of sample size required for a given power at some α level requires an estimate of the anticipated effect size. This estimate can be obtained using estimated effect sizes from previous similar studies and/or from theory.

8. We illustrated the PASS 6.0 program, which is very nice for obtaining power estimates very quickly. This program can be used to try out different

sample sizes for different alpha levels and determine which sample size provides adequate power.

EXERCISES

1. Graphically, type I error is the area under the F distribution (for H_0 true) in the critical region, while type II error is the area under the F distribution (for H_0 false) *not* in the critical region. Below are given the F distributions for H_0 true and for a case when it is not true for the situation of 4 groups and 30 error degrees of freedom. Also shown are the critical values for $\alpha = .10$ and $.01$.

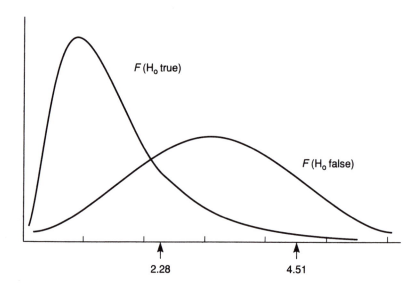

$F (H_0 \text{ true})$

$F (H_0 \text{ false})$

2.28   4.51

(a) Using different degrees of shading, indicate what areas correspond to alpha levels of .10 and .01.
(b) Now, using lining, cross hatching, etc., indicate what areas correspond to type II errors for the above alpha levels.
(c) As the alpha level decreases in (a), what happens to the sizes of the areas?
(d) As the alpha level decreases, what happens to the sizes of the areas corresponding to type II error? Thus, what have we shown graphically?

2. Starting from the following form for the t test for independent samples

$$t = \frac{\bar{x}_1 - \bar{x}_2}{\sqrt{\dfrac{(n_1 - 1) \cdot s_1^2 + (n_2 - 1) \cdot s_2^2}{n_1 + n_2 - 2} \left(\dfrac{1}{n_1} + \dfrac{1}{n_2} \right)}}$$

show that $\hat{d} = t\sqrt{1/n_1 + 1/n_2}$ as given in Equation 2.

3. Explain why for the same alpha level a one tail test is more powerful than a two tail test.

4. A marketing research study by Sternthal, Dholakia, and Leavitt (1978) was designed to test cognitive response theory predictions about the persuasive efforts of source credibility and initial opinion on number of counterarguments generated. There were 37 subjects—17 who had a positive prior opinion and 20 who were initially negative. Each of these subjects was assigned to either a moderate or high source credibility condition. As predicted, the moderate credibility source subjects generated more counterarguments; however, the t statistic was not significant ($t = 1.43$, $df = 35$).
   (a) What is the effect size in this study?
   (b) Estimate power at the .05 level.
   (c) What might the investigators consider doing in a future replication study?

5. A researcher in counselor education reviews a small number of studies that have compared (a) counselors in training who participate in a classroom discussion on counseling skills and (b) counselors in training who both participate in a classroom discussion and also observe a videotape of expert counselors outside of the classroom. The dependent measure is empathy. He finds that only one of 10 such studies shows statistical significance at the .05 level. He thus concludes that the effectiveness of the videotape has not been established. Below are the sample sizes and associated t values for the studies:

Study	Classroom Discussion and Videotape	Classroom Discussion	t
1	10	8	1.46
2	12	12	1.76
3	11	13	1.37
4	25	20	1.23
5	6	8	1.64
6	49	36	3.08*
7	20	20	−1.13
8	21	23	1.59
9	8	9	1.92
10	10	10	−.45

The results favor the classroom discussion and videotape group in all cases except studies 7 and 10.

(a) Calculate the effect size for each of the studies.

(b) From an examination of the effect sizes, and considering power, might you come to a different conclusion concerning the effectiveness of the combined treatment?

6. Show that $\hat{f} = \sqrt{(k-1) \cdot F/N}$ as given in Equation 4.

7. An ANOVA is run with 5 groups and 25 subjects per group. The F value is 2.03, which is not significant at the .05 level. What is power at the .05 level? at the .10 level?

8. An investigator is in the process of planning a 4 group study in which she will use ANOVA to analyze the results. From previous related literature she estimates that the expected effect size for her study will be .35. How many subjects will she need per group for power = .70 at $\alpha = .05$? at $\alpha = .10$? How many subjects would be needed per group at the same alpha levels if she wanted power to be .80?

9. A survey researcher compares four religious groups on their attitude toward education. The survey is sent out to 1200 subjects, of which 823 eventually responded. Ten items, Likert scaled from 1 to 5, are used to assess attitude. A higher positive score indicates a more positive attitude. There are only 800 usable responses. The Protestants are split into two groups for analysis purposes. The group sizes, along with the means and standard deviations, are given below:

	Protestant1	Catholic	Jewish	Protestant2
n_i	238	182	130	250
$\bar{x}$	32.0	33.1	34.0	31.0
s_i	7.09	7.62	7.80	7.49

An analysis of variance on these four groups yields $F = 311.66/55.58 = 5.61$, which is significant at the .001 level.

(a) Estimate power at the .05 level for the above example.

(b) Calculate the effect size, and discuss the practical significance issue.

10. (a) Using SPSS MANOVA, obtain estimates of power for the t test example in Table 3.2 at $\alpha = .10, .15,$ and .20.

(b) Does power become adequate for any of the above alpha levels?

(c) What does the above suggest might be done in small sample studies?

11. Use the PASS 6.0 program and the t test for independent samples template in Table 3.3. Note that you have a small effect size (.2sd), according to Cohen. Does power become adequate for any of the group sizes?

12. Use the PASS 6.0 program to run power analysis for a 5 group ANOVA, using the template in Table 3.4.

(a) What is the magnitude of the effect size?

(b) How many subjects are needed per group for adequate power at the .05 level?

4 Factorial Analysis of Variance

4.1 INTRODUCTION

In Chapter 2 we considered the effect of a single independent (grouping) variable on a dependent variable, called one way ANOVA. In this chapter we extend the discussion to examine the effect of two or more independent variables (factors) on some dependent variable, which is called factorial analysis of variance. Often the interest is in whether the additional independent variable moderates or changes the effect of a primary treatment variable. For example, suppose an investigator believes the effect of three treatments on changing attitude toward minorities will vary according to whether the subjects are male or female. That is, the investigator feels treatments will work differently with these subgroups. Since there are two levels for sex and three levels for treatment, we have what is called a 2 × 3 factorial design. As another example, suppose an educational psychologist has reason to believe from previous research that teaching method 1 will yield

145

highest achievement for urban elementary children while teaching method 3 will work best with rural children. He is not sure which method works best with suburban children. He can check out these beliefs by setting up a 3 × 3 factorial design: three levels for location (urban, suburban, and rural) by three teaching methods.

One broad area of research that utilizes factorial designs is called aptitude by treatment interaction (ATI) research. This research is concerned with the effect of any individual difference characteristic of subjects on their response to treatments. The definitive source on this type of research is *Aptitudes and Instructional Methods* by Cronbach and Snow (1977). Aptitude is defined very generally and includes ability, personality, and nontest factors such as social class, ethnic background, sex, etc. Cronbach and Snow discuss numerous ATI studies that have been done in various areas: (1) interactions of abilities with variations in instructional programming, (2) interactions in reading and arithmetic instruction, (3) interactions of abilities with variations in curriculum and instruction, and (4) interactive effects of making instruction less verbal. The reader with interest in any of the above areas will find the Cronbach and Snow book very interesting, critical, and informative. For applied researchers with a clinical orientation, there is an interesting review article by Dance and Neufeld (1988) on ATI research in the clinical setting. Here the focus is on client variables that predict differential treatment responsiveness. They review the literature encompassing cognitive and/or behavioral treatments for anxiety, depression, pain, obesity, and tobacco dependence.

The previous discussion has focused on one experimentally induced factor (treatments) and some individual difference characteristic of subjects that might moderate the effect of the treatments. Factorial ANOVA can be appropriate, however, any time the subjects are cross-classified on two factors and measured on some dependent variable. For example, suppose a survey researcher cross-classified 200 subjects on sex and religion (Catholic, Jewish, and Protestant) and wished to determine whether attitude toward abortion is influenced by sex and religion. She could test this out with a 2 × 3 (sex × religion) factorial design.

Advantages of a Two Way Analysis of Variance

A two way design enables us to examine the *joint* (*interactive*) effect of the independent variables on the dependent variable. We cannot get this information by running two separate one way analyses. An interaction means that the effect one independent variable has on the dependent variable is *not* the same for all levels of the other independent variable. This moderating effect can take two forms:

(a) The degree of superiority changes, but one subgroup always does better than another. To illustrate this, consider the following ability by teaching methods design:

Methods of Teaching

	T_1	T_2	T_3
High Ability	85	80	76
Low Ability	60	63	68

The numbers in each cell represent the mean achievement for subjects in that cell; that is, 85 is average achievement for high ability subjects under teaching method 1, and so on. Note that the high ability students do better than the low ability for all teaching methods (as we would expect). However, the superiority of the high ability students changes from 25 for T_1 to only 8 for T_3. Since the order of superiority is maintained, however, this is called an *ordinal* interaction.

(b) The superiority reverses; that is, one treatment is best with one group, but another treatment is better for a different group. A study by Daniels and Stevens (1976) provides an illustration of this more dramatic type of interaction, called a *disordinal* interaction. Using a group of college undergraduates, they considered two types of instruction: (1) a traditional, teacher controlled (lecture type) and (2) a contract for grade plan. The subjects were classified as internally or externally controlled, using Rotter's scale. An internal orientation means that those subjects perceive positive events occur as a consequence of their actions (i.e., they are in control), while external subjects feel that positive and/or negative events occur more because of powerful others, or due to chance or fate. The design and the means for the subjects on an achievement posttest in psychology are given below:

		Instruction	
		Contract for Grade	Teacher Controlled
	Internal	50.52	38.01
Locus of Control			
	External	36.33	46.22

The moderator variable in this case is locus of control, and it has a substantial effect on the efficacy of an instructional method. When the subject's locus of control is matched to the teaching method (internals with contract for grade and externals with teacher controlled) the subject does quite well in terms of achievement; where there is a mismatch, achievement suffers.

This study also illustrates how a one way design can lead to quite misleading results. Suppose that Daniels and Stevens had just considered the two methods, ignoring locus of control. The means for achievement for the contract for grade plan and for teacher controlled are 43.42 and 42.11, nowhere near significant. The conclusion would have been that teaching methods don't make a difference. The factorial study showed, however, that methods definitely do make a difference, a quite positive difference if subject locus of control is matched to teaching methods, and an undesirable effect if there is a mismatch.

A second advantage of factorial designs is that they can lead to more powerful tests by reducing error (within cell) variance. If performance on the dependent variable is related to the individual difference characteristic (the blocking variable), then the reduction can be substantial. Consider the hypothetical sex × treatment design below:

	T_1	T_2
Males	18, 19, 21 20, 22 (2.5)	17, 16, 16 18, 15 (1.3)
Females	11, 12, 11 13, 14 (1.7)	9, 9, 11 8, 7 (2.2)

Notice that *within* each cell there is very little variability. The within cell variances quantify this, and are given in parentheses. Recall from Chapter 3 that for equal group sizes the error term was just the average of the group variances. In two way ANOVA, for equal cell sizes, the error term is simply the average of the *cell* variances, which here is 1.925. On the other hand, if this had been considered as a two group design, combining males and females together, then the variability is considerably greater, as evidenced by within group (treatment) variances for T_1 and T_2 of 18.766 and 17.6, and a pooled error term for the t test of 18.18.

A third advantage of a factorial design is *economy of subjects*. We only need *half* as many subjects to do a two way ANOVA as would be needed for *two* one way ANOVAs with the same number of levels for each factor. We use a 3 × 4 (A × B) factorial design with 10 subjects per cell to illustrate. Here we need a total of 12(10) = 120 subjects to test whether A and B have a systematic effect on the dependent variable *and* to test for the joint effect of A and B (the interaction effect). To test whether A and B have systematic effects using two one way ANOVAs is going to require 40 S's per level for A and 30 S's per level for B, or a total of 240 subjects, as can be seen from the diagram below:

		B			
	10	10	10	10	40
A	10	10	10	10	40
	10	10	10	10	40
	30	30	30	30	

Overview of the Five Major Sections in the Chapter

Since this is a long chapter, we have split it up into five major sections to help the reader organize and see the different main thrusts. The first major section involves a numerical example, where we show how the sums of squares are calculated for the various effects in a two way ANOVA, and how to test each of the effects for significance. The second major section deals with equal and unequal cell size factorial analysis of variance. It is noted that although equal n is desirable, often in practice unequal cell size occurs. Also, we discuss different ways of analyzing unequal n designs and indicate which method should generally be used. The third major section discusses higher order 3 and 4 way ANOVA designs. A three way ANOVA would arise, for example, if we wished to determine whether *both* sex and race moderated the effect of treatments. We would have a treatment by sex by race design. The focus in this chapter for higher order designs is *not* on calculating sums of squares for the various effects, but rather on interpreting effects that are significant. The fourth major section involves a comprehensive computer example that ties together various concepts that were discussed earlier in the chapter. The final major section deals with power analysis for two and three way ANOVA, and the use of SPSS MANOVA for obtaining power estimates is illustrated.

4.2 NUMERICAL CALCULATIONS
FOR TWO WAY ANOVA*

Now that the reader has examples of two way ANOVAs in mind and reasons why a two way ANOVA is advantageous, we consider a small data set to illustrate what the hypotheses are that we are testing and how they are tested. In the one way ANOVA there were just two sources of variation (between and within). In a two way ANOVA ($A \times B$ design) there are four sources of variation:

1. Variation due to factor A.
2. Variation due to factor B.
3. Variation due to the interactive effect of A and B.
4. Within cell (error) variation.

Consider the following 2×3 design with 3 observations per cell.

---

*We again have the same assumptions as for a one way ANOVA, except now they apply to cells, that is, normality on the dependent variable in each cell and equal cell population variances.

| | Treatments(B) | | | |
	1	2	3	*Row Means*
1 (males)	12, 16, 17 $\bar{x}_{11} = 15$	13, 9, 8 $\bar{x}_{12} = 10$	14, 15, 13 $\bar{x}_{13} = 14$	$\bar{x}_{1.} = 13$
Sex (A) 2 (females)	6, 10, 8 $\bar{x}_{21} = 8$	11, 8, 8 $\bar{x}_{22} = 9$	12, 10, 8 $\bar{x}_{23} = 10$	$\bar{x}_{2.} = 9$
Column Means	$\bar{x}_{.1} = 11.5$	$\bar{x}_{.2} = 9.5$	$\bar{x}_{.3} = 12$	$\bar{x} = 11$ grand mean

The first number in the subscript for each cell mean refers to the level for Sex, while the second number refers to the level for Treatment. Thus, $\bar{x}_{12}$ refers to the mean for males in treatment 2, while $\bar{x}_{23}$ refers to the mean for females in treatment 3. The dot notation in the second part of the subscript means we are summing across the columns or levels of factor B in obtaining the row means. The dot notation in the first part of the subscript indicates we are summing across the rows or levels of factor A to obtain the column means.

As for the one way ANOVA, we will use *definitional* formulas to compute the sums of squares for factor A, factor B, interaction and error, that is, SS_A, SS_B, SS_{AB} and SS_w. Before we give these formulas, let us have clearly in mind what hypotheses are being tested. The first two involve what are called *main effects* for factors A and B. The null hypothesis being tested for the A main effect is:

$$H_0: \mu_{1.} = \mu_{2.} = \cdots = \mu_{I.} \text{ (population row means are equal)}$$

In the above table $\bar{x}_{1.} = 13 = \hat{\mu}_{1.}$ and $\bar{x}_{2.} = 9 = \hat{\mu}_{2.}$ are estimates of the population means for males and females, and the inferential question is, "Are the differences in the sample row means large enough, given sampling error, to suggest that the underlying population row means are different?" Also, I in the above null hypothesis refers to the general number of levels for factor A.

The null hypothesis for the B main effect is:

$$H_0: \mu_{.1} = \mu_{.2} = \cdots = \mu_{.J} \text{ (population column means are equal)}$$

In the above data table $\bar{x}_{.1} = 11.5 = \hat{\mu}_{.1}$, $\bar{x}_{.2} = 9.5 = \hat{\mu}_{.2}$, and $\bar{x}_{.3} = 12 = \hat{\mu}_{.3}$ are estimates of the underlying population column means. Also, J refers to the general number of levels for factor B.

Thus, in general we are talking about an $I \times J$ design. We further restrict matters, at this point in the chapter, to what are called *balanced* designs, which are designs with an equal number of observations (n) per cell.

Sums of Squares for Factor A and Factor B

The definitional formula for sum of squares for factor A (SS_A) is given by:

$$SS_A = nJ \sum (\bar{x}_{i.} - \bar{x})^2$$
$$= nJ \left[(\bar{x}_{1.} - \bar{x})^2 + (\bar{x}_{2.} - \bar{x})^2 + \cdots + (\bar{x}_{I.} - \bar{x})^2 \right] \tag{1}$$

Note that nJ is the number of observations on which each row mean is based. Thus, this sum of squares merely reflects variability of the row means about the grand mean. It is analogous to the sum of squares between in the one way ANOVA. For our example we have

$$SS_A = 3(3) \left[(13 - 11)^2 + (9 - 11)^2 \right] = 72$$

We want the mean sum of squares for factor A (MS_A), which is given by

$$MS_A = SS_A / (I - 1) = 72/1 = 72$$

The definitional formula for the sum of squares for factor B (SS_B) is given by

$$SS_B = nI \sum (\bar{x}_{.j} - \bar{x})^2 \tag{2}$$
$$= nI \left[(\bar{x}_{.1} - \bar{x})^2 + (\bar{x}_{.2} - \bar{x})^2 + \cdots + (\bar{x}_{.J} - \bar{x})^2 \right]$$

This sum reflects variability of the column means about the grand mean. For our example it is

$$SS_B = 3(2) \left[(11.5 - 11)^2 + (9.5 - 11)^2 + (12 - 11)^2 \right]$$
$$= 21$$

We want mean sum of squares for factor B (MS_B), which is

$$MS_B = SS_B / (J - 1) = 21/2 = 10.5$$

Error Term

To test each of these main effects for significance we need an error term. That error term is a pooled within cell measure of variability. Verbally, for each cell we deviate the scores in the cell about the mean for the cell, square the deviations, and add them up across all the cells. Recall that exactly the same process was followed in obtaining the error term for the one way ANOVA, except that the scores were deviated about the *group* means. In symbols we can write the factorial error term as:

$$SS_w = \sum_{\text{cells}} (x - \bar{x}_{ij})^2 \qquad (3)$$

$$SS_w = \underbrace{\sum (x - \bar{x}_{11})^2}_{\substack{\text{variability} \\ \text{within cell 11}}} + \underbrace{\sum (x - \bar{x}_{12})^2}_{\substack{\text{variability} \\ \text{within cell 12}}} + \cdots + \underbrace{\sum (x - \bar{x}_{IJ})^2}_{\substack{\text{variability} \\ \text{within cell } IJ}}$$

Now we compute this for the example:

$$SS_w = (12 - 15)^2 + (16 - 15)^2 + (17 - 15)^2 \quad \text{(cell 11)}$$
$$+ (13 - 10)^2 + (9 - 10)^2 + (8 - 10)^2 \quad \text{(cell 12)}$$
$$+ (14 - 14)^2 + (15 - 14)^2 + (13 - 14)^2 \quad \text{(cell 13)}$$
$$+ \cdots + (12 - 10)^2 + (10 - 10)^2 + (8 - 10)^2 \quad \text{(cell 23)}$$
$$SS_w = 52$$

We want MS_w, which, as mentioned earlier, represents the average of the cell variances. This is given by

$$MS_w = SS_w / (N - IJ)$$

A degree of freedom is lost in estimating each cell mean, hence the degrees of freedom for error is $N - IJ$. For the example, we have

$$MS_w = 52/(18 - 6) = 4.33$$

F Tests for The Main Effects

The F tests for the main effects are analogous to doing two one way ANOVAs on the data, although the error term here is different. One can think of "slicing the data cake" first horizontally, and then vertically. The F ratio for the A main effect is given by

$$F_A = MS_A / MS_w$$

which for our data becomes

$$F_A = 72/4.33 = 16.63$$

The critical value at the .05 level is given by

$$F_{.05;I-1,N-IJ} = F_{.05;1,12} = 4.75$$

Because the value of the test statistic is greater than the critical value (i.e., 16.63 > 4.75), we reject and conclude that males did significantly better than females.

The F ratio for the B main effect is given by:

$$F_B = MS_B/MS_w,$$

which for this data is

$$F_B = 10.5/4.33 = 2.42$$

The critical value at the .05 level is given by

$$F_{.05;J-1,N-IJ} = F_{.05;2,12} = 3.89$$

Since 2.42 < 3.89, we fail to reject and conclude that treatments did not have a differential effect on performance. Or, to put it another way, the sample column means are estimating equal population column means.*

The Interaction Effect

We will define the interaction sum of squares (SS_{AB}) in terms of the *cell* interaction effects. A cell interaction effect, which we denote by ϕ_{ij}, is that part of the cell mean that can *not* be accounted for by overall effect (grand mean) and by main effects for A and B. The main effects for A and B respectively are: $\alpha_i = \mu_{i.} - \mu$ and $\beta_j = \mu_{.j} - \mu$, where μ is the grand (overall) population mean. Thus, the cell interaction effect is:

$$\phi_{ij} = (\mu_{ij} - \mu) - (\mu_{i.} - \mu) - (\mu_{.j} - \mu)$$
$$= \mu_{ij} - \mu_{i.} - \mu_{.j} + \mu$$

Now, the sum of squares for interaction is

$$SS_{AB} = n \sum \hat{\phi}_{ij}^2,$$

where

---

*The reader needs to understand that although we are doing the tests on main effects first because of their simplicity, if a significant interaction effect is found then interpretation of the results needs to be focused on the interaction. An interaction effect means that the explanation of the data requires a more complex model.

$$\hat{\phi}_{ij} = \bar{x}_{ij} - \bar{x}_{i.} - \bar{x}_{.j} + \bar{x} \qquad (4)$$

is the estimated cell interaction effect.

Let us bring back the data again, but this time just with the row and column means and grand mean:

		(B) Treatments			
		1	2	3	Row Means
	1	$\bar{x}_{11} = 15$ $\hat{\phi}_{11} = 1.5$	$\bar{x}_{12} = 10$ $\hat{\phi}_{12} = -1.5$	$\bar{x}_{13} = 14$ $\hat{\phi}_{13} = 0$	13
Sex (A)	2	$\bar{x}_{21} = 8$ $\hat{\phi}_{21} = -1.5$	$\bar{x}_{22} = 9$ $\hat{\phi}_{22} = 1.5$	$\bar{x}_{23} = 10$ $\phi_{23} = 0$	9
Column Means		11.5	9.5	12	11

$$\downarrow$$
grand mean

The estimated cell interaction effects above were obtained using Equation 4. To illustrate, we calculate the first two:

$$\hat{\phi}_{11} = 15 - 13 - 11.5 + 11 = 1.5$$

and

$$\hat{\phi}_{12} = 10 - 13 - 9.5 + 11 = -1.5$$

It can be shown that for a fixed effects design the sum of the interaction effects for *every* row and column add to 0. Thus, for the above design, once the above two effects are calculated the others are determined. For example, since the sum of the interaction effects for row 1 must be 0, we have

$$1.5 + (-1.5) + x = 0 \text{ or } x = 0$$

Similarly, since the sum of the interaction effects for column 1 must be 0, it follows that $\hat{\phi}_{21} = -1.5$.

Plugging the interaction effects into the equation above:

$$SS_{AB} = 3 \ [(1.5)^2 + (-1.5)^2 + (-1.5)^2 + (1.5)^2]$$
$$SS_{AB} = 3 \ (9) = 27$$

Now, the mean sum of squares (MS_{AB}) is given by

$$MS_{AB} = SS_{AB}/(I - 1)(J - 1)$$

where $(I - 1)(J - 1)$ is the degrees of freedom for interaction. For this problem we have

$$MS_{AB} = 27/(2 - 1)(3 - 1) = 13.5$$

The F ratio for interaction is

$$F_{AB} = MS_{AB}/MS_w = 13.5/4.33 = 3.12$$

The critical value at the .05 level is given by

$$F_{.05;(I - 1)(J - 1),N - IJ} = F_{.05;2,12} = 3.89$$

Since $3.12 < 3.89$, the interaction effect is not significant (the null hypothesis is H_0: All $\phi_{ij} = 0$).

Another way of characterizing an interaction effect is as "a difference in the differences." The differences across sex for the different treatments are respectively 7, 1, and 4. Although these differences may appear to be large, the test statistic indicates that they are likely to occur from populations with equal differences. This is due to considerably sampling error present here because of the very small cell size of 3.*

Graphically, if there is no interaction, then the *population profile of means will be parallel.* When plotting real data, however, the profiles of sample means will essentially always be non-parallel. For the previous example the interaction effect was not significant at the .05 level, and yet when the profiles of means are plotted (see Figure 4.1) for A_1 and A_2 they are strikingly non-parallel. For this example there was a power problem due to small cell size (3), because the estimated interaction effect size is very large: $f = \sqrt{(2 - 1)(3 - 1)(3.12)/18} = .59$.

Still another example to illustrate that the sample mean profiles will be non-parallel even when the interaction F is less than 1 is provided in later in this section (where we consider three way ANOVA). The social class by grade level interaction F was .868. When the profiles of means were plotted (Figure 4.1) for social class they even cross, although just slightly. The F test is telling us, however, that these sample mean profiles are estimating parallel *population* profiles.

---

*In the Appendix we illustrate how to do an equal n ANOVA using a calculator.

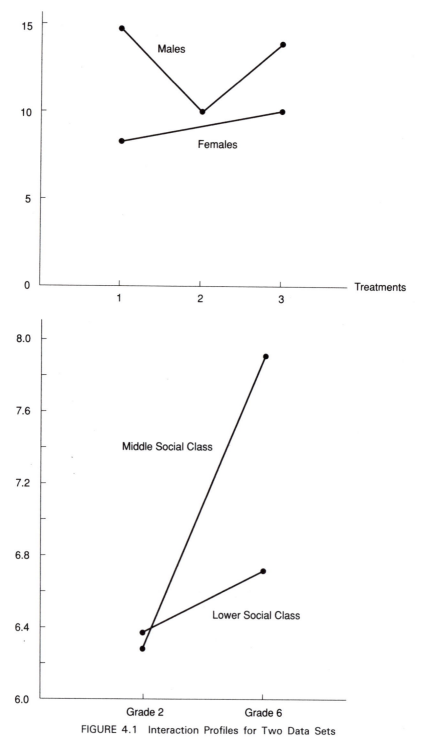

FIGURE 4.1 Interaction Profiles for Two Data Sets

Finally, note that the degrees of freedom for interaction, $(I-1)(J-1)$, is directly related to the fact that the sum of the interaction effects for every row and column must add to 0. Recall from our example, once we had computed the first two interaction effects, the others were determined. That is, they were *not* free to vary. This was because for the 2×3 design there are only 2 degrees of freedom.

Linear Model for the Data

Recall that the linear model for a subject's score (y_{ij}) in one way ANOVA was

$$y_{ij} = \mu + \alpha_j + e_{ij},$$

where μ was the grand mean (general effect), $\alpha_j = \mu - \mu_j$ was an effect unique to the jth treatment, and e_{ij} was random error. The subjects score was decomposed into three components. In two way ANOVA we still have a linear model, although now there will be a component for factor A, a component for factor B, and a component to represent the joint effect of A and B. The model looks like this:

$$
\begin{array}{ccccc}
y_{ijk} = & \mu & + \alpha_i + \beta_j + & \phi_{ij} & + e_{ijk} \\
& \text{general} & \text{main} & \text{interaction} & \text{error} \\
& \text{effect} & \text{effects} & \text{effect} &
\end{array}
\qquad (5)
$$

where $\alpha_i = \mu_i - \mu$ (deviation of ith row mean from grand mean), $\beta_j = \mu_j - \mu$ (deviation of the jth column mean from the grand mean), and ϕ_{ij} is the interaction effect, which was defined in the previous section. The triple subscript for the subject's score is read, "the score for subject k in cell ij."

Now we show for a few selected subjects from the example in the section on Interaction Effect how their scores can be decomposed into the four parts given by the linear model for a two way ANOVA design. We start with the first subject in cell 11. That score can be expressed as:

$$
\begin{array}{cccccc}
12 = & 11 & + (13-11) + & (11.5-11) + & (1.5) & + e_{111} \\
& \text{general} & A \text{ main} & B \text{ Main} & \text{Interaction} & \text{Error} \\
& \text{effect} & \text{effect} & \text{effect} & \text{effect} &
\end{array}
$$

Thus, the error component for this subject is -3.

Or, consider the second subject in cell 21. That score of 8 can be decomposed as follows:

$$
\begin{array}{cccccc}
8 = & 11 & + (9-11) + & (9.5-11) + & (1.5) & + e_{212} \\
& \text{general} & A \text{ main} & B \text{ Main} & \text{Interaction} & \text{Error} \\
& \text{effect} & \text{effect} & \text{effect} & \text{effect} &
\end{array}
$$

Therefore, the error component for this subject is -1.

4.3   BALANCED AND UNBALANCED DESIGNS

Balanced Designs

In one way ANOVA the total sum of squares was partitioned into two independent sources of variation (sum of squares between and within). In a two way ANOVA, for *equal cell size*, the sums of squares for the main effects, interaction, and error are also independent. That is, SS_A, SS_B, SS_{AB}, and SS_w are independent. Of course, the corresponding mean squares will also be independent. But the F ratios for A, B, and AB interaction are *not* independent. Why? Because they all share the *same* error term, that is, MS_w. However, research has shown that if the total N is even moderately large, then the amount of dependence will be small and can be ignored for practical purposes. Thus, we will regard the F tests as independent. This is important in terms of clarity of interpretation, since significance on one effect is not dependent on (or confounded with) significance on the other effects. We see later on in this chapter that for disproportional cell sizes the effects are correlated or confounded.

Factorial ANOVA on SAS and SPSS

Now we show how easy it is to run the data from the numerical example on SAS and SPSS. The control lines, along with annotation, are given in Table 4.1. Annotated printout from SAS is presented in Table 4.2 and printout for SPSS is given below:

Dependent Variable: DEP

Source	Type III Sum of Squares	df	Mean Square	F	Sig.
Corrected Model	120.000[a]	5	24.000	5.538	.007
Intercept	2178.000	1	2178.000	502.615	.000
SEX	72.000	1	72.000	16.615	.002
TREAT	21.000	2	10.500	2.423	.131
SEX * TREAT	27.000	2	13.500	3.115	.081
Error	52.000	12	4.333		
Total	2350.000	18			
Corrected Total	172.000	17			

Unbalanced Designs

For the equal cell size designs the sums of squares for the different effects are uncorrelated, and for moderately large N the F ratios for the effects are essentially uncorrelated. This is important in interpreting results since significance on one effect implies nothing about significance on another. This makes for a clean and clear interpretation of results. However, often in real world data situations we will not have equal cell size, for at least two reasons:

TABLE 4.1
SAS and SPSS Control Lines for 2 × 3 Factorial ANOVA

SAS (Release 5.16)	SPSS
TITLE ' TWO WAY ANOVA';	TITLE 'TWO WAY ANOVA EQUAL N'.
DATA TWOWAY;	DATA LIST FREE/FACA FACB DEP.
① INPUT FACA FACB DEP @@;	BEGIN DATA.
LINES;	1 1 12 1 1 16 1 1 17
② 1 1 12 1 1 16 1 1 17	1 2 13 1 2 9 1 2 8
1 2 13 1 2 9 1 2 8	1 3 14 1 3 15 1 3 13
1 3 14 1 3 15 1 3 13	2 1 6 2 1 10 2 1 8
2 1 6 2 1 10 2 1 8	2 2 11 2 2 8 2 2 8
2 2 11 2 2 8 2 2 8	2 3 12 2 3 10 2 3 8
2 3 12 2 3 10 2 3 8	END DATA.
PROC PRINT;	LIST.
PROC GLM;	MANOVA DEP BY FACA(1,2)
③ CLASS FACA FACB;	FACB(1,3)/
④ MEANS FACA FACB FACA*FACB;	DESIGN/.
⑤ MODEL DEP=FACA FACB FACA*FACB;	

①Recall that the @@ is necessary in order to put the data for more than one subject on the same data line.

②The first two numbers of each triple here are for the cell ID for the subject. Thus, the first triple here indicates the first subject in cell 11 has a score of 12 on the dependent variable, the second triple that the score for the next subject in cell 11 is 16, and the first triple for the *fourth* data line that the score for the first subject in cell 21 is 6.

③This CLASS statement indicates which of the variables in the INPUT statement are the grouping variables.

④This MEANS statement is required to obtain the level (row and column) means and the cell means.

⑤In the MODEL statement we put the dependent variable(s) on the left side and the effects in the design on the right side. Since we wish to test the full factorial model we put in the main effects and the interaction. Observe that the interaction effect is indicated by placing an * between the factors.

⑥We are using the MANOVA program here, a very powerful and general program within the SPSSX package. The numbers within the parentheses for each factor indicate the levels of the factor that are being used. Here we are using all levels of each factor.

⑦The DESIGN subcommand indicates the effects in the design that are being tested. We could have put DESIGN=FACA,FACB,FACA*FACB/ , but for a full model DESIGN/ can be used.

1. Even if we started with equal cell size in an experimental study, because of experimental mortality (subjects dropping out of the study for various reasons—parents moving, boredom, annoyance with the treatment, treatment schedule becomes inconvenient, etc.) we wind up with unequal cell sizes.

2. We are studying intact groups, which when cross-classified produce quite different subgroup (cell) sizes. Of course, we could in some instances simply

TABLE 4.2

Factorial ANOVA run for Numerical Example on SAS General Linear Models (GLM) Procedure

DEPENDENT VARIABLE: DEP

TWO WAY EQUAL N ANOVA
GENERAL LINEAR MODELS PROCEDURE

SOURCE	DF	SUM OF SQUARES	MEAN SQUARE	F VALUE	PR > F
MODEL	5	① 120.00000000	24.00000000	5.54	0.0071
ERROR	12	52.00000000	③ 4.33333333		
CORRECTED TOTAL	17	172.00000000			

SOURCE	DF	TYPE I SS	F VALUE	PR > F	DF	TYPE III SS
FACA	1	72.00000000	16.62	0.0015	1	72.00000000
FACB	2	① 21.00000000	② 2.42	0.1306	2	21.00000000
FACA*FACB	2	27.00000000	3.12	0.0813	2	27.00000000

MEANS

FACA	N	DEP
1	9	13.0000000 ④
2	9	9.0000000

FACB	N	DEP
1	6	11.5000000
2	6	9.5000000 ⑤
3	6	12.0000000

(continued)

160

TABLE 4.2 *(Continued)*

FACA	FACB	N	DEP
1	1	3	15.0000000
1	2	3	10.0000000
1	3	3	14.0000000
2	1	3	8.0000000
2	2	3	9.0000000
2	3	3	10.0000000

①The model sum of squares is in the total of the sums of squares for the effects in the model. Here $120 = 72$ (ss for FACA) + 21 (ss for FACB) + 27 (ss for FACA*FACB).

②Notice from the tail probabilities to the right of the F ratios, that only FACA is significant at the .05 level, since only that probability is less than .05.

③The mean square error (4.333), which we denoted by MS_w in the chapter, is the denominator for each of the F ratios.

④Row means for factor A.

⑤Column means for factor B.

161

randomly discard subjects from cells to achieve equal n, but in other cases this may cause a loss of too many subjects.

Thus it becomes imperative to be able to analyze and properly interpret unequal cell size factorial designs. The problem with disproportional cell size designs is that the effects become correlated (confounded), and unless these correlations are taken into account we may misinterpret the results. There is a considerable amount of literature on the topic, particularly from the late 1960s through the 1970s. Overall and Spiegel (1969), in a classic paper on analyzing factorial designs, discuss three basic methods of analysis:

Method 1: Adjust each effect for all other effects in the design to obtain its unique contribution (regression approach).

Method 2: Estimate the main effects ignoring the interaction, but estimate the interaction effect adjusting for the main effects (experimental method).

Method 3: Based on theory and/or previous research, establish an ordering for the effects, and then adjust each effect only for those effects preceding it in the ordering (hierarchical approach).

For equal cell size designs all three of the above methods yield the same results, that is, the same F tests. Therefore, it will not make any difference, in terms of the conclusions a researcher draws, which of these methods is used on one of the packages. For unequal cell sizes, however, these methods can yield quite different results.

Two Examples for Unbalanced Designs

We give two examples for unequal n factorial designs. The first example uses artificial data, but shows that the method of analysis can affect the conclusions drawn. The second example uses real data, and also illustrates bringing data in from disk. For our first example, consider the following 2×3 design:

	B		
A	3, 5, 6	2, 4, 8	11, 7, 8, 6, 9
	9, 14, 5, 11	6, 7, 7, 8, 10, 5, 6	9, 8, 10

The control lines for running the analysis on SPSS and on SAS are the same as for the equal cell n case. With both programs the regression approach (Method 1) is the *default* option; that is, it is used automatically unless something else is specified. In both programs the unique sum of squares (regression approach) is called type III sum of squares. Type I sum of squares in both programs refers to the sequential sum of squares. In the sequential approach (also called hierarchical) a given effect is adjusted for all effects to its left (or preceding it) in the ordering. Suppose the effects went in the following order: *FACA, FACB, FACA*FACB*. Then, in the sequential approach, the *A* main effect is not adjusted for anything. The *B* main effect is adjusted for the *A* main effect, and the interaction is adjusted for both main effects. In this approach the sums of squares for the terms in the model do add up to the total sum of squares.

We ran the above data on SAS GLM and on the SPSS GLM program (*SPSS Base 8.0*, p. 239). Both sums of squares come out in one run on SAS; recall that type III sum of squares is the unique sum of squares, while type I is the sequential sum of squares. Two runs are required for SPSS, although we just present the type III (unique) sum of squares for the SPSS run in Table 4.3.

If we use the unique sum of squares approach we would conclude that only the factor *A* main effect is significant at the .05 level of significance, because only that *p* value is less than .05. On the other hand, with the sequential sum of squares the conclusion would be that both main effects are significant at the .05 level (*p* values of .048 and .043, respectively). Thus, the method used with disproportional designs can make a difference in terms of the conclusions drawn from an experiment. Importantly, however, the interaction *F* is the *same* for both approaches, because all other effects (main effects) are partialed from it with the unique sum of squares approach, and also both main effects are partialed in the sequential approach since the interaction effect is last in the ordering.

Our research example involves data from a study by Philips and Jahanshahi of the London University Institute of Psychiatry (Hand & Taylor, 1987). The study examined the effectiveness of different kinds of psychological treatment on the sensitivity of headache sufferers to noise. Each subject was first pretested on sensitivity, then given relaxation training (to be defined shortly), then given one of 4 treatments, and finally posttested on sensitivity. The sensitivity scores were obtained by listening to a tone that gradually increased in volume and having the subjects rate the levels at which the tone became (1) uncomfortable and (2) definitely unpleasant. These ratings are the dependent variables for the study. We denote the pretest and posttest ratings by PREU, PREUP, POSTU, and POSTUP.

1. The subjects were asked to listen to the tone at their definitely unpleasant level for up to two minutes, with the option of terminating the exposure if they wished.

2. The subjects were then given instruction on breathing techniques and the use of visual imagery to act as a controlled distraction.

The design was a 2 × 4 factorial because there were two types of headache sufferers involved (migraine and tension) and four treatments, which were as follows:

T_1: Subjects in this group listened to the tone again at their initial definitely unpleasant (POSTUP) level for the length of time that they were able to stand it in the relaxation training phase.

TABLE 4.3
Factorial Unequal *n* Printouts From SAS GLM and SPSS GLM Program

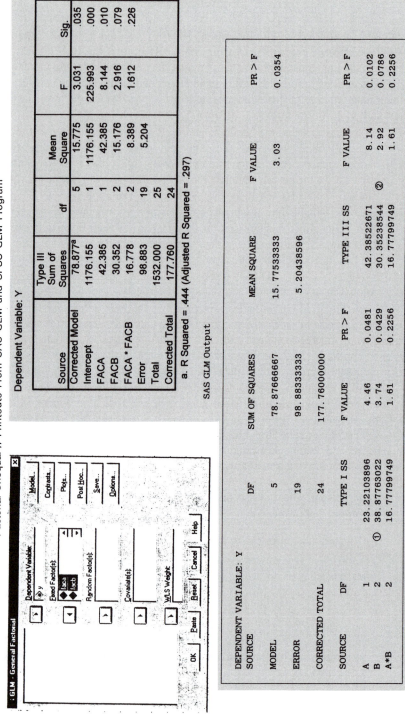

Dependent Variable: Y

Source	Type III Sum of Squares	df	Mean Square	F	Sig.
Corrected Model	78.877a	5	15.775	3.031	.035
Intercept	1176.155	1	1176.155	225.993	.000
FACA	42.385	1	42.385	8.144	.010
FACB	30.352	2	15.176	2.916	.079
FACA * FACB	16.778	2	8.389	1.612	.226
Error	98.883	19	5.204		
Total	1532.000	25			
Corrected Total	177.760	24			

a. R Squared = .444 (Adjusted R Squared = .297)

SAS GLM Output

DEPENDENT VARIABLE: Y

SOURCE	DF	SUM OF SQUARES	MEAN SQUARE	F VALUE	PR > F
MODEL	5	78.87666667	15.77533333	3.03	0.0354
ERROR	19	98.88333333	5.20438596		
CORRECTED TOTAL	24	177.76000000			

SOURCE	DF	TYPE I SS	F VALUE	PR > F	TYPE III SS	F VALUE	PR > F
A	1	23.22103896	4.46	0.0481	42.38522671	8.14	0.0102
B	2	① 38.87763022	3.74	0.0429	30.35238544 ②	2.92	0.0786
A*B	2	16.77799749	1.61	0.2256	16.77799749	1.61	0.2256

①Note, as mentioned in the chapter, that the sequential sums of squares from SPSSX are the same as the type I sums of squares from SAS.

②Unique sums of squares from SPSSX are the same as type III sums of squares from SAS.

T_2: This treatment was the same as T_1, but with one extra minute's exposure to the tone.

T_3: The subjects in this treatment group had the same exposure to the tone as those in treatment group 2, but they were *instructed* to use the relaxation techniques of breathing and visual imagery.

T_4: This was a control group, in that the subjects had no exposure to the tone between the relaxation training and the posttest measurement.

From within migraine and tension, the subjects were randomly assigned to the treatment groups. However, missing data reduced an initial balanced design to the following unequal n situation:

	T_1	T_2	T_3	T_4
Migraine	11	11	12	11
Tension	14	11	16	12

Here we consider analysis on only the definitely unpleasant posttest rating (DEFUNPL) of the subjects. The raw data for this study is given in Appendix A in the back of the book. I had the data on a 3.5-inch disk, along with several other data sets, and ran the analysis using the GLM program of SPSS for Windows 8.0. In Table 4.4 I present selected printout from that run.

For those who are interested, Stevens (1996, pp. 294–301) shows through dummy coding of the effects that the effects are indeed uncorrelated for balanced designs and correlated for disproportional designs.

Which Method Should Be Used?

After much debate in the statistical literature in the 1970s, there seem now to be a consensus that Method 1 (obtaining the unique sum of squares for each effect) *generally should be used*. For example, this is what Carlson and Timm (1974)

TABLE 4.4
Selected Printout From SPSS GLM for Headache Data

Dependent Variable: DEFUNPL

Source	Type III Sum of Squares	df	Mean Square	F	Sig.	Noncent. Parameter	Observed Power[a]
Corrected Model	119.454[b]	7	17.065	.965	.462	6.754	.394
Intercept	2853.922	1	2853.922	161.367	.000	161.367	1.000
HEADACHE	24.381	1	24.381	1.379	.243	1.379	.213
TREAT	83.655	3	27.885	1.577	.201	4.730	.402
HEADACHE * TREAT	6.784	3	2.261	.128	.943	.384	.073
Error	1591.732	90	17.686				
Total	4728.943	98					
Corrected Total	1711.186	97					

a. Computed using alpha = .05
b. R Squared = .070 (Adjusted R Squared = -.003)

recommend, and what Myers (1979) recommends for experimental studies (random assignment involved), or, as he puts it, "whenever variations in cell frequencies can reasonably be assumed due to chance" (p. 403).

When an a priori ordering of the effects can be established, then Method 3 (hierarchical or sequential sum of squares) makes sense. Pedhazur (1982) gives the following example. There is a 2 × 2 design in which one of the classification variables is race (black or white) and the other classification variable is education (high school or college). The dependent variable is income. In this case one can argue that race affects one's level of education, but obviously not vice versa. Thus, it makes sense to enter race first to determine its effect on income, then to enter education to determine how much it adds in predicting income. Finally, the race × education interaction is entered.

4.4   HIGHER ORDER DESIGNS

Three Way Analysis of Variance

Here we are examining the effect of three independent variables or factors on some dependent variable. We present three examples to illustrate:

1. An instructional technologist wishes to determine whether teaching method (2), teacher (2), and sex of the child each have an effect on achievement in reading. She has a 2 × 2 × 2 factorial design. This design enables her to determine whether all 3 factors jointly affect achievement in some unique way. For example, perhaps method 1 is particularily effective with teacher 1 working with girls, while method 2 is not effective with teacher 2 working with boys.

2. Consider again the aptitude treatment interaction study by Daniels and Stevens (1976) mentioned earlier. That study examined the effect of locus of control and teaching method on achievement in an introductory psychology course, and found a disordinal interaction. Internals did better with the contract for grade plan while externals did better with the teacher controlled method of instruction. As a heuristic followup to their study, Daniels and Stevens broke the subjects down into males and females and ran a sex by locus of control by method ANOVA to determine whether the nature of the interaction might be different for males and females (it was not).

3. A study by Marwit and Neumann (1974) provides another illustration of a three way ANOVA. Two black and two white examiners administered standard and nonstandard English forms of the California Reading Test to 60 black and 53 white second graders from a St. Louis public school. Here the race of the subject is one factor, the race of the examiner the second factor, and the format the third factor, while achievement is the dependent variable. The design schematically is this:

Format

		Standard English	Nonstandard English
Subject	Examiner		
	Black		
Black	White		
	Black		
White	White		

Recall that in a one way ANOVA there were two sources of variation (between and within), in a two way ANOVA there were four sources of variation (factor A, factor B, interaction of A and B, and within cell or error variation), and three hypotheses that were tested: A and B main effects and interaction effect. How many sources of variation are there in a three way design? The number of sources of variation in general for a k way factorial design is 2^k. Thus, for a 3 way design there are $2^3 = 8$ sources of variation, while for a 4 way ANOVA there are $2^4 = 16$ sources of variation. Consider the methods $\times$ teacher $\times$ sex design again. The sources of variation are

```
METHOD (A)    ⎫
TEACHER (B)   ⎬ MAIN EFFECTS
SEX (C)       ⎭
METHOD × TEACHER ⎫
METHOD × SEX     ⎬ FIRST ORDER INTERACTIONS
TEACHER × SEX    ⎭
METHOD × TEACHER × SEX
WITHIN CELLS (ERROR)
```

Each of the 7 effects in the design is tested against the *same* error term, that is, within cells variability (MS_w). Thus, the F ratios would look like this: $F_A = MS_A/MS_w$, $F_B = MS_B/MS_w$, . . . , $F_{BC} = MS_{BC}/MS_w$, $F_{ABC} = MS_{ABC}/MS_w$. The process of computing SS_w is exactly the same as for the two way ANOVA, that is, deviate the scores about the means in each cell, square the deviations and then add the squared deviations. The degrees of freedom for error for the two way ANOVA was $N - IJ$ (total number of subjects – number of cells). If we denote the number of levels for the factors in a 3 way ANOVA by I, J, and K, then the degrees of freedom for error in a 3 way is $N - IJK$ (again, the total number of subjects – number of cells).

The main effects involve comparing level means, analogous to comparing row and column means for the two way ANOVA. The first order (or two way) interactions are assessed by examining the pattern of means for the two factors combined over the third factor. For example, the method $\times$ teacher interaction is assessed by examining the means for those two factors with boys and girls combined together. Finally, the three way interaction is going to tell us whether the patterns of means for any two factors differs across the levels of the third factor.

Interpretation of Effects for An Example from Literature

To make this more concrete we consider data from a study by Cradler and Goodwin (1971). They were interested in comparing the way in which three types of reinforcement affected children's ability to use the word *they* when making up sentences. The children were randomly assigned to three groups: (1) material reinforcement condition—subjects received an M&M candy immediately after using the word *they* at the beginning of a sentence; (2) praise reinforcement—the children were reinforced by the experimenter's saying "good"; and (3) symbolic reinforcement—the children were simply given a plus mark. The investigators were also interested in whether the reinforcements worked differently for middle and lower class children (second factor in the design), and for different aged children (2nd and 6th graders—the third factor in the design). Below are the means (M) and standard deviations (SD):

		Grade Level				
Social		*Grade 2*			Grade 6	
Class	Mat.	Praise	Symb.	Mat.	Praise	Symb.
Middle						
M	5.66	6.64	6.58	5.75	8.25	9.66
SD	2.32	3.28	2.98	1.63	4.12	3.37
Lower						
M	8.41	5.41	5.25	6.75	7.00	6.33
SD	4.23	3.63	2.74	4.20	4.16	3.22

There were 12 subjects in each of the cells. The following ANOVA table was obtained:

Source	df	MS	F
Social Class (A)	1	12.250	.957
Grade Level (B)	1	25.000	1.954
Type of Reinforce (C)	2	1.465	.114
A × B	1	11.111	.868
A × C	2	41.646	3.255*
B × C	2	47.396	3.704*
A × B × C	2	5.298	.414
Error	132	12.792	

*$p < .05$

Note that none of the main effects is significant, although grade level is closest. Recall that in three way ANOVA main effects test whether the underlying *population* level means are different for the factor under consideration. The level mean for grade 2 is obtained by adding up all the means for grade 2 and dividing by 6:

$$(5.66 + 6.64 + 6.58 + 8.41 + 5.41 + 5.25)/6 = 6.325$$

and similarly for grade 6.

The reinforcement level means are obtained by adding the 4 means for each reinforcement condition and then dividing by 4. Thus, for material, we have

$$(5.66 + 8.41 + 5.75 + 6.75)/4 = 6.6425$$

The social class level means are obtained by adding up the 6 means for each social class across grades and reinforcement conditions. Thus, for middle social class we have:

$$(5.66 + 6.64 + 6.58 + 5.75 + 8.25 + 9.66)/6 = 7.09$$

All the sample level means are given below:

Grade Level Means: Grade 2: 6.325, Grade 6: 7.29
Social Class Means: Middle: 7.09, Lower: 6.525
Reinforcement Level Means: Mat.: 6.643, Praise: 6.825, Sym: 6.955

The reinforcement means are very close, making it quite likely that they are estimating equal population values, which is reflected in the very small $F = .111$.

Now, let us turn to the 2 way interaction effects that were significant, that is, AC (Social class × reinforcement) and BC (grade × reinforcement). To interpret these we need the means for social class by reinforcement combined over grade and the means for grade by reinforcement combined over social class. These means are presented below:

	Reinforcement				*Reinforcement*		
	Mat.	Praise	Symb.		Mat.	Praise	Symb.
Middle	5.71	7.45	8.12	Grade 2	7.04	6.03	5.92
Lower	7.58	6.21	5.79	Grade 6	6.25	7.63	8.00

The mean of 5.71 for the middle class and material reinforcement cell is obtained by adding the means for this set of conditions for the two grades, that is, $(5.66 + 5.75)/2 = 5.71$, and similarly for the other means. The mean of 7.04 for the grade 2 by material reinforcement condition is obtained by adding the means for this set of conditions for the two social classes, i.e., $(5.66 + 8.41)/2 = 7.04$ and similarly for the other means.

The interaction for social class $\times$ reinforcement is disordinal. That is, the lower class children respond better to the material reinforcement and then the means "flip flop"; the middle class children respond better to the praise and symbolic reinforcement.

The grade by reinforcement interaction is also *disordinal*; that is, the younger children respond better to the material reinforcement, and then the means "flip flop"; the older children respond better to praise and symbolic reinforcement.

The Three Way Interaction Effect

Why was the three way interaction not significant? As was mentioned earlier, *a significant three way interaction implies that the two way interaction profiles are different for different levels of the third factor.* If the patterns of means (profiles) are similar, then no interaction will be found. We present the means again below:

	Grade 2			Grade 6		
	Mat.	Praise	Symb.	Mat.	Praise	Symb.
Middle	5.66	6.64	6.58	5.75	8.25	9.66
Lower	8.41	5.41	5.25	6.75	7.00	6.33

Note that the profile of means for second graders is very similar to that for sixth graders. In both cases the mean is higher for lower social class under material reinforcement, and then reverses and is higher for praise and symbolic reinforcement for both grade levels. That is, for both the second and sixth grade we have the same type disordinal interaction.

Now we consider two hypothetical situations in which a significant three way interaction is present, and illustrate these graphically. The first example is a sex $\times$ treatment by race design while the second example involves a counseling methods $\times$ counselors $\times$ sex design. Suppose that the means for the two way design (collapsed on race) and for counseling methods $\times$ counselors (collapsed on sex) were as follows:

	Example 1			*Example 2*	
	T_1	T_2		C_1	C_2
Males	60	50	Method 1	85	72.5
Females	40	42	Method 2	75	76

Example 1 shows a clear ordinal interaction while example 2 shows a disordinal interaction, but neither of these tells the whole story. We now present the two way profiles of means for whites and blacks for example 1 and for males and females for example 2:

	Whites		Blacks			Males		Females	
	T_1	T_2	T_1	T_2		C_1	C_2	C_1	C_2
Male	65	50	55	50	Method 1	80	70	90	75
Female	40	47	40	37	Method 2	70	78	80	74

For example 1 we can see that the profiles of means for whites and blacks are distinctly different. Race further moderates the sex by treatment interaction. For whites we have a strong ordinal interaction while for blacks there is no interaction effect. For the counseling example (example 2), we see that the disordinal interaction effect apparent when males and females were combined together was due to the males. We see a clear disordinal method by counselor interaction for males, while for females there is an ordinal interaction. Here, sex moderates the method by counselor interaction. The practical implications for this example are that counselor 1 does uniformly better with method 1 regardless of sex. Method 2 is optimal for counselor 2 working with males, but for females counselor 2 is equally effective with both methods. We display graphically the interaction profiles for these two examples in Figure 4.2. It is important to emphasize again that a significant three way interaction means that the two way interaction profiles for *any two* of the factors are different for the levels of the third factor. Thus, in the sex by treatment by race example above, a significant three way interaction means that:

1. The sex by treatment profiles are different for the races (which is what we illustrated).
2. The sex by race profiles are different for the treatments.
3. The treatment by race profiles are different for the two sexes.

In the context of aptitude-treatment interaction (ATI) research, Cronbach (1975) had an interesting way of characterizing higher order interactions:

When ATI's are present, a general statement about a treatment effect is misleading because the effect will come or go depending on the kind of person treated. . . . An ATI result can be taken as a general conclusion only if it is not in turn moderated by further variables. If Aptitude × Treatment × Sex interact, for example, then the Aptitude × Treatment effect does not tell the story. Once we attend to interactions, we enter a hall of mirrors that extends to infinity. (p. 119)

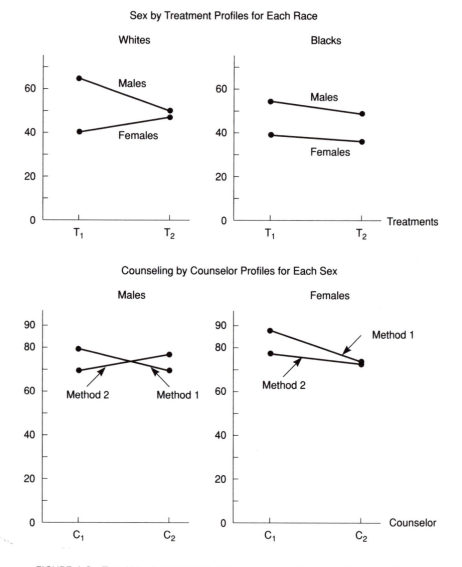

FIGURE 4.2   Two Way Interaction Profiles for Sex by Treatment by Race Design and for the Counseling by Counselor by Sex Design

Interpreting Patterns of Significant Effects

To further continue our discussion of interpreting effects from a three way ANOVA, we consider an *A* (methods) × *B* (teacher) × *C* (sex) example. We examine three possible patterns of significant results, and how one would interpret those patterns.

Pattern 1

A* (method)
B (teacher)
C (sex)
AB
AC
BC
ABC

*p < .05

Here only the method main effect is significant. Since there are no significant interactions we needn't qualify our statement on the efficacy of methods. It can be stated that one method produces *uniformly* higher achievement than the other regardless of teacher and regardless of sex of the child. A pattern of means that would be congruent with the above results is

	T_1	T_2
M_1	72	70
M_2	63	62

Pattern 2

A* (method)
B (teacher)
C (sex)
AB*
AC
BC
ABC

*p < .05

Here we have a method main effect again, but this time there is also a significant method by teacher interaction. Thus the efficacy of method needs to be *qualified*. The interaction is telling us that how much better one method is than another depends on the teacher. A pattern of means congruent for the above would be

	T_1	T_2	
M_1	70	65	67.5
M_2	60	62	61.0
	65	63.5	

Method 1 is superior to method 2; however, the degree of superiority depends sharply on the teacher. For teacher 1 method 1 is vastly superior, while for teacher 2 method 1 is only slightly better than method 2.

Pattern 3

A	(method)
B*	(teacher)
C	(sex)
AB	*p* < .05
AC	
BC	
ABC*	

The teacher main effect here needs to be considerably qualified because of the significant three way interaction. This could be discussed in terms of differences between two way profiles, as was done previously. Or we might think of it as follows. Call the two teachers Ms. Jones and Mr. Morton. The main effect is telling us that one teacher tends to get higher achievement regardless of method and sex of child (suppose this is Ms. Jones). The three way interaction is telling us that how much better achievement Ms. Jones obtains *depends on both* the method being taught and on the sex of the child. For example, Ms. Jones might do much better than Mr. Morton working with method 1 and girls, while she gets only slightly better achievement working with method 2 and boys.

Three Way ANOVA on SAS and SPSS

To illustrate the setup of the control lines for running a three way ANOVA on SAS we consider the following sex × age × treatment data set:

			Treatments	
	Age	1	2	3
	14	4,6,9	2,3,8	11,9,16
Males		(111)	(112)	(113)
	17	9,11,8	11,7,8	10,14,9
		(121)	(122)	(123)
	14	10,2,8	12,7,15	3,7,4
Females		(211)	(212)	(213)
	17	7,6,12	9,11,7	10,15,8
		(221)	(222)	(223)

The numbers in parentheses are the cell identifications, and are very important in identifying to the packages where the data originate. The 111 cell ID means the first level for each factor, while 113 means the first level for factors 1 and 2 and the third level for factor 3, and 213 means the subject is in the second level for factor 1 (female), the first level for factor 2 (age 14) and the third level for factor 3 (treatment 3). Once the cell identification is clear the rest of the setup is relatively straightforward (see Table 4.5).

Selected printout from SPSS GLM for Windows 8.0 for this data is given in Table 4.6. The SPSS options screen (used for obtaining marginal means) is given in Table 4.7.

TABLE 4.5
SAS Control Lines for Sex × Age(2) × Treat (3) ANOVA

```
    TITLE ' THREE WAY ANOVA';
    DATA THREEWAY;
①  INPUT SEX AGE TREAT Y @@;
    LINES;
②  1 1 1 4 1 1 1 6 1 1 1 9
    1 1 2 2 1 1 2 3 1 1 2 8
    1 1 3 11 1 1 3 9 1 1 3 16
    1 2 1 9 1 2 1 11 1 2 1 8
    1 2 2 11 1 2 2 7 1 2 2 8
    1 2 3 10 1 2 3 14 1 2 3 9
    2 1 1 10 2 1 1 2 2 1 1 8
    2 1 2 12 2 1 2 7 2 1 2 15
    2 1 3 3 2 1 3 7 2 1 3 4
    2 2 1 7 2 2 1 6 2 2 1 12
    2 2 2 9 2 2 2 11 2 2 2 7
    2 2 3 10 2 2 3 15 2 2 3 8
    PROC PRINT;
    PROC GLM;
③  CLASS SEX AGE TREAT;
    MEANS SEX AGE TREAT SEX*AGE
④  SEX*TREAT AGE*TREAT
    SEX*AGE*TREAT;
⑤  MODEL Y=SEX|AGE|TREAT;
```

①In the INPUT statement we list the variables in the analysis.

②The first 3 numbers for each block of 4 numbers is the cell ID, with the fourth number being the score on the dependent variable. Thus, the first subject in cell 111 has a score of 4, the second subject in cell 111 has a score of 6 and the third subject a score of 9. Although not necessary, we have put the data for each cell on a separate line for ease of reading.

③This CLASS statement lists the grouping variables (factors) for the ANOVA.

④The MEANS statement is needed to obtain the level means (SEX AGE TREAT), the means for the two way interactions (SEX*AGE SEX*TREAT AGE*TREAT) and the cell means.

⑤This is the abbreviated way of representing a full three way factorial model in SAS (see SAS USER'S GUIDE, Version 5, p. 436)

TABLE 4.6
SPSS GLM Printout for Three Way ANOVA:
Tests of Significance and Marginal Means for All Effects

Dependent Variable: DEP

Source	Type III Sum of Squares	df	Mean Square	F	Sig.	Noncent. Parameter	Observed Power[a]
Corrected Model	221.556[b]	11	20.141	2.224	.049	24.466	.804
Intercept	2635.111	1	2635.111	290.994	.000	290.994	1.000
AGE	36.000	1	36.000	3.975	.058	3.975	.482
SEX	.111	1	.111	.012	.913	.012	.051
TREAT	24.889	2	12.444	1.374	.272	2.748	.266
AGE * SEX	.111	1	.111	.012	.913	.012	.051
AGE * TREAT	4.667	2	2.333	.258	.775	.515	.086
SEX * TREAT	80.889	2	40.444	4.466	.022	8.933	.710
AGE * SEX * TREAT	74.889	2	37.444	4.135	.029	8.270	.674
Error	217.333	24	9.056				
Total	3074.000	36					
Corrected Total	438.889	35					

a. Computed using alpha = .05
b. R Squared = .505 (Adjusted R Squared = .278)

Estimated Marginal Means

1. AGE

Dependent Variable: DEP

AGE	Mean	Std. Error	95% Confidence Interval Lower Bound	Upper Bound
1.00	7.556	.709	6.092	9.019
2.00	9.556	.709	8.092	11.019

2. SEX

Dependent Variable: DEP

SEX	Mean	Std. Error	95% Confidence Interval Lower Bound	Upper Bound
1.00	8.611	.709	7.147	10.075
2.00	8.500	.709	7.036	9.964

3. TREAT

Dependent Variable: DEP

TREAT	Mean	Std. Error	95% Confidence Interval Lower Bound	Upper Bound
1.00	7.667	.869	5.874	9.460
2.00	8.333	.869	6.540	10.126
3.00	9.667	.869	7.874	11.460

TABLE 4.6
(Continued)

4. AGE * SEX

Dependent Variable: DEP

AGE	SEX	Mean	Std. Error	95% Confidence Interval	
				Lower Bound	Upper Bound
1.00	1.00	7.556	1.003	5.485	9.626
	2.00	7.556	1.003	5.485	9.626
2.00	1.00	9.667	1.003	7.596	11.737
	2.00	9.444	1.003	7.374	11.515

5. AGE * TREAT

Dependent Variable: DEP

AGE	TREAT	Mean	Std. Error	95% Confidence Interval	
				Lower Bound	Upper Bound
1.00	1.00	6.500	1.229	3.964	9.036
	2.00	7.833	1.229	5.298	10.369
	3.00	8.333	1.229	5.798	10.869
2.00	1.00	8.833	1.229	6.298	11.369
	2.00	8.833	1.229	6.298	11.369
	3.00	11.000	1.229	8.464	13.536

6. SEX * TREAT

Dependent Variable: DEP

SEX	TREAT	Mean	Std. Error	95% Confidence Interval	
				Lower Bound	Upper Bound
1.00	1.00	7.833	1.229	5.298	10.369
	2.00	6.500	1.229	3.964	9.036
	3.00	11.500	1.229	8.964	14.036
2.00	1.00	7.500	1.229	4.964	10.036
	2.00	10.167	1.229	7.631	12.702
	3.00	7.833	1.229	5.298	10.369

TABLE 4.6
(Continued)

7. AGE * SEX * TREAT

Dependent Variable: DEP

AGE	SEX	TREAT	Mean	Std. Error	95% Confidence Interval Lower Bound	Upper Bound
1.00	1.00	1.00	6.333	1.737	2.748	9.919
		2.00	4.333	1.737	.748	7.919
		3.00	12.000	1.737	8.414	15.586
	2.00	1.00	6.667	1.737	3.081	10.252
		2.00	11.333	1.737	7.748	14.919
		3.00	4.667	1.737	1.081	8.252
2.00	1.00	1.00	9.333	1.737	5.748	12.919
		2.00	8.667	1.737	5.081	12.252
		3.00	11.000	1.737	7.414	14.586
	2.00	1.00	8.333	1.737	4.748	11.919
		2.00	9.000	1.737	5.414	12.586
		3.00	11.000	1.737	7.414	14.586

Calculation of Sums of Squares in Three Way ANOVA

We illustrate here, using definitional type formulas, how some of the sums of squares given in Table 4.6 are obtained, and leave the calculation of the others as exercises. In doing this we link the process to what was done for two way ANOVA, since it is similar. Recall that earlier in calculating the sum of squares for the main effects for A and B the definitional formulas were

$$SS_A = nJ \sum (\bar{x}_{i.} - \bar{x})^2 \text{ and } SS_B = nI \sum (\bar{x}_{.j} - \bar{x})^2$$

That is, the row and column means were deviated about the grand mean, and the weighting factor in each case is the number of observations on which each row mean (nJ) or column mean (nI) is based. In calculating the sums of squares for the main effects in three way ANOVA we simply deviate the *level* means about the grand mean, and the weighting factor in each case is the number of observations on which each level mean is based. Now the grand mean for the ANOVA in Table 4.6 is the average of the level means for sex and is thus 8.5555. Since each sex level mean is based on 18 observations, the sum of squares for the sex main effect is:

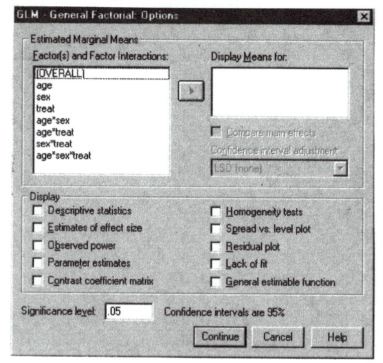

$$SS_{sex} = 18 \ [(8.6111 - 8.5555)^2 + (8.5000 - 8.5555)^2]$$
$$= .11129$$

The discrepancy from the value in Table 4.6 is due to rounding error. Similarly, the sum of squares for treatment is given by

$$SS_{tr} = 12 \ [(7.6666 - 8.5555)^2 + (8.3333 - 8.5555)^2 + (9.6666 - 8.5555)^2]$$
$$= 24.88864$$

The calculations for a two way interaction effect are exactly the same as for the two way ANOVA (see Table 4.6), *after* one has collapsed on the levels of the third factor. To illustrate we consider the calculation of sum of squares for the sex by treatment interaction. The means for sex by treatment combined over the two age groups, along with the row and column means and the interaction effects (in parentheses) are:

	Treatments			
	1	2	3	
1	7.8333	6.5000	11.5000	8.6111
	(.1111)	(−1.89)	(1.78)	
Sex				
2	7.5000	10.1667	7.8333	8.5000
	(−.1111)	(1.89)	(−1.78)	
	7.6667	8.3333	9.6666	8.5555

Recall that the formula for sum of squares interaction is

$$SS = n \sum \hat{\phi}_{ij}^2$$

where n is the number of observations in each cell and $\hat{\phi}_{ij}$ is the estimated interaction effect for the ijth cell, and

$$\hat{\phi}_{ij} = \bar{x}_{ij} - \bar{x}_{i.} - \bar{x}_{.j} + \bar{x}$$

Thus, the sum of squares here is

$$SS = 6[(.1111)^2 + (−1.89)^2 + (1.78)^2 + (−.1111)^2 + (1.89)^2 + (−1.78)^2]$$
$$= 80.89$$

The calculations for interaction sum of squares for sex by age and age by treatment are similar, and are left as exercises.

To calculate sum of squares for the three way interaction effect we first compute variability of the cell means about the grand mean (denote this by $SS_{cell(ABC)}$). The means are:

		Males			Females		
		1	2	3	1	2	3
	14	6.3333	4.3333	12.0	6.6667	11.3333	4.6667
Age							
	17	9.3333	8.6667	11.0	8.3333	9.0000	11.0000

$$SS_{cell(ABC)} = 3[(6.3333 − 8.5555)^2 + (4.3333 − 8.5555)^2 + (12 − 8.5555)^2$$
$$+ \cdots + (9 − 8.5555)^2 + (11 − 8.5555)^2] = 221.556$$

From this quantity we subtract all variation due to the main effects and the first order interactions. What remains is variability due to the three way interaction effect;

$$SS_{ABC} = SS_{cell(ABC)} - SS_A - SS_B - SS_C - SS_{AB} - SS_{AC} - SS_{BC}$$

$SS_{ABC} = 221.556 - .1111 - 36 - .1111 - 24.8888 - 80.8888 - 4.6667$
$= 74.889$

The error term for equal cell size, as was true for two way ANOVA, is simply the *average* of the cell variances.

$MS_w = (6.3333 + 10.3333 + 13 + \cdots + 10.3333 + 4 + 13)/12$
$= 9.0555$

Four Way Analysis of Variance

In a four way analysis of variance we are examining the effect of 4 independent variables on some dependent variable. We consider an example from the literature to illustrate. Chase (1986) examined the effect of penmanship quality, sex, race, and reader expectation on the grade given an essay test. The graders were 80 elementary and middle school inservice teachers in an integrated large urban area of the Midwest. Each grader was given contrived student school records, some of which contained mainly A's and B's while others contained mostly D's and U's. These records were intended to create in the essay reader a set as to the level of achievement expected from the students whose paper was being graded. Thus there were two levels for reader expectation. The essays were written in poor and good quality of penmanship, as judged by the Ayres handwriting scale. Thus, a $2 \times 2 \times 2 \times 2$ four way ANOVA was run. As mentioned earlier, in a 4 way design there are 16 sources of variation and 15 hypotheses that are tested. For the Chase example the 15 effects are:

$$
\left.
\begin{array}{l}
\text{Penmanship (A)} \\
\text{Sex (B)} \\
\text{Race (C)} \\
\text{Expectation (D)}
\end{array}
\right\} \text{Main Effects}
$$

$$
\left.
\begin{array}{l}
A \times B \\
A \times C \\
A \times D \\
B \times C \\
B \times D \\
C \times D
\end{array}
\right\} \text{First Order Interactions}
$$

$$
\left.
\begin{array}{l}
A \times B \times C \\
A \times B \times D \\
A \times C \times D \\
B \times C \times D
\end{array}
\right\} \text{Second Order Interactions}
$$

$$A \times B \times C \times D$$

One does not see very many 4 or 5 way ANOVAs in the literature. A couple of reasons for this are (1) the difficulty of interpreting higher order interactions and (2) sample size required so that some of cell frequencies are *not* extremely small (like 1 or 2 subjects).

We wish to discuss a caution in using such designs for another reason. While the use of complex ANOVA designs is the only way to get at higher order interactions, and their "real" existence may have important practical implications, the key word here is real. Remember in a 4 way ANOVA we are testing 15 hypotheses. To some researchers this may seem like a boon, but it can be a bane if one is not careful. Researchers using such designs often interpret any effects that are significant at the .05 level. The potential danger with this for 3, 4, or 5 way ANOVAs is that the overall α level gets out of control. Recall again from Chapter 2 that if we are testing k hypotheses, each at the .05 level, then an upper bound on overall α is given by $1 - (1 - .05)^k$. Below we list the upper bound on overall α for 3, 4, and 5 way ANOVAs if .05 level is used for each effect:

	Three Way	Four Way	Five Way
Number of hypotheses being tested	7	15	31
Upper Bound on Overall α	.30	.536	.79

The results of the Chase study mentioned previously provide a perfect illustration of the danger. In that study the focus was on looking for interactions, but *no specific interactions were hypothesized a priori to be significant.* However, two significant higher order interactions were found at the .05 level, and these were the only significant results. The cell size was equal so that the overall α = .536. But this is saying that the probability of *at least one* false rejection is uncomfortably high. Thus, the two significant results found could very well be type I errors or spurious results. At the very least, the reader should be warned of this possibility.

A simple way of controlling the escalating overall α level for 3 and 4 way designs is to test each effect at a more stringent α level, say α = .01. Then we are assured that overall $\alpha \le .07$ for the 3 way and overall $\alpha \le .15$ for the 4 way design because of the Bonferroni inequality. But the price of this is even worse power for detecting interactions. Now, if sample size is large enough, then we can have the luxury of setting α = .01 and still have adequate power. For example, if $n = 270$ in a $2 \times 3 \times 3$ design, then power will be good to adequate for detecting all effects (although marginally so for the BC and ABC interactions). The reader may verify this by running PASS 6.0 with $n = 15$ for the above design.

Table 4.8 has the PASS 6.0 screen for a $2 \times 3 \times 3$ design with a medium effect size and both 5 and 10 subjects per cell. The results are presented in Table 4.9. Also, Table 4.9 shows that if you have 8 subjects per cell and are attempting to detect a medium effect, with the alpha level set somewhat higher for the

TABLE 4.8
PASS 6.0 Screen for Three Way ANOVA
(Medium Effect Size and $\alpha = .05$ for All Effects)

Terms	Categories df	Sigma m	Alpha Level
A	2 ◄► 1	.25	0.05
B	3 ◄► 2	.25	0.05
C	3 ◄► 2	.25	0.05
AB	6 2	.25	0.05
AC	6 2	.25	0.05
BC	9 4	.25	0.05
ABC	18 4	.25	0.05

n per cell
5,10

Sigma
1

Template File: default

interaction effects (since this is the main reason for setting up a factorial design), power is adequate for the AB, AC, and ABC interaction effects. If a large effect is present, then the bottom of Table 4.9 shows that power is good (or very close to good) for all effects with only 5 subjects per cell.

An Improved Bonferroni Type Procedure

Holland and Copenhaver (1988) discuss several new and improved competitors to the Bonferroni procedure. The one we consider here and illustrate is due to Holm (1979). For this procedure one needs the p values (tail probabilities) for each hypothesis being tested, but since these are printed out on the major statistical packages this is no problem.

The general problem then is to keep overall α under control when testing a set of k hypotheses. The k hypotheses could be of a variety of forms: (1) the numerous F tests from a complex factorial design, (2) the numerous t tests involved if one compares two groups on large set of dependent variables, (3) examining a large number of 2×2 contingency tables from say an original $5 \times$

TABLE 4.9
Power Values From PASS 6.0 for Medium Effect Size
in a 2 × 3 × 3 Design With 5, 8, and 10 Subjects
per Cell and for Large Effect Size With $n = 5$

Term	Power	n	N	df1	df2	n'	Sigma m	Effect Size	Alpha
A	0.56432	5.00	90	1	72	37.00	0.25	0.2500	0.05000
B	0.46008	5.00	90	2	72	25.00	0.25	0.2500	0.05000
C	0.46008	5.00	90	2	72	25.00	0.25	0.2500	0.05000
AB	0.46008	5.00	90	2	72	25.00	0.25	0.2500	0.05000
AC	0.46008	5.00	90	2	72	25.00	0.25	0.2500	0.05000
BC	0.35897	5.00	90	4	72	15.40	0.25	0.2500	0.05000
ABC	0.35897	5.00	90	4	72	15.40	0.25	0.2500	0.05000

Term	Power	n	N	df1	df2	n'	Sigma m	Effect Size	Alpha
A	0.58525	8.00	144	1	126	64.00	0.25	0.2500	0.01000
B	0.47148	8.00	144	2	126	43.00	0.25	0.2500	0.01000
C	0.47148	8.00	144	2	126	43.00	0.25	0.2500	0.01000
AB	0.71015	8.00	144	2	126	43.00	0.25	0.2500	0.05000
AC	0.71015	8.00	144	2	126	43.00	0.25	0.2500	0.05000
BC	0.59766	8.00	144	4	126	26.20	0.25	0.2500	0.05000
ABC	0.71734	8.00	144	4	126	26.20	0.25	0.2500	0.10000

Term	Power	n	N	df1	df2	n'	Sigma m	Effect Size	Alpha
A	0.88925	10.00	180	1	162	82.00	0.25	0.2500	0.05000
B	0.82038	10.00	180	2	162	55.00	0.25	0.2500	0.05000
C	0.82038	10.00	180	2	162	55.00	0.25	0.2500	0.05000
AB	0.82038	10.00	180	2	162	55.00	0.25	0.2500	0.05000
AC	0.82038	10.00	180	2	162	55.00	0.25	0.2500	0.05000
BC	0.72269	10.00	180	4	162	33.40	0.25	0.2500	0.05000
ABC	0.72269	10.00	180	4	162	33.40	0.25	0.2500	0.05000

LARGE EFFECT SIZE

Term	Power	n	N	df1	df2	n'	Sigma m	Effect Size	Alpha
A	0.92432	5.00	90	1	72	37.00	0.40	0.4000	0.05000
B	0.86886	5.00	90	2	72	25.00	0.40	0.4000	0.05000
C	0.86886	5.00	90	2	72	25.00	0.40	0.4000	0.05000
AB	0.86886	5.00	90	2	72	25.00	0.40	0.4000	0.05000
AC	0.86886	5.00	90	2	72	25.00	0.40	0.4000	0.05000
BC	0.78454	5.00	90	4	72	15.40	0.40	0.4000	0.05000
ABC	0.78454	5.00	90	4	72	15.40	0.40	0.4000	0.05000

7 contingency table, and (4) determining which of 50 individual between correlations are significant, in analyzing the association between two sets of variables (5 in one set and 10 in the other set).

In the Holm procedure the p values for the k hypotheses are ordered from smallest to largest: $p_{(1)} < p_{(2)} < \cdots < p_{(k)}$. Tied p values can be ordered arbitrarily.

Let $H_{(1)}, \ldots, H_{(k)}$ denote the hypotheses corresponding to these ordered p values. Suppose i^* is the smallest integer from 1 to k such that

$$p_{(i)} > \alpha/(k - i^* + 1)$$

Then the Holm procedure rejects $H_{(1)}, \ldots, H_{(i-1)}$ and retains $H_{(i)}, \ldots, H_{(k)}$. The increased power for the Holm procedure comes from the fact that $\alpha/(k - i + 1)$ is larger than α/k.

To illustrate the use of the Holm procedure consider a hypothetical 4 way ANOVA. Suppose we wish to control overall α at .10 for the $k = 15$ hypotheses and that the ordered p values are:

i	$p(i)$	$\alpha/(k - i + 1)$
1	.0001	.0067
2	.0001	.0071
3	.0017	.0077
4	.0046	.0083
5	.0053	.0091
6	.0078	.0100
7	.0094	.0111
8	.0113	.0125
9	.0435	.0143
10	.0896	.0167
11	.1342	.0200
12	.2689	.0250
13	.4625	.0333
14	.5813	.0500
15	.6437	.1000

We see here that i^* is 9, where $p(i) = .0435 > .0143$. Thus, by the Holm procedure we would declare 8 effects in the design significant, with assurance that overall $\alpha = .10$. If Bonferroni had been used, an effect would need a $p < .067$ to be declared significant, and only 5 effects would have been significant.

4.5 A COMPREHENSIVE COMPUTER
EXAMPLE USING REAL DATA

To tie together several elements discussed in this chapter, we consider a computer analysis of the CARTOON data set. In this study an instructional slide presentation (18 slides) was developed, with the topic being the behavior of people in a group situation, and in particular the various roles or character types that group members often assume. Each role was identified by an animal. Each animal was shown on two slides, once in a cartoon sketch and once in a realistic picture. A random half of the 179 subjects saw the slides in black and white and the other half saw the slides in color. The subjects were immediately posttested for the number of cartoon characters they could identify (CARTOON1) and for the number of realistic characters they could identify (REAL1). They were retested 4 weeks later on the same two variables. Three groups of subjects were involved in the study: preprofessional and professional personnel from three hospitals and a group of Penn State college students. For the computer analysis, in contrast to the first edition of this text, I just consider the REAL2 variable for this 2 × 3 design (color of presentation by type of subject). Our analysis serves to illustrate and integrate several aspects of practical data analysis.

The analysis was run on SPSS MANOVA, and only on subjects for which there is complete data. Note that that this reduces the effective sample size substantially (from 179 to 105). Immediately we encounter a couple of problems that typify "real world" data analysis. First, the cell sizes are sharply unequal. Second, there is a fair amount of missing data (many subjects did not show up for the retest). Missing data is a fairly common occurrence in certain areas of research, and there is no simple solution for this problem. If it can be assumed that the data is missing *at random*, then there is a sophisticated procedure available for obtaining good estimates (Johnson & Wichern, 1988, pp. 197–202). On the other hand, if the random missing data assumption is not tenable (usually the case), then there is no general consensus as to what should be done. There are various suggestions, like using the mean of the scores on the variable as an estimate, or using regression analysis (Frane, 1976). Probably the "best" solution is to make every attempt to minimize the problem before and during the study, rather than having to manufacture data. The statistical packages SAS and SPSS have various ways of handling missing data. The default option for both, however, is to delete the case if there is missing data on any variable for the subject (called listwise deletion).

Now recall that the homogeneity of variance assumption for factorial designs is that the *cell* population variances are equal. Since the cell sizes are sharply unequal, a violation of this assumption will distort the type I error rate, and it is important to check this assumption. Fortunately this assumption is tenable (using Cochran's test, $p = .401$).

The significant main effect for REAL2 is an overall test that merely tells us the three population column means differ. It does not indicate which particular column means are different. For this we need a post hoc procedure, just as we did in one way ANOVA. We use the Tukey procedure. Recall that for one way ANOVA the endpoints for the confidence intervals were given by

$$(\bar{x}_i - \bar{x}_j) \pm q_{\alpha;k,N-k} \sqrt{MS_w/n}$$

where n was the assumed common group size. Remember also that when the group sizes were unequal the Tukey was still applicable, provided that the population

TABLE 4.10
SPSS MANOVA Control Lines and Selected Printout for CARTOON Data

```
TITLE 'TWO WAY ANOVA ON CARTOON DATA FOR REAL2'.
DATA LIST FIXED/ID 1-3 COLOR 5 ED 7 LOCATION 9 OTIS 11-13 CARTOON1
  15 REAL1 17 CARTOON2 19 REAL2 21.
BEGIN DATA.

DATA (FROM 3.5 FLOPPY DISK)

END DATA.
MANOVA REAL2 BY COLOR(0,1) ED(0,2)/
  PRINT=CELLINFO(MEANS)/.
```

Tests of Significance for REAL2 using UNIQUE sums of squares

Source of Variation	SS	DF	MS	F	Sig of F
WITHIN CELLS	532.74	99	5.38		
COLOR	15.04	1	15.04	2.79	.098
ED	79.95	2	39.98	7.43	.001
COLOR BY ED	12.62	2	6.31	1.17	.314
(Model)	95.89	5	19.18	3.56	.005
(Total)	628.63	104	6.04		

R-Squared =   .153
Adjusted R-Squared =   .110

variances were equal and that n was replaced by the harmonic mean for each pair of groups.

In application of the Tukey to factorial designs the n is replaced by the number of observations on which each row or column mean is based, for equal cell size. When the cell sizes are unequal, as in the study we are examining, we again employ the harmonic mean, but now for each pair of row and/or column sizes.

Below we present the cell sizes for the REAL2 variable. From this table we see that the column sizes are 24, 26, and 55.

		Real2	
Preprof	*Prof*	*Coll*	*Row Mean*
3.667	3.937	4.852	4.33
(2.43)	(2.05)	(2.23)	
$n = 12$	$n = 16$	$n = 27$	
2.333	2.700	4.964	3.88
(1.97)	(1.89)	(2.73)	
$n = 12$	$n = 10$	$n = 28$	
3.0	3.46	4.91	4.11

Thus, the harmonic means for each pair of column sizes are given by

$$2(24)(26)/50 = 25, \ 2(24)(55)/79 = 33.42 \text{ and } 2(26)(55)/81 = 35.31$$

Below are the calculations and the intervals:

Groups Compared	Harmonic Mean	Critical Value	Interval
Prof-Preprof Mean diff = .46	25	$3.356\sqrt{5.381/25} = 1.56$	(−1.1, 2.02)
Coll-Preprof Mean diff = 1.91	33.42	$3.356\sqrt{5.381/33.42} = 1.35$	(.56, 3.26)
Coll-Prof Mean diff = 1.45	35.31	$3.356\sqrt{5.381/35.31} = 1.31$	(.14, 2.76)

These intervals show that the college students differed significantly from both the preprofessional and the professional groups, and examination of the column means in the above table shows that the college students scored higher in each case.

4.6 POWER ANALYSIS

Power Estimation for Two Way Analysis of Variance

Because we are basing our treatment of power on Cohen's book (1977, revised edition), it is very important to note here that estimation of power for factorial designs changed significantly from the first edition (Cohen, 1969) to the second edition. We quote from a couple of footnotes in Cohen's (1977) edition:

> Readers familiar with the first edition should note that the treatment of main effects (and even more so, of interactions) in factorial design differs considerably here. The systematic overestimation of power for main effects by the former method proved to be unacceptably large in some applications. The present method gives quite accurate and unbiased results. . . . In the case of interactions, both the *ES* (effect size measure) of formula (8.3.6) below and the *n* used for table entry have been changed in this edition, thus avoiding substantial underestimation of power for interactions. (footnotes 2 and 3, p. 364 and p. 369)

The main reason for setting up a factorial design is to test for an interaction effect. Unfortunately, as we will see shortly, the power for detecting this interaction can be inadequate. Suppose that we have an $A \times B$ design, with r levels for factor A and c levels for factor B. The effect sizes for the main effects and interaction may be expressed as follows:

$$A \text{ main effect: } \hat{f}_A = \sqrt{(r-1)F_A/N} \qquad (5)$$

$$B \text{ main effect: } \hat{f}_B = \sqrt{(c-1)F_B/N} \qquad (6)$$

$$AB \text{ interaction:} \hat{f}_{AB} = \sqrt{(r-1)(c-1)F_{AB}/N} \qquad (7)$$

To illustrate the power calculations we consider a 2×3 design with 10 observations per cell:

$$
\begin{array}{ccccc}
 & & & B & \\
 & 10 & 10 & 10 & 30 \\
A & & & & \\
 & 10 & 10 & 10 & 30 \\
 & 20 & 20 & 20 & 60 = N
\end{array}
$$

It might appear that the n we should use to enter the power tables for the A main effect is 30, since the row mean is based on 30 subjects. However, a slight adjustment is necessary (Cohen, 1977, p. 365). The same is true for the B main effect and the interaction, and the following ns are what are needed:

Effect	*n used to enter the table*
A main effect	$n_A = [(N - rc)/r] + 1$
B main effect	$n_B = [(N - rc)/c] + 1$
AB interaction	$n_{AB} = [(N - rc)/((r - 1)(c - 1) + 1)] + 1$

The F ratios from the above study, along with the corresponding effect sizes and power are presented below:

Effect	F	Effect Size	n to enter table	Power
A main	1.8	$\sqrt{1(1.8)/60} = .173$	$(60 - 6)/2 + 1 = 28$	.25
B main	3.6	$\sqrt{2(3.6)/60} = .346$	$(60 - 6)/3 + 1 = 19$	.64
AB inter	2.1	$\sqrt{2(2.1)/60} = .265$	$[(60 - 6)/2 + 1] + 1 = 19$	.40

Since there is a fairly large effect size for the B main effect, power is at least fair. However, for the interaction with a medium effect size, power is poor.

For a priori estimation of power in two way ANOVA the PASS 6.0 program is very helpful. We simply specify what size effect we wish to detect (small, medium, or large), and different cell sizes (n), and we will see in a matter of seconds whether any of the cell sizes specified yield adequate power. Table 4.11 shows power for $n = 10$, 20, and 30 for a medium effect size at alpha = .05 in the top portion. This shows that to have near adequate power (.66353) we need 20 subjects per cell. If we can tolerate a 10% chance of a type I error for the interaction, then the middle

TABLE 4.11
Power Values From PASS 6.0 for 2 × 3 Design With 10, 20, and 30
Subjects per Cell for Medium Effect Size and n = 10 for Large Effect Size

MEDIUM EFFECT SIZE

Term	Power	n	N	df1	df2	n'	Sigma m	Effect Size	Alpha
A	0.45135	10.00	60	1	54	28.00	0.25	0.2500	0.05000
B	0.35675	10.00	60	2	54	19.00	0.25	0.2500	0.05000
AB	0.35675	10.00	60	2	54	19.00	0.25	0.2500	0.05000
A	0.76111	20.00	120	1	114	58.00	0.25	0.2500	0.05000
B	0.66353	20.00	120	2	114	39.00	0.25	0.2500	0.05000
AB	0.66353	20.00	120	2	114	39.00	0.25	0.2500	0.05000
A	0.90960	30.00	180	1	174	88.00	0.25	0.2500	0.05000
B	0.84827	30.00	180	2	174	59.00	0.25	0.2500	0.05000
AB	0.84827	30.00	180	2	174	59.00	0.25	0.2500	0.05000

MEDIUM EFFECT SIZE

Term	Power	n	N	df1	df2	n'	Sigma m	Effect Size	Alpha
A	0.45135	10.00	60	1	54	28.00	0.25	0.2500	0.05000
B	0.35675	10.00	60	2	54	19.00	0.25	0.2500	0.05000
AB	0.48598	10.00	60	2	54	19.00	0.25	0.2500	0.10000
A	0.76111	20.00	120	1	114	58.00	0.25	0.2500	0.05000
B	0.66353	20.00	120.	2	114	39.00	0.25	0.2500	0.05000
AB	0.77218	20.00	120	2	114	39.00	0.25	0.2500	0.10000
A	0.90960	30.00	180	1	174	88.00	0.25	0.2500	0.05000
B	0.84827	30.00	180	2	174	59.00	0.25	0.2500	0.05000
AB	0.91139	30.00	180	2	174	59.00	0.25	0.2500	0.10000

LARGE EFFECT SIZE

Term	Power	n	N	df1	df2	n'	Sigma m	Effect Size	Alpha
A	0.83639	10.00	60	1	54	28.00	0.40	0.4000	0.05000
B	0.75172	10.00	60	2	54	19.00	0.40	0.4000	0.05000
AB	0.75172	10.00	60	2	54	19.00	0.40	0.4000	0.05000

portion of the table shows that power = .77218 for 20 subjects per cell. If a large main or interaction effect is present, then the bottom portion of the table shows that we have adequate power with only 10 subjects per cell.

Power Estimation for Three Way Analysis of Variance

Power analysis for three way ANOVA is a straightforward generalization of that for two way ANOVA. Consider a general three way design: factor A—a levels, factor B—b levels, and factor C—c levels. We simply need the following effect size for the three way interaction:

$$\hat{f} = \hat{\sigma}_{ABC}/\hat{\sigma}, \text{ where } \hat{\sigma}^2 = MS_w \text{ and } \hat{\sigma}_{ABC} = SS_{ABC}/N$$

It can be shown that f is related to the F statistic for the three way interaction as follows:

$$\hat{f} = \sqrt{[(a - 1)(b - 1)(c - 1)/N]\, F_{ABC}} \tag{8}$$

In the above, $u = (a - 1)(b - 1)(c - 1)$ is the degrees of freedom for the three way interaction. The n that is used to enter the power tables for *each* effect in the design (i.e., main effects, first order interactions and the second order interaction) is

$$n' = (N - abc)/(u + 1) + 1$$

where $(N - abc)$ is the degrees of freedom for the error term, and u is the degrees of freedom for the effect in question: for example, $(a - 1)$ for the A main effect, $(b - 1)$ for the B main effect, $(a - 1)(b - 1)$ for the AB interaction, etc.

To illustrate power estimation we consider a $2 \times 3 \times 3$ design with 5 subjects per cell. For example, the design might be sex by treatments by social class. The power values are given for differing α and for different effect sizes.

Power as a Function of Effect Size & α Level
in a $2 \times 3 \times 3$ Design with $n = 5$

Effect	u	n'	$f = .10$		$f = .25$		$f = .40$	
			.05	.10	.05	.10	.05	.10
A	1	37	.13	.22	.58	.70	.93	.96
B	2	25	.10	.19	.47	.60	.87	.93
C	2	25	.10	.19	.47	.60	.87	.93
AB	2	25	.10	.19	.47	.60	.87	.93
AC	2	25	.10	.19	.47	.60	.87	.93
BC	4	16	.09	.16	.38	.51	.81	.88
ABC	4	16	.09	.16	.38	.51	.81	.88

The power values at $\alpha = .05$ for small and medium effect sizes are boxed in. Notice that almost all (only 1 exception) these values are less than .50, that is, poor.

In Chapter 3 on power analysis we indicated that SPSS MANOVA can be used to obtain estimates of power for various fixed effects univariate and multivariate tests, and showed in Table 3.2 the control lines for obtaining the power estimates for the t test and a one way ANOVA. To obtain power estimates for the various effects in a factorial design is equally as simple. For example, for the data on page 174, we simply insert after the MANOVA command the following subcommands

```
POWER=F(.05)/
PRINT=CELLINFO(MEANS) SIGNIF(EFSIZE)/
```

Directly beneath the ANOVA table SPSS prints out the effect sizes and power estimates for each effect in the design. It looks like this:

EFFECT SIZE MEASURES AND OBSERVED POWER AT THE .05 LEVEL

SOURCE OF VARIATION	PARTIAL ETA SQD	NONCENTRALITY	POWER
SEX	.00051	.01227	.042
AGE	.14211	3.97546	.481
TREAT	.10275	2.74847	.266
SEX BY AGE	.00051	.01227	.042
SEX BY TREAT	.27124	8.93252	.710
AGE BY TREAT	.02102	.51534	.088
SEX BY AGE BY TREAT	.25627	8.26994	.674

Recall from Chapter 3 that a partial η^2 around .01 indicates a small effect size, a partial η^2 around .06 a medium effect size, and a partial η^2 around .14 was a large effect size. For the above design there are three large effect sizes (for age main effect, the sex by treat interaction, and for the three way interaction). Recall that the above two interaction effects were significant at the .05 level, while the age main effect was not significant. Here, because of the very small sample size (only 3 subjects per cell), power was only adequate (around .70) when the effect size was very large.

4.7   FIXED AND RANDOM FACTORS

At this point it is important to distinguish between fixed and random factors. All that we have considered to this point is what is called *fixed effects* ANOVA. For example, in comparing three different diets (one way ANOVA), the diets are not randomly sampled from some population of diets, but rather they are fixed by the experimenter. Furthermore, the experimenter is not interested in generalizing to some population of diets but wishes to determine which of the diets in the study is superior to the others. Thus, inferences in the study are "fixed" or limited to the diets under consideration. There are situations in factorial designs where the experimenter may wish to generalize beyond the given levels of a factor in the study, and in this case the factor is considered random. Let us consider two examples to illustrate.

First, suppose we want to compare three different teaching methods (fixed factor) in 7 randomly selected schools in some metropolitan area. The investigator wishes to generalize to the population of schools in this area. Schools is the random factor and we have what is called in the literature a *mixed model*, since one factor (methods) is fixed while the other factor is random.

As a second example suppose we are comparing the effect of two reading methods on comprehension for second graders. We select 5 stories that we consider to be representative of second grade reading material. We have a 2(methods) $\times$ 5(stories) design. We wish to generalize the results to all stories, so that stories is the random factor.

A random factor(s) in the design introduces another complication; different error terms (something other than MS_w) are needed for testing some of the effects for significance. For instance, for the teaching methods by schools example, while MS_w is appropriate for testing the school main effect and the interaction effect for significance, the method $\times$ school interaction mean square is the appropriate error term for testing the method main effect.

4.8 SUMMARY

1. In two way ANOVA we are examining the effect of two independent variables (factors) on some dependent variable.

2. For an $A \times B$ design there are 3 hypotheses to be tested: the A main effect (that the population row means are equal), the B main effect (that the population column means are equal), and the $A \times B$ interaction effect.

3. An interaction means that the effect one factor has on the dependent variable is not the same for all levels of the other factor. Two types of interaction, ordinal and disordinal, were discussed.

4. The same error term, MS_w, is used for testing each of the 3 effects. It is a pooled estimate of within cell variability, and for equal cell size is just the average of the cell variances.

5. For balanced designs (equal cell n) the sums of squares are independent, although the F tests are not independent because they share a common error term. However, for total N even moderately large the amount of dependence is small and can be ignored for practical purposes.

6. *For disproportional cell size the sums of squares are correlated (confounded)*. Several methods have been suggested in the literature for analyzing such designs. There is now a consensus that generally the regression approach, where the unique contribution of each effect is obtained, should be used. If, however, an a priori ordering of the effects can be established, then the sequential sum of squares approach makes sense.

7. The regression approach, which yields the unique variation due to each effect, is denoted by type III sum of squares in SAS and SPSS for Windows 7.5 and 8.0.

8. Aptitude × treatment interaction (ATI) is a broad area of research that uses factorial designs, and is concerned with the possible moderating effect any individual difference characteristic (sex, age, locus of control, etc.) of subjects may have on their response to treatments.

9. In a three way ANOVA there are 7 hypotheses that are tested. The 3 main effects test whether the population level means are equal. The nature of the two way interactions is ascertained by examining the means for each pair of factors lumped over the third factor. The three way interaction indicates whether the patterns of means (profiles) for any two factors are different for the levels of the third factor.

10. Power estimation for two and three way ANOVA was discussed using Cohen's approach. The PASS 6.0 program was used to obtain power estimates quickly for different sample sizes and different alpha levels.

11. An improved Bonferroni type procedure, which makes use of p values, is discussed and illustrated.

12. A comprehensive computer example, using real data, is used to illustrate and integrate several important concepts from the chapter, as well as indicating some aspects of practical data analysis.

13. For 3 and 4 way ANOVA there are many hypotheses being tested (7 for three way and 15 for four way). It is important to note that if the .05 level is used for each effect, then the overall α level becomes quite high. Thus, 1 or 2 significant results from such a design, if not hypothesized a priori, could well be spurious.

14. The distinction between fixed and random factors is illustrated with some examples.

APPENDIX: DOING A BALANCED TWO WAY ANOVA WITH A CALCULATOR

1. Obtain the mean and variance for each cell.
2. Obtain the row, column, and grand means.
3. Obtain the error term (MS_w) as the average of the cell variances.

4. Obtain the sum of squares and mean squares for the main effects.
5. Test each of the main effects for significance.
6. Obtain the sum of squares and mean square for the interaction effect.
7. Test the interaction effect for significance.

To illustrate the above process, we consider the following age by treatment design:

		Treatments		
		1	2	3
	10 yrs	21, 27, 23	24, 32, 30	19, 30, 27
		28, 20	35, 32	20, 21
AGE				
	12 yrs	18, 25, 27	24, 16, 18	34, 28, 21
		20, 23	19, 20	30, 29

The means, cell variance, and the row, column, and grand means are as follows:

	TREATS			ROW MEANS	
	23.8	30.6	23.4	25.93	
	(12.7)	(16.8)	(23.3)		
AGE					
	22.6	19.4	28.4	23.47	
	(13.3)	(8.8)	(22.3)		
COLUMN	23.2	25	25.9	24.70	(GRAND MEAN)
MEANS					

Now we move to step 3 and obtain the error term: Recall from the chapter that for equal cell size the error term is just the average of the cell variances. Therefore,

$$MS_w = (12.7 + 16.8 + 23.3 + 13.3 + 8.8 + 22.3)/6 = 16.2$$

In step 4 we obtain the sum of squares and mean squares for the main effects (note that cell size = 5):

$$SS_{age} = 15[(25.93 - 24.7)^2 + (23.47 - 24.7)^2] = 45.39$$
$$MS_{age} = 45.39/1 = 45.39$$
$$SS_{trts} = 10[(23.2 - 24.7)^2 + (25 - 24.7)^2 + (25.9 - 24.7)^2]$$
$$= 37.8$$
$$MS_{trts} = 37.8/2 = 18.9$$

In step 5 we test the main effects for significance (we use the .05 level here).

$$F_{age} = MS_{age}/MS_w = 45.39/16.2 = 2.80$$

Since the critical value at the .05 level, based on 1 and 24 degrees of freedom, is 4.26, we fail to reject.

$$F_{trts} = MS_{trts}/MS_w = 18.9/16.2 = 1.17$$

Here the critical value, based on 2 and 24 df, is 3.40, and we once again fail to reject.

In step 6 we obtain the sum of squares and mean square for the interaction effect. Recall that the sum of squares for interaction involved cell interaction effects, and that each cell interaction effect, in words, is given by cell interaction = cell mean + grand mean − row mean − column mean. The cell interaction effects are given below:

	TREATMENTS		
	−.63	4.37	−3.74
AGE			
	.63	−4.37	3.74

Therefore,

$$SS_{int} = 5[(-.63)^2 + (4.37)^2 + (3.74)^2 + (.63)^2 + (-4.37)^2 + (3.74)^2]$$
$$= 334.814$$
$$MS_{int} = 334.814/2 = 167.407$$

Finally, in step 7 we test the interaction effect for significance:

$$F_{int} = MS_{int}/MS_w = 167.407/16.2 = 10.33$$

The critical value is 3.40. Thus, there is a significant interaction effect.

EXERCISES

1. Can you think of a fourth advantage of a factorial design?

2. Consider the following hypothetical data for an Age by Treatments factorial design:

	Treatments		
	1	2	3
10 yrs	21, 27, 23	24, 32, 30	19, 30, 27
	28, 20	35, 32	20, 21
AGE			
12 yrs	18, 25, 27	24, 16, 18	34, 28, 21
	20, 23	19, 20	30, 29

(a) Test each of the effects for significance at the .05 level using the definitional formulas given in the text. Use your calculator to obtain the mean and variance for each cell and then go from there.

(b) Which of the effects, if any, are significant? Interpret any effect which is significant.

3. Run problem 2 on the SAS GLM program.

4. Suppose that a study like that for problem 2 had been conducted, starting with 5 subjects per cell, but that for various reasons several subjects dropped out of the study leaving the following disproportional cell size data set:

	TREATMENTS		
	1	2	3
10 yrs	21, 27, 23	24, 35, 32	19, 30,
	28, 20		20, 21
AGE			
12 yrs	25, 20	24, 16, 18	28, 21
		19, 20	30, 29

(a) Run this data set on both SAS GLM and on SPSSX MANOVA. Which effects are significant at the .05 level? Interpret any significant effects.

(b) Are the Type I and Type III sums of squares different for all the effects? Explain.

5. Consider the following results from a 2×3 factorial ANOVA (4 subjects per cell) study by Pukulski (*The Reading Teacher*, 1970, 515–522):

Source of Variation	df	MS	F
Sex	1	308.16	.528
Reinforcement	2	3251.29	5.57*
Sex by Reinforcement	2	1094.29	1.87
Error	18	583.78	

$*p < .05$

(a) Estimate what his power was at $\alpha = .10$ for detecting the reinforcement main effect?

(b) Estimate power at $\alpha = .10$ for detecting the interaction effect.

(c) Given the result in (b), what would you recommend Pukulski do in a followup study?

6. Explain what Cronbach meant when he said, "Once we attend to interactions we enter a hall of mirrors that extends to infinity."

7. Suppose an investigator in a heuristic study has a two way design and 5 dependent variables. He runs 5 univariate two way ANOVA's, that is, he does a two way ANOVA on each dependent variable separately. Four of the effects are significant at the .05 level, and he is excited by these results and discusses them in some detail.

(a) What is the total number of statistical tests that was done here?

(b) What is the upper bound on overall α?

(c) Given the result in (b), should the investigator be excited, or should he be cautiously optimistic?

8. Consider again the method by teacher by sex example on p. 173.

(a) Suppose that only the AC interaction was significant. Interpret what this result means. Give a pattern of means that is congruent with the above result.

(b) Suppose that the A and C main effects and the AC interaction were the only significant effects. Interpret these results, and give a pattern of means that is congruent with these results.

9. In Section 4.4 we indicated, using definitional formulas, how various sums of squares for a three way ANOVA are calculated. Finish the calculations for that example by

(a) calculating the age by treatment sum of squares

(b) calculating the sex by age sum of squares

(c) calculating the age main effect sum of squares

10. Construct the treatment by race profiles for example 1 on p. 171 and interpret.

11. An investigator has a 3×3 (treatments by social class) factorial design and from previous literature anticipates a medium treatment main effect and a medium interaction effect. She wishes to know if having 10 subjects in each cell will yield adequate power (> .70) for detecting these two effects. Given these results, what is the estimated power for detecting the interaction at $\alpha = .10$? Is power now adequate? Obtain a somewhat rough estimate (since it involves extrapolation) of power at $\alpha = .15$.

12. Suppose an investigator actually hypothesized a significant three way inter-action effect (don't expect to find this very often in the literature). He wishes to detect a medium or larger three way interaction effect with power = .70 at α = .10. He has a $2 \times 2 \times 3$ design. How many subjects per cell are needed?

13. A study by Tuckman, Steber, and Hyman (1979) had principals rate teachers in their schools, whom they had previously nominated as effective or ineffective, on the four dimensions of the Tuckman Teacher Feedback Form: creativity, dynamism, organized demeanor, and warmth and acceptance. There were 180 teachers rated, one-third each at the elementary, intermediate, and high school levels. The primary question in the study, in the authors words was, "Do prin-cipals' judgments across the four dimensions of teaching style vary from ele-mentary to intermediate to senior high school principals? That is, do principals at the three levels perceive the four dimensions differently as elements of effective versus ineffective teaching?" They hypothesized elementary principals would see warmth and acceptance and creativity as contributing most to the discrepancy between most effective and least effective teachers while dynamism and organized demeanor were expected to be higher in importance for intermediate and high school principals.

To test their hypothesis, four two way ANOVA's were run, a separate ANOVA for each dimension of the TTFF. The independent or grouping variables are school level and effective-ineffective dimension. The following results were obtained:

		CREATIVITY		DYNAMISM		ORGANIZED DEMEANOR		WARMTH AND ACCEPTANCE	
SOURCE	DF	MS	F	MS	F	MS	F	MS	F
SCHOOL LEVEL	2	461.1	8.3*	295.6	5.1*	39.5	.8	93.0	1.6
EFFECT.	1	2268.4	40.9*	760.5	13.0*	4108.9	81.2*	4331.6	73.3*
SL × EFF.	2	64.9	1.2	717.5	12.3*	94.4	1.9	414.4	7.0*

The asterisks indicate those effects with a p value less than .01.

Also, the following means were obtained on the four variables for the six cells in the factorial design:

	CREATIVITY		DYNAMISM		ORGANIZED DEMEANOR		WARMTH AND ACCEPTANCE	
	M.E.	L.E.	M.E.	L.E.	M.E.	L.E.	M.E.	L.E.
ELEM.	27.3	22.4	25.7	28.9	34.8	27.9	39.3	23.9
INTERM.	29.2	21.8	27.9	22.8	36.8	27.0	35.6	26.5
SENIOR	24.9	15.9	28.2	17.6	36.3	24.4	31.7	26.7

(a) What are the significant interaction effects on DYNAMISM and WARMTH AND ACCEPTANCE telling us?

(b) Explain why these interaction effects occurred, using the cell means.

(c) What part(s) of their hypotheses are confirmed by the above analysis?

(d) Is further analysis necessary to validate or invalidate some of their hypotheses?

14. A study by Bryan (1974) investigated the peer popularity of learning disabled children. The learning disabled and a sample of control "normal" subjects each consisted of 35 white and 29 black boys and 10 white and 10 black girls. The children were in grades 3, 4, and 5. A combination of two sociometric techniques was used to assess peer popularity. The measures included: (a) the choice of three classmates as friends, classroom neighbors, and invitees to a birthday party; (b) the choice of three classmates who are not friends or neighbors or invitees to a birthday party; and (c) the Guess Who Technique. Sample items from this procedure include: "Who finds it hard to sit still in class? Who is handsome or pretty? Who is always worried or scared?" The scores of the children on items from the above three categories were the sum of the number of classmates who nominated the subject on that item, divided by the total number of votes cast within the classroom. The relationships among the items indicated that the 20 items could be divided into two scales: social acceptance and social rejection. These were the two dependent variables for the study. The percentages on these two variables were transformed into arc sine equivalents before analysis. This transformation is appropriate when there is reason to believe there may be a relationship between the means and the variances. Such is the case when the dependent variable involves proportions or percentages (see Myers, 1979, p. 73), as in this study. Subjects were cross classified on group (learning disabled or control), sex, and race, and three way ANOVA's were run on each dependent variable, using a least square analysis. The following results were obtained:

	Social Acceptance		Social Rejection	
		F		F
	Mean Sq	$df = 1,160$	Mean Sq	$df = 1,60$
Group (A)	.809	19.896***	.589	9.118**
Sex (B)	.149	3.667	.004	.055
Race (C)	.000	.008	.007	.112
A × B	.032	.797	.313	4.850*
A × C	.233	5.737**	.932	14.415***
B × C	.001	.019	.029	.447
A × B × C	.094	2.320	.173	.104

*p < .05
**p < .01
***p < .001

(a) Why is the degrees of freedom for error = 160?

(b) What is the numerical value of the error term for social acceptance and social rejection?

(c) The cell sizes in the study were unequal, but the exact cell sizes were not reported. Given this, should the author have checked the homogeneity of variance assumption? Why, or why not?

(d) The author presents the following table for interpreting the significant AC interactions for social acceptance and rejection:

	SOCIAL REJECTION		SOCIAL ACCEPTANCE	
	WHITE	BLACK	WHITE	BLACK
LEARNING DISABLED	15	8	4	6
CONTROL	5	9	10	7

What type of interaction (ordinal or disordinal) resulted for social rejection? for social acceptance? Does there seem to be a particular cell that is primarily responsible for the interactions in each case?

(e) Calculate the effect size for the $A \times B \times C$ interaction on social acceptance. Is this a practically significant effect which we failed to detect because of inadequate power?

16. Run a three way ANOVA on the data given below for a sex(2) $\times$ age(2) $\times$ treat(3) design. *sex / higher for treatment 2*

SEX	AGE	TREAT 1	2	3
1	1	19,16,18,17	23,24,25,28	16,12,24,10
	2	20,17,18,19	27,31,28,25	19,18,23,27
2	1	17,18,14,22	26,19,13,17	15,17,15,12
	2	13,18,20,19	14,13,21,18	14,18,19,11

(a) Test each of the effects at the .01 level. Which are significant?

(b) Interpret any significant effects using the appropriate means.

17. Consider the following subset of data (all of site 1) for a SETTING (1 for home and 2 for school) by VIEWCAT (1 for rarely watches Sesame St to 4 for watches the show on average of more than 5 times a week) factorial design. The dependent variable is LETDIFF = POSTLET-PRELET, that is, a measure of how much the children have gained in their knowledge of letters:

	VIEWCAT1	VIEWCAT2	VIEWCAT3	VIEWCAT4
HOME	0, 4	6, 4, 10, 9	14, 7, 7, 28, 16, 32	27, 21, 4
		11, 1, −2, 6, −10	8, −1, 10, 26, −22	24, 35, 5
SCHOOL	7, 3, 8, −1	−1, 4, 17, 6	11, 32, 10, 33, 14	6, 6, 4, 4
	2, −1, −1	9, 21, 5, 7	33, 30, 31, 5	24, −15, 8, 7

(a) Run a two way ANOVA on this data using either SAS or SPSS. For both the default is the unique variability due to each effect (called type III sum of squares). Which effect(s) is(are) significant at the .05 level?

(b) Using the appropriate means, interpret each of the significant effects.

18. Consider the following approximate 33% random sample of the ATTITUDE data. Here we focus on the SEX and GRADE factors and the change in mathematics attitude (CHGMATH).

		GRADE		
	3	4	5	6
MALE	−1, 0, 2, 2	0, −3, 0, −1	−1, 1, 1, −1	1, 2, 0, 3, 1
	−1, 0, 2, 2	3, −5, 0, 3		1, −4, 1, 0
FEMALE	3, −2, −2, 2, −2	−1, −1, −3, 0	−1, −1, 0, 0	−1, 1, 1, −4, −1
	−3, −1, 0, 0, −1, 1	2, 0, 0, 0	0, 0, −1, 0, 0	0, 4, 1, −1, 0

(a) Using either SPSS or SAS, test each of the effects for significance at the .05 level. Which, if any, are significant?

5
Repeated Measures Analysis

5.1 INTRODUCTION

In our discussion of one way ANOVA and factorial ANOVA the subjects were only measured once on the dependent variable. In this chapter we consider designs that measure subjects several times, either on the same dependent variable or on different measures. The simplest repeated measures design measures the subjects twice, with an intervening treatment. Schematically, we have

Pretest   Treatment   Posttest

203

In this case the student may recall that the t test for correlated (dependent) samples applies. Repeated measures analysis of variance (where the subjects are measured more than twice) is the generalization of the t test for correlated samples, just as ANOVA (k groups) was the generalization of the t test (two groups) for independent samples.

There are many situations in which repeated measures are either appropriate or the natural thing to use. For example, if we are concerned with performance trends over time. Bock (1975) presented an example comparing boys' and girls' performance on vocabulary acquisition over grades 8 through 11. Here the focus is often on the mathematical form of the trend, that is, whether it is linear, quadratic, etc. The same type of analysis applies whether we are concerned with cognitive variables (as above), or personality changes for a group of subjects over time, or developmental (physiological) changes for a group of infants (children).

Another class of repeated measures situations occurs when we are comparing the same subjects under several different treatments (drugs, stimulus displays of different complexity, etc.). For example, we may be interested in the effects of 4 drugs on reaction time for a group of subjects, or in the effects of repeated practice (say over 3 sessions) on a learning task.

Another useful application of repeated measures occurs in combination with a one way ANOVA design. In a one way design involving treatments the subjects are posttested to determine which treatment is best. If we are interested in the lasting or residual effects of treatments, then we need to measure the subjects a few more times. Huck, Cormier, and Bounds (1974) present an example in which three teaching methods are being compared, but in addition the subjects are again measured 6 weeks and 12 weeks later to determine the residual effect of the methods on achievement. A repeated measures analysis of such data *could* yield a quite different conclusion as to which method might be preferred. Suppose the pattern of means looked as follows:

	Posttest	Six Weeks	12 Weeks
Method 1	66	64	63
Method 2	69	65	59
Method 3	62	56	52

Just looking at a one way ANOVA on posttest scores (if significant) could lead one to conclude that method 2 is best. Examination of the pattern of achievement over time shows however that for lasting effect method 1 is to be preferred, because after 12 weeks the achievement for method 1 is superior to method 2 (63 vs. 59). What we have here is an example of a method by time interaction effect.

Another class of situations in which repeated measures designs apply is when the same subjects are given a series of tests or subtests. For instance, Glass and

Hopkins (1984) present the following example. A group of 12 neurologically handicapped children are measured on the information, vocabulary, digit span, and block design subtests of the Wechsler Intelligence Scale for Children (WISC). If the 12 fall into, say, 3 different types of neurological handicaps, then we may be interested in whether certain deficits on WISC are particularly associated with different types of handicaps. Here a subject by subtest interaction is the focus.

In this chapter we consider repeated measures designs of varying complexity. The simplest design involves a single group of subjects measured under various treatments (conditions), or at different points in time. Schematically, it looks like this:

$$\textit{Treatments}$$

		1	2	3	....	k
	1					
Subjects	2					
	n					

We then consider a one between and one within design. Many texts use the terms "between" and "within" in referring to repeated measures factors. A be-tween variable is simply a grouping or classification variable such as sex, age, or social class. A within variable is one on which the subjects have been measured repeatedly (like time). Some authors even refer to repeated measures designs as within designs (Keppel, 1983). An example of a one between and one within design is

DRUGS

	1	2	3
Schizophrenics			
Depressives			

Here the *same* schizophrenics and depressives are given three drugs to deter-mine which of them is best in inhibiting some undesirable response. The teaching methods study mentioned previously is another example of a one between and one within design, where methods is the between variable (different subjects taught by different methods) and time is the within variable. The reader should be aware that there are three other names that are used by some authors for the same design: Lindquist Type I, split plot, and two way ANOVA, with repeated measures on one factor.

Next we consider a one between and two within design. As an example, suppose a researcher in child development is interested in observing three groups of children (ages 3, 4, and 5) in two situations at two different times (morning and afternoon) of the day. She is concerned with the extent of their social interaction, and will measure this by having two observers independently rate the amount of social interaction. The average of the two ratings will serve as the dependent variable. The age of the children is the grouping or between variable here. The two within variables are situation and time of day. There are four scores for each child: social interaction in situation 1 in the morning, social interaction in situation 1 in the afternoon, social interaction in situation 2 in the morning, and social interaction for situation 2 in the afternoon.

Schematically, the design is as follows:

	SITUATION	1		2	
	TIME	Morn.	After	Morn.	After
	3 years	y_1	y_2	y_3	y_4
AGE	4 years				
	5 years				

where the y's represent the four social interaction measures for each subject. One can think of this as a three way ANOVA, but it is a *different* type of analysis of variance from that in Chapter 4, because the subjects' scores are correlated across situation and across time, and this must be taken into account in the analysis.

Finally, we discuss planned comparisons in repeated measures designs.

5.2 ADVANTAGES AND DISADVANTAGES OF REPEATED MEASURES DESIGNS

Recall that the two basic objectives in experimental design are elimination of systematic bias and the reduction of error (within gp or cell) variance. The main reason for within group variability is individual differences among the subjects. One way of reducing error variance is considered in Chapter 7 on factorial designs, and that is by blocking on a variable. One may block on sex, social class, I.Q., etc. All of the variability between blocks is removed from the error term, yielding a more powerful test. In repeated measures designs, blocking is carried to its extreme. We are blocking on each subject. Thus, variability among the subjects due to individual differences is completely removed from the error term. This makes these designs much more powerful than completely randomized designs, where different subjects are randomly assigned to different treatments.

Another distinct advantage of repeated measures designs is that far fewer subjects are required for the study. For example, if three treatments are involved in a completely randomized design, we may require 60 subjects (20 per treatment). With a repeated measures design, we would need only 20 subjects. This can be a very important practical advantage in many cases, since numerous subjects are not readily available in some areas like counseling, school psychology, clinical psychology, and nursing.

Although increased precision and economy of subjects are two distinct advantages of repeated measures designs, these designs have two potentially serious disadvantages, unless care is taken. When several treatments are involved, the *order* in which treatments are administered might make a difference in the subjects' performance. Thus, it is important to *counterbalance* the order of treatments. For three treatments, counterbalancing involves randomly assigning one third of the subjects to each of the following sequences:

Order of Administration of Treatments

A	B	C
B	C	A
C	A	B

Another potential disadvantage is the possibility of carryover effects. Thus, it is important to allow sufficient time between treatments to minimize carryover effects, which could occur for example if the treatments were drugs. How much time is necessary is of course a substantive, not a statistical question. Keppel (1983) and Myers (1979) provide further discussion of the two above potential disadvantages.

5.3 SINGLE GROUP REPEATED MEASURES

To illustrate how the variance is partitioned for this simplest design we consider the following data set:

Subjects	Treatments 1	2	3	Means
1	30	28	34	30.667
2	14	18	22	18.000
3	24	20	30	24.667
4	38	34	44	38.667
5	26	28	30	28.000
Column Means	26.4	25.6	32	28.000 (grand mean)

We analyze this data in two different ways: (1) as a completely randomized design (pretending there are different subjects for the different treatments), and (2) as a univariate repeated measures analysis. The purpose of including approach 1 is to contrast the error variance that results against the markedly smaller error variance found with the repeated measures design. The reason we mention *univariate* repeated measures analysis is because there is a multivariate approach that can be employed. We discuss and compare the univariate and multivariate approaches after presenting this numerical example.

5.4   COMPLETELY RANDOMIZED DESIGN

This simply involves doing a one way ANOVA, as was done in Chapter 2. Thus, we compute the sums of squares between (SS_b) and the sum of squares within (SS_w):

$$SS_b = 5[(26.4 - 28)^2 + (25.6 - 28)^2 + (32 - 28)^2] = 121.6$$
$$SS_w = (30 - 26.4)^2 + (14 - 26.4)^2 + \cdots + (26 - 26.4)^2 \quad \text{treatment 1}$$
$$\qquad + (28 - 25.6)^2 + (18 - 25.6)^2 + \cdots + (28 - 25.6)^2 \quad \text{treatment 2}$$
$$\qquad + (34 - 32)^2 + (22 - 32)^2 + \cdots + (30 - 32)^2 \quad \text{treatment 3}$$
$$SS_w = 734.4$$

Now, we need the mean squares:

$$MS_b = SS_b/(k - 1) = 121.6/2 = 60.80 \quad \text{and}$$
$$MS_w = SS_w/(N - k) = 734.4/12 = 61.20$$

Therefore, $F = MS_b/MS_w = 60.80/61.20 = .99$, which is clearly not significant at the .05 level since we have more error variation than effect variation.

5.5   UNIVARIATE REPEATED MEASURES ANALYSIS

Notice that the mean responses for the subjects over the 3 treatments vary considerably (ranging from 18 to 38.667). We quantify this variability through the so-called sum of squares for blocks (SS_{bl}), where here we are blocking on subjects. The error variability that was calculated for the completely randomized analysis is split up into two parts, that is, $SS_w = SS_{bl} + SS_{res}$, where SS_{res} stands for the sum of squares residual. Denote the number of repeated measures by k. Now we calculate the sum of squares for blocks:

$$SS_{bl} = k \cdot \Sigma (\bar{x}_i - \bar{x})^2$$
$$\qquad = 3[(30.667 - 28)^2 + (18 - 28)^2 + \cdots + (28 - 28)^2] = 696.02$$

Our error term for the repeated measures analysis is formed by subtracting the sum of squares for blocks from the sum of squares within, $SS_{res} = SS_w - SS_{bl} = 734.4 - 696.02 = 38.38$. Note that the vast majority of the within variability is due to individual differences (696.02 out of 734.4), and that we have removed all of this from our error term. The variability that remains is due to *within subject* variability over treatments. Now,

$$MS_{res} = SS_{res}/(n - 1)(k - 1) = 38.38/4(2) = 4.8$$

and our F ratio for the repeated measures analysis is

$$F = MS_b/MS_{res} = 60.80/4.8 = 12.67$$

with $(k - 1) = 2$ and $(n - 1)(k - 1) = 4(2) = 8$ degrees of freedom. This is significant at the .05 level (critical value $= 4.46$), in contrast to the F for the randomized analysis, which was less than 1.

5.6 ASSUMPTIONS IN REPEATED MEASURES ANALYSIS

The three assumptions for a single group univariate repeated measures analysis are:

1. independence of the observations
2. multivariate normality
3. sphericity (sometimes called circularity)

The first two assumptions are also required for the multivariate approach, but the sphericity assumption is not necessary. The reader should recall from Chapter 2 that a violation of the independence assumption is very serious for independent samples ANOVA, and the same holds true for repeated measures analysis. Multivariate normality is somewhat difficult to characterize; however, it does require normality on each of the individual measures. Recall again from Chapter 2 that ANOVA was robust against non-normality. There is also a fair amount of evidence to suggest (Stevens, 1986, p. 207) that MANOVA is also robust against lack of multivariate normality, with respect to type I error.

Before we specify what sphericity means, we wish to note that for many years it was thought that a *stronger* condition called uniformity (compound symmetry) was necessary. The uniformity condition required equality of the population variances for all treatments and also that all population covariances be equal. Schematically for three repeated measures the uniformity condition looks like this:

	1	2	3
1	σ^2	σ_c	σ_c
2	σ_c	σ^2	σ_c
3	σ_c	σ_c	σ^2

In the above, σ^2 represents the common population variance for the three repeated measures, and σ_c represents the common population covariance. Huynh and Feldt (1970) and Rounet and Lepine (1970) independently showed that sphericity is an *exact* condition for the F test to be valid. Sphericity only requires that the variances of the differences for *all pairs* of repeated measures need to be equal. Sphericity is a weaker condition than uniformity, and defines an additional class of situations where the univariate approach is valid. Consider the covariance matrix below:

$$S = \begin{array}{c} \\ \\ \\ \end{array} \begin{array}{ccc} y_1 & y_2 & y_3 \\ \left[\begin{array}{ccc} 1.0 & .5 & 1.5 \\ .5 & 3.0 & 2.5 \\ 1.5 & 2.5 & 5.0 \end{array} \right] \end{array}$$

The formula for the variance of the difference scores for the ith and jth repeated measures is given by

$$s^2_{i-j} = s^2_i + s^2_j - 2 s_{ij}$$

Now we calculate the variance for the differences for each pair of repeated measures

$$s^2_{1-2} = s^2_1 + s^2_2 - 2 s_{12} = 1 + 3 - 2(.5) = 3$$
$$s^2_{1-3} = 1 + 5 - 2(1.5) = 3$$
$$s^2_{2-3} = 3 + 5 - 2(2.5) = 3$$

The variances are the same for all difference variables, which means the sphericity condition is met, even though uniformity is most definitely not satisfied (all the variances are unequal and the covariances are all unequal).

The multivariate approach to repeated measures is valid for *any* covariance matrix for the repeated measures.

Box (1954) showed that if the sphericity assumption is not met, then the F ratio for the univariate approach is positively biased (we are rejecting falsely too often). In other words, we may set our α level at .05, but may be rejecting falsely 8% or 10% of the time. The extent to which the covariance matrix deviates from sphericity is reflected in a parameter called ε (Greenhouse & Geisser, 1959). We give the formula in Exercise 3 for those who are interested. Since $\hat{\varepsilon}$ is printed out by SPSS and SAS, there is no need to go through all the tedious calculations. If sphericity is met, then $\varepsilon = 1$, while for the worst possible violation the value of $\varepsilon = 1/(k-1)$, where k is the number of repeated measures. To adjust for the positive bias Greenhouse and Geisser suggest altering the degrees of freedom from

$$(k - 1) \text{ and } (k - 1)(n - 1) \text{ to } 1 \text{ and } (n - 1)$$

that is, dividing both degrees of freedom by $(k - 1)$.

Doing this makes the test *very* conservative, since adjustment is made for the worst possible case, and we don't recommend it. A more reasonable approach is to estimate ε. Then adjust the degrees of freedom from

$$(k - 1) \text{ and } (k - 1)(n - 1) \text{ to } \hat{\varepsilon} \, (k - 1) \text{ and } \hat{\varepsilon} \, (k - 1)(n - 1)$$

Results from Collier, Baker, Mandeville, and Hayes (1967) and Stoloff (1967) show that this approach keeps the actual α very close to the level of significance.

Huynh and Feldt (1976) found that even multiplying the degrees of freedom by $\hat{\varepsilon}$ is somewhat conservative when the true value of ε is above about .70. They recommended using the following for those situations:

$$\hat{\varepsilon} = \frac{n(i - 1)\hat{\varepsilon} - 2}{(i - 1)[(n - 1) - (i - 1)\hat{\varepsilon}]}$$

The above Huynh epsilon can be printed out by both SPSS MANOVA and SAS GLM.

There are statistical tests for checking sphericity, for example, the Mauchley test presented on SPSS. However, based on the results of Monte Carlo studies (Keselman, Rogan, Mendoza, & Breen, 1980), we don't recommend using these tests.

5.7   SHOULD WE USE THE UNIVARIATE OR MULTIVARIATE APPROACH?

In terms of controlling on type I error, there is no real basis for preferring the multivariate approach, since use of the modified (adjusted) univariate test (i.e., multiplying the degrees of freedom by $\hat{\varepsilon}$) yields an honest error rate. The choice then involves a question of power. Now assuming sphericity, the univariate test is more powerful. When sphericity is violated, however, the situation is much more complex. Davidson (1972) has stated, "when small but reliable effects are present with the effects being highly variable . . . the multivariate test is far more powerful than the univariate test" (p. 452). And O'Brien and Kaiser (1985), after mentioning several studies that compared the power of the multivariate and modified univariate tests, state, "Even though a limited number of situations has been investigated, this work found that no procedure is uniformly more powerful or even usually the most powerful" (p. 319). Thus, given an exploratory study, we agree with Barcikowski and Robey (1984), who recommend that *both* the univariate and multivariate tests be routinely used because they may differ in the treatment effects that they discern. In such a study half the experimentwise level of significance might be set for each test. Thus, if we wish our overall $\alpha = .05$, simply do each test at $\alpha = .025$.

5.8 COMPUTER ANALYSIS ON SAS AND SPSS FOR EXAMPLE

In Table 5.1 we present the complete control lines for running the single group repeated measures example given in Section 5.3 on SAS GLM and SPSS MANOVA. Table 5.2 gives the means and standard deviations for the three

TABLE 5.1
SAS and SPSS Control Lines for Single Group Repeated Measures

SAS	SPSS

TITLE 'SINGLE GP REPEATED MEASURES';
DATA SINGLE;
① INPUT SUBJ TREAT REAC @@;
LINES;
② 1 1 30   1 2 28   1 3 34
  2 1 14   2 2 18   2 3 22
  3 1 24   3 2 20   3 3 30
  4 1 38   4 2 34   4 3 44
  5 1 26   5 2 28   5 3 30
PROC PRINT;
PROC GLM;
③ CLASS SUBJ TREAT;
MODEL REAC=SUBJ TREAT;
	TITLE 'REPEATED MEASURES'.
	DATA LIST FREE/Y1 Y2 Y3.
	BEGIN DATA.
	30 28 34 14 18 22 24 20 30
	38 34 44 26 28 30
	END DATA.
	LIST.
	MANOVA Y1 Y2 Y3/
	④ WSFACTOR=TREAT(3)/
	    WSDESIGN/
	⑤⑥ ANALYSIS(REPEATED)/
	    PRINT=TRANSFORM CELLINFO(MEANS)
	    SIGNIF(UNIV AVERF)/.

①In order to run the single group repeated measures on SAS we treat it as a two way ANOVA, with subjects and treatments as the grouping variables and reaction as the dependent variable.

②The first two numbers of each block of three gives the cell identification. Thus, the first subject in treatment 1 (1 1) had a reaction score of 30, the second subject in treatment 3 (2 3) had a reaction score of 22, etc.

③In the CLASS statement we list the classification or grouping variables, which here are subject and treatment.

④The WSFACTOR (within subject factor) and the WSDESIGN (within subject design) are fundamental to running repeated measures analysis on SPSS MANOVA. In the WSFACTOR subcommand we specify which are the repeated measures, or within subject, factors. And we indicate, in parentheses, the number of levels for each repeated measures factor. The WSDESIGN specifies the design on the repeated measures. Here it is simply the treatment effect.

⑤The TRANSFORM part of the PRINT subcommand prints out in columns the uncorrelated, transformed variables that are created by the program for the multivariate approach (cf. Stevens, 1986, Chapter 13).

⑥The UNIV is necessary to obtain the significance tests for each of the transformed variables created by the program for the multivariate approach to repeated measures. The AVERF yields the *unadjusted*, overall univariate test for repeated measures.

TABLE 5.2
Means and Standard Deviations for the Drug Data

CELL MEANS AND STANDARD DEVIATIONS		
VARIABLE . . Y1		
	MEAN	STD. DEV.
FOR ENTIRE SAMPLE	26.400	8.764
VARIABLE . . Y2		
	MEAN	STD. DEV.
FOR ENTIRE SAMPLE	25.600	6.542
VARIABLE . . Y3		
	MEAN	STD. DEV.
FOR ENTIRE SAMPLE	32.000	8.000

repeated measures variables, and Table 5.3 presents selected, annotated output from SAS GLM.

5.9 POST HOC PROCEDURES
IN REPEATED MEASURES ANALYSIS

As in a one way ANOVA, if an overall difference is found, one would almost always want to determine where the differences lie. This involves a post hoc procedure. There are several reasons for preferring pairwise procedures: (1) they are easily interpreted, (2) they are quite meaningful, and (3) some of these procedures are fairly powerful. The Tukey procedure is appropriate in repeated measures analysis, provided that the sphericity assumption is met. For the drug example this assumption is tenable. We apply the Tukey there, setting overall α = .05. Thus, we take at most a 5% chance of one or more false rejections. Recall that we discussed the Tukey procedure in Chapter 2. Remember that the studentized range statistic (denoted by q) is used in the procedure. If there are k groups and the total sample size is N, then any two means are declared significantly different at the .05 level if the following inequality is satisfied:

$$|\bar{x}_i - \bar{x}_j| > q_{.05;k,N-k} \sqrt{MS_w/n},$$

where MS_w is the error term for the one way ANOVA, and n is the common group size. The modification of the Tukey for the one sample repeated measures design is

$$|\bar{x}_i - \bar{x}_j| > q_{.05;k,(n-1)(k-1)} \sqrt{MS_{res}/n}, \tag{1}$$

TABLE 5.3
Selected Output From SAS GLM for Single Group Repeated Measures

SINGLE SAMPLE REP MEASURES
General Linear Models Procedure

Dependent Variable: REAC

Source	DF	Sum of Squares	Mean Square	F Value	Pr > F
Model	6	817.60000000	136.26666667	28.39	0.0001
Error	8	38.40000000	4.80000000		
Corrected Total	14	856.00000000			

R-Square	C.V.	Root MSE	REAC Mean
0.955140	7.824608	2.19089023	28.00000000

Source	DF	Type I SS	Mean Square	F Value	Pr > F
SUBJ	4	696.00000000	174.00000000	36.25	0.0001
TREAT	2	121.60000000	60.80000000	12.67	0.0033

Source	DF	Type III SS	Mean Square	F Value	Pr > F
SUBJ	4	696.00000000	174.00000000	36.25	0.0001
TREAT	2	121.60000000	60.80000000	12.67	0.0033

where $(n - 1)(k - 1)$ is the error degrees of freedom and MS_{res} is the error term, replacing MS_w.

The means, from Table 5.2 are 26.4, 25.6, and 32. If we set overall $\alpha = .05$, then the appropriate studentized range value is $q_{.05;3,8} = 4.041$. The error term, from Table 5.3, is 4.8 and the number of subjects is $n = 5$. Therefore, two treatments will be declared significantly different if

$$|\bar{x}_i - \bar{x}_j| > 4.041 \sqrt{4.8/5} = 3.96$$

Thus, treatment 3 differs from" treatments 1 and 2, but treatments 1 and 2 are not significantly different (as one would have suspected).

There are several other pairwise procedures that Maxwell (1980) discusses in a Monte Carlo study that compared the procedures control on overall α when the sphericity assumption is violated. We present his results for the Tukey and Bonferroni approaches in Table 5.4. The Bonferroni approach in the repeated measures context involves the use of multiple *dependent* t tests. For example, if there are five treatments, then there will be ten paired comparisons. If we wish overall $\alpha = .05$, then we simply do each dependent t test at the $.05/10 = .005$ level of significance. Results from Table 5.4 show that the Bonferroni approach keeps the actual $\alpha <$ level of significance in all cases, even when there is a severe

TABLE 5.4

Type I Error Rates for the Tukey and Bonferroni Procedures under Different Violations of the Sphericity Assumption

| | | k = 3 | | k = 4 | | k = 5 | |
		Tukey	Bonf	Tukey	Bonf	Tukey	Bonf
n	ϵ	min ϵ = .50		min ϵ = .33		min ϵ = .25	
15	1.00	.041	.039	.045	.043	.050	.040
15	.86	.043	.036				
15	.74	.051	.033				
15	.54	.073	.033				
15	.53			.081	.030		
15	.49			.087	.036		
15	.831					.061	.044
15	.752					.067	.042
15	.522					.081	.038
8	.860	.048	.042				
8	.740	.054	.038				
8	.540	.078	.036				
8	.530			.084	.042		
8	.490			.095	.032		
8	.831					.058	.044
8	.752					.060	.042
8	.522					.076	.044

violation of the sphericity assumption (e.g., for $k = 3$ the min $\varepsilon = .50$ and one of the conditions modeled had $\varepsilon = .54$). Because of this, Maxwell recommended the Bonferroni approach for post hoc pairwise comparisons in repeated measures analysis if the sphericity assumption is violated. Maxwell also studied the power of the five approaches, and found the Tukey to be most powerful. When $\varepsilon > .70$ in Table 5.4, the deviation of actual α from the level of significance is less than .02 for the Tukey procedure. This, coupled with the fact that the Tukey tends to be most powerful, would lead us to prefer the Tukey when $\varepsilon > .070$. When $\varepsilon < .70$, however, then we agree with Maxwell that the Bonferroni approach should be used.

5.10   ONE BETWEEN AND ONE WITHIN FACTOR—
A TREND ANALYSIS

We now consider a slightly more complex design, adding a grouping (between) variable. An investigator interested in verbal learning randomly assigns 12 subjects to two treatments. She obtains recall scores on verbal material after 1, 2, 3, 4, and 5 days. Treatments is the grouping variable. She expects them to be a significant effect over time, but wishes a more focused assessment. She wants to mathematically model the form of the decline in verbal recall. For this, trend analysis is appropriate and in particular orthogonal (uncorrelated) polynomials are in order. If the decline in recall is essentially constant over the days, then a significant linear (straight line) trend, or first degree polynomial, will be found. On the other hand, if the decline in recall is slow over the first two days and then drops sharply over the remaining 3 days, a quadratic trend (part of a parabola), or second degree polynomial, will be found. Finally, if the decline is slow at first, then drops off sharply for the next few days and finally levels off, we will find a cubic trend, or third degree polynomial. We illustrate each of these cases below:

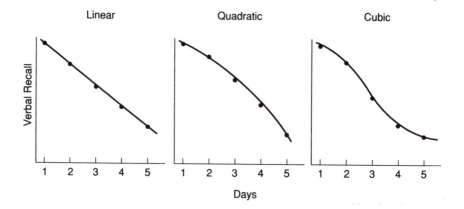

The fact that the polynomials are uncorrelated means that the linear, quadratic, cubic, and quartic components are partitioning distinct (different) parts of the variation in the data.

In Table 5.5 we present the SAS and SPSS control lines for running the trend analysis on this verbal recall data. In Chapter 2, in discussing planned comparisons, we indicated that several types of contrasts are available in SPSS MANOVA (Helmert, special, polynomial, etc.), and we also illustrated the use of the Helmert and special contrasts; here the polynomial contrast option is used. Recall these are built into the program, so that all we need do is request them, which is what has been done in the CONTRAST subcommand.

When several groups are involved, as in our verbal recall example, an *additional* assumption is homogeneity of the covariance matrices on the repeated measures for the groups. In our example the group sizes are equal, and in this case a violation of the equal covariance matrices assumption is not serious. That is, the test statistic is robust (with respect to type I error) against a violation of this assumption (cf. Stevens, 1986, Chapter 6). However, if the group sizes are substantially unequal, then a violation is serious, and we indicate in Table 5.5 what should be added to test the assumption.

Table 5.6 gives the means and standard deviations for the two groups on the 5 repeated measures. In Table 5.7 we present selected, annotated output from SPSS MANOVA for the trend analysis. Results from that table show that the groups do not differ significantly ($F = .04$, $p < .837$) and that there is not a significant group by days interaction ($F = 1.2$, $p < .323$). There is, however, a quite significant days main effect, and in particular, the LINEAR and CUBIC trends are significant at the .05 level ($F = 239.14$, $p < .000$ and $F = 10.51$, $p < .006$, respectively). The linear trend is by far the most pronounced, and a graph of the means for the data in Figure 5.1 shows this, although a cubic curve (with a few bends) will fit the data slightly better.

In concluding this example, the following from Myers (1979) is important:

Trend or orthogonal polynomial analyses should never be routinely applied whenever one or more independent variables are quantitative. . . . It is dangerous to identify statistical components freely with psychological processes. It is one thing to postulate a cubic component of A, to test for it, and to find it significant, thus substantiating the theory. It is another matter to assign psychological meaning to a significant component that has not been postulated on a priori grounds. (p. 456)

5.11 POST HOC PROCEDURES FOR THE ONE BETWEEN AND ONE WITHIN DESIGN

In the one between and one within, or mixed model, repeated measures design, we have both the assumption of sphericity *and* homogeneity of the covariance matrices for the different levels of the between factor. This combination of assumptions has been called multisample sphericity. Keselman and Keselman (1988) conducted a

TABLE 5.5
SAS Control Lines and SPSS Command Syntax File
for One Between and One Within Repeated Measures Analysis

SAS	SPSS
TITLE '1 BETW & 1 WITHIN';	TITLE 'ONE BETWEEN AND ONE WITHIN –
DATA TREND;	INTERM. BOOK P.204'.
INPUT GPID Y1 Y2 Y3 Y4 Y5;	DATA LIST FREE/GPID Y1 Y2 Y3 Y4 Y5.
CARDS;	BEGIN DATA.
1 26 20 18 11 10	1 26 20 18 11 10 1 34 35 29 22 23
1 34 35 29 22 23	1 41 37 25 18 15
1 41 37 25 18 15	1 29 28 22 15 13 1 35 34 27 21 17
1 29 28 22 15 13	1 28 22 17 14 10
1 35 34 27 21 17	1 38 34 28 25 22 1 43 37 30 27 25
1 28 22 17 14 10	2 42 38 26 20 15 2 31 27 21 18 13
1 38 34 28 25 22	2 45 40 33 25 18
1 43 37 30 27 25	2 29 25 17 13 8 2 39 32 28 22 18
2 42 38 26 20 15	2 33 30 24 18 7
2 31 27 21 18 13	2 34 30 25 24 23 2 37 31 25 22 20
2 45 40 33 25 18	END DATA.
2 29 25 17 13 8	LIST.
2 29 32 28 22 18	MANOVA Y1 TO Y5 BY GPID(1,2)/
2 33 30 24 18 7	③ WSFACTOR=DAY(5)/
2 34 30 25 24 23	④ CONTRAST(DAY)=POLYNOMIAL/
2 37 31 25 22 20	③ WSDESIGN=DAY/
PROC GLM;	⑤ RENAME=MEAN,LINEAR,QUAD,CUBIC,QUART/
CLASS GPID;	PRINT=TRANSFORM CELLINFO(MEANS)
MODEL Y1 Y2 Y3 Y4 Y5=GPID;	SIGNIF(AVERF)/
① REPEATED DAY 5 (1 2 3 4 5)	ANALYSIS(REPEATED)/
② POLYNOMIAL/SUMMARY;	⑥ DESIGN=GPID/.

①The REPEATED statement is fundamental for running repeated measures designs on SAS. The general form is REPEATED factorname levels (level values) transformation/options; Note that the level values are in parentheses. We are interested in polynomial contrasts on the repeated measures, and so that is what has been requested. Other transformations are available (HELMERT, PROFILE, etc.—see SAS USER's GUIDE: STATISTICS, Version 5, p. 454).

②SUMMARY here produces ANOVA tables for each contrast defined by the within subject factors.

③Recall again that the WSFACTOR (within subject factor) and the WSDESIGN (within subject design) subcommands are fundamental for running multivariate repeated measures analysis on SPSS.

④If we wish trend analysis on the DAY repeated measure variable, then all we need do is request POLYNOMIAL on the CONTRAST subcommand.

⑤In this RENAME subcommand we are giving meaningful names to the polynomial contrasts being generated.

⑥It is important to realize that with SPSS MANOVA there is a design subcommand (WSDESIGN) for the within or repeated measures factor(s) and a *separate* DESIGN subcommand for the between(grouping) factor(s).

TABLE 5.6
Means and Standard Deviations for One Between and
One Within Repeated Measures

CELL MEANS AND STANDARD DEVIATIONS				
VARIABLE . . Y1				
FACTOR	CODE	MEAN	STD. DEV.	N
GPID	1	34.250	6.228	8
GPID	2	36.250	5.523	8
FOR ENTIRE SAMPLE		35.250	5.779	16
VARIABLE . . Y2				
FACTOR	CODE	MEAN	STD. DEV.	N
GPID	1	30.875	6.728	8
GPID	2	31.625	5.097	8
FOR ENTIRE SAMPLE		31.250	5.779	16
VARIABLE . . Y3				
FACTOR	CODE	MEAN	STD. DEV.	N
GPID	1	24.500	4.986	8
GPID	2	24.875	4.704	8
FOR ENTIRE SAMPLE		24.687	4.686	16
VARIABLE . . Y4				
FACTOR	CODE	MEANS	STD. DEV.	N
GPID	1	19.125	5.592	8
GPID	2	20.250	3.882	8
FOR ENTIRE SAMPLE		19.687	4.686	16
VARIABLE . . Y5				
FACTOR	CODE	MEAN	STD. DEV.	N
GPID	1	16.875	5.890	8
GPID	2	15.250	5.651	8
FOR ENTIRE SAMPLE		16.062	5.639	16

Monte Carlo study examining how well four post hoc procedures controlled overall alpha under various violations of multisample sphericity. The four procedures were: the Tukey, a modified Tukey employing a nonpooled estimate of error, a Bonferroni t statistic, and a t statistic with a multivariate critical value. These procedures were also used in the Maxwell (1980) study of post hoc procedures for the single group repeated measures design.

Keselman and Keselman set the number of groups at 3 and considered 4 and 8 levels for the within (repeated) factor. They considered both equal and unequal group sizes for the between factor. Recall that ε quantifies departure from sphericity, and $\varepsilon = 1$ means sphericity, with $1/(k - 1)$ indicating maximum departure from sphericity. They investigated $\varepsilon = .75$ (a relatively mild departure) and $\varepsilon = .40$ (a severe departure for the 4 level case, given the minimum value there would

TABLE 5.7
Selected Output from SPSS for One Between and One Within

```
ORTHONORMALIZED TRANSFORMATION MATRIX (TRANSPOSED)

        MEAN      LINEAR        QUAD        CUBIC       QUART

Y1     .44721    -.63246      .53452      -.31623      .11952
Y2     .44721    -.31623     -.26726       .63246     -.47809
Y3     .44721     .00000   ② -.53452       .00000      .71714
Y4     .41721     .31623     -.26726      -.63246     -.47809
Y5     .44721     .63246      .53452       .31623      .11952
```

TESTS OF BETWEEN-SUBJECTS EFFECTS.

TESTS OF SIGNIFICANCE FOR MEAN USING UNIQUE SUMS OF SQUARES

SOURCE OF VARIATION	SS	DF	MS	F	SIG OF F
WITHIN CELLS	1764.67	14	126.05		
CONSTANT	51562.01	1	51562.01	409.07	.000
GPID	5.51	1	5.51	.04 ①	.837

TESTS INVOLVING 'DAYS' WITHIN-SUBJECT EFFECT.

```
MAUCHLY SPHERICITY TEST, W =        .09678
CHI-SQUARE APPROX. =              28.99686 WITH 9 D. F.
SIGNIFICANCE =                      .001

GREENHOUSE-GEISSER EPSILON =    ③  .44629
HUYNH-FELDT EPSILON =               .54366
LOWER-BOUND EPSILON =               .25000
```

EFFECT . . DAYS (CONT.)
UNIVARIATE F-TESTS WITH (1, 14) D. F.

①The group and group by days interaction are not significant, although the unadjusted DAYS main effect is significant at the .05 level.

②The last four columns of numbers are the coefficients for orthogonal polynomials, although they may look strange since each column is scaled such that the sum of the squared coefficients equals 1. Textbooks typically present the coefficients for 5 levels as follows:

Linear	-2	-1	0	1	2
Quadratic	2	-1	-2	-1	2
Cubic	-1	2	0	-2	1
Quartic	1	-4	6	-4	1

Compare, for example, *Fundamentals of Experimental Design*, Myers, 1979, p. 548.

③This value of $\hat{\varepsilon}$ indicates a severe violation of the sphericity assumption, although the adjusted univariate test is still easily significant at the .05 level.

(Continued)

TABLE 5.7
(Continued)

Tests involving 'DAY' Within-Subject Effect

AVERAGED Tests of Significance for Y using UNIQUE sums of squares

Source of Variation	SS	DF	MS	F	Sig of F
WITHIN+RESIDUAL	338.70	56	6.05		
DAY	4025.18	4	1006.29	166.38	.000
GPID BY DAY	28.92	4	7.23	1.20	.323

Estimates for LINEAR
- - - Individual univariate .9500 confidence intervals

DAY

Parameter	Coeff.	Std. Err.	t-Value	Sig. t	Lower -95%	CL- Upper
1	-15.791624	1.02118	-15.46415	.00000	-17.98183	-13.60142

GPID BY DAY

Parameter	Coeff.	Std. Err.	t-Value	Sig. t	Lower -95%	CL- Upper
2	1.08703295	1.02118	1.06449	.30512	-1.10317	3.27724

(Continued)

TABLE 5.7
(Continued)

Estimates for QUAD
--- Individual univariate .9500 confidence intervals

	Coeff.	Std. Err.	t-Value	Sig. t	Lower -95%	CL- Upper
DAY						
Parameter						
1	.618041622	.49014	1.26096	.22793	-.43320	1.66928
GPID BY DAY						
Parameter						
2	.250557414	.49014	.51120	.61718	-.80068	1.30180

Estimates for CUBIC
--- Individual univariate .9500 confidence intervals

	Coeff.	Std. Err.	t-Value	Sig. t	Lower -95%	CL- Upper
DAY						
Parameter						
1	1.24514683	.38404	3.24221	.00590	.42146	2.06884
Parameter						
2	.691748238	.38404	1.80123	.09324	-.13194	1.51544

Estimates for QUART
--- Individual univariate .9500 confidence intervals

	Coeff.	Std. Err.	t-Value	Sig. t	Lower -95%	CL- Upper
DAY						
Parameter						
1	-.51544234	.28553	-1.80519	.09259	-1.12785	.09696
GPID BY DAY						
Parameter						
2	.291336974	.28553	1.02033	.32488	-.32107	.90374

be .33). Selected results from their study are presented below for the four level within factor case.

		Tukey(pooled)	Bonferroni	Multivariate
$\epsilon = .75$	equal covariance matrices & gp sizes	6.34	3.46	1.70
	unequal covariance matrices, but equal group sizes	7.22	4.32	2.48
	unequal covariance matrices and gp sizes—larger variability with smaller group size	14.78	11.38	7.04
$\epsilon = .40$	equal covariance matrices & gp sizes	11.36	2.38	1.16
	unequal covariance matrices, but equal group sizes	10.08	2.70	1.56
	unequal covariance matrices and gp sizes—larger variability with smaller group size	17.80	6.34	3.94

The group sizes for the values presented above were 13, 10, and 7. The entries in the body of the table are to be compared against an overall alpha of .05.

The above results show that the Bonferroni approach keeps the overall alpha less than .05, provided you do not have *both* unequal group sizes and unequal covariance matrices. If you want to be confident that you will be rejecting falsely no more than your level of significance, then this is the procedure of choice. In my opinion, the Tukey procedure is acceptable for $\epsilon = .75$, as long as there are *equal* group sizes. For the other cases, the error rates for the Tukey are at least double the level of significance, and therefore not acceptable.

Recall that the pooled Tukey procedure for the single group repeated measures design was to reject if

$$|\bar{x}_i - \bar{x}_j| > q_{.05;k,(n-1)(k-1)} \sqrt{MS_{res}/n},$$

where n is the number of subjects, k is the number of levels, and MS_{res} is the error term (Equation 1).

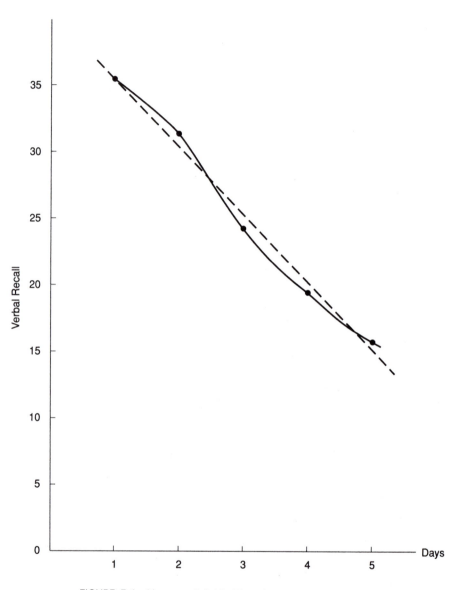

FIGURE 5.1   Linear and Cubic Plots for Verbal Recall Data

For the one between and one within design with J groups and k within levels, we declare two marginal means (means for the repeated measures levels over the J groups) different if

$$\left| \bar{x}_i - \bar{x}_j \right| > q_{.05;k,(N-J)(k-1)} \sqrt{MS_{kxs/J}/N} \tag{2}$$

where the mean square is the within subjects error term for the mixed model and N is total number of subjects.

5.12   ONE BETWEEN AND TWO WITHIN FACTORS

We now consider the repeated measures analysis for a one between and two within design, using data from Elashoff (1981). Two groups of subjects are given three different doses of two drugs. There are several different questions of interest in this study. Will the drugs be differentially effective for different groups? Is the effectiveness of the drugs dependent on dose level? Is the effectiveness of the drugs dependent on both dose level and on the group?

The design for this study is given below schematically:

	Dose	Drug 1			Drug 2		
		D_1	D_2	D_3	D_1	D_2	D_3
	S_1	Y_1	Y_2	Y_3	Y_4	Y_5	Y_6
Gp 1	S_2						
	S_8						
	S_9						
Gp 2	S_{10}						
	S_{16}						

Note that there are six measures for each subject (Y_1 to Y_6). Also, we have a crossed design on the within variables of drug and dose.

The complete control lines for running this analysis on SAS are given in Table 5.8. The means and standard deviations for the six repeated measures are given in Table 5.9. Table 5.10 presents the univariate analyses for this design from the SAS GLM program. Although the control lines for SAS in Table 5.8 yield *both* the univariate and multivariate analyses, we have just presented the univariate analyses because the Greenhouse–Geisser epsilons in Table 5.10 are greater than .70. For such a relatively mild violation of sphericity, it has been shown that the type I error rate remains at essentially the level of significance.

Results from Table 5.10 show that we have significant drug, group, and dose main effects and a significant drug by group interaction at the .05 level. To ascertain what was responsible for the drug, group and drug by group interactions we take the means from Table 5.9 and insert them into the design, yielding:

	Drug					
	1			2		
Dose	1	2	3	1	2	3
Group 1	17.5	22.5	27	19	21.88	26.50
Group 2	19.63	22.38	24	26.88	28.63	33.00

TABLE 5.8
SAS Control Lines for One Between and Two Within Repeated Measures

```
            SAS
TITLE 'ELASHOFF DATA';
DATA ELAS;
INPUT GP Y1 Y2 Y3 Y4 Y5 Y6;
CARDS;
1 19 22 28 16 26 22
1 11 19 30 12 28 28
1 20 24 24 24 22 29
1 21 25 25 15 10 26
1 18 24 29 19 26 28
1 17 23 28 15 23 22
1 20 23 23 26 21 28
1 14 20 29 25 29 29
2 16 20 24 30 34 36
2 26 26 26 24 30 32
2 22 27 23 33 36 45
2 16 18 29 27 26 34
2 19 21 20 22 22 21
2 20 25 25 29 29 33
2 21 22 23 27 26 35
2 17 20 22 23 26 28
PROC GLM;
CLASS GP;
① MODEL Y1 Y2 Y3 Y4 Y5 Y6=GP;
② REPEATED DRUG 2, DOSE 3;
```

①Recall that in the MODEL statement the dependent variables, the repeated measures here, go on the left side and the classification or grouping variable(s) go on the right side.

②When there is more than one repeated measures factor, they *must* be separated by a comma, and the product of the levels of all factors must equal the number of dependent variables in the MODEL statement.

Now, collapsing on dose, the group by drug means are obtained:

	Drug	
	1	2
Group 1	22.3	22.46
Group 2	22.00	29.50

The mean in cell 11 (22.33) is simply the average of 17.5, 22.5, and 27, the mean in cell 12 (22.46) is the average of 19, 21.88, and 26.5, etc. Now it is apparent that the "outlier" cell mean of 29.50 is what was responsible for both main effects and the interaction being significant. Note that if this cell mean were about 22 or 23, as the others, then none of the effects would have been significant.

TABLE 5.9
Means and Standard Deviations for One
Between and Two Within Repeated Measures

CELL MEANS AND STANDARD DEVIATIONS

VARIABLE . . Y1

FACTOR	CODE	MEAN	STD. DEV.
GPID	1	17.50000	3.42261
GPID	2	19.62500	3.42000
FOR ENTIRE SAMPLE		18.56250	3.48270

VARIABLE . . Y2

FACTOR	CODE	MEAN	STD. DEV.
GPID	1	22.50000	2.07020
GPID	2	22.37500	3.24863
FOR ENTIRE SAMPLE		22.43750	2.63233

VARIABLE . . Y3

FACTOR	CODE	MEAN	STD. DEV.
GPID	1	27.00000	2.61861
GPID	2	24.00000	2.72554
FOR ENTIRE SAMPLE		25.50000	3.01109

VARIABLE . . Y4

FACTOR	CODE	MEAN	STD. DEV.
GPID	1	19.00000	5.34522
GPID	2	26.87500	3.75832
FOR ENTIRE SAMPLE		22.93750	6.03842

VARIABLE . . Y5

FACTOR	CODE	MEAN	STD. DEV.
GPID	1	21.87500	5.89037
GPID	2	28.62500	4.62717
FOR ENTIRE SAMPLE		25.25000	6.19139

VARIABLE . . Y6

FACTOR	CODE	MEAN	STD. DEV.
GPID	1	26.50000	2.92770
GPID	2	33.00000	6.84523
FOR ENTIRE SAMPLE		29.75000	6.09371

TABLE 5.10
Univariate Analyses from SAS GLM for One Between and Two Within

UNIVARIATE TESTS OF HYPOTHESES FOR WITHIN SUBJECT EFFECTS

SOURCE	DF	TYPE III SS	MEAN SQUARE	F VALUE	PR > F
DRUG	1	348.84375000	348.84375000	13.00	0.0029
DRUG*GPID	1	326.34375000	326.34375000	12.16 ③	0.0036
ERROR (DRUG)	14	375.64583333 ⑥	26.83184524		

SOURCE	DF	TYPE III SS	MEAN SQUARE	F VALUE	PR > F
DOSE	2	758.77083333	379.38541667	36.51	0.0001
DOSE*GPID	2	42.27083333	21.13541667	2.03 ④	0.1497
ERROR (DOSE)	28	290.95833333 ⑥	10.39136905		

GREENHOUSE-GEISSER EPSILON = 0.8787
HUYNH-FELDT EPSILON = 1.0667

SOURCE	DF	TYPE III SS	MEAN SQUARE	F VALUE	PR > F
DRUG*DOSE	2	12.06250000	6.03125000	0.68	0.5140
DRUG*DOSE*GPID	2	14.81250000	7.40625000	0.84	0.4436
ERROR(DRUG*DOSE)	28	247.7916667 ⑤	8.84970238		

GREENHOUSE-GEISSER EPSILON = 0.7297 ①
HUYNH-FELDT EPSILON = 0.8513

TESTS OF HYPOTHESES FOR BETWEEN SUBJECTS EFFECTS

SOURCE	DF	TYPE III SS	MEAN SQUARE	F VALUE	PR > F
GPID	1	270.01041667	270.01041667	7.09 ②	0.0185
ERROR	14	532.97916667 ⑤	38.06994048		

①Since both ε̂'s are > .70, the univariate approach is preferred, since the type I error rate is controlled and it may be more powerful than the multivariate approach.

②Groups differ significantly at the .05 level, since .0185 < .05.

③ & ④The drug main effect and drug by group interaction are significant at the .05 level, while the dose main effect is also significant at the .05 level.

⑤Note that 4 different error terms are involved in this design, an additional complication with complex repeated measures designs. The error terms are boxed.

Now, we obtain the level means for DOSE and then apply the Tukey procedure to see which dose levels differ significantly. The dose level means are 20.753, 23.848, and 27.625. Now, two DOSE level means will differ significantly if

$$|\bar{x}_i - \bar{x}_j| > q_{.05;3,28} \sqrt{10.391/16},$$

where 10.391 is the mean square error term for DOSE (cf. Table 5.9), 16 is the number of subjects for each dose, and 28 is the error degrees of freedom. Calculation yields:

$$|\bar{x}_i - \bar{x}_j| > 3.486 \sqrt{10.391/16} = 2.809$$

Since the smallest difference between any two level means is 3.095 for levels 1 and 2, this means that all dose levels differ significantly from one another.

One Between and Two Within on SPSS for Windows 8.0

Once the data are in the Editor, click on STATISTICS and scroll down to GENERAL LINEAR MODEL. At this point the screen appears as at the top of Table 5.11. When you scroll across to GLM-REPEATED MEASURES and click the screen at the left middle of Table 5.11 appears. Click within the WITHIN SUBJECT FACTOR NAME box and type in drug. Then click within the NUMBER OF LEVELS box and type in 2. The ADD box will light up; click on it. Do the same for DOSE (remember DOSE has 3 levels), click on ADD, and at this point the screen will appear as at the right middle in Table 5.11. When you click on DEFINE, the screen at the bottom of Table 5.11 appears. Click on y1 and then click on the forward arrow to put y1 in position 1,1. Do the same for y2 through y6. Finally, click on GP and click on the forward arrow to make GP a between subjects factor. The OK box will light up. Simply click on OK to run the analysis.

5.13   TOTALLY WITHIN DESIGNS

There are research situations where the *same* subjects are measured under various treatment combinations, that is, where the same subjects are in each cell of the design. This may particularly be the case when not many subjects are available. We consider three examples to illustrate:

Example 1

A researcher in child development is interested in observing the same group of preschool children (all 4 years of age) in two situations at two different times (morning and afternoon) of the day. She is concerned with the extent of their social interaction, and will measure this by having two observers independently rate the amount of social interaction. The average of the two ratings will serve as the dependent variable. The within factors here are situation and time of day.

There are 4 scores for each child: social interaction in situation 1 in the morning and afternoon, and social interaction in situation in the morning and afternoon. We denote the four scores by Y1, Y2, Y3, and Y4.

Such a totally within repeated measures design is easily setup on SPSS MANOVA. The command syntax file is given below:

```
TITLE 'TWO WITHIN DESIGN'.
DATA LIST FREE/Y1 Y2 Y3 Y4.
BEGIN DATA.
     DATA LINES
END DATA.
MANOVA Y1 TO Y4/
 WSFACTOR=SIT(2),TIME(2)/
 WSDESIGN/
 PRINT=TRANSFORM CELLINFO(MEANS)/
 ANALYSIS(REPEATED)/.
```

TABLE 5.11
SPSS for Windows 8.0 Screens for One Between
and Two Within Repeated Measures on Elashoff Data

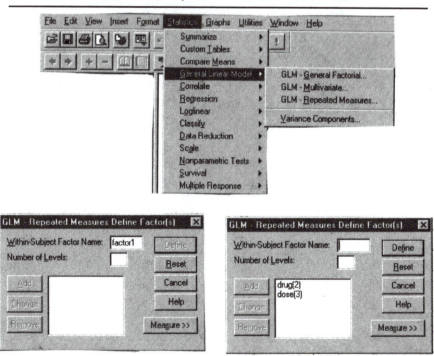

(Continued)

TABLE 5.11
(Continued)

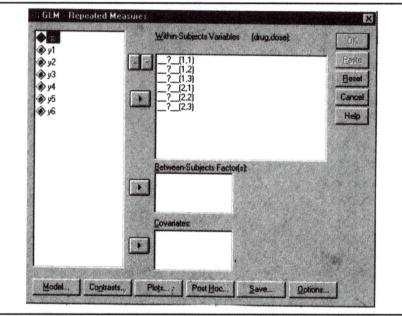

Example 2

A social psychologist is interested in determining how self-reported anxiety level for 35–45 year old men varies as a function of situation, who they are with, and how many people are involved. A questionnaire will be administered to 20 such men, asking them to rate their anxiety level (on a Likert scale from 1 to 7) in 3 situations (going to the theater, going to a football game, and going to a dinner party), with primarily friends and primarily strangers, and with a total of 6 people and with 12 people. Thus, the men will be reporting anxiety for 12 different contexts. This is a three within, crossed repeated measures design, where situation (3 levels) is crossed with nature of group (2 levels) and with number in group (2 levels).

Example 3

Suppose in an ergonomic study we are interested in the effects of day of the work week and time of the day (AM or PM) on various measures of posture. We select 30 computer operators and for this example we consider just one measure of posture called shoulder flexion. We then have a two factor totally within design which looks as follows:

	Monday		Wednesday		Friday	
	AM	PM	AM	PM	AM	PM
1						
2						
3						
.						
.						
.						
30						

5.14 PLANNED COMPARISONS
IN REPEATED MEASURES DESIGNS

Planned comparisons can be easily set up on SPSS MANOVA or on SAS GLM for repeated measures factors. To illustrate, we consider data from a study reported by Bock (1975). The study involved the effect of three drugs on the duration of sleep for 10 mental patients. The drugs were given orally on alternate evenings, and the hours of sleep were compared with an intervening control night. Each of the drugs was tested a number of times with each patient. The average number of hours of sleep was the dependent measure. Schematically, we have

	Control	Drug Type I	Drug Type II	Drug Type III
Subjects				
1				
2				
.				
.				
.				
10				

Drug Type I was distinctly different from the remaining two drugs, which were somewhat similar in composition. Three relevant questions here are:

1. Does drug have a different effect on duration of sleep than no drug?
2. Does drug Type I produce a different effect from types II and III?
3. Do drug types II and III, which are similar, have a differential effect on sleep?

These questions correspond to the following contrasts on the repeated measures:

	y_1	y_2	y_3	y_4
L_1	1	$-.33$	$-.33$	$-.33$
L_2	0	1	$-.50$	$-.50$
L_3	0	0	1	-1

Notice in the above that each level of the repeated measure is contrasted against the *average* of the remaining levels. This kind of set of contrasts are called Helmert contrasts. They are built into the SPSS and SAS packages. All one need do is request them. In Table 5.12 we present the complete command syntax for running the Helmert contrasts on SPSS MANOVA.

5.15   SUMMARY

1. Repeated measures designs are more powerful than completely randomized designs, since the variability due to individual differences is removed from the error term, and individual differences are the major reason for error variance.

2. Two major advantages of repeated measures designs are increased precision (because of the smaller error term), and economy of subjects. Two potential

TABLE 5.12
SPSS 7.5 Command Syntax File for Helmert
Contrasts for a Repeated Measures Factor

```
TITLE 'HELMERT CONTRASTS FOR REPEATED MEASURES'.
DATA LIST FREE/Y1 Y2 Y3 Y4.
BEGIN DATA.
.6 1.3 2.5 2.1  3 1.4 3.8 4.4   4.7 4.5 5.8 4.7
6.2 6.1 6.1 6.7  3.2 6.6 7.6 8.3   2.5 6.2 8 8.2
2.8 3.6 4.4 4.3  1.1 1.1 5.7 5.8   2.9 4.9 6.3 6.4
5.5 4.3 5.6 4.8
END DATA.
LIST.
① MANOVA Y1 TO Y4/
   WSFACTOR=DRUGS(4)/
② CONTRAST(DRUGS)=HELMERT/
   WSDESIGN=DRUGS/
③ RENAME=MEAN,HELMERT1,HELMERT2,HELMERT3/
   PRINT=CELLINFO(MEANS)TRANSFORM/
   ANALYSIS(REPEATED)/.
```

①Recall that the four repeated measures are treated as 4 dependent variables.
②Since HELMERT is one of the standard set of contrasts available in SPSS MANOVA, all we need do is request it in the CONTRAST subcommand.
③We have simply given meaningful names to the transformed variables. The first transformed variable is a general mean, and the last 3 transformed variables are the Helmert contrasts that we wish to test the significance of.

disadvantages are that the order of treatments may make a difference (this can be dealt with by counterbalancing) and carryover effects.

3. Either a univariate or multivariate approach can be used for repeated measures analysis. If the sphericity assumption is tenable, then the univariate approach is preferred as it is more powerful.

4. If sphericity is violated, then the type I error rate for the univariate approach is inflated. However, a modified univariate approach (obtained by multiplying each of the degrees of freedom by $\hat{\varepsilon}$) yields an honest type I error rate.

5. *As both the modified univariate and multivariate approaches control type I error, the choice between them involves the issue of power.* To keep things simpler in this text, I simply illustrate and use the modified univariate approach. However, as I point out in my multivariate text, neither approach is even usually more powerful, and therefore I recommend there that both approaches should be used, since they may differ in the effects they will discern.

6. If sphericity is tenable, then the Tukey is a good post hoc procedure for locating pairwise differences. If sphericity is not tenable, then the Bonferroni approach should be used. That is, do multiple correlated *t* tests, but use the Bonferroni Inequality to keep the overall α level under control.

7. When several groups are involved, then an additional assumption is homogeneity of the covariance matrices for the groups. This can be checked with the Box test, and would be of most concern when the group sizes are sharply unequal.

EXERCISES

1. Consider the following data for a single group repeated measures with 8 subjects measured for 4 treatments:

		Treatments		
Subjects	1	2	3	4
1	5	6	2	5
2	3	4	1	6
3	3	7	4	10
4	6	8	3	3
5	4	9	7	8
6	5	7	4	9
7	2	10	1	2
8	4	3	2	5

(a) Do a univariate repeated measures analysis on this data, testing for significance at the .05 level.

(b) Use the Tukey post hoc procedure to locate the significant pairwise differences at the .05 level.

(c) Run the above data on SPSS MANOVA to check your results.

2. Give an example or two where a two or three within subjects design would make sense. As a starter for you, consider driving behavior (measured by number of steering errors) or smoking behavior (number of cigarettes smoked) for a group of subjects, and a few key factors that you think might influence such behavior.

3. Output from SPSS MANOVA for the single sample (5 subjects and 3 levels) repeated measures design in Table 5.1 includes the following:

$$
\begin{aligned}
\text{GREENHOUSE-GEISSER EPSILON} &= .66564 \\
\text{HUYNH-FELDT EPSILON} &= .87240 \\
\text{LOWER-BOUND EPSILON} &= .50000
\end{aligned}
$$

The covariance matrix for the three measures is

$$
\mathbf{S} = \begin{bmatrix} 76.8 & 53.2 & 69.0 \\ 53.2 & 42.8 & 47.0 \\ 69.0 & 47.0 & 64.0 \end{bmatrix}
$$

The formula for the Greenhouse-Geisser epsilon is:

$$
\hat{\varepsilon} = \frac{k^2 \, (\bar{s}_{ii} - \bar{s})^2}{(k - 1)(\sum\sum s_{ij}^2 - 2k\sum_i \bar{s}_i^2 + k^2 \, \bar{s}^2)}
$$

where

$\bar{s}$ is the mean of all entries in the covariance matrix $\mathbf{S}$

$\bar{s}_{ii}$ is mean of entries on main diagonal of $\mathbf{S}$

$\bar{s}_i$ is mean of all entries in row i of $\mathbf{S}$

s_{ij} is ijth entry of $\mathbf{S}$

(a) Using this formula, verify the SPSS value of .66564.

(b) Using the equation given in the chapter relating the Greenhouse-Geisser and the Huynh-Feldt epsilons, verify the value of .87240.

(c) Why is the LOWER-BOUND EPSILON value given as .500?

(d) For the one between and one within design in Table 5.7, the Greenhouse-Geisser epsilon = .44629 and Huynh-Feldt epsilon = .54366 on the SPSS printout. A generalized formula relating these measures for this design is given by

$$\tilde{\varepsilon} = \frac{ng(k-1)\hat{\varepsilon} - 2}{(k-1)[g(n-1) - (k-1)\hat{\varepsilon}]}$$

where g is the number of groups, n is the number of subjects per group, and k is the number of levels for the within variable. Using this relationship, show how the Huynh-Feldt value of .54366 follows from the Greenhouse-Geisser value of .44629.

4. Consider the following hypothetical data from a study comparing the relative efficacy of a behavior modification approach to dieting vs. a behavior modification approach + exercise on weight loss for a group of overweight women. There is also a control group. First, 18 women who are between 20 and 30 years old are randomly assigned to one of the three groups. Then, six each of women 30 to 40 years old are randomly assigned to one of the three groups. The investigator wishes to determine whether age might moderate the effect of the diet approaches. The weight loss for the women is measured two months, four months, and six months after the diets begin. Thus, we have a two between and one within repeated measures design.

	DIET	AGE	WGTLOSS1	WGTLOSS2	WGTLOSS3
	1.00	1.00	4.00	3.00	3.00
	1.00	1.00	4.00	4.00	3.00
	1.00	1.00	4.00	3.00	1.00
CONTROL	1.00	1.00	3.00	2.00	1.00
20–30 YRS	1.00	1.00	5.00	3.00	2.00
	1.00	1.00	6.00	5.00	4.00
	1.00	2.00	6.00	5.00	4.00
	1.00	2.00	5.00	4.00	1.00
CONTROL	1.00	2.00	3.00	3.00	2.00
30–40 YRS	1.00	2.00	5.00	4.00	1.00
	1.00	2.00	4.00	2.00	2.00
	1.00	2.00	5.00	2.00	1.00
	2.00	1.00	6.00	3.00	2.00
	2.00	1.00	5.00	4.00	1.00
BEH. MOD	2.00	1.00	7.00	6.00	3.00
20–30 YRS	2.00	1.00	6.00	4.00	2.00
	2.00	1.00	3.00	2.00	1.00
	2.00	1.00	5.00	5.00	4.00
	2.00	2.00	4.00	3.00	1.00
BEH. MOD	2.00	2.00	4.00	2.00	1.00
30–40 YRS	2.00	2.00	6.00	5.00	3.00
	2.00	2.00	7.00	6.00	4.00
	2.00	2.00	4.00	3.00	2.00
	2.00	2.00	7.00	4.00	3.00
	3.00	1.00	8.00	4.00	2.00

BEH. MOD. + EXER.	3.00	1.00	3.00	6.00	3.00
20–30 YRS	3.00	1.00	7.00	7.00	4.00
	3.00	1.00	4.00	7.00	1.00
	3.00	1.00	9.00	7.00	3.00
	3.00	1.00	2.00	4.00	1.00
	3.00	2.00	3.00	5.00	1.00
BEH. MOD. + EXER.	3.00	2.00	6.00	5.00	2.00
30–40 YRS	3.00	2.00	6.00	6.00	3.00
	3.00	2.00	9.00	5.00	2.00
	3.00	2.00	7.00	9.00	4.00
	3.00	2.00	8.00	6.00	1.00

(a) Run the analysis on SPSS MANOVA, obtaining both the multivariate and univariate results.

(b) Which of the between effects are significant at the .05 level?

(c) Given the values of the Greenhouse-Geisser and Huynh-Feldt epsilons, would the univariate or multivariate approach be preferred?

(d) Which of the within effects are significant at the .05 level?

(e) Using the appropriate means (cell, row or column), interpret the results.

5. Run the Helmert planned comparisons given in Table 5.12 on SPSS MANOVA. If overall alpha is set at .10, then which are significant? What do the significant contrasts represent?

6. Recall that in the Elashoff data example in section 5.12 two groups of subjects were given three different doses of two drugs, which yielded a one between and two within repeated measures design. Suppose that the two groups of subjects had been given the different doses of the drugs under two different conditions. Then we would have a one between and three within design. Show the SPSS MANOVA control lines for running this analysis.

6 Simple and Multiple Regression

CONTENTS

6.1   SIMPLE REGRESSION

Here we are predicting a dependent (outcome) variable from a single predictor. Several examples come to mind. One may wish to predict chemistry achievement from I.Q. One may wish to predict a person's heart rate from blood pressure. A farmer may wish to predict yield from level of the fertilizer.

Before we get into simple regression, let us review some basic concepts from high school. Recall that in high school you may have been told to graph an equation such as $y = 1 + .5x$. To do so you take a range of x values, determine the corresponding y values, and then plot the points. It would look like this:

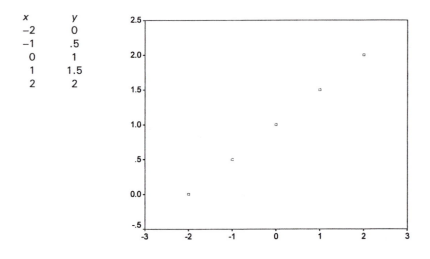

x	y
-2	0
-1	.5
0	1
1	1.5
2	2

When you did this each y value was *exactly* determined once the x value was specified. You probably did not think a lot about that fact. This is called a deterministic model. When we collect data and are attempting to predict some y (like college GPA) from a single x (like high school GPA), it should be obvious that perfect prediction is not going to happen. Why? Because there are many other factors that determine college GPA, like what your major is, where you go to college, boyfriends and girlfriends, a death in the family, a divorce, attitude toward school, etc. Because of all these other factors we need to set up what is called a *probabilistic* model, where we allow for error in prediction. We will assume a linear relationship between y and x. The probabilistic model is as follows:

$$y_i = \underline{\beta_0 + \beta_1 x_i} + e_i \qquad i = 1, 2, \ldots, n$$

The part I have underlined corresponds to the linear relationship, and the other part is the error of prediction.

To illustrate the above, consider the following data set and scatterplot:

x	y
2	3
3	6
4	8
6	4
7	10
8	14
9	8
10	12
11	14
12	12
13	16

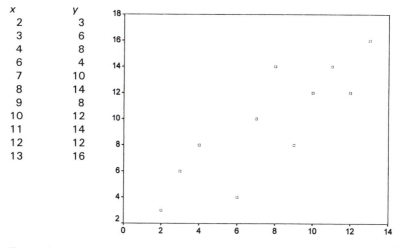

From the above plot it is obvious that a straight line will not fit the points perfectly. Yet it is also clear that as x increases y increases and that the relationship seems primarily linear. We wish to model this linear relationship, and we will see that a "least squares" regression line does a pretty good job.

We consider two examples to illustrate simple regression. The first example uses artificial data for a small data set. The second example, based on real data, provides a more realistic use of simple regression in practice.

Before we get into the examples, let us consider more precisely what is done in simple regression. First, we are assuming a *linear* relationship exists between the dependent variable and the predictor. This means there is a significant correlation between x and y. We are modeling y, assuming it is linearly related to x (predictor). The mathematical model looks like this:

$$y_i = \beta_0 + \beta_1 x_i + e_i \qquad i = 1, 2, \ldots, n$$

where β_0 and β_1 are to be estimated, and the e_i are the errors of prediction. There are assumptions concerning the e_i which we get to later. How do we estimate the β's? The *least squares* criterion is used; that is, the sum of the squared estimated errors of prediction is minimized.

$$\hat{e}_1^2 + \hat{e}_2^2 + \cdots + \hat{e}_n^2 = \sum_{i=1}^{n} \hat{e}_i^2 = \min$$

Now, $\hat{e}_i = y_i - \hat{y}_i$, where y_i is the actual score on the dependent variable and $\hat{y}_i$ is the estimated score for the ith subject.

The score for each subject defines a point in the plane. What the least squares criterion does is find the line that best fits the points. Geometrically this corre-

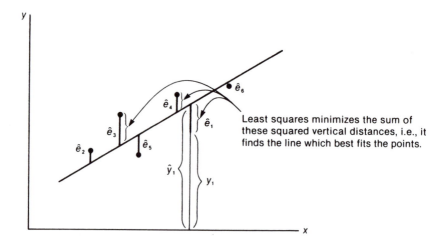

FIGURE 6.1   Geometrical Representation of Least Squares Criterion

sponds to *minimizing* the sum of the squared vertical distances $(\hat{e}_i^2)$ of each subject's score from their estimated score. This is illustrated in Figure 6.1.

Example 1

The above is abstract. To give the reader a feel for the errors of prediction and just plotting of points, we consider our first example with just 11 data points. In Table 6.1 we present selected printout from the SPSS for Windows 7.5 regression run of this data. First, the correlation of .841 shows that there is a strong linear relationship. Second, from the unstandardized coefficients we can construct the prediction equation. We have put that equation on the diagram below. Third, in Table 6.1 we have the unstandardized predicted values and errors. In Figure 6.2 we present the regression line, along with geometric illustrations of what some of the estimated y values look like and how the errors of prediction are obtained by simply taking the difference between the person's actual y score and the person's predicted score.

Example 2

For our second example, using real data, we consider part of a Sesame Street database from Glasnapp and Poggio (1985), who present data on many variables, including 12 background variables and 8 achievement variables, for 240 subjects. Sesame Street was developed as a television series aimed mainly at teaching preschool skills to three to five year old children. Data was collected on many achievement variables both before (pretest) and after (posttest) viewing of the series. We consider here only one of the achievement variables, knowledge of body parts. In particular, we consider pretest and posttest data on body parts for a sample of 80 children.

TABLE 6.1
Selected Simple Regression Output From SPSS for Windows 7.5

Regression

Descriptive Statistics

	Mean	Std. Deviation	N
Y	9.7273	4.2916	11
X	7.7273	3.6903	11

Correlations

		Y	X
Pearson Correlation	Y	1.000	.841
	X	.841	1.000
Sig. (1-tailed)	Y	.	.001
	X	.001	.
N	Y	11	11
	X	11	11

Coefficients[a]

Model		Unstandardized Coefficients		Standardized Coefficients		
		B	Std. Error	Beta	t	Sig.
1	(Constant)	2.170	1.781		1.218	.254
	X	.978	.210	.841	4.662	.001

[a]Dependent Variable: Y.

Case Summaries[a]

	Unstandardized Predicted Value	Unstandardized Residual e_i
1	4.12617	−1.12617
2	5.10414	.89586
3	6.08211	1.91789
4	8.03805	−4.03805
5	9.01602	.98398
6	9.99399	4.00601
7	10.97196	−2.97196
8	11.94993	0.5007
9	12.92790	1.07210
10	13.90587	−1.90587
11	14.88385	1.11615
Total N	11	11

[a]Limited to first 100 cases.

These are the coefficients that define the prediction equation:

$$\hat{y}_i = .978x_i + 2.17$$

Thus, the predicted score for subject 1 is

$$\hat{y}_1 = .978 (2) + 2.17 = 4.126,$$

as given on the left, and the residual for subject 1 is $3 - 4.126 = -1.126$. The predicted score for subject 2 is

$$\hat{y}_2 = .978(3) + 2.17 = 5.104$$

And so on.

TABLE 6.2
SPSS Command Syntax for Simple Regression
on Sesame Street Data and Selected Printout

```
TITLE 'SIMPLE REGRESSION ON SESAME DATA'.
DATA LIST FREE/PREBODY POSTBODY.
BEGIN DATA.
    DATA LINES
END DATA.
REGRESSION DESCRIPTIVES = DEFAULT/
    VARIABLES = PREBODY POSTBODY/
    DEPENDENT = POSTBODY/
①  METHOD = ENTER/
②  SCATTERPLOT (POSTBODY,PREBODY)/.
```

①DESCRIPTIVES = DEFAULT subcommand yields the means, standard deviations and the correlation matrix for the variables.

②This SCATTERPLOT subcommand yields the scatterplot for the variables. Note that the variables have been standardized (z scores) and then plotted.

(Continued)

The command syntax for running the regression analysis, along with selected printout, is presented in Table 6.2. Part of the printout is a standardized scatterplot (recall that when variables are standardized this does *not* affect the magnitude of the correlation).

6.2 ASSUMPTIONS FOR THE ERRORS

The errors (e_i) are assumed to be independent, with constant variance and normally distributed with a mean of 0. If these assumptions are valid for a given set of

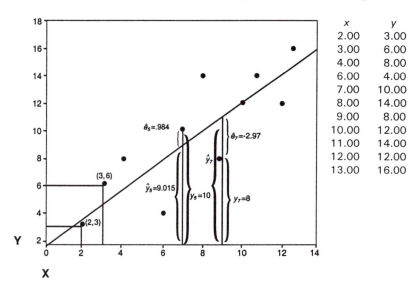

FIGURE 6.2 Errors of Prediction

244

TABLE 6.2
(Continued)

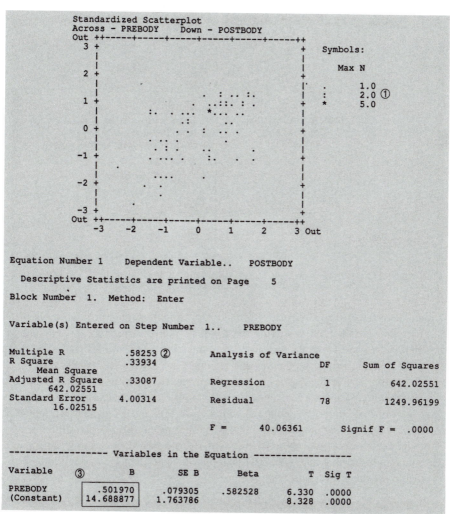

```
Standardized Scatterplot
Across - PREBODY    Down - POSTBODY
Out ++-----+-----+-----+-----+-----+-----++
  3 +                                      +    Symbols:
    |                                      |
  2 +                                      +    Max N
    |                                      |
    |              .           .          |.
  1 +          . : .. :.        |    .        1.0
    |         ..::: : .         +    :     2.0 ①
    |  :. . ... *.... ..        |    *     5.0
    |      .:       ..          |
  0 +       .  : ...  .         +
    |       . . :  ...  .       |
    |      ..: :      . .       |
 -1 +    .... .   :.      .     +
    |   .                       |
    |  .    ....    .           |
 -2 +      .  .                 +
    |        .                  |
    |  .                        |
 -3 +                           +
Out ++-----+-----+-----+-----+-----+-----++
    -3    -2    -1     0     1     2     3 Out
```

Equation Number 1   Dependent Variable..   POSTBODY

Descriptive Statistics are printed on Page   5

Block Number 1. Method: Enter

Variable(s) Entered on Step Number 1..   PREBODY

		Analysis of Variance		
Multiple R	.58253 ②			
R Square	.33934		DF	Sum of Squares
Mean Square				
Adjusted R Square	.33087	Regression	1	642.02551
642.02551				
Standard Error	4.00314	Residual	78	1249.96199
16.02515				

F =   40.06361   Signif F = .0000

------------------ Variables in the Equation ------------------

Variable ③	B	SE B	Beta	T	Sig T
PREBODY	.501970	.079305	.582528	6.330	.0000
(Constant)	14.688877	1.763786		8.328	.0000

①This legend means there is one observation whenever a single dot appears, two observations whenever a : appears, and 5 observations where there is an asterisk (*).

②The multiple correlation here is in fact the simple correlation between postbody and prebody, since there is just one predictor.

③These are the raw coefficients which define the prediction equation: POSTBODY = .50197 PREBODY + 14.6888.

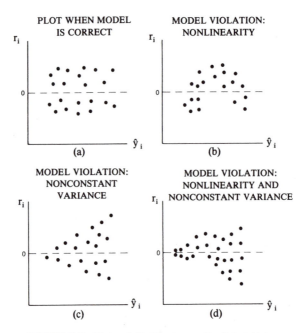

FIGURE 6.3   Plots of Residuals vs. Predicted Values

data, then the estimated errors ($\hat{e}_i$), called the residuals, should behave similarly. There are various plots involving the residuals that are available for assessing potential problems with a linear regression model. One of the most useful plots, in my opinion, involves graphing the residuals against the predicted values. If the assumptions of the regression model are tenable, then the residuals should scatter randomly about a horizontal line of 0. *Any systematic pattern or clustering of the residuals suggests a model violation(s).* In Figure 6.3 I present four plots: one in which the assumptions are tenable, while in the other 3 plots there is a model violation(s). We obtained this plot for the first data example, and the results are presented in Figure 6.4. This plot indicates that the assumptions are tenable for this set of data.

6.3   INFLUENTIAL DATA POINTS

There is one additional point we wish to make before moving into multiple regression. There are situations where a single point may have a big influence on the resulting prediction equation; such a point is called an influential point. A statistic that is quite useful for detecting such influential points is called *Cook's distance.* Cook and Weisberg (1982) indicate that if Cook's distance (which is readily obtained from SPSS or SAS) is > 1, then generally that point will be influential. As a vivid illustration of such a point, consider Case B from Chapter

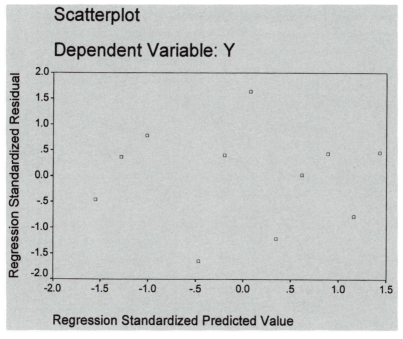

FIGURE 6.4   Plots of Residuals vs. Predicted Values for Example 1 Data

1, Section 1.6. The last data point (24,5) is an outlier. Without that point we get a nice regression line. When that point is included, however, it pulls the regression line down considerably. The two regression lines are shown in Figure 6.5.

How Summary Statistics Can Be Misleading

One of the reviewers of this second edition noted that data sets provided by Anscombe (1973) can show why summary statistics can be misleading, and hence the need for plotting the data. I commented on these data sets in the first edition of my multivariate text (Stevens, 1986, p. 86), but did not show the plots. The actual data are as follows:

X	Y1	Y2	Y3
4	4.26	3.10	5.39
5	5.68	4.74	5.73
6	7.24	6.13	6.08
7	4.82	7.26	6.42
8	6.95	8.14	6.77
9	8.81	8.77	7:11
10	8.04	9.14	7.46
11	8.33	9.26	7.81
12	10.84	9.13	8.15
13	7.58	8.74	12.74
14	9.96	8.10	8.84

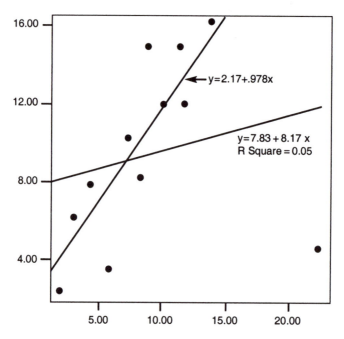

FIGURE 6.5   Regression Lines With and Without Influential Point

These data sets have exactly the same correlation (.816) and the same regression line: $y = 3 + .5x$. Yet the situations are quite different. The plots, from SPSS for Windows 8.0, are given in Figure 6.6. These plots show that only in the first case are the summary statistics an accurate indication of the situation. In the second case there is a curvilinear relationship, and in the last case there is an outlier.

6.4   MULTIPLE REGRESSION

In multiple regression we are interested in predicting a dependent variable from a set of predictors. Since human behavior is complex and influenced by many factors, single predictor studies are limited in their predictive power. For example, in a college GPA study, we are able to predict college GPA better by considering predictors other than high school GPA. Some other factors would be scores on standardized tests (verbal and quantitative), and some noncognitive variables, such as study habits and attitude toward education. That is, we look to other predictors (often test scores) that tap other aspects of criterion behavior.

Consider three other examples of multiple regression studies:

1. Feshbach, Adelman, and Williamson (1977) conducted a study of 850 middle class children. The children were measured in kindergarten on a battery

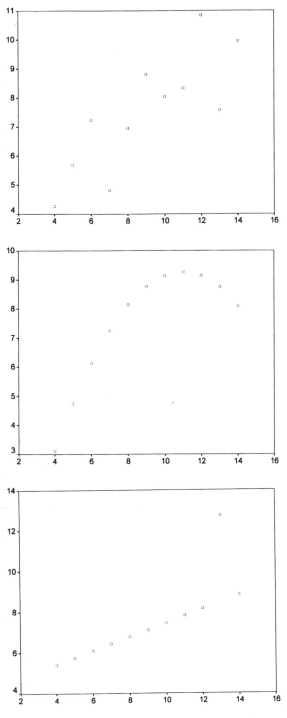

FIGURE 6.6 Plots for Anscombe (1973) Data Sets

of variables: WPPSI, deHirsch–Jansky Index (assessing various linguistic and perceptual motor skills), the Bender Motor Gestalt, and a Student Rating Scale developed by the authors that measures various cognitive and affective behaviors and skills. These measures were used to predict reading achievement for these same children in grades 1, 2, and 3.

2. Crystal (1988) attempted to predict chief executive officer (CEO) pay for the top 100 of last year's Fortune 500 and the 100 top entries from last year's Service 500. He used the following predictors: company size, company performance, company risk, government regulation, tenure, location, directors, ownership, and age. He found that only about 39% of the variance in CEO pay can be accounted for by these factors.

3. Agresti (1990) gives an example based on real data for 93 homes that were sold in Florida. The dependent variable is price of the home and the predictors were size, number of bathrooms, number of bedrooms, and whether the home was new or not.

In discussing simple regression we mentioned that least squares was used to estimate the parameters and that this procedure minimized the sum of the squared errors of prediction. In multiple regression we will use least squares again. It is very important for the reader to realize that *minimizing the sum of the squared errors of prediction is equivalent to maximizing the correlation between the observed and predicted scores*. This maximized correlation is called the multiple correlation, i.e., $R = r_{y_i y_i'}$. Nunnally (1978) characterized the procedure as "wringing out the last ounce of predictive power" (obtained from the linear combination of the x's, i.e., from the regression equation). Since the correlation is maximum for the sample from which it is derived, when the regression equation is applied to an *independent* sample from the same population (i.e., cross-validated) the predictive power drops off. If the predictive power drops off sharply, then the equation is of very limited utility. That is, it has little generalizability, and hence is of limited scientific value. After all, we derive the prediction equation for the purpose of predicting with it on future (other) samples. If the equation does not predict well on other samples, then it is not fulfilling the purpose for which it was designed.

Sample size (n) and the number of predictors (k) are two crucial factors that determine how well a given equation will cross validate. In particular, the n/k *ratio is crucial*. For small ratios (5:1 or less) the shrinkage can be substantial.

Since the rest of this chapter is rather lengthy, we give the reader an overview of the critical topics. As we will show shortly, how the predictors are correlated can have a big impact on the multiple correlation. This will take us into the topic of multicollinearity (Section 6.7). In Section 6.8 we discuss several methods for selecting a "good" set of predictors. In Section 6.9 we give two computer examples, using real data, to illustrate some of the methods discussed in Section 6.8. In Section 6.10 we discuss assumptions underlying the regression analysis, and how they can be checked. The crucial topic of model validation is discussed in Section 6.11. Since multiple regression is a *mathematical maximization* procedure, it is very important to check the generalizability of the equation.

6.5 BREAKDOWN OF SUM OF SQUARES IN REGRESSION AND *F* TEST FOR MULTIPLE CORRELATION

In analysis of variance we broke down variability about the grand mean into between and within variability. In regression analysis variability about the mean is broken down into variability due to regression and variability about the regression. To get at the breakdown, we start with the following identity:

$$y_i - \hat{y}_i = (y_i - \bar{y}) - (\hat{y}_i - \bar{y})$$

Now we square both sides, obtaining

$$(y_i - \hat{y}_i)^2 = [(y_i - \bar{y}) - (\hat{y}_i - \bar{y})]^2$$

Then we sum over the subjects, from 1 to n:

$$\sum_{i=1}^{n} (y_i - \hat{y}_i)^2 = \sum_{i=1}^{n} [(y_i - \bar{y}) - (\hat{y}_i - \bar{y})]^2$$

By algebraic manipulation (see Draper & Smith, 1981, pp. 17–18), this can be rewritten as:

$$
\begin{array}{ccccc}
\sum (y_i - \bar{y})^2 & = & \sum (y_i - \hat{y}_i)^2 & + & \sum (\hat{y}_i - \bar{y})^2 \\
\text{sum of squares} & & \text{sum of squares} & & \text{sum of squares} \\
\text{about mean} & = & \text{about regression} & + & \text{due to regression} \\
& & (SS_{res}) & & (SS_{reg}) \\
df: \quad n - 1 & = & (n - k - 1) & + & k \ (df = \text{degrees of freedom})
\end{array}
\tag{3}
$$

This results in the following analysis of variance table and the *F* test for determining whether the population multiple correlation is different from 0.

Source	SS	df	MS	F
Regression	SS_{reg}	k	S_{reg}/k	$\dfrac{MS_{reg}}{MS_{res}}$
Residual (error)	SS_{res}	$n - k - 1$	$SS_{res}/(n - k - 1)$	

Recall that since the residual for each subject is $\hat{e}_i = y_i - \hat{y}_i$, the mean square error term can be written as $MS_{res} = \Sigma \hat{e}_i^{\,2}/(n - k - 1)$. Now, R^2 (squared multiple correlation) is given by:

$$R^2 = \frac{\text{sum of squares due to regression}}{\text{sum of squares about the mean}} = \frac{\sum (\hat{y}_i - \bar{y})^2}{\sum (y_i - \bar{y})^2} = \frac{SS_{reg}}{SS_{tot}}$$

Thus, R^2 measures the proportion of total variance on y that is accounted for by the set of predictors. By simple algebra then we can rewrite the F test in terms of R^2 as follows:

$$F = \frac{R^2/k}{(1 - R^2)/(n - k - 1)} \text{ with } k \text{ and } (n - k - 1) \, df \qquad (1)$$

We feel this test is of limited utility, since it does *not necessarily* imply that the equation will cross-validate well, and this is the crucial issue in regression analysis.

Example 3

An investigator obtains $R^2 = .50$ on a sample of 50 subjects with 10 predictors. Do we reject the null hypothesis that the population multiple correlation $= 0$?

$$F = \frac{.50/10}{(1 - .50)/(50 - 10 - 1)} = 3.9 \text{ with } 10 \text{ and } 39 \, df$$

This is significant at .01 level, since the critical value is 2.8.

However, since the n/k ratio is only 5/1, the prediction equation will probably not predict well on other samples and is therefore of questionable utility.

Myers' (1990) response to the question of what constitutes an acceptable value for R^2 is illuminating:

This is a difficult question to answer, and, in truth, what is acceptable depends on the scientific field from which the data were taken. A chemist, charged with doing a linear calibration on a high precision piece of equipment, certainly expects to experience a very high R^2 value (perhaps exceeding .99), while a behavioral scientist, dealing in data reflecting human behavior, may feel fortunate to observe an R^2 as high as .70. An experienced model fitter senses when the value of R^2 is large enough, given the situation confronted. Clearly, some scientific phenomena lend themselves to modeling with considerably more accuracy than others. (p. 37)

His point is that how well one can predict depends on *context*. In the physical sciences, generally quite accurate prediction is possible. In the social sciences, where we are attempting to predict human behavior (which can be influenced by many systematic and some idiosyncratic factors), prediction is much more difficult.

6.6   RELATIONSHIP OF SIMPLE CORRELATIONS
TO MULTIPLE CORRELATION

The ideal situation, in terms of obtaining a high R would be to have each of the predictors significantly correlated with the dependent variable and for the predictors to be uncorrelated with each other, so that they measure different constructs and are able to predict different parts of the variance on y. Of course, in practice we will not find this because almost all variables are correlated to some degree. A good situation in practice then would be one in which most of our predictors correlate significantly with y and the predictors have relatively low correlations among themselves. To illustrate the above points further, consider the following three patterns of intercorrelations for three predictors.

		X_1	X_2	X_3			X_1	X_2	X_3			X_1	X_2	X_3
(1)	Y	.20	.10	.30	(2)	Y	.60	.50	.70	(3)	Y	.60	.70	.70.
	X_1		.50	.40		X_1		.20	.30		X_1		.70	.60
	X_2			.60		X_2			.20		X_2			.80

In which of these cases would you expect the multiple correlation to be the largest and the smallest respectively? Here it is quite clear that R will be the smallest for 1 because the highest correlation of any of the predictors with y is .30, whereas for the other two patterns at least one of the predictors has a correlation of .70 with y. Thus, we know that R will be at least .70 for cases 2 and 3, whereas for case 1 we only know that R will be at least .30. Furthermore, there is no chance that R for case 1 might become larger than that for cases 2 and 3, because the intercorrelations among the predictors for 1 are approximately as large or larger than those for the other two cases.

We would expect R to be largest for case 2 because each of the predictors is moderately to strongly tied to y and there are low intercorrelations (i.e., little redundancy) among the predictors, exactly the kind of situation we would hope to find in practice. We would expect R to be greater in case 2 than in case 3, because in case 3 there is considerable redundancy among the predictors. Although the correlations of the predictors with y are slightly higher in case 3 (.60, .70, .70) than in case 2 (.60, .50, .70), the much higher intercorrelations among the predictors for case 3 will severely limit the ability of X_2 and X_3 to predict additional variance beyond that of X_1 (and hence significantly increase R), whereas this will not be true for case 2.

6.7   MULTICOLLINEARITY

When there are moderate to high intercorrelations among the predictors, as is the case when several cognitive measures are used as predictors, the problem is referred to as *multicollinearity*. Multicollinearity poses a real problem for the researcher using multiple regression for three reasons:

1. It severely limits the size of R, because the predictors are going after much of the same variance on y. A study by Dizney and Gromen (1967) illustrates very nicely how multicollinearity among the predictors limits the size of R. They studied how well reading proficiency (x_1) and writing proficiency (x_2) would predict course grade in college German. The following correlation matrix resulted:

	x_1	x_2	y
x_1	1.00	.58	.33
x_2		1.00	.45
y			1.00

Note the multicollinearity for x_1 and x_2 $(r_{x_1x_2} = .58)$, and also that x_2 has a simple correlation of .45 with y. The multiple correlation R was only .46. Thus, the relatively high correlation between reading and writing severely limited the ability of reading to add hardly anything (only .01) to the prediction of German grade above and beyond that of writing.

2. Multicollinearity makes determining the importance of a given predictor difficult because the effects of the predictors are confounded due to the correlations among them.

3. Multicollinearity increases the variances of the regression coefficients. The greater these variances, the more unstable the prediction equation will be.

The following are two methods for diagnosing multicollinearity:

1. Examine the simple correlations among the predictors from the correlation matrix. These should be observed, and are easy to understand, but the researcher need be warned that they do not always indicate the extent of multicollinearity. More subtle forms of multicollinearity may exist. One such more subtle form is discussed next.

2. Examine the variance inflation factors for the predictors.

The quantity $1/(1 - R_j^2)$ is called the jth *variance inflation factor*, where R_j^2 is the squared multiple correlation for predicting the jth predictor from all other predictors.

The variance inflation factor for a predictor indicates whether there is a strong linear association between it and all the remaining predictors. It is distinctly possible for a predictor to have only moderate and/or relatively weak associations with the other predictors in terms of simple correlations, and yet to have a quite high R when regressed on all the other predictors. When is the value for a variance inflation factor large enough to cause concern? Myers (1990) offers the following suggestion: "Though no rule of thumb on numerical values is foolproof, it is generally believed that if any VIF exceeds 10, there is reason for at least some concern; then one should consider variable deletion or an alternative to least squares estimation to combat the problem" (p. 369). The variance inflation factors are easily obtained from SAS REG (cf. Table 6.6).

There are at least three ways of combating multicollinearity. One way is to combine predictors that are highly correlated. For example, if there are three measures relating to a single construct which have intercorrelations of about .80 or larger, then add them to form a single predictor. The two other ways (factor analysis and ridge regression) are more advanced; see Stevens (1996).

6.8 MODEL SELECTION

There are various methods available for selecting a good set of predictors:

Substantive Knowledge.   As Weisberg (1985) has noted, "The single most important tool in selecting a subset of variables for use in a model is the analyst's knowledge of the substantive area under study" (p. 210). It is important for the investigator to be judicious in selection of predictors. Far too many investigators have abused multiple regression by "throwing everything in the hopper," often merely because the variables are available. Cohen (1990), among many others, has commented on the indiscriminate use of variables; "I have encountered too many studies with prodigious numbers of dependent variables, or with what seemed to me far too many independent variables, or (heaven help us) both."

There are several good reasons for generally preferring to work with a small number of predictors: (a) principle of scientific parsimony; (b) reducing the number of predictors improves the n/k ratio, and this helps cross-validation prospects; and (c) note the following from Lord and Novick (1968):

> Experience in psychology and in many other fields of application has shown that it is seldom worthwhile to include very many predictor variables in a regression equation, for the incremental validity of new variables, after a certain point, is usually very low. This is true because tests tend to overlap in content and consequently the addition of a fifth or sixth test may add little that is new to the battery and still relevant to the criterion. (p. 274)

Sequential Methods.   These are the forward, stepwise, and backward selection procedures that are very popular with many researchers. All these procedures involve a partialling-out process; that is, they look at the contribution of a predictor with the effects of the other predictors partialled out, or held constant. Many readers may have been exposed in a previous statistics course to the notion of a partial (and maybe a part) correlation, but a review is nevertheless in order.

We consider a procedure that, for a *given ordering* of the predictors, will enable us to determine the unique contribution each predictors is making in accounting for variance on y. This procedure, which uses semipartial correlations, will disentangle the correlations among the predictors.

The partial correlation between variables 1 and 2 with variable 3 partialled from both 1 and 2 is the correlation with variable 3 held constant, as the reader may recall. The formula for the partial correlation is given by

$$r_{12.3} = \frac{r_{12} - r_{13}\,r_{23}}{\sqrt{1 - r_{13}^2}\ \sqrt{1 - r_{23}^2}}$$

We have introduced the partial correlation first for two reasons: (1) the semipartial correlation is a variant of the partial correlation, and (2) the partial correlation will be involved in computing more complicated semipartial correlations.

For breaking down R^2 we will want to work with the semipartial, sometimes called part, correlation. The formula for the semipartial correlation is:

$$r_{12.3(s)} = \frac{r_{12} - r_{13}\,r_{23}}{\sqrt{1 - r_{23}^2}}$$

The only difference between this equation and the previous one is that the denominator here doesn't contain the standard deviation of the partialled scores for variable 1.

In multiple correlation we wish to partial the independent variables (the predictors) from one another, but not from the dependent variable. We wish to leave the dependent variable intact, and not partial any variance attributable to the predictors. Let $R^2_{y12\ldots k}$ denote the squared multiple correlation for the k predictors, where the predictors appear after the dot. Consider the case of one dependent variable and three predictors. It can be shown that:

$$R^2_{y.123} = r_{y1}{}^2 + r_{y2.1(s)}^2 + r_{y3.12(s)}^2$$

where

$$r_{y2.1(s)} = \frac{r_{y2} - r_{y1}\,r_{21}}{\sqrt{1 - r_{21}^2}} \tag{2}$$

is the semipartial correlation between y and variable 2, with variable 1 partialled only from variable 2, and $r_{y3.12(s)}$ is the semipartial correlation between y and variable 3 with variables 1 and 2 partialled only from variable 3:

$$r_{y3.12(s)} = \frac{r_{y3.1(s)} - r_{y2.1(s)}\, r_{23.1}}{\sqrt{1 - r_{23.1}^2}} \qquad (3)$$

Thus, through the use of semipartial correlations we disentangle the correlations among the predictors and determine how much *unique* variance on each predictor is related to variance on *y*.

We now consider two examples to illustrate the meaning of squared semipartial correlations; the first example is a verbal explanation, while the second is a graphical representation.

Example 4—Verbal Explanation of Variance Breakdown

y—freshman college GPA
predictor 1—high school GPA
predictor 2—SAT total score
predictor 3—attitude toward education

$$R_{y.123}^2 = r_{y1}{}^2 + r_{y2.1(s)}^2 + r_{y3.12(s)}^2$$

$r_{y1}{}^2$ gives the variance in college GPA scores that is predictable from variability on high school GPA scores. That is, because of differences in high school GPA the subject will differ (vary) in college GPA.

$r_{y2.1(s)}^2$ gives the residual variance in SAT scores (i.e., variance *unrelated* to variance on high school GPA) which is related to variance in college GPA.

$r_{y3.12(s)}^2$ gives the residual variance on attitude (i.e., variance *not* related to its correlations with high school GPA and SAT score) which is related to variance on college GPA.

Example 5—Graphical Representation of Variance Breakdown

This is easiest to see for 2 predictors. Therefore, suppose we have the following: $r_{y1} = .60$, $r_{y2} = .50$ and $r_{12} = .70$. We will use a Venn diagram, where a circle represents variance for a variable, and overlap between two circles indicates amount of variance the two variables share.

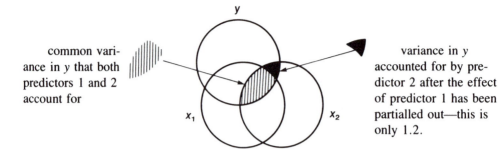

common variance in y that both predictors 1 and 2 account for

variance in y accounted for by predictor 2 after the effect of predictor 1 has been partialled out—this is only 1.2.

Below we present the semipartial correlation, showing how the 1.2% is arrived at:

$$r_{y2.1(s)} = \frac{r_{y2} - r_{y1}\, r_{21}}{\sqrt{1 - r^2_{21}}} = \frac{.50 - .60(.70))}{\sqrt{1 - .49}} = .11 \Rightarrow r^2_{y2.1(s)} = .012$$

FORWARD—The first predictor that has an opportunity to enter the equation is the one which has the largest simple correlation with y. If this predictor is significant, then the predictor with the largest semipartial correlation with y is considered, etc. At some stage a given predictor will not make a significant contribution to prediction, and the procedure terminates. It is important to remember that with this procedure, once a variable gets into the equation it stays.

STEPWISE—This is basically a variation on the forward selection procedure. However, at each stage of the procedure, a test is made of the least useful predictor. The importance of each predictor is constantly reassessed. Thus, a predictor that may have been the best entry candidate earlier may now be superfluous.

BACKWARD SELECTION—The steps are as follows: (a) An equation is computed with all the predictors. (b) The partial F is calculated for every predictor, treated as though it were the last predictor to enter the regression equation. (c) The smallest partial F value, say F_1, is compared to a preselected significance value (F_0), or to an F to remove, as in the BMDP2R program. If $F_1 < F_0$, remove that predictor and recompute the equation with the remaining variables. Reenter stage B.

Use of Mallow's C_p. Before we introduce Mallows' C_p, it is important to consider the consequences of underfitting (important variables are left out of the model) and overfitting (having variables in the model that make essentially no contribution or are marginal). Myers (1990, pp. 178–180) has an excellent discussion on the impact of underfitting and overfitting, and notes that, "A model that is too simple may suffer from biased coefficients and biased prediction, while an overly complicated model can result in large variances, both in the coefficients and in the prediction."

This measure was introduced by C. L. Mallows (1973) as a criterion for selecting a model. It measures total squared error, and it was recommended by Mallows to choose the model(s) where $C_p \approx p$. For these models the amount of underfitting and/or overfitting is minimized. Mallows' criterion may be written as

$$C_p = p + \frac{(s^2 - \hat{\sigma}^2)(N - p)}{\hat{\sigma}^2} \qquad (p = k + 1) \qquad (4)$$

where s^2 is the residual variance for the model being evaluated and $\hat{\sigma}^2$ is an estimate of the residual variance that is usually based on the full model.

Use of MAXR Procedure From SAS.   There are *nine* methods of model selection in the SAS REG program (*SAS/STAT User's Guide*, Volume 2, 1990), MAXR being one of them. This procedure produces several models; the best one variable model, the best two variable model, etc. Here is the description of the procedure from the *SAS/STAT* manual:

> The MAXR method begins by finding the one variable model producing the highest R^2. Then another variable, the one that yields the greatest increase in R^2, is added. Once the two variable model is obtained, each of the variables in the model is compared to each variable not in the model. For each comparison, MAXR determines if removing one variable and replacing it with the other variable increases R^2. After comparing all possible switches, MAXR makes the switch that produces the largest increase in R^2. Comparisons begin again, and the process continues until MAXR finds that no switch could increase R^2. . . . Another variable is then added to the model, and the comparing and switching process is repeated to find the best three variable model. (p. 1398)

Use of one or more of the above methods will often yield a number of models of roughly equal efficacy. As Myers (1990) noted, "The successful model builder will eventually understand that with many data sets, several models can be fit that would be of nearly equal effectiveness. Thus the problem that one deals with is the selection of *one model* from a pool of *candidate models*" (p. 164). One of the problems with the stepwise methods, which are very frequently used, is that they have led many investigators to conclude that they have found *the* best model, when in fact there may be some better models and/or several other models that are about as good. As Huberty notes (1989), "And one or more of these subsets may be more interesting or relevant in a substantive sense" (p. 46).

As mentioned earlier, Mallows' criterion is useful in guarding against both underfitting and overfitting. Three other very important criteria that can be used to select from the candidate pool all relate to the generalizability of the prediction equation, that is, how well will the equation predict on an independent sample(s) of data. The 3 methods of model validation, which are discussed in detail in Section 6.11, are:

1. Data splitting—Randomly split the data, obtain a prediction equation on one half of the random split and then check its predictive power (cross validate) on the other sample.
2. Use of the PRESS statistic.
3. Obtain an *estimate* of the average predictive power of the equation on many other samples from the same population, using a formula due to Stein (Herzberg, 1969).

The *SPSS Base 7.5 Applications Guide* (pp. 184–185) and *SPSS Base 8.0 Applications Guide* (pp. 216–217) comment on overfitting and the use of several models. There is no one test to determine the dimensionality of the best submodel. Some researchers find it tempting to include too many variables in the model. This is called *overfitting*. Such a model will perform poorly when applied to a new sample drawn from the same population. Automatic stepwise procedures cannot do all the work for you. Use them as a tool to determine roughly the number of predictors needed (for example, you might find three to five variables). If you try several methods of selection, you may identify candidate predictors that are not included by any method. Ignore them, and fit models, say, with three to five variables, selecting alternative subsets from among the better candidates. You may find several subsets that perform equally as well. Then knowledge of the subject matter, how accurately individual variables are measured, and what a variable "communicates" may guide selection of the model to report.

6.9   TWO COMPUTER EXAMPLES

To illustrate the use of several of the aforementioned model selection methods, we consider two computer examples. The first example illustrates the SPSS REGRESSION program, and uses data from Morrison (1983) on 32 students enrolled in an MBA course. We predict instructor course evaluation from 5 predictors. The second example illustrates SAS REG on quality ratings of 46 research doctorate programs in psychology, where we are attempting to predict quality ratings from factors such as number of program graduates, percentage of graduates that received fellowships or grant support, etc. (Singer & Willett, 1988).

Example 6—SPSS REGRESSION on Morrison MBA Data

The data for this problem are from Morrison (1983). The dependent variable is instructor course evaluation in an MBA course, with the five predictors being clarity, stimulation, knowledge, interest, and course evaluation. We illustrate two of the sequential procedures, stepwise and backward selection, using the SPSS REGRESSION program. The control lines for running the analyses, along with the correlation matrix, are given in Table 6.3.

SPSS REGRESSION has "p values," denoted by PIN and POUT, which govern whether a predictor will enter the equation and whether it will be deleted. The default values are PIN = .05 and POUT = .10. In other words, a predictor must be "significant" at the .05 level to enter, or must not be significant at the .10 level to be deleted.

First, we discuss the stepwise procedure results. Examination of the correlation matrix in Table 6.3 reveals that three of the predictors (CLARITY, STIMUL, and COUEVAL) are strongly related to INSTEVAL (simple correlations of .862, .739, and .738, respectively). Because clarity has the highest correlation, it will enter the equation first. Superficially, it might appear that STIMUL or COUEVAL would enter next; however, we must take into account how these predictors are correlated with CLARITY, and indeed both have fairly high correlations with CLARITY (.617 and .651 respectively). Thus, they will not account for as much unique variance on INSTEVAL, above and beyond that of CLARITY, as first appeared. On the other hand, INTEREST, which has a considerably lower correlation with INSTEVAL (.44), is only correlated .20 with CLARITY. Thus, the variance on INSTEVAL it accounts for is relatively independent of the variance CLARITY accounted for. And, as seen in Table 6.4, it is INTEREST that enters the regression equation second.

STIMUL is the third and final predictor to enter, since its p value (.0086) is less than the default value of .05. Finally, the other predictors (KNOWLEDGE and COUEVAL) don't enter since their p values (.0989 and .1288) are greater than .05.

Selected printout from the backward selection procedure appears in Table 6.5. First, all of the predictors are put into the equation. Then, the procedure determines which of the predictors makes the *least* contribution when entered last in the equation. That predictor is INTEREST, and since its p value is .9097, it is deleted from the equation. None of the other predictors can be further deleted because their p values are much less than .10.

Interestingly, note that two *different* sets of predictors emerge from the two sequential selection procedures. The stepwise procedure yields the set (CLARITY, INTEREST, and STIMUL), while the backward procedure yields the set (COUEVAL, KNOWLEDGE, STIMUL, and CLARITY). However, CLARITY and STIMUL are common to both sets. On the grounds of parsimony, we might prefer the set (CLARITY, INTEREST, and STIMUL), especially since the adjusted R^2's for the two sets are quite close (.84 and .87).

There are three other things that should be checked out before settling on this as our chosen model:

1. We need to determine if the assumptions of the linear regression model are tenable.

TABLE 6.3
SPSS Control Syntax for Stepwise Regression Run
on MORRISON Data and Correlation Matrix

```
TITLE 'MULTIPLE REGRESSION - MORRISON DATA'.
DATA LIST FREE/INSTEVAL CLARITY STIMUL KNOWLEDG INTEREST COUEVAL.
BEGIN DATA.
1 1 2 1 1 2    1 2 2 1 1 1    1 1 1 1 1 2    1 1 2 1 1 2
2 1 3 2 2 2    2 2 4 1 1 2    2 3 3 1 1 2    2 3 4 1 2 3
2 2 3 1 3 3    2 2 2 2 2 2    2 2 3 2 1 2    2 2 2 3 3 2
2 2 2 1 1 2    2 2 4 2 2 2    2 3 3 1 1 3    2 3 4 1 1 2
2 3 2 1 1 2    3 4 4 3 2 2    3 4 3 1 1 4    3 4 3 1 2 3
3 4 3 2 2 3    3 3 4 2 3 3    3 3 4 2 3 3    3 4 3 1 1 2
3 4 5 1 1 3    3 3 5 1 2 3    3 4 4 1 2 3    3 4 4 1 1 3
3 3 3 2 1 3    3 3 5 1 1 2    4 5 5 2 3 4    4 4 5 2 3 4
END DATA.
LIST.
① REGRESSION DESCRIPTIVES=DEFAULT/
  VARIABLES=INSTEVAL TO COUEVAL/
② STATISTICS=DEFAULTS TOL SELECTION/
  DEPENDENT=INSTEVAL/
③ METHOD=STEPWISE/
④ CASEWISE=ALL PRED RESID ZRESID LEVER COOK/
⑤ SCATTERPLOT(*RES,*PRE)/.
```

CORRELATION MATRIX

	INSTEVAL	CLARITY	STIMUL	KNOWLDGE	INTEREST	COUEVAL
INSTEVAL	1.000	.862	.739	.282	.435	.738
CLARITY	.862	1.000	.617	.057	.200	.651
STIMUL	.739	.617	1.000	.078	.317	.523
KNOWLEDGE	.282	.057	.078	1.000	.583	.041
INTEREST	.435	.200	.317	.583	1.000	.448
COUEVAL	.738	.651	.523	.041	.448	1.000

①The DESCRIPTIVES=DEFAULT subcommand yields the means, standard deviations and the correlation matrix for the variables.

②This STATISTICS subcommand TOL part yields useful information concerning multicollinearity. In particular it yields the VIF's (variance inflation factors). The SELECTION part yields, among other things, Mallows' prediction criterion, which is very useful in selecting a set of predictors.

③To obtain the backward selection procedure, we would simply put METHOD=BACKWARD/

④This CASEWISE subcommand yields important regression diagnostics: ZRESID (standardized residuals—for identifying outliers on y), LEVER (hat elements—for identifying outliers on predictors), and COOK (Cook's distance—for identifying influential data points).

⑤This SCATTERPLOT subcommand yields the plot of the residuals vs. the predicted values, which is very useful for determining whether any of the assumptions underlying the linear regression model may be violated.

TABLE 6.4
Selected Printout From SPSS Syntax Editor Stepwise
Regression Run on the Morrison MBA Data

Regression

Descriptive Statistics

	Mean	Std. Deviation	N
INSTEVAL	2.4063	.7976	32
CLARITY	2.8438	1.0809	32
STIMUL	3.3125	1.0906	32
KNOWLEDG	1.4375	.6189	32
INTEREST	1.6563	.7874	32
COUEVAL	2.5313	.7177	32

Correlations

		INSTEVAL	CLARITY	STIMUL	KNOWLEDG	INTEREST	COUEVAL
Pearson Correlation	INSTEVAL	1.000	.862	.739	.282	.435	.738
	CLARITY	.862	1.000	.617	.057	.200	.651
	STIMUL	.739	.617	1.000	.078	.317	.523
	KNOWLEDG	.282	.057	.078	1.000	.583	.041
	INTEREST	.435	.200	.317	.583	1.000	.448
	COUEVAL	.738	.651	.523	.041	.448	1.000

Variables Entered/Removed[a]

Model	Variables Entered	Variables Removed	Method
1	CLARITY	.	Stepwise (Criteria: Probability-of-F-to-enter <= .050, Probability-of-F-to-remove >= .100).
2	INTEREST	.	Stepwise (Criteria: Probability-of-F-to-enter <= .050, Probability-of-F-to-remove >= .100).
3	STIMUL	.	Stepwise (Criteria: Probability-of-F-to-enter <= .050, Probability-of-F-to-remove >= .100).

a. Dependent Variable: INSTEVAL

This predictor enters the equation first, since it has the highest simple correlation (.862) with the dependent variable INSTEVAL.

INTEREST has the opportunity to enter the equation next since it has the largest partial correlation of .528 (see the box with EXCLUDED VARIABLES), and does enter since its p value (.002) is less than the default entry value of .05.

Since STIMULUS has the strongest tie to INSTEVAL, after the effects of CLARITY and INTEREST are partialed out, it gets the opportunity to enter next. STIMULUS does enter, since its p value (.009) is less than .05.

(Continued)

TABLE 6.4
(Continued)

Model Summary[d]

Model	R	R Square	Adjusted R Square	Std. Error of the Estimate	Selection Criteria			
					Akaike Information Criterion	Amemiya Prediction Criterion	Mallows' Prediction Criterion	Schwarz Bayesian Criterion
1	.862[a]	.743	.734	.4112	-54.936	.292	35.297	-52.004
2	.903[b]	.815	.802	.3551	-63.405	.224	19.635	-59.008
3	.925[c]	.856	.840	.3189	-69.426	.186	11.517	-63.563

a. Predictors: (Constant), CLARITY

b. Predictors: (Constant), CLARITY, INTEREST

c. Predictors: (Constant), CLARITY, INTEREST, STIMUL

d. Dependent Variable: INSTEVAL

With just CLARITY in the equation we account for 74.3% of the variance; adding INTEREST increases the variance accounted for to 81.5%, and finally with 3 predictors (STIMUL added) we account for 85.6% of the variance in this sample.

ANOVA[d]

Model		Sum of Squares	df	Mean Square	F	Sig.
1	Regression	14.645	1	14.645	86.602	.000[a]
	Residual	5.073	30	.169		
	Total	19.719	31			
2	Regression	16.061	2	8.031	63.670	.000[b]
	Residual	3.658	29	.126		
	Total	19.719	31			
3	Regression	16.872	3	5.624	55.316	.000[c]
	Residual	2.847	28	.102		
	Total	19.719	31			

a. Predictors: (Constant), CLARITY

b. Predictors: (Constant), CLARITY, INTEREST

c. Predictors: (Constant), CLARITY, INTEREST, STIMUL

d. Dependent Variable: INSTEVAL

Coefficients[a]

Model		Unstandardized Coefficients		Standardized Coefficients	t	Sig.	Collinearity Statistics	
		B	Std. Error	Beta			Tolerance	VIF
1	(Constant)	.598	.207		2.882	.007		
	CLARITY	.636	.068	.862	9.306	.000	1.000	1.000
2	(Constant)	.254	.207		1.230	.229		
	CLARITY	.596	.060	.807	9.887	.000	.960	1.042
	INTEREST	.277	.083	.273	3.350	.002	.960	1.042
3	(Constant)	2.137E-02	.203		.105	.917		
	CLARITY	.482	.067	.653	7.158	.000	.619	1.616
	INTEREST	.223	.077	.220	2.904	.007	.900	1.112
	STIMUL	.195	.069	.266	2.824	.009	.580	1.724

a. Dependent Variable: INSTEVAL

These are the raw regression coefficients that define the prediction equation, i.e., INSTEVAL = .482 CLARITY + .223 INTEREST + .195 STIMUL + .021. The coefficient of .482 for CLARITY means that for every unit change on CLARITY there is a change of .482 units on INSTEVAL. The coefficient of .223 for INTEREST means that for every unit change on INTEREST there is a change of .223 units on INSTEVAL.

(Continued)

TABLE 6.4
(Continued)

Excluded Variables[d]

Model		Beta In	t	Sig.	Partial Correlation	Collinearity Statistics Tolerance	VIF	Minimum Tolerance
1	STIMUL	.335[a]	3.274	.003	.520	.619	1.616	.619
	KNOWLEDG	.233[a]	2.783	.009	.459	.997	1.003	.997
	INTEREST	.273[a]	3.350	.002	.528	.960	1.042	.960
	COUEVAL	.307[a]	2.784	.009	.459	.576	1.736	.576
2	STIMUL	.266[b]	2.824	.009	.471	.580	1.724	.580
	KNOWLEDG	.116[b]	1.183	.247	.218	.656	1.524	.632
	COUEVAL	.191[b]	1.692	.102	.305	.471	2.122	.471
3	KNOWLEDG	.148[c]	1.709	.099	.312	.647	1.546	.572
	COUEVAL	.161[c]	1.567	.129	.289	.466	2.148	.451

a. Predictors in the Model: (Constant), CLARITY
b. Predictors in the Model: (Constant), CLARITY, INTEREST
c. Predictors in the Model: (Constant), CLARITY, INTEREST, STIMUL
d. Dependent Variable: INSTEVAL

Since neither of these *p* values is less than .05, no other predictors can enter, and the procedure terminates.

2. We need an estimate of the cross-validity power of the equation.

3. We need to check for the existence of outliers and/or influential data points.

Figure 6.4 showed the plot of the residuals versus the predicted values from SPSS. This plot showed essentially random variation of the points about the horizontal line of 0, indicating no violations of assumptions.

The issues of cross-validity power and outliers are considered later in this chapter, and are applied to this problem in Section 6.15, after both topics have been covered.

Example 7—SAS REG on Doctoral Programs in Psychology

The data for this example come from a National Academy of Sciences report (Jones, Lindzey, & Coggsdall, 1982) that, among other things, provided ratings on the quality of 46 research doctoral programs in psychology. The six variables used to predict quality are:

NFACULTY—number of faculty members in the program as of December 1980.

NGRADS—number of program graduates from 1975 through 1980.

PCTSUPP—percentage of program graduates from 1975–1979 that received fellowships or training grant support during their graduate education.

Variables Entered/Removed[b]

Model	Variables Entered	Variables Removed	Method
1	COUEVAL, KNOWLED G, STIMUL, INTEREST, CLARITY[a]	.	Enter
2		INTEREST	Backward (criterion: Probability of F-to-remov e >= .100).

a. All requested variables entered.

b. Dependent Variable: INSTEVAL

Model Summary[c]

Model	R	R Square	Adjusted R Square	Std. Error of the Estimate	Akaike Information Criterion	Amemiya Prediction Criterion	Mallows' Prediction Criterion	Schwarz Bayesian Criterion
						Selection Criteria		
1	.946[a]	.894	.874	.2831	-75.407	.154	6.000	-66.613
2	.946[b]	.894	.879	.2779	-77.391	.145	4.013	-70.062

a. Predictors: (Constant), COUEVAL, KNOWLEDG, STIMUL, INTEREST, CLARITY

b. Predictors: (Constant), COUEVAL, KNOWLEDG, STIMUL, CLARITY

c. Dependent Variable: INSTEVAL

Coefficients[a]

Model		Unstandardized Coefficients B	Std. Error	Standardized Coefficients Beta	t	Sig.	Collinearity Statistics Tolerance	VIF
1	(Constant)	-.443	.235		-1.886	.070		
	CLARITY	.386	.071	.523	5.415	.000	.436	2.293
	STIMUL	.197	.062	.269	3.186	.004	.569	1.759
	KNOWLEDG	.277	.108	.215	2.561	.017	.579	1.728
	INTEREST	1.114E-02	.097	.011	.115	.910	.441	2.266
	COUEVAL	.270	.110	.243	2.459	.021	.416	2.401
2	(Constant)	-.450	.222		-2.027	.053		
	CLARITY	.384	.067	.520	5.698	.000	.471	2.125
	STIMUL	.198	.059	.271	3.335	.002	.592	1.690
	KNOWLEDG	.285	.081	.221	3.518	.002	.994	1.006
	COUEVAL	.276	.094	.249	2.953	.006	.553	1.810

a. Dependent Variable: INSTEVAL

(Continued)

				Collinearity Statistics			
Model	Beta In	t	Sig.	Partial Correlation	Tolerance	VIF	Minimum Tolerance
2 INTEREST	.011[a]	.115	.910	.022	.441	2.266	.416

Excluded Variables[b]

a. Predictors in the Model: (Constant), COUEVAL, KNOWLEDG, STIMUL, CLARITY
b. Dependent Variable: INSTEVAL

PCTGRANT—percentage of faculty members holding research grants from the Alcohol, Drug Abuse, and Mental Health Administration, the National Institute of Health or the National Science Foundation at any time during 1978–1980.

NARTICLE—number of published articles attributed to program faculty members from 1978–1980.

PCTPUB—percentage of faculty with one or more published articles from 1978–1980.

Both the stepwise procedure and the MAXR procedure were used on this data to generate several regression models. The control lines for doing this, along with the correlation matrix, are given in Table 6.6.

The stepwise procedure terminated after 4 predictors entered. Below is the summary table, exactly as it appears on the printout:

Summary of Stepwise Procedure for Dependent Variable QUALITY

Step	Variable Entered	Removed	Partial $R**2$	Model $R**2$	$C(p)$	F	$Prob > F$
1	NARTIC		0.5809	0.5809	55.1185	60.9861	0.0001
2	PCTGRT		0.1668	0.7477	18.4760	28.4156	0.0001
3	PCTSUPP		0.0569	0.8045	7.2970	12.2197	0.0011
4	NFACUL		0.0176	0.8221	5.2161	4.0595	0.0505

This four predictor model appears to be a reasonably good one. First, Mallows' C_p is very close to p (recall $p = k + 1$), that is, $5.216 \approx 5$, indicating that there is not much bias in the model. Second, $R^2 = .8221$, indicating that we can predict quality quite well from the 4 predictors. Although this R^2 is *not* adjusted, the adjusted value will not differ much because we have not selected from a large pool of predictors.

Selected printout from the MAXR procedure run appears in Table 6.7. From Table 6.7 we can construct the following results:

BEST MODEL	VARIABLE(S)	MALLOWS' C_p
for 1 variable	NARTIC	55.118
for 2 variables	PCTGRT, NFACUL	16.859
for 3 variables	PCTPUB, PCTGRT, NFACUL	9.147
for 4 variables	NFACUL, PCTSUPP, PCTGRT, NARTIC	5.216

TABLE 6.6
SAS REG Control Lines for Stepwise and MAXR Runs on the
National Academy of Sciences Data and the Correlation Matrix

DATA SINGER;
INPUT QUALITY NFACUL NGRADS PCTSUPP PCTGRT NARTIC PCTPUB;
CARDS;

DATA LINES

① PROC REG SIMPLE CORR;
② MODEL QUALITY = NFACUL NGRADS PCTSUPP PCTGRT NARTIC PCTPUB/
  SELECTION = STEPWISE VIF R INFLUENCE;
  MODEL QUALITY = NFACUL NGRADS PCTSUPP PCTGRT NARTIC PCTPUB/
  SELECTION = MAXR VIF R INFLUENCE;

① SIMPLE is needed to obtain descriptive statistics (means, variances, etc) for all
variables.
CORR is needed to obtain the correlation matrix for the variables.

② In this MODEL statement, the dependent variable goes on the left and all predictors to
the right of the equals.
SELECTION is where we indicate which of the 9 procedures we wish to use. There is a
wide variety of other information we can get printed out. Here we have selected VIF
(variance inflation factors), R (analysis of residuals — standard residuals, hat elements,
Cooks D), and INFLUENCE (influence diagnostics).

Note that there are two separate MODEL statements for the two regression procedures
being requested. Although multiple procedures can be obtained in one run, you *must*
have separate MODEL statement for each procedure.

CORRELATION MATRIX

		NFACUL 2	NGRADS 3	PCTSUPP 4	PCTGRT 5	NARTIC 6	PCTPUB 7	QUALITY 1
NFACUL	2	1.000						
NGRADS	3	0.692	1.000					
PCTSUPP	4	0.395	0.337	1.000				
PCTGRT	5	0.162	0.071	0.351	1.000			
NARTIC	6	0.755	0.646	0.366	0.436	1.000		
PCTPUB	7	0.205	0.171	0.347	0.490	0.593	1.000	
QUALITY	1	0.622	0.418	0.582	0.700	0.762	0.585	1.000

In this case, the *same* 4 predictor model is selected by the MAXR procedure
that was selected by the stepwise procedure.

Caveat on p Values for the "Significance" of Predictors

The p values that are given by SPSS and SAS for the "significance" of each
predictor at each step for stepwise or the forward selection procedures should be
treated tenuously, especially if your initial pool of predictors is moderate (15) or

TABLE 6.7
Selected Printout From the MAXR Run on the National Academy of Sciences Data

Maximum R-square Improvement for Dependent Variable QUALITY

Step 1   Variable NARTIC Entered   R-square = 0.58089673   C(p) = 55.11853652
The above model is the best 1-variable model found.
Step 2   Variable PCTGRT Entered   R-square = 0.74765405   C(p) = 18.47596774
Step 3   Variable NARTIC Removed   R-square = 0.75462892   C(p) = 16.85968570
       Variable NFACUL Entered
The above model is the best 2-variable model found.
Step 4   Variable PCTPUB Entered   R-square = 0.79654184   C(p) = 9.14723035
The above model is the best 3-variable model found.
Step 5   Variable PCTSUPP Entered   R-square = 0.81908649   C(p) = 5.92297432
Step 6   Variable PCTPUB Removed   R-square = 0.82213698   C(p) = 5.21608457
       Variable NARTIC Entered

	DF	Sum of Squares	Mean Square	F	Prob>f
Regression	4	3752.82298869	938.20574717	47.38	0.0001
Error	41	811.89440261	19.80230250		
Total	45	4564.71739130			

Variable	Parameter Estimate	Standard Error	Type II Sum of Squares	F	Prob>F
INTERCEP	9.06132974	1.64472577	601.05272060	30.35	0.0001
NFACUL	0.13329934	0.06615919	80.38802096	4.06	0.0505
PCTSUPP	0.09452909	0.03236602	168.91497705	8.53	0.0057
PCTGRT	0.24644511	0.04414314	617.20528404	31.17	0.0001
NARTIC	0.05455483	0.01954712	154.24691982	7.79	0.0079

The above model is the best 4-variable model found.

large (30). The reason is that the ordinary F distribution is *not* appropriate here, because the largest F is being selected out of all F's available. Thus, the appropriate critical value will be larger (and can be considerably larger) than would be obtained from the ordinary null F distribution. Draper and Smith (1981) note, "Studies have shown, for example, that in some cases where an entry F test was made at the α level, the appropriate probability was $q\alpha$, where there were q entry candidates at that stage" (p. 311). This is saying, for example, that an experimenter may think his or her probability of erroneously including a predictor is .05, when in fact the *actual* probability of erroneously including the predictor is .50 (if there were 10 entry candidates at that point)!

Thus, the F tests are positively biased, and the greater the number of predictors, the larger the bias. Hence, these F tests should be used only as rough guides to the usefulness of the predictors chosen. The acid test is how well the predictors do under cross-validation. It can be unwise to use *any* of the stepwise procedures with 20 or 30 predictors and only 100 subjects, since capitalization on chance is great, and the results may well not cross-validate. To find an equation that probably will have generalizability, it is best to carefully select (using substantive knowledge and/or any previous related literature) a small or relatively small set of predictors.

6.10   CHECKING ASSUMPTIONS
FOR THE REGRESSION MODEL

Recall that in the linear regression model it is assumed that the errors are independent and follow a normal distribution with constant variance. The normality assumption can be checked through use of the histogram of the standardized residuals. The independence assumption implies that the subjects are responding independently of one another. This is an important assumption. Even a slight violation can cause the type I error rate to be several times greater than what one desires.

Let us consider a situation where the independence assumption would not be tenable. Suppose we had 50 college freshmen each write 4 in class essays. Then, although we have 200 essays to grade, we have only 50 independent responses, since the responses for each student are going to be correlated.

Residual Plots

There are various plots available for assessing potential problems with the regression model (Draper & Smith, 1981; Weisberg, 1985). A very useful plot graphs the standardized residuals (y) vs. the predicted values (x). If the assumptions of the linear regression model are tenable, then the standardized residuals should scatter randomly about a horizontal line of 0, as shown in Figure 6.3a (see Section 6.3). *Any systematic pattern or clustering of the residuals suggests a model violation(s).* Three such systematic patterns are shown in Figures 6.3b to 6.3d. Figure 6.3b shows a systematic quadratic (second degree equation) clustering of the residuals. For Figure 6.3c the variability of the residuals increases systematically as the predicted values increase, suggesting a violation of the constant variance assumption.

In Figure 6.7 we present residual plots for three real data sets. The first plot is for the Morrison data (the first computer example), and shows essentially random scatter of the residuals, suggesting no violations of assumptions. The remaining two plots are from a study by a statistician who analyzed the salaries of over 260 major league hitters, using predictors such as career batting average, career home runs per time at bat, years in the major leagues, etc. These plots are from Moore and McCabe (1989), and are used with permission. Figure 6.7b, which plots the residuals versus predicted salaries, shows a clear violation of the constant variance assumption. For lower predicted salaries there is little variability about 0, but for the high salaries there is considerable variability of the residuals. The implication of this is that the model will predict lower salaries quite accurately, but not so for the higher salaries.

Figure 6.7c plots the residuals versus number of years in the major leagues. This plot shows a clear curvilinear clustering, that is, quadratic. The curved lines encompass the vast majority of points to make this trend even more evident. The implication of this curvilinear trend is that the regression model will tend to overestimate the salaries of players who have been in the major leagues only a few years or over 15 years, while it will underestimate the salaries of players who have been in the majors about 5 to 9 years.

In concluding this section, note that if nonlinearity or nonconstant variance is found, there are various remedies. For nonlinearity, perhaps a polynomial model is needed. Or sometimes a transformation of the data will enable a nonlinear model to be approximated by a linear one. For nonconstant variance, weighted least squares is one possibility, or more commonly, a variance stabilizing transformation (such as square root or log) may be used. I refer the reader to Weisberg (1985, Chapter 6) for an excellent discussion of remedies for regression model violations.

6.11   MODEL VALIDATION

We indicated earlier that it was crucial for the researcher to obtain some measure of how well the regression equation will predict on an independent sample(s) of data. That is, it was important to determine whether the equation had generalizability. We discuss here two methods of model validation: one empirical, and the other involving an estimate of average predictive power on other samples. A third method of model validation, particularly useful when one has a small

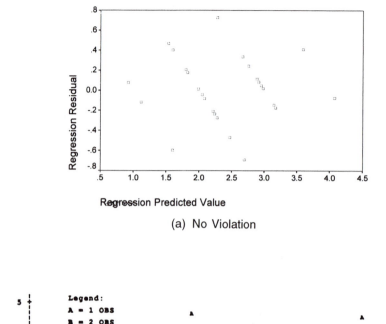

Regression Residual

Regression Predicted Value

(a) No Violation

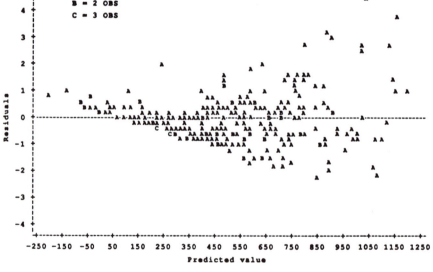

(b) Model Violation: Heterogeneous Variance

FIGURE 6.7   Residual Plots for Three Real Data Sets Showing No Violations, Heterogenous Variance, and Curvilinearity

272

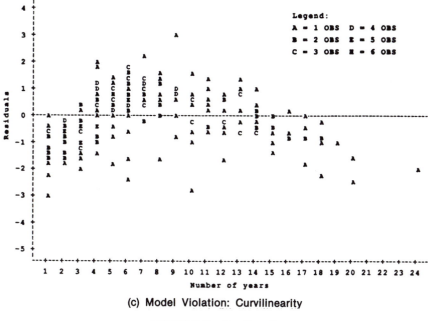

(c) Model Violation: Curvilinearity

FIGURE 6.7 *(Continued)*

or moderate sample, utilizes what is called the PRESS statistic. This is a nice empirical measure, but it is more complicated, so I have put it in an Appendix to this chapter for those who are interested. Let me give a brief description of the two methods, and then I will elaborate on each form of validation.

Data Splitting. Here the sample is randomly split in half. It does not have to be split evenly, but we use this for illustration. The regression equation is found on the so-called derivation sample (also called the screening sample, or the sample that "gave birth" to the prediction equation by Tukey). This prediction equation is then applied to the other sample of data (called the validation sample) to see how well it predicts the y score there.

Compute an Adjusted R^2. There are various adjusted R^2 measures, or measures of shrinkage in predictive power, but they do not estimate the same thing. The one most commonly used, and that which is printed out by SPSS and SAS, is due to Wherry. It is very important to note that the Wherry formula estimates how much variance on *y* would be accounted for if we had derived the equation in the population from which the sample was drawn. The Wherry formula does *not* indicate how well the derived equation will predict on other samples from the same population. A formula due to Stein (1960) does estimate average cross-validation predictive power. Unfortunately, it was not printed out by SPSS and SAS about 10 years ago, and it is still not printed out by either package.

Data Splitting

Recall that the sample is randomly split. The regression equation is found on the derivation sample and then is applied to the other sample (validation) to determine how well it will predict y there. Below we give a hypothetical example, randomly splitting 100 subjects.

Derivation Sample $n = 50$		Validation Sample $n = 50$		
Prediction Equation $\hat{y}_i = 4 + .3x_1 + .7x_2$		y	x_1	x_2
		6	1	.5
		4.5	2	.3
		. . . .		
		7	5	.2

Now, using the above prediction equation we predict the y scores in the validation sample:

$$\hat{y}_1 = 4 + .3(1) + .7(.5) = 4.65$$
$$\hat{y}_2 = 4 + .3(2) + .7(.3) = 4.81$$
.

.

.

$$\hat{y}_{50} = 4 + .3(5) + .7(.2) = 5.64$$

The cross-validated R then is the correlation for the following set of scores:

y	$\hat{y}_i$
6	4.65
4.5	4.81
.	
.	
.	
7	5.64

Adjusted R^2

Herzberg (1969) presents a discussion of various formulas that have been used to estimate the amount of shrinkage found in R^2. As mentioned earlier, the one most commonly used, and due to Wherry, is given by

$$\hat{\rho}^2 = 1 - \frac{(n-1)}{(n-k-1)}(1-R^2) \tag{5}$$

where $\hat{\rho}$ is the estimate of ρ, the population multiple correlation coefficient. This is the adjusted R^2 printed out by SAS and SPSS. Draper and Smith (1981) comment on Equation 5: "A related statistic . . . is the so called adjusted r (R_a^2), the idea being that the statistic R_a^2 can be used to compare equations fitted not only to a specific set of data but also to two or more entirely different sets of data. The value of this statistic for the latter purpose is, in our opinion, not high" (p. 92).

Herzberg notes that, "In applications, the population regression function can never be known and one is more interested in how effective the *sample* regression function is in *other* samples. A measure of this effectiveness is r_c, the sample cross-validity. For any given regression function r_c will vary from validation sample to validation sample. The average value of r_c will be approximately equal to the correlation, in the *population*, of the sample regression function with the criterion. This correlation is the population cross-validity, ρ_c. Wherry's formula estimates ρ rather than ρ_c." (p. 4).

There are two possible models for the predictors: (1) regression—the values of the predictors are fixed, i.e., we study y only for certain values of x, and (2) correlation—the predictors are random variables—this is a much more reasonable model for social science research. Herzberg presents the following formula for estimating ρ_c^2 under the correlation model:

$$\hat{\rho}_c^2 = 1 - \left(\frac{n-1}{n-k-1}\right)\left(\frac{n-2}{n-k-2}\right)\left(\frac{n+1}{n}\right)(1-R^2) \tag{6}$$

where n is sample size and k is the number of predictors. It can be shown that $\rho_c < \rho$.

If you are interested in cross-validity predictive power, then the Stein formula (Equation 6) should be used. As an example, suppose $n = 50$, $k = 10$, and R^2 .50. If you use the Wherry formula (Equation 5), then your estimate is

$$\hat{\rho}^2 = 1 - 49/39\,(.50) = .372$$

whereas with the proper Stein formula you would obtain

$$\hat{\rho}_c^2 = 1 - (49/39)(48/38)(51/50)(.50) = .191$$

In other words, use of the Wherry formula would give a misleadingly positive impression of the cross validity predictive power of the equation.

TABLE 6.8
Estimated Predictive Power Using the Stein Formula
for Small to Fairly Large Subject/Variable Ratios

Subject/Variable Ratio	Stein Estimate $$1 - \left(\frac{n-1}{n-k-1}\right)\left(\frac{n-2}{n-k-2}\right)\left(\frac{n+1}{n}\right)(1 - R^2)$$	Comment
Small (5:1) $n = 50$, $k = 10$ $R^2 = .50$ ②	$1 - (49/39)\,(48/38)\,(51/50)\,(.5)$ $= .191$ ①	The estimated amount of shrinkage is great, i.e., on the average we expect the predictive power to be reduced by about 60%.
Moderate (10:1) $n = 100$, $k = 10$ $R^2 = .50$	$1 - (99/98)\,(98/88)\,(101/100)\,(.5)$ $= .374$	The shrinkage is still fairly substantial.
Fairly Large (15:1) $n = 150$, $k = 10$ $R^2 = .50$	$1 - (149/139)\,(148/138)\,(151/150)\,(.5)$ $= .421$	We finally reach a point where the expected amount of shrinkage is fairly small, i.e., about 16%.

① If we were to apply the prediction equation to many other samples from the same population, then on the *average* we would account for 19.1% of the variance on y.

② We have chosen this value to illustrate since the typical R^2 values found in social science are often around .50.

Table 6.8 shows how the estimated predictive power drops off using the Stein formula (Equation 6) for small to fairly large subject/variable ratios when $R^2 = .50$.

6.12 IMPORTANCE OF THE ORDER OF THE PREDICTORS IN REGRESSION ANALYSIS

The order in which the predictors enter a regression equation can make a great deal of difference with respect to how much variance on y they account for, especially for moderate or highly correlated predictors. Only for uncorrelated predictors (which would rarely occur in practice) does the order not make a difference. We give two examples to illustrate.

Example 8

A dissertation by Crowder (1975) attempted to predict ratings of trainably mentally retarded individuals (TMs) using I.Q. (x_2) and scores from a TEST of Social Inference (TSI). He was especially interested in showing that the TSI had incremental predictive validity. The criterion was the average ratings by two individuals in charge of the TMs. The intercorrelations among the variables were:

$$r_{x_1x_2} = .59, r_{yx_2} = .54, r_{yx_1} = .566$$

Now, consider two orderings for the predictors, one where TSI is entered first, and the other ordering where I.Q. is entered first.

	First Ordering % of variance		Second Ordering % of variance
TSI	32.04	I.Q.	29.16
I.Q.	6.52	TSI	9.40

The first ordering conveys an overly optimistic view of the utility of the TSI scale. Since we know that I.Q. will predict ratings it should be entered first in the equation (as a control variable), and then TSI to see what its incremental validity is, i.e., how much it *adds* to predicting ratings above and beyond what I.Q. does. Because of the moderate correlation between I.Q. and TSI, the amount of variance accounted for by TSI differs considerably when entered first vs. second (32.04 vs. 9.4).

The 9.4% of variance accounted for by TSI when entered second is obtained through the use of the semipartial correlation previously introduced:

$$r_{y1.2(s)} = \frac{.566 - .54(.59)}{\sqrt{1 - 59^2}} = .306 \Rightarrow r^2_{y1.2(s)} = 0.94$$

Example 9

Consider the following matrix of correlations for a three predictor problem:

	x_1	x_2	x_3
y	.60	.70	.70
x_1		.70	.60
x_2			.80

How much variance on y will x_3 account for if entered first, and if entered last? If x_3 is entered first, then it will account for $(.7)^2 \times 100$ or 49% of the variance on y. If x_3 is entered last, we need to compute a second order semipartial correlation (see Stevens, 1996, p. 102 for details). The answer is only 4.8% of the variance on y. Because the predictors are so highly correlated, most of the variance on y that x_3 could have accounted for has already been accounted for by x_1 and x_2.

Controlling the Order of Predictors in the Equation

With the forward and stepwise selection procedures, the order of entry of predictors into the regression equation is determined via a mathematical maximization procedure. That is, the first predictor to enter is the one with the largest (maximized) correlation with y, the second to enter is the predictor with the largest semipartial correlation, etc. However, there are situations where one may not want the mathematics to determine the order of entry of predictors. For example, suppose we have a five predictor problem, with two proven predictors from previous research. The other three predictors are included to see if they have any incremental validity. In this case we would want to enter the two proven predictors in the equation first (as control variables), and then let the remaining three predictors "fight it out" to determine whether any of them add anything significant to predicting y above and beyond the proven predictors.

With SPSS REGRESSION or SAS REG we can control the order of predictors, and in particular, we can *force* predictors into the equation. In Table 6.9 we illustrate how this is done for SPSS and SAS for the above five predictor situation.

TABLE 6.9
Controlling the Order of Predictors and Forcing Predictors
Into the Equation With SPSS REGRESSION and SAS REG

```
                        SPSS REGRESSION
    TITLE 'FORCING X3 AND X4 & USING STEPWISE SELECTION FOR OTHERS'.
    DATA LIST FREE/Y X1 X2 X3 X4 X5
    BEGIN DATA.
       DATA LINES
    END DATA.
    REGRESSION VARIABLES = Y X1 X2 X3 X4 X5/
       DEPENDENT = Y/
①  ENTER X3/ENTER X4/STEPWISE/.
                        SAS REG
    DATA FORCEPR;
    INPUT Y X1 X2 X3 X4 X5;
    CARDS;
       DATA LINES
    PROC REG SIMPLE CORR;
②  MODEL Y = X3 X4 X1 X2 X5/INCLUDE = 2 SELECTION = STEPWISE;
```

①These two ENTER subcommands will force the predictors in the specific order indicated. Then the STEPWISE subcommand will determine whether any of the remaining predictors (X1, X2 or X5) have semipartial correlations large enough to be "significant." If we wished to force in predictors X1, X3, and X4 and then use STEPWISE, the subcommand is ENTER X1 X3 X4/STEPWISE/

②The INCLUDE = 2 forces the *first 2* predictors listed in the MODEL statement into the prediction equation. Thus, if we wish to force X3 and X4 we must list them first on the MODEL statement.

6.13   OTHER IMPORTANT ISSUES

Preselection of Predictors

An industrial psychologist hears about the predictive power of multiple regression and is excited. He wants to predict success on the job, and gathers data for 20 potential predictors on 70 subjects. He obtains the correlation matrix for the variables, and then picks out 6 predictors that correlate significantly with success on the job and that have low intercorrelations among themselves. The analysis is run, and the R^2 is highly significant. Furthermore, he is able to explain 52% of the variance on y (more than other investigators have been able to do). Are these results generalizable? Probably not, since what he did involves a *double* capitalization on chance:

1. First, in preselecting the predictors from a larger set, he is capitalizing on chance. Some of these variables would have high correlations with y because of sampling error, and consequently their correlations would tend to be lower in another sample.
2. Second, the mathematical maximization involved in obtaining the multiple correlation involves capitalizing on chance.

Preselection of predictors is common among many researchers, who are unaware of the fact that this tends to make their results sample specific. Nunnally (1978) has a nice discussion of the preselection problem, and Wilkinson (1979) has shown the considerable positive bias preselection can have on the test of significance of R^2 in forward selection. The following example from his tables illustrates. The critical value for a 4 predictor problem ($n = 35$) at .05 level is .26, while the appropriate critical value for the *same* n and α level, when preselecting 4 predictors from a set of 20 predictors is .51! Unawareness of the positive bias has led to many results in the literature that are not replicable, for as Wilkinson notes, "A computer assisted search for articles in psychology using stepwise regression from 1969 to 1977 located 71 articles. Out of these articles, 66 forward selections analyses reported as significant by the usual F tests were found. Of these 66 analyses, 19 were *not* significant by [his] Table 1."

It is important to note that both the Wherry and Herzberg formulas do *not* take into account preselection. Hence, the following from Cohen and Cohen (1983) should be seriously considered: "A more realistic estimate of the shrinkage is obtained by substituting for k the *total* number of predictors from which the selection was made" (p. 107). In other words, they are saying if 4 predictors were selected out of 15, use $k = 15$ in the Herzberg formula. While this may be conservative, using 4 will certainly lead to a positive bias. Probably a median value between 4 and 15 would be closer to the mark, although this needs further investigation.

Positive Bias of R^2

A study by Schutz (1977) on California principals and superintendents illustrates how capitalization on chance in multiple regression (if the researcher is unaware of it) can lead to misleading conclusions. Schutz was interested in validating a "contingency theory of leadership," that is, that success in administering schools calls for different personality styles depending on the social setting of the school. The theory seems plausible, and in what follows we are not criticizing the theory per se, but the empirical validation of it. Schutz's procedure for validating the theory involved establishing a relationship between various personality attributes (24 predictors) and several measures of administrative success in heterogeneous samples with respect to social setting using multiple regression, that is, find the multiple R for each measure of success on 24 predictors. Then he showed that the magnitude of the relationships was greater for subsamples homogeneous with respect to social setting. The problem was that he had nowhere near adequate sample size for a reliable prediction equation. Below we present the total sample sizes and the subsamples homogeneous with respect to social setting:

	Superintendents	*Principals*
Total	$n = 77$	$n = 147$
Subsample(s)	$n = 29$	$n_1 = 35, n_2 = 61, n_2 = 36$

Indeed, Schutz did find that the R's in the homogeneous subsamples were on the average .34 greater than in the total samples; however, this was an artifact of the multiple regression procedure in this case. As Schutz went from total to his subsamples the number of predictors (k) approached sample size (n). For this situation the multiple correlation increases to 1 *regardless* of whether there is any relationship between y and the set of predictors. And in 3 of 4 of Schutz's subsamples the n/k ratios became dangerously close to 1. In particular it is the case that $E(R^2) = k/(n - 1)$, when the population multiple correlation = 0 (Morrison, 1976).

To dramatize this, consider subsample 1 for the principals. Then $E(R^2) = 24/34$ = .706, even when there is *no* relationship between y and the set of predictors. The critical value required just for statistical significance of R at .05 is 2.74, which implies $R^2 > .868$, just to be confident that the population multiple correlation is different from 0!

6.14   OUTLIERS AND INFLUENTIAL DATA POINTS

Since multiple regression is a mathematical maximization procedure, it can be very sensitive to data points that "split off" or are different from the rest of the points, that is, to outliers. Just 1 or 2 such points can affect the interpretation of results, and it is certainly moot as to whether 1 or 2 points should be permitted to have such a profound influence. Therefore, it is important to be able to detect outliers and influential points. There is a distinction between the two because a point that is an outlier (either on y or for the predictors) will *not necessarily* be influential in affecting the regression equation.

There are two basic approaches that can be used in dealing with outliers and influential points. We consider the approach of having an arsenal of tools for isolating these important points for further study, with the possibility of deleting some or all of the points from the analysis. The other approach is to develop procedures that are relatively insensitive to wild points (i.e., robust regression techniques).

Data Editing

Outliers and influential cases can occur because of recording errors. Consequently, researchers should give more consideration to the data editing phase of the data analysis process (i.e., *always* listing the data and examining the list for possible errors). There are many possible sources of error, from the initial data collection to the final keypunching. First, some of the data may have been recorded incorrectly. Second, even if recorded correctly, when all of the data are transferred to a single sheet or a few sheets in preparation for keypunching, errors may be made. Finally, even if no errors are made in these first two steps, an error(s) could be made in entering the data into the terminal.

There are various statistics for identifying outliers on y and on the set of predictors, as well as for identifying influential data points. We discuss first, in brief form, a statistic for each, with advice on how to interpret that statistic. Equations for the statistics are given in my multivariate text (Stevens, 1996), along with a more extensive and somewhat technical discussion for those who are interested.

Measuring Outliers on y

For finding subjects whose predicted scores are quite different from their actual y scores (i.e., they do not fit the model well), the *standardized residuals* (r_i) can be used. If the model is correct, then they have a normal distribution with a mean of 0 and a standard deviation of 1. Thus, about 95% of the r_i should lie within two standard deviations of the mean and about 99% within three standard deviations. Therefore, any standardized residual greater than about 3 in absolute value is unusual and should be carefully examined.

Measuring Outliers on Set of Predictors

The *hat elements* (h_{ii}) can be used here. It can be shown that the hat elements lie between 0 and 1, and that the average hat element is p/n, where $p = k + 1$. Because of this, Hoaglin and Welsch (1978) suggest that $2p/n$ may be considered large. However, this can lead to more points then we really would want to examine, and the reader should consider using $3p/n$. For example, with 6 predictors and 100 subjects, any hat element (also called leverage) greater than $3(7)/100 = .21$ should be carefully examined. This is a very simple and useful rule of thumb for quickly identifying subjects who are very different from the rest of the sample on the set of predictors.

Measuring Influential Data Points

An influential data point is one that when deleted produces a substantial change in at least one of the regression coefficients. That is, the prediction equations with and without the influential point are quite different. *Cook's distance* (1977) is very useful for identifying influential points. It measures the *combined* influence of the case being an outlier on y and on the set of predictors. Cook and Weisberg (1982) have indicated that a Cook's distance > *1 would generally be considered large*. This provides a "red flag," when examining computer printout, for identifying influential points.

All of the above diagnostic measures are easily obtained from SPSS REGRESSION (cf. Table 6.3) or SAS REG (cf. Table 6.6).

6.15   FURTHER DISCUSSION OF THE TWO COMPUTER EXAMPLES

Morrison Data

Recall that for Morrison data the stepwise procedure yielded the more parsimonious model involving 3 predictors: CLARITY, INTEREST, and STIMUL. If we were interested in an estimate of the predictive power in the population, then the Wherry estimate given by Equation 5 is appropriate. This is given in Table 6.4 under model 3 as ADJUSTED R SQUARE .840. Here the estimate is used in a descriptive sense; to describe the relationship in the population. However, if we are interested in the cross-validity predictive power, then the Stein estimate (Equation 6) should be used. The Stein adjusted R^2 in this case is

$$\rho_c^2 = 1 - (31/28)(30/27)(33/32)(1 - .856) = .82$$

This estimates that if we were to cross-validate the prediction equation on many other samples from the same population, then *on the average* we would account for about 82% of the variance on the dependent variable. In this instance the estimated dropoff in predictive power is very little from the maximized value of 85.56%. The reason is that the association between the dependent variable and the set of predictors is *very* strong. Thus, we can have confidence in the future predictive power of the equation.

It is also important to examine the regression diagnostics to check for any outliers and/or influential data points. Table 6.10 presents the appropriate statistics, as discussed in Section 6.14, for identifying outliers on the dependent variable (standardized residuals), outliers on the set of predictors (hat elements), and influential data points (Cook's distance).

First, we would expect only about 5% of the standardized residuals to be > |2| if the linear model is appropriate. From Table 6.10 we see that 2 of the ZRESID are > |2|, and we would expect about 32(.05) = 1.6, so nothing seems to be awry here. Next, we check for outliers on the set of predictors. The rough "critical value" here is $3p/n = 3(4)/32 = .375$. Since there are no values under LEVER in Table 6.10 exceeding this value, we have no outliers on the set of predictors. Finally, and perhaps most importantly, we check for the existence of influential data points using Cook's *D*. Recall that Cook (1982) has suggested if $D > 1$, then the point is influential. All the Cook *D*'s in Table 6.10 are far less than 1, so we have no influential data points.

In summary then, the linear regression model is quite appropriate for the Morrison data. The estimated cross validity power is excellent, and there are no outliers or influential data points.

National Academy of Sciences Data

Recall that both the stepwise procedure and the MAXR procedure yielded the same "best" 4-predictor set: NFACUL, PCTSUPP, PCTGRT, and NARTIC. The maximized $R^2 = .8221$, indicating that 82.21% of the variance in quality can be accounted for by these 4 predictors in *this* sample. Now we obtain two measures of the cross-validity power of the equation. First, from the SAS REG printout, we have PREDICTED RESID SS (PRESS) = 1350.33. Furthermore, the variance for QUALITY is 101.438, so that $\Sigma (Y_i - Y)^2 = 4564.71$. From these numbers we can compute

$$R^2_{PRESS} = 1 - (1350.33)/4564.71 = .7042$$

This is a good measure of the external predictive power of the equation, where we have *n* validations, each based on $(n - 1)$ observations.

The Stein *estimate* of how much variance on the average we would account for if the equation were applied to many other samples is

$$\rho_c^2 = 1 - (45/41)(44/40)(47/46)(1 = .822) = .7804$$

Now we turn to the regression diagnostics from SAS REG, which are presented in Table 6.11. In terms of the standardized residuals for *y*, there are two that stand

TABLE 6.10
Regression Diagnostics (Standardized Residuals, Hat Elements, and Cook's Distance) for Morrison MBA Data

Casewise Diagnostics[a]

Case Number	Std.[3] Residual	INSTEVAL	[1] Predicted Value	[2] Residual	Centered Leverage [4] Value	[5] Cook's Distance
1	-.363	1.00	1.1156	-.1156	.102	.006
2	-1.875	1.00	1.5977	-.5977	.054	.090
3	.248	1.00	.9209	7.911E-02	.154	.004
4	-.363	1.00	1.1156	-.1156	.102	.006
5	1.464	2.00	1.5330	.4670	.135	.128
6	.040	2.00	1.9872	1.277E-02	.122	.000
7	-.861	2.00	2.2746	-.2746	.028	.012
8	-2.170	2.00	2.6920	-.6920	.018	.064
9	-.746	2.00	2.2378	-.2378	.138	.034
10	.563	2.00	1.8204	.1796	.071	.010
11	.651	2.00	1.7925	.2075	.041	.009
12	-.135	2.00	2.0431	-4.31E-02	.203	.002
13	1.262	2.00	1.5977	.4023	.054	.041
14	-.658	2.00	2.2099	-.2099	.086	.016
15	-.861	2.00	2.2746	-.2746	.028	.012
16	-1.472	2.00	2.4693	-.4693	.054	.055
17	-.250	2.00	2.0799	-7.99E-02	.095	.003
18	-.546	3.00	3.1741	-.1741	.039	.006
19	.763	3.00	2.7567	.2433	.104	.026
20	.065	3.00	2.9794	2.062E-02	.093	.000
21	.065	3.00	2.9794	2.062E-02	.093	.000
22	.268	3.00	2.9147	8.532E-02	.098	.003
23	.268	3.00	2.9147	8.532E-02	.098	.003
24	.763	3.00	2.7567	.2433	.104	.026
25	-.458	3.00	3.1462	-.1462	.141	.013
26	.355	3.00	2.8868	.1132	.112	.006
27	-.546	3.00	3.1741	-.1741	.039	.006
28	.152	3.00	2.9514	4.855E-02	.076	.001
29	2.275	3.00	2.2746	.7254	.028	.087
30	1.054	3.00	2.6641	.3359	.174	.090
31	-.231	4.00	4.0736	-7.36E-02	.186	.005
32	1.281	4.00	3.5915	.4085	.131	.095

a. Dependent Variable: INSTEVAL

[1] These are the predicted values.

[2] These are the raw residuals, that is, $\hat{e}_i = y_i - \hat{y}_i$. Thus, for the first subject we have $\hat{e}_1 = 1 - 1.1156 = -.1156$.

[3] These are the standardized residuals.

[4] The hat elements—they have been called leverage elements elsewhere; hence the abbreviation LEVER.

[5] Cook's distance—useful for identifying influential data points. Cook suggests if $D > 1$, then the point generally would be considered influential.

TABLE 6.11
Regression Diagnostics (Standardized Residuals, Hat Elements, and Cook's Distance) for National Academy of Science Data

Obs	Student Residual	-2-1-0 1 2	Cook's D	Rstudent	Hat Diag H
1	-0.708	*	0.007	-0.7039	0.0684
2	-0.078		0.000	-0.0769	0.1064
3	0.403		0.003	0.3992	0.0807
4	0.424		0.009	0.4193	0.1951
5	0.800	*	0.012	0.7968	0.0870
6	-1.447	**	0.034	-1.4677	0.0742
7	1.085	**	0.038	1.0874	0.1386
8	-0.300		0.002	-0.2968	0.1057
9	-0.460		0.010	-0.4556	0.18765
10	1.694	* ***	0.48	1.7346	0.0765
11	-0.694	*	0.004	-0.6892	0.0433
12	-0.870	*	0.016	-0.8670	0.0956
13	-0.732		0.007	-0.7276	0.0652
14	0.359	*	0.003	0.3556	0.0885
15	-0.942	**	0.054	-0.9403	0.2328
16	1.282		0.063	1.2927	0.1613
17	0.424		0.001	0.4200	0.0297
18	0.227		0.001	0.2241	0.1196
19	0.877	*	0.007	0.8747	0.0464
20	0.643	*	0.004	0.6382	0.0456
21	-0.417		0.002	-0.4127	0.0429
22	0.193		0.001	0.1907	0.0696
23	0.490		0.002	0.4856	0.0460
24	0.357		0.001	0.3533	0.0503
25	-2.756	*****	2.292	-3.0154	0.6014
26	-1.370	**	0.068	-1.3855	0.1533
27	-0.799	*	0.017	-0.7958	0.1186
28	0.165		0.000	0.1629	0.0573
29	0.995	*	0.018	0.9954	0.0844
30	-1.786	***	0.241	-1.8374	0.2737
31	-1.171	**	0.018	-1.1762	0.0613
32	-0.994	*	0.017	-0.9938	0.0796
33	1.394	**	0.037	1.4105	0.0859
34	1.568	***	0.051	1.5978	0.0937
35	-0.622	*	0.006	-0.6169	0.0714
36	0.282		0.002	0.2791	0.1066
37	-0.831	*	0.009	-0.8277	0.0643
38	1.516	***	0.039	1.5411	0.0789
39	1.492	**	0.081	1.5151	0.1539
40	0.314		0.001	0.3108	0.0638
41	-0.977	*	0.016	-0.9766	0.0793
42	-0.581	*	0.006	-0.5766	0.0847
43	0.059		0.000	0.0584	0.0877
44	2.376	****	0.164	2.5276	0.1265
45	-0.508	*	0.003	-0.5031	0.0592
46	-1.505	***	0.085	-1.5292	0.1583

out (-3.0154 and 2.5276 for observations 25 and 44). These are for the University of Michigan and Virginia Polytech. In terms of outliers on the set of predictors, using $2p/n = 2(5)/46 = .217$, there are outliers for observation 15 (University of Georgia), observation 25 (University of Michigan again), and observation 30 (Northeastern).

Using the criterion of Cook $D > 1$, there is one influential data point, observation 25 (University of Michigan). Recall that whether a point will be influential is a *joint* function of being an outlier on y and on the set of predictors. In this case, the University of Michigan definitely doesn't fit the model and it differs dramatically from the other psychology departments on the set of predictors. A check of the DFBETAS reveals that it is very different in terms of number of faculty (DFBETA $= -2.7653$), and a scan of the raw data shows the number of faculty at 111, while the average number of faculty members for all the departments is only 29.5. The question needs to be raised as to whether the University of Michigan is "counting" faculty members in a different way from the rest of the schools. For example, are they including part time and adjunct faculty, and if so, is the number of these quite large?

For comparison purposes, the analysis was also run with the University of Michigan deleted. Interestingly, the same 4 predictors emerge from the stepwise procedure, although the results are better in some ways. For example, Mallows' C_p is now 4.5248, whereas for the full data set it was 5.216. Also, the PRESS residual sum of squares is now only 899.92, whereas for the full data set it was 1350.33.

6.16   SAMPLE SIZE DETERMINATION FOR A RELIABLE PREDICTION EQUATION

The reader may recall that in power analysis one is interested in determining a priori how many subjects are needed per group to have, say, power $= .80$ at the .05 level. Thus, planning is done ahead of time to ensure that one has a good chance of detecting an effect of a given magnitude. Now, in multiple regression the focus is different and the concern, or at least one very important concern, is development of a prediction equation that has generalizability. A study by Park and Dudycha (1974) provides several tables that, given certain input parameters, enable one to determine how many subjects will be needed for a reliable prediction equation. They considered from 3 to 25 random variable predictors, and found that with about 15 subjects per predictor the amount of shrinkage is small ($<.05$) with high probability (.90), if the squared population multiple correlation (ρ^2) is .50. In Table 6.12 we present selected results from the Park and Dudycha study for 3, 4, 8, and 15 predictors.

To use Table 6.12 we need an estimate of ρ^2, that is, the squared *population* multiple correlation. Unless an investigator has a good estimate from a previous study that used similar subjects and predictors, we feel taking $\rho^2 = .50$ is a reasonable guess for social science research. In the physical sciences, estimates $>.75$ are quite

TABLE 6.12
Sample Size Such That the Difference Between the Squared Multiple Correlation and Squared Cross-Validated Correlation is Arbitrarily Small with Given Probability

Three Predictors

ρ^2	ϵ	.99	.95	.90	.80	.60	.40
.05	.01	858	554	421	290	158	81
	.03	269	166	123	79	39	18
.10	.01	825	535	410	285	160	88
	.03	271	174	133	91	50	27
	.05	159	100	75	51	27	14
.25	.01	693	451	347	243	139	79
	.03	232	151	117	81	48	27
	.05	140	91	71	50	29	17
	.10	70	46	36	25	15	7
	.20	34	22	17	12	8	6
.50	.01	464	304	234	165	96	55
	.03	157	104	80	57	34	21
	.05	96	64	50	36	22	14
	.10	50	34	27	20	13	9
	.20	27	19	15	12	9	7
.75	.01	235	155	120	85	50	30
	.03	85	55	43	31	20	13
	.05	51	35	28	21	14	10
	.10	28	20	16	13	9	7
	.20	16	12	10	9	7	6
.98	.01	23	17	14	11	9	7
	.03	11	9	8	7	6	6
	.05	9	7	7	6	6	5
	.10	7	6	6	6	5	5
	.20	6	6	5	5	5	5

Four Predictors

ρ^2	ϵ	.99	.95	.90	.80	.60	.40
.05	.01	1041	707	559	406	245	144
	.03	312	201	152	103	54	27
.10	.01	1006	691	550	405	253	155
	.03	326	220	173	125	74	43
	.05	186	123	95	67	38	22
.25	.01	853	587	470	348	221	140
	.03	283	195	156	116	73	46
	.05	168	117	93	69	43	28
	.10	84	58	46	34	20	14
	.20	38	26	20	15	10	7
.50	.01	573	396	317	236	152	97
	.03	193	134	108	81	53	35
	.05	117	82	66	50	33	23
	.10	60	43	35	27	19	13
	.20	32	23	19	15	11	9
.75	.01	290	201	162	121	78	52
	.03	100	70	57	44	30	21
	.05	62	44	37	28	20	15
	.10	34	25	21	17	13	11
	.20	19	15	13	11	9	7
.98	.01	29	22	19	15	12	10
	.03	14	11	10	9	8	7
	.05	10	9	8	8	7	7
	.10	8	8	7	7	7	6
	.20	7	7	7	6	6	6

TABLE 6.12
(Continued)

Eight Predictors
probability

ρ^2	ϵ	.99	.95	.90	.80	.60	.40
.05	.01	1640	1226	1031	821	585	418
	.03	447	313	251	187	116	71
.10	.01	1616	1220	1036	837	611	450
	.03	503	373	311	246	172	121
	.05	281	202	166	128	85	55
.25	.01	1376	1047	893	727	538	404
	.03	453	344	292	237	174	129
	.05	267	202	171	138	101	74
	.10	128	95	80	63	45	33
	.20	52	37	30	24	17	12
.50	.01	927	707	605	494	368	279
	.03	312	238	204	167	125	96
	.05	188	144	124	103	77	59
	.10	96	74	64	53	40	31
	.20	49	38	33	28	22	18
.75	.01	470	360	308	253	190	150
	.03	162	125	108	90	69	54
	.05	100	78	68	57	44	35
	.10	54	43	38	32	26	22
	.20	31	25	23	20	17	15
.98	.01	47	38	34	29	24	21
	.03	22	19	18	16	15	14
	.05	17	16	15	14	13	12
	.10	14	13	12	12	11	11
	.20	12	11	11	11	11	10

Fifteen Predictors
probability

ϵ	.99	.95	.90	.80	.60	.40	ρ^2
.01	2523	2007	1760	1486	1161	918	.05
.03	640	474	398	316	222	156	
.01	2519	2029	1794	1532	1220	987	.10
.03	762	600	524	438	337	263	
.05	403	309	265	216	159	119	
.01	2163	1754	1557	1339	1079	884	.25
.03	705	569	504	431	345	280	
.05	413	331	292	249	198	159	
.10	191	151	132	111	87	69	
.20	76	58	49	40	30	24	
.01	1461	1188	1057	911	738	608	.50
.03	489	399	355	306	249	205	
.05	295	261	214	185	151	125	
.10	149	122	109	94	77	64	
.20	75	62	55	48	40	34	
.01	741	605	539	466	380	315	.75
.03	255	210	188	164	135	113	
.05	158	131	118	103	86	73	
.10	85	72	65	58	49	43	
.20	49	42	39	35	31	28	
.01	75	64	59	53	46	41	.98
.03	36	33	31	29	27	25	
.05	28	26	25	24	23	22	
.10	23	21	21	20	20	19	
.20	20	19	19	19	18	18	

*Entries in the body of the table are the sample size such that $P(\rho^2 - \rho_c^2 < \epsilon) = \gamma$ where ρ is population multiple correlation, ϵ is some tolerance and γ is the probability.

reasonable. If we set $\rho^2 = .50$ and want the loss in predictive power to be less than .05 with probability $= .90$, then the required sample sizes are as follows:

	Number of Predictors			
$\rho^2 = .50$ $\varepsilon = .05$	3	4	8	15
n	50	66	124	214
n/k ratio	16.7	16.7	15.5	14.3

The n/k ratios in all 4 cases are around 15/1.

We had indicated earlier that *generally* about 15 subjects per predictor are needed for a reliable regression equation in the social sciences, that is, an equation that will cross-validate well. There are three converging lines of evidence that support this conclusion:

1. The Stein formula for estimated shrinkage (Table 6.8).
2. My own experience.
3. The results just presented from the Park and Dudycha study.

However, the Park and Dudycha study (cf. Table 6.12) clearly shows that *the magnitude of* ρ (population multiple correlation) strongly affects how many subjects will be needed for a reliable regression equation. For example, if $\rho^2 = .75$, then for 3 predictors only 28 subjects are needed, whereas 50 subjects were needed for the same case when $\rho^2 = .50$.

Also, from the Stein formula (Table 6.8), you will see if you plug in .40 for R^2 that more than 15 subjects per predictor will be needed to keep the shrinkage fairly small, while if you insert .70 for R^2, significantly less than 15 will be needed.

6.17   ANOVA AS A SPECIAL CASE
OF REGRESSION ANALYSIS

This section is presented to show that ANOVA is just a special case of regression analysis, i.e., the general linear model. Cohen's (1968) seminal article was primarily responsible for bringing the general linear model to the attention of social science researchers. The regression approach to ANOVA is accomplished by dummy coding group membership. We will illustrate with two examples that were analyzed in Chapter 2 with traditional ANOVA. The first example had 3 groups, with the following data:

GROUP 1	GROUP 2	GROUP 3
3	4	4
6	7	5
8	9	2
	8	3
		5

We create two dummy variables (DUM1 and DUM2) to identify group membership, and use a 1 on the dummy variable to indicate group membership. The entities in the third group are uniquely identified by 0 and 0 on the two dummy variables, i.e., not in groups 1 or 2. Thus, we have

DEP	DUM1	DUM2	DEP	DUM1	DUM2
3	1	0	4	0	0
6	1	0	5	0	0
8	1	0	2	0	0
4	0	1	3	0	0
7	0	1	5	0	0
9	0	1			
8	0	1			

The second example had four groups, with the following data:

GROUP 1	GROUP2	GROUP3	GROUP4
2	7	4	8
3	9	4	4
5	11	5	7
6		8	7
		3	

In this case we need 3 dummy variables to identify group membership (DUM1, DUM2, and DUM3):

2	1	0	0
3	1	0	0
5	1	0	0
6	1	0	0
7	0	1	0
9	0	1	0
11	0	1	0
4	0	0	1
4	0	0	1
5	0	0	1
8	0	0	1
3	0	0	1
8	0	0	0
4	0	0	0
7	0	0	0
7	0	0	0

Note, that again the subjects in the last group (4th group here) are identified by 0's on all dummy variables, i.e., not in groups 1, 2, or 3. In general, we need $(k - 1)$ dummy variables for k groups.

When the above two data sets were run on SPSS or Windows 7.5 as regression analyses, predicting the dependent variable from group membership (DUM1 and DUM2 were the predictors in the first analysis and DUM1, DUM2, and DUM3 were the predictors in the second analysis), the results were as follows:

Variables Entered/Removed[b]

Model	Variables Entered	Variables Removed	Method
1	DUM2, DUM1[a]		Enter

a. All requested variables entered.

b. Dependent Variable: DEP

Model Summary

Model	R	R Square	Adjusted R Square	Std. Error of the Estimate
1	.640[a]	.409	.278	1.9283

a. Predictors: (Constant), DUM2, DUM1

ANOVA[b]

Model		Sum of Squares	df	Mean Square	F	Sig.
1	Regression	23.200	2	11.600	3.120	.093[a]
	Residual	33.467	9	3.719		
	Total	56.667	11			

a. Predictors: (Constant), DUM2, DUM1

b. Dependent Variable: DEP

Variables Entered/Removed[b]

Model	Variables Entered	Variables Removed	Method
1	DUM3, DUM2, DUM1[a]		Enter

a. All requested variables entered.

b. Dependent Variable: DEP

Model Summary

Model	R	R Square	Adjusted R Square	Std. Error of the Estimate
1	.740[a]	.548	.435	1.8664

a. Predictors: (Constant), DUM3, DUM2, DUM1

ANOVA[b]

Model		Sum of Squares	df	Mean Square	F	Sig.
1	Regression	50.638	3	16.879	4.846	.020[a]
	Residual	41.800	12	3.483		
	Total	92.438	15			

a. Predictors: (Constant), DUM3, DUM2, DUM1

b. Dependent Variable: DEP

Note that the results are *identical* to what was obtained in Chapter 2. The mean square due to regression corresponds to mean square between, while the residual corresponds to mean square error. The mean square due to regression is just variability due to group membership. We will see in the next chapter, on analysis of covariance (which combines ANOVA and regression analysis), that analysis of covariance can be done through regression analysis also.

6.18   SUMMARY OF IMPORTANT POINTS

1. A particularly good situation for multiple regression is where each of the predictors is correlated with y and the predictors have low intercorrelations, for then each of the predictors is accounting for a relatively distinct part of the variance on y.

2. Moderate to high correlations among the predictors (multicollinearity) creates three problems: it (a) severely limits the size of R, (b) makes determining the importance of given predictor difficult, and (c) increases the variance of regression coefficients, making for an unstable prediction equation. One way of

combating this problem is to combine into a single measure a set of predictors that are highly correlated.

3. Preselecting a small set of predictors by examining a correlation matrix from a large initial set, or by using one of the stepwise procedures (forward, stepwise, backward) to select a small set, is likely to produce an equation that is sample specific. If one insists on doing this, and I do not recommend it, then the onus is on the investigator to demonstrate that the equation has adequate predictive power beyond the derivation sample.

4. Mallows' C_p was presented as a measure that minimizes the effect of underfitting (important predictors left out of the model) and overfitting (having predictors in the model that make essentially no contribution or are marginal). This will be the case if one chooses models for which $C_p \approx p$.

5. With many data sets, more than one model will provide a good fit to the data. Thus, one deals with selecting a model from a *pool* of candidate models.

6. There are various graphical plots for assessing how well the model fits the assumptions underlying linear regression. One of the most useful graphs the standardized residuals (y axis) versus the predicted values (x axis). If the assumptions are tenable, then one should observe roughly a random scattering. Any *systematic clustering* of the residuals indicates a model violation(s).

7. It is crucial to validate the model(s) by either randomly splitting the sample and cross-validating, or using the PRESS statistic, or by obtaining the Stein estimate of the *average* predictive power of the equation on other samples from the same population. Studies in the literature that have not cross-validated should be checked with the Stein estimate to assess the generalizability of the prediction equation(s) presented.

8. Results from the Park and Dudycha study indicate that the magnitude of the *population* multiple correlation strongly affects how many subjects will be needed for a reliable prediction equation. If your estimate of the squared population value is .50, then about 15 subjects per predictor are needed. On the other hand, if your estimate of the squared population value is substantially *larger* than .50, then far less than 15 subjects per predictor will be needed.

9. Influential data points, that is, points that strongly affect the prediction equation, can be identified by seeing which cases have Cook distances >1. These points need to be examined very carefully. If such a point is due to a recording error, then one would simply correct it and redo the analysis. Or if it is found that the influential point is due to an instrumentation error or that the process that generated the data for that subject was different, then it is legitimate to drop the case from the analysis. If, however, none of these appears to be the case, then one should *not* drop the case, but perhaps report the results of several analyses: one analysis with all the data and an additional analysis(ses) with the influential point(s) deleted.

10. It was shown that analysis of variance can be considered as a special case of regression analysis by dummy coding group membership.

APPENDIX: THE PRESS STATISTIC

As pointed out by several authors, in many instances one does not have enough data to do a random split. One can obtain a good measure of the *external* predictive power by use of the PRESS statistic. In this approach the y value for each subject is set aside and a prediction equation is derived on the remaining data. Thus, n prediction equations are derived and n true prediction errors are found. To be very specific, the prediction error for subject 1 is computed from the equation derived on the remaining $(n - 1)$ data points, the prediction error for subject 2 is computed from the equation derived on the other $(n - 1)$ data points, etc. As Myers (1990) put it, "PRESS is important in that one has information in the form of n validations in which the fitting sample for each is of size $n - 1$" (p. 171).

The PRESS statistic is especially important when one does not have large sample size, for in this case data splitting is really not practical. For example, if $n = 60$ and we have 6 predictors, randomly splitting the sample involves obtaining a prediction equation on only 30 subjects.

Recall that in deriving the prediction (via the least squares approach), the sum of the squared errors is *minimized*. The PRESS residuals, on the other hand, are true prediction errors, since the y value for each subject was not simultaneously used for fit and model assessment. Let us denote the predicted value for subject i, where that subject was *not* used in developing the prediction equation, by $y_{(-i)}$. Then the PRESS residual for each subject is given by

$$\hat{e}_{(-i)} = y_i - \hat{y}_{(-i)}$$

and the PRESS sum of squared residuals is given by

$$\text{PRESS} = \Sigma \, \hat{e}_{(-i)}^2$$

Therefore, one might prefer the model with the smallest PRESS value. The above PRESS value can be used to calculate an R^2-like statistic that more accurately reflects the generalizability of the model. It is given by

$$R^2_{\text{PRESS}} = 1 - (\text{PRESS})/\Sigma \, (y_i - \bar{y})^2$$

Importantly, the SAS REG program does routinely print out PRESS, although it is called PREDICTED RESID SS (PRESS). Given this value, it is a simple matter to calculate the R^2 PRESS statistic, since $s_y^2 = \Sigma \, (y_i - \bar{y})^2/(n - 1)$.

EXERCISES

1. Consider this set of data:

x	y
2	3
3	6
4	8
6	4
7	10
8	14
9	8
10	12
11	14
12	12
13	16

(a) Plot the data. Does there appear to be a linear relationship?
(b) Run this data on SPSS, obtaining the case analysis.
(c) Do you see any pattern in the plot of the standardized residuals? What does this suggest?
(d) Sketch in the regression line, and indicate the raw residuals by vertical lines.

2. Consider the following small set of data:

PREDX	DEP
0	1
1	4
2	6
3	8
4	9
5	10
6	10
7	8
8	7
9	6
10	5

(a) Plot the points. What type of relationship does this suggest?
(b) Run this data on SPSS, forcing the predictor in and obtaining the case analysis.

(c) Do you see any pattern in the plot of the standardized residuals? What does this suggest?

3. Consider the following correlation matrix:

	y	x_1	x_2
y	1.00	.60	.50
x_1	.60	1.00	.80
x_2	.50	.80	1.00

(a) How much variance on y will x_1 account for if entered first?
(b) How much variance on y will x_1 account for if entered second?
(c) What, if anything, do the above results have to do with the multicollinearity problem?

4. A medical school admissions official has two proven predictors (x_1 and x_2) of success in medical school. He has two other predictors under consideration (x_3 and x_4), of which he wishes to choose just one which will add the most (beyond what x_1 and x_2 already predict) to predicting success. Below is the matrix of intercorrelations he has gathered on a sample of 100 medical students:

	x_1	x_2	x_3	x_4
y	.60	.55	.60	.46
x_1		.70	.60	.20
x_2			.80	.30
x_3				.60

(a) What procedure would he use to determine which predictor has the greater incremental validity? Do *not* go into any numerical details, just indicate the general procedure. Also, what is your educated guess as to which predictor (x_3 or x_4) will probably have the greater incremental validity.

5. Consider the following random sample of about 50% from the Agresti data (in Appendix A in the back of the book) on home sales in Florida. We wish to predict PRICE from the other 4 variables as predictors. The other variables are NEW (whether the home was new or not), NOBATH (number of bathrooms), NOBED (number of bedrooms) and SIZE (size of the house).
(a) Run stepwise regression analysis on this data. What model is selected?
(b) Run backward elimination on this data. What model is selected?

Case Summaries[a]

	NEW	NOBATH	NOBED	PRICE	SIZE
1	.00	1.00	3.00	48.50	1.10
2	.00	2.00	3.00	55.00	1.01
3	.00	3.00	3.00	137.00	2.40
4	1.00	3.00	4.00	309.40	3.30
5	.00	1.00	3.00	19.60	1.28
6	.00	1.00	3.00	24.50	.74
7	.00	1.00	2.00	34.80	.78
8	.00	1.00	3.00	32.00	.97
9	.00	1.00	3.00	28.00	.84
10	.00	2.00	2.00	49.90	1.08
11	.00	2.00	3.00	61.50	1.01
12	.00	2.00	3.00	68.90	1.29
13	.00	2.00	3.00	70.50	1.25
14	.00	2.00	3.00	72.90	1.28
15	.00	2.00	3.00	72.00	1.36
16	.00	2.00	3.00	71.00	1.20
17	.00	2.00	3.00	73.00	1.22
18	.00	2.00	2.00	70.00	1.40
19	.00	2.00	2.00	76.00	1.15
20	.00	2.00	3.00	75.50	1.62
21	.00	2.00	3.00	76.00	1.66
22	.00	2.00	3.00	81.80	1.33
23	.00	2.00	3.00	84.50	1.34
24	1.00	2.00	3.00	86.90	1.58
25	.00	2.00	3.00	88.10	2.10
26	.00	2.00	3.00	89.50	1.34
27	.00	2.00	3.00	90.00	1.55
28	1.00	2.00	3.00	95.50	1.54
29	1.00	2.00	4.00	99.90	1.62
30	1.00	2.00	3.00	102.30	1.42
31	1.00	2.00	3.00	110.80	1.56
32	.00	2.00	3.00	97.90	2.00
33	1.00	2.00	3.00	106.30	1.45
34	.00	2.00	3.00	106.50	1.65
35	1.00	2.00	4.00	109.90	2.06
36	.00	2.00	4.00	110.00	1.76
37	1.00	2.00	4.00	115.00	1.80
38	.00	2.00	3.00	114.90	1.57
39	.00	2.00	4.00	115.00	2.07
40	.00	2.00	4.00	117.90	1.99
41	.00	2.00	3.00	110.00	1.55
42	1.00	2.00	3.00	128.00	1.88
43	1.00	2.00	4.00	139.30	2.05
44	.00	3.00	3.00	142.00	2.12
45	.00	2.00	5.00	148.00	2.40
46	.00	3.00	3.00	150.00	2.04
Total N	46	46	46	46	46

a. Limited to first 100 cases.

6. An investigator has 15 variables on a file. Denote them by $x1, x2, x3, \ldots,$ $x15$. Assume there are spaces between all variables, so that free format can be used to read the data. The investigator wishes to predict $x4$. First, however, he obtains the correlation matrix among the predictors and finds that variables 7 and 8 are highly correlated, and decides to combine those as a single predictor. He will also use variables 1, 3, 11, 12, 13, and 14 as predictors. Show the set of control lines for running a stepwise analysis and also obtaining a scatterplot of the residuals vs predicted values of y.

7. A different investigator has 8 variables on a file, with no spaces between the variables, so that fixed format will be needed to read the data. The data looks as follows:

2534674823178659
3645738234267583
    ETC.

The first two variables are single digit integers, the next three variables are two digit integers, the next two variables are three digit integers and the 8th variable is a two digit integer. The 8th variable is the dependent variable. She wishes to force in variables 1 and 2, and then determine whether variables 3 through 5 (as a block) have any incremental validity. Show the complete SPSS REGRESSION control lines for doing this analysis.

8. A regression analysis was run on the Sesame St ($n = 240$) data set, predicting postbody from the following 5 pretest measures: prebody, prelet, preform, prenumb and prerelat. This was run in the syntax editor on SPSS for Windows 7.5. The control lines for doing a stepwise regression, obtaining the 10 largest values for the standardized residuals, the hat elements and Cook's distance, and for obtaining a plot of the standardized residuals versus the predicted y values are given below:

```
TITLE 'MULT REG ON POSTBODY - 5 PREDICTORS'.
DATA LIST FREE/ID SITE SEX AGE VIEWCAT SETTING VIEWENC
    PREBODY PRELET PREFORM
    PRENUMB PRERELAT PRECLASF POSTBODY POSTLET POSTFORM
    POSTNUMB POSTREL
    POSTCLAS PEABODY.
BEGIN DATA.

DATA LINES.
END DATA.
REGRESSION DESCRIPTIVES=DEFAULT/
    VARIABLES=PREBODY TO PRERELAT POSTBODY/
    STATISTICS=DEFAULTS TOL SELECTION/
```

```
DEPENDENT=POSTBODY/
METHOD=STEPWISE/
RESIDUALS=OUTLIERS (ZRESID,LEVER,COOK)/
SCATTERPLOT (*RES,*PRE)/.
```

The SPSS Windows 7.5 printout follows. Answer the following questions:
(a) Why did PREBODY enter the prediction equation first? highest corr.
(b) Why did PREFORM enter the prediction equation second? Second highest corr.
(c) Write the prediction equation, rounding off to 3 decimals.
(d) Is multicollinearity present? Explain. yes. other
(e) Compute the Stein estimate and indicate in words exactly what it represents.
(f) Refer to the standardized residuals. Is the number of these greater than |2| about what you would expect if the model is appropriate? Why, or why not?
(g) Are there are outliers on the set of predictors?
(h) Are there any influential data points? Explain.
(i) From examination of the residual plot, does it appear there may be some model violation(s)? Why, or why not?
(j) Are the values of VIF (variance inflation factor) for the predictors in the equation reasonable, according to Myers?
(k) Does the value of Mallows prediction criterion for model 2 seem reasonable? What about for model 1?

Descriptive Statistics

	Mean	Std. Deviation	N
PREBODY	21.4000	6.3909	240
PRELET	15.9375	8.5364	240
PREFORM	9.9208	3.7369	240
PRENUMB	20.8958	10.6854	240
PRERELAT	9.9375	3.0738	240
POSTBODY	25.2625	5.4121	240

Correlations

	PREBODY	PRELET	PREFORM	PRENUMB	PRERELAT	POSTBODY
PREBODY	1.000	.453	.680	.698	.623	.650
PRELET	.453	1.000	.506	.717	.471	.371
PREFORM	.680	.506	1.000	.673	.596	.551
PRENUMB	.698	.717	.673	1.000	.718	.527
PRERELAT	.623	.471	.596	.718	1.000	.449
POSTBODY	.650	.371	.551	.527	.449	1.000

Model	Variables Entered	Variables Removed	Method
1	PREBODY	.	Stepwise (Criteria: Probability-of-F-to-enter <= .050, Probability-of-F-to-remove >= .100).
2	PREFORM	.	Stepwise (Criteria: Probability-of-F-to-enter <= .050, Probability-of-F-to-remove >= .100).

a. Dependent Variable: POSTBODY

Model Summary[c]

Model	R	R Square	Adjusted R Square	Std. Error of the Estimate	Selection Criteria			
					Akaike Information Criterion	Amemiya Prediction Criterion	Mallows' Prediction Criterion	Schwarz Bayesian Criterion
1	.650[a]	.423	.421	4.1195	681.539	.587	8.487	688.500
2	.667[b]	.445	.440	4.0491	674.253	.569	1.208	684.695

a. Predictors: (Constant), PREBODY
b. Predictors: (Constant), PREBODY, PREFORM
c. Dependent Variable: POSTBODY

ANOVA[c]

Model		Sum of Squares	df	Mean Square	F	Sig.
1	Regression	2961.602	1	2961.602	174.520	.000[a]
	Residual	4038.860	238	16.970		
	Total	7000.462	239			
2	Regression	3114.883	2	1557.441	94.996	.000[b]
	Residual	3885.580	237	16.395		
	Total	7000.462	239			

a. Predictors: (Constant), PREBODY
b. Predictors: (Constant), PREBODY, PREFORM
c. Dependent Variable: POSTBODY

Coefficients[a]

Model		Unstandardized Coefficients		Standardized Coefficients	t	Sig.	Collinearity Statistics	
		B	Std. Error	Beta			Tolerance	VIF
1	(Constant)	13.475	.931		14.473	.000		
	PREBODY	.551	.042	.650	13.211	.000	1.000	1.000
2	(Constant)	13.062	.925		14.120	.000		
	PREBODY	.435	.056	.513	7.777	.000	.538	1.860
	PREFORM	.292	.096	.202	3.058	.002	.538	1.860

a. Dependent Variable: POSTBODY

Excluded Variables[c]

Model		Beta In	t	Sig.	Partial Correlation	Collinearity Statistics		
						Tolerance	VIF	Minimum Tolerance
1	PRELET	.096[a]	1.742	.083	.112	.795	1.258	.795
	PREFORM	.202[a]	3.058	.002	.195	.538	1.860	.538
	PRENUMB	.143[a]	2.091	.038	.135	.513	1.950	.513
	PRERELAT	.072[a]	1.152	.250	.075	.612	1.634	.612
2	PRELET	.050[b]	.881	.379	.057	.722	1.385	.489
	PRENUMB	.075[b]	1.031	.304	.067	.439	2.277	.432
	PRERELAT	.017[b]	.264	.792	.017	.557	1.796	.464

a. Predictors in the Model: (Constant), PREBODY
b. Predictors in the Model: (Constant), PREBODY, PREFORM
c. Dependent Variable: POSTBODY

Casewise Diagnostics[a]

Case Number	Std. Residual	POSTBODY
139	-3.056	11.00
219	3.138	31.00

a. Dependent Variable: POSTBODY

Outlier Statistics[a]

		Case Number	Statistic	Sig. F
Std. Residual	1	219	3.138	
	2	139	-3.056	
	3	125	-2.873	
	4	155	-2.757	
	5	39	-2.629	
	6	147	2.491	
	7	210	-2.345	
	8	40	-2.305	
	9	135	2.203	
	10	36	2.108	
Cook's Distance	1	219	.081	.970
	2	125	.078	.972
	3	39	.042	.988
	4	38	.032	.992
	5	40	.025	.995
	6	139	.025	.995
	7	147	.025	.995
	8	177	.023	.995
	9	140	.022	.996
	10	13	.020	.996
Centered Leverage Value	1	140	.047	
	2	32	.036	
	3	23	.030	
	4	114	.028	
	5	167	.026	
	6	52	.026	
	7	233	.025	
	8	8	.025	
	9	236	.023	
	10	161	.023	

a. Dependent Variable: POSTBODY

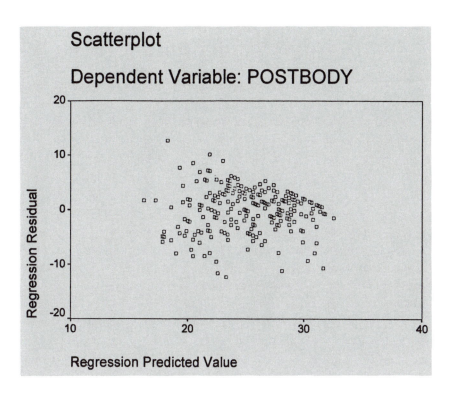

Scatterplot

Dependent Variable: POSTBODY

7
Analysis of Covariance

7.1 INTRODUCTION

In Chapter 4 we examined the effect of two or more independent variables (factors) in explaining variation on the dependent variable. We set up an experimental design, and thus this method is called experimental control. In this chapter we consider explaining variation on the dependent variable by measuring the subjects on some other variable(s), called covariates, that are correlated with the dependent variable. Recall that the square of a correlation can be interpreted as "proportion of variance accounted for." Thus, if we find that I.Q. is correlated

305

with achievement (dependent variable), say .60, we will be able to attribute 36% of the within group variance on the dependent variable to variability on I.Q. In analysis of covariance (ANCOVA), this part of the variance is removed from the error term, and yields a more powerful test. This method of explaining variation is called statistical control. We now consider an example to illustrate how ANCOVA can be very useful in an experimental study in which the subjects have been randomly assigned to groups.

Example

Suppose an investigator is comparing the effects of two treatments on achievement in science. He assesses achievement through the use of a 50 item multiple choice test. He has 24 students and is able to randomly assign 12 of them to each of the treatments. I.Q. scores are also available for these subjects. The data are as follows:

	Treat. 1		Treat. 2	
	I.Q.	Ach.	I.Q.	Ach.
	100	23	96	19
	113	31	108	26
	98	35	122	31
	110	28	103	22
	124	40	132	36
	135	42	120	38
	118	37	111	31
	93	29	93	25
	120	34	115	29
	127	45	125	41
	115	33	102	27
	104	25	107	21
Means	113.08	33.5	111.17	28.83

The investigator feels no need to use the I.Q. data for analysis purposes since the groups have been "equated" on all variables because of the random assignment. He therefore runs a t test for independent samples on achievement at the .05 level. He finds $t = 1.676$, which is not significant because the critical values are ± 2.074.

Because of small sample size we have a power problem. The estimated effect size is $\hat{d} = (33.5 - 28.83)/6.83 = .68$ (cf. Section 3.2), which is undoubtedly of practical significance since the groups differ by about two-thirds of a standard deviation. We have not detected it because of the power problem *and* because there is considerable within group variability on achievement. In fact, the pooled within correlation of I.Q. with achievement for the above data is about .80. This means that 64% of the variation in achievement test scores is associated with variation (individual differences) on I.Q. An analysis of covariance removes that portion from the error term and yields a t value significant at the .05 level ($t = 2.25$). Actually it comes out as an F statistic, so you need to take the square root. Recall that $F = t^2$ for two groups. After reading this chapter, the reader will be able to verify the above t value by running the ANCOVA on SAS or SPSS.

The above example showed that analysis of covariance is very useful in creating a more powerful test in an experimental study. ANCOVA is also used to reduce bias when comparing intact or self-selected groups, such as males and females, Head Start and non-Head Start. A classical use is adjusting posttest means on the dependent variable for any initial differences that may have been present on a pretest. Another typical use is in teaching methods studies that use intact classrooms. If the average I.Q.'s for the classrooms differ by 10 points, then an adjustment of the posttest achievement is done. Although the use of analysis of covariance in this context may seem reasonable, it is quite controversial, which we discuss in detail in Section 7.8.

The first 10 sections of this chapter cover the basics for ANCOVA with one covariate. We discuss the purposes of covariance, the underlying concepts, the assumptions, interpretation of results, the relationship of ANOVA and ANCOVA, and the running of ANCOVA on SAS and SPSS. The last five sections are more advanced, especially the section on the Johnson–Neyman technique, and may be skipped without loss of continuity. Much has been written about analysis of covariance, and the reader should at least be aware of two classic review articles by Cochran (1957) and Elashoff (1969), and a very comprehensive and thorough book on covariance and alternatives by Huitema (1980).

7.2 PURPOSES OF COVARIANCE

Analysis of covariance is related to the following two basic objectives in experimental design:

1. Elimination of systematic bias.
2. Reduction of within group or error variance.

Systematic bias means that the groups differ systematically on some key variable(s) that are related to performance on the dependent variable. If the groups involve treatments, then a significant difference on a posttest at the end of treatments will be confounded (mixed in with) with initial differences on a key variable. It would not be clear whether the treatments were making the difference, or whether initial differences simply transferred to posttest means. A simple example is a teaching methods study with initial differences between groups on I.Q. Suppose two methods of teaching algebra are compared (same teacher for both methods) with two classrooms in the same school. The following summary data, means for the groups, are available:

	Method 1	Method 2
I.Q.	120.2	105.8
Posttest	73.4	67.5

If the t test for independent samples on the posttest is significant, then it isn't clear whether it was method 1 that made the difference, or the fact that the children in that class were "brighter" to begin with, and thus would be expected to achieve higher scores.

As another example, suppose we are comparing the effect of four stress situations on blood pressure (the dependent variable). It is found that situation 3 is significantly more stressful than the other three situations. However, we note that the blood pressure of the subjects in group 3 under minimal stress is greater than for the subjects in the other groups. Then, it isn't clear that situation 3 is necessarily most stressful. We need to determine whether the blood pressure for group 3 would still be higher if the posttest means for all 4 groups were "adjusted" in some way to account for initial differences in blood pressure. We see later that the posttest means are adjusted in a linear fashion to what they would be if all groups started out equally on the covariate, that is, at the grand mean.

The best way of dealing with systematic bias is to randomly assign subjects to groups. Then we can be confident, within sampling error, that the groups don't differ systematically *on any variables*. Of course, in many studies random assignment is not possible, so we look for ways of at least partially equating groups. One way of partially controlling for initial differences is to match on key variables. Of course, then we can only be sure the groups are equivalent on those matched variables. Analysis of covariance is a *statistical* way of controlling on key variables. Once again, as with matching, ANCOVA can only *reduce* bias, and not eliminate it.

Why is reduction of error variance, the second purpose of analysis of covariance, important? Recall from Chapter 2 on one way ANOVA that the F statistic was $F = MS_b/MS_w$, where MS_w was the estimate of error. If we can make MS_w smaller, then F will be larger and we will obtain a more sensitive or powerful test. And from Chapter 3 on power, remember that power is generally poor in small or medium sample size studies. Thus the use of perhaps 2 or 3 covariates in such studies should definitely be considered. The use of covariates that have relatively low correlations with each other are particularly helpful because each covariate removes a somewhat different part of the error variance from the dependent variable.

Analysis of covariance is a *statistical* way of reducing error variance. There are several other ways of reducing error variance. One way is through sample selection; subjects who are more homogeneous vary less on the dependent measure. Another way, discussed in Chapter 4 on factorial designs, was to block on a variable, or consider it as another factor in the design.

7.3   ADJUSTMENT OF POSTTEST MEANS

As mentioned earlier, analysis of covariance adjusts the posttest means to what they would be if all groups started out equally on the covariate; at the grand mean. In this section we derive the general equation for linearly adjusting the posttest means for one covariate. Before we do that, however, it is important to discuss one of the assumptions underlying the analysis of covariance. That assumption for one covariate requires *equal population regression slopes* for all groups. Consider a three group situation, with 15 subjects per group. Suppose that the scatterplots for the 3 groups looked as given below.

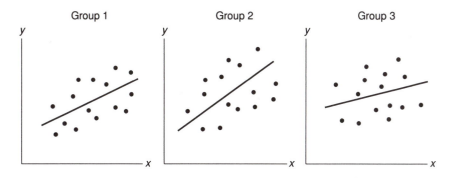

Recall from beginning statistics that the x and y scores for each subject determine a point in the plane. Requiring that the slopes be equal is equivalent to saying that the nature of the linear relationship is the *same* for all groups, or that the rate of change in y as a function of x is the same for all groups. For the above scatterplots the slopes are different, with the slope being the largest for group 2 and smallest for group 3. But the issue is whether the *population* slopes are different, and whether the sample slopes differ sufficiently to conclude that the population values are different. With small sample sizes as in the above scatterplots, it is dangerous to rely on visual inspection to determine whether the population values are equal, because of considerable sampling error. Fortunately there is a statistic for this, and later we indicate how to obtain it on SPSS and SAS. In deriving the equation for the adjusted means we are going to assume the slopes are equal. What if the slopes are not equal? Then ANCOVA is *not* appropriate, and we indicate alternatives later on in the chapter.

The details of obtaining the adjusted mean for the ith group (i.e., any group) are given in Figure 7.1. The general equation follows from the definition for the slope of a straight line and some basic algebra.

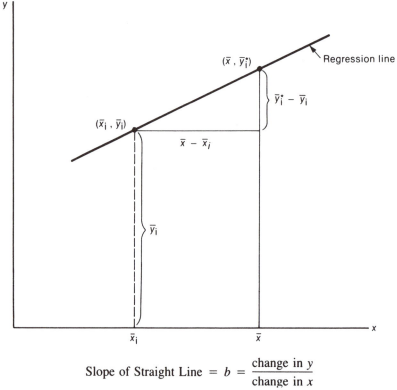

$$\text{Slope of Straight Line} = b = \frac{\text{change in } y}{\text{change in } x}$$

$$b = \frac{\bar{y}_i^* - \bar{y}_i}{\bar{x} - \bar{x}_i}$$

$$b(\bar{x} - \bar{x}_i) = \bar{y}_i^* - \bar{y}_i$$
$$\bar{y}_i^* = \bar{y}_i + b\,(\bar{x} - \bar{x}_i)$$
$$\bar{y}_i^* = \bar{y}_i - b\,(\bar{x}_i - \bar{x})$$

FIGURE 7.1   Deriving the General Equation for Adjusted Means in Covariance

In Figure 7.2 we show the adjusted means geometrically for a hypothetical 3 group data set. A positive correlation is assumed between the covariate and the dependent variable, so that a higher mean on x implies a higher mean on y. Note that since group 1 scored below the grand mean on the covariate, its mean is adjusted upward. On the other hand, since the mean for group 3 on the covariate is *above* the grand mean, covariance estimates that it would have scored lower on y if its mean on the covariate was lower (at grand mean), and therefore the mean for group 3 is adjusted downward.

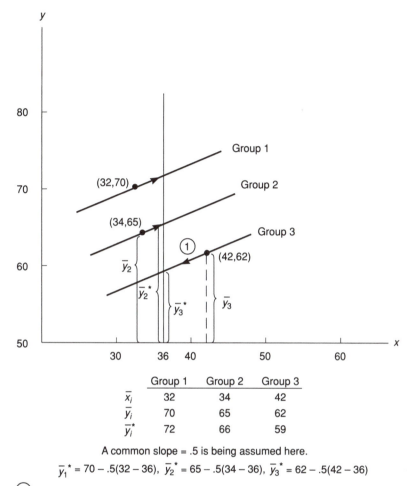

	Group 1	Group 2	Group 3
$\bar{x}_i$	32	34	42
$\bar{y}_i$	70	65	62
$\bar{y}_i^*$	72	66	59

A common slope = .5 is being assumed here.

$$\bar{y}_1^* = 70 - .5(32 - 36),\ \bar{y}_2^* = 65 - .5(34 - 36),\ \bar{y}_3^* = 62 - .5(42 - 36)$$

① The arrows on the regression lines indicate that the means are adjusted linearly upward or downward to what they would be if the groups had started out at the grand mean on the covariate.

FIGURE 7.2   Means and Adjusted Means for Hypothetical Three Group Data Set

7.4   REDUCTION OF ERROR VARIANCE

It is relatively simple to derive the approximate error term for covariance. Denote the correlation between the covariate (x) and the dependent variable (y) by r_{xy}. The square of a correlation can be interpreted as "proportion of variance accounted for." The within group variance for ANOVA is MS_w. Thus, the part of the within group variance on y that is accounted for by the covariate is $r_{xy}^2 \, MS_w$. The within variability left, after the portion due to the covariate is removed, is

$$MS_w - MS_w \, r_{xy}^2 = MS_w \, (1 - r_{xy}^2) \tag{1}$$

and this becomes our new error term for the analysis of covariance, which we denote by MS_w^*. Technically, there is an additional part to the adjusted error term:

$$MS_w^* = MS_w \, (1 - r_{xy}^2) \, [1 + 1/ (f_e - 2)]$$

where f_e is the error degrees of freedom. However, the effect of this additional factor is slight as long as $N > 50$.

To show how much of a difference a covariate can make in increasing the sensitivity of an experiment, we consider a hypothetical study. An investigator runs a one-way ANOVA (3 groups and 20 subjects per group), and obtains $F = 200/100 = 2$, which is not significant, because the critical value at .05 is 3.18. He pretested the subjects, but didn't use the pretest as a covariate (even though the correlation between covariate and posttest was .71) because the groups didn't differ significantly on the pretest. This is a common mistake made by some researchers who are unaware of the other purpose of covariance, that of reducing error variance. The analysis is redone by another investigator using ANCOVA. Using the equation we just derived she finds

$$MS_w^* \approx 100[1 - (.71)^2] = 50$$

Thus, the error term for the ANCOVA is only half as large as the error term for ANOVA. It is also necessary to obtain a new MS_b^* for ANCOVA, call it MS_b^*. In Section 7.6 we show how to calculate MS_b^*. Let us assume here that the investigator obtains the following F ratio for the covariance analysis:

$$F^* = 190/50 = 3.8$$

This is significant at the .05 level. Therefore, the use of covariance can make the difference between finding and not finding significance. Finally, we wish to note that MS_b^* can be smaller or larger than MS_b although in a randomized study the expected values of the two are equal.

7.5 CHOICE OF COVARIATES

In general, any variables that theoretically should correlate with the dependent variable, or variables that have been shown to correlate on similar types of subjects, should be considered as possible covariates. The ideal is to choose as covariates variables that of course are significantly correlated with the dependent variable *and* have low correlations among themselves. If two covariates are highly correlated (say .80), then they are removing much of the *same* error variance from *y*; x_2 will not have much incremental validity. On the other hand, if two covariates (x_1 and x_2) have a low correlation (say .20), then they are removing relatively distinct pieces of the error variance from *y*, and we will obtain a much greater total error reduction. This is illustrated graphically below using Venn diagrams, where the circle represents error variance on *y*.

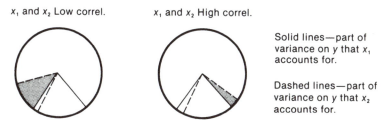

The shaded portion in each case represents the incremental validity of x_2, that is, the part of error variance on *y* it removes that x_1 did not.

Huitema (1980, p. 161) has recommended limiting the number of covariates to the extent that the ratio

$$\frac{[C + (J - 1)]}{N} < .10$$

where *C* is the number of covariates, *J* is the number of groups, and *N* is total sample size. Thus, if we had a four group problem with a total of 80 subjects, then ($C + 3)/80 < .10$ or $C < 5$. Less than 5 covariate should be used. If the above ratio is > .10, then the adjusted means are likely to be unstable.

7.6   NUMERICAL EXAMPLE

We now consider an example to illustrate how to calculate an ANCOVA and to make clear what the null hypothesis is that is being tested. We use the following 3 group data set from Myers (1979, p. 417), where *x* indicates the covariate:

Group 1		Group 2		Group 3	
x	*y*	*x*	*y*	*x*	*y*
12	26	11	32	6	23
10	22	12	31	13	35
7	20	6	20	15	44
14	34	18	41	15	41
12	28	10	29	7	28
11	26	11	31	9	30

Recall that in the one way ANOVA the null hypothesis was H_0: $\mu_1 = \mu_2 = \cdots = \mu_k$ (population means are equal). But in analysis of covariance we are adjusting the means (Section 7.3), so that the null hypothesis becomes H_0: μ_1^* $= \mu_2^* = \cdots = \mu_k^*$, that is, the *adjusted* population means are equal. In the above example, the specific null hypothesis is H_0: $\mu_1^* = \mu_2^* = \mu_3^*$. In ANCOVA we adjust sums of squares corresponding to the sums of squares total, within and between from ANOVA. We denote these adjusted sums of squares by SS_t^*, SS_w^*, and SS_b^* respectively. SS_b^* is obtained by subtracting SS_w^* from SS_t^*.

An ANOVA on the above Myers data, as the reader should check, yields a within cells sum of squares of 666.83 and a group sum of squares of 172.11. We will need these results in obtaining the ANCOVA. Recall that SS_t from ANOVA measures variability of the subjects scores about the grand mean;

$$SS_t = \sum (x_{ij} - \bar{x})^2$$

Let r_{xy} denote the correlation between the covariate and the dependent variable for all the scores, disregarding group membership. Remember that r_{xy}^2 can be interpreted as proportion of variance accounted for. Thus, $r_{xy}^2 SS_t$ represents the amount of variability on y that is accounted for by its relationship with the covariate. Therefore, the remaining variability on y, or the adjusted total sum of squares, is given by

$$SS_t^* = (1 - r_{xy}^2) SS_t \tag{2}$$

Now consider the pooled within correlation for x and y, that is, where group membership is taken into account. Although not strictly true, this correlation can be thought of as the average (or weighted average for unequal group sizes) of the correlations within the groups. Denote this correlation by $r_{xy(w)}$. Then the amount of within group variability on y accounted for by the covariate is given by $r_{xy}^2{}_{(w)}SS_w$. Therefore, the remaining within variability on y, or the adjusted within sum of squares, is given by

$$SS_w^* = (1 - r_{xy}^2{}_{(w)}) SS_w \tag{3}$$

Finally, the adjusted between sum of squares is obtained as the difference between the adjusted total and adjusted within:

$$SS_b^* = SS_t^* - SS_w^* \tag{4}$$

The F ratio for analysis of covariance is then given by

$$F^* = (SS_b^*/(k-1))/SS_w^*/(N-k-C) = MS_b^*/MS_w^* \tag{5}$$

where C is the number of covariates. Note that one degree of freedom for error is lost for each covariate used.

This method of computing the ANCOVA is conceptually fairly simple, and importantly shows its direct linkage with the results from an ANOVA on the same data. The SAS GLM control lines for running the ANCOVA are presented in Table 7.1, along with selected printout. The total correlation is .85286 and the within group correlations are gp 1: .9316, gp 2: .9799, and gp 3: .9708. Using these results, the F ratio for the ANCOVA is easily obtained. First, from Equation 2 we have that

$$SS_t^* = (1 - (.85286)^2) \, 838.94 = 228.72$$

Now, using the average of the within correlations as a rough estimate of the pooled within correlation, we find that $r = (.9316 + .9799 + .9708)/3 = .9608$ (the actual pooled correlation is .965). Now, using Equation 3 we find the adjusted within sum of squares:

$$SS_w^* = (1 - (.965)^2) \, (666.83) = 45.86$$

Therefore, the adjusted between sum of squares is:

$$SS_b^* = 228.72 - 45.86 = 182.86$$

TABLE 7.1

SAS GLM Control Lines and Selected Printout for ANCOVA on Myers Data and SPSS Windows 8.0 Interactive Plots and Regression Lines

```
TITLE 'ANCOVA MYERS DATA 164';
DATA MYERS;
INPUT GP X Y @@;
LINES;
1 12 26    1 10 22    1  7 20    1 14 34    1 12 28    1 11 26
2 11 32    2 12 31    2  6 20    2 18 41    2 10 29    2 11 31
3  6 23    3 13 35    3 15 44    3 15 41    3  7 28    3  9 30
PROC PRINT;
PROC GLM;
CLASSES GP;
MODEL Y=GP X;
```

Source	DF	Type I SS	Mean Square	F Value	Pr > F
GP	2	172.11111111	86.05555556	26.25	0.0001
X	1	620.94132730	620.94132730	189.43	0.0001

Source	DF	Type III SS	Mean Square	F Value	Pr > F
GP	2	182.82232259	91.41116130	27.89	0.0001
X	1	620.94132730	620.94132730	189.43	0.0001

(Continued)

TABLE 7.1
(Continued)

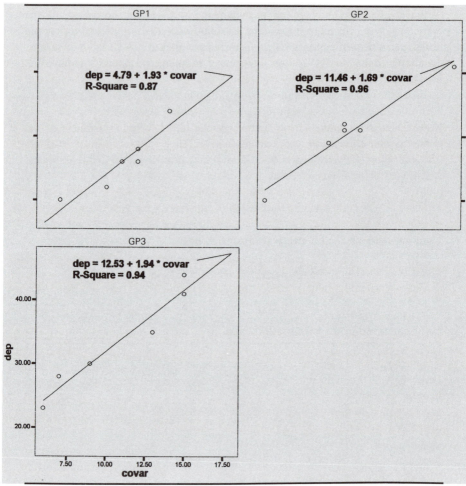

and the *F* ratio for the analysis of covariance is

$$F^* = (182.86/2)/45.86/(18 - 3 - 1) = 27.87$$

ANCOVA as a Special Case of Multiple Regression

Since analysis of covariance involves both analysis of variance and regression analysis, we can do an ANCOVA using multiple regression. Recall that in the last chapter on regression analysis we showed that ANOVA was a special case of regression analysis. We dummy coded group membership and used these dummy variables to predict the dependent variable.

We will illustrate how an ANCOVA can be done using multiple regression with the Myers data. First, we shall check the homogeneity of regression slopes assumption. For a one way design, as Myers and Well (1991, p. 567) point out, "Performing an ANCOVA on a design that has a single factor A can now be seen as determining whether A has effects over and above those of the covariate x. "Thus, we *force* the covariate in and then determine whether group membership has an effect above and beyond the covariate. Since we have 3 groups here, we will need two dummy variables to code group membership (we denote them by DUM1, DUM2). Recall that a violation of the slopes assumption meant there was a group by covariate interaction. Thus, we set up an interaction effect and test it for significance. We create the group by covariate interaction effects by multiplying (we denote them by COVDUM1 and COVDUM2) and then test these for significance. The complete control lines for testing homogeneity of slopes and doing the ANCOVA are presented in Table 7.2.

Selected printout from SPSS for Windows 8.0 is presented in Table 7.3. Note that the assumption of equal regression slopes is tenable ($F = .354$), and that the ANCOVA is significant ($F = 27.886$).

7.7   ASSUMPTIONS IN ANALYSIS OF COVARIANCE

Analysis of covariance rests on the same assumptions as the analysis of variance *plus* three additional assumptions regarding the regression part of the covariance analysis. ANCOVA also assumes

1. A linear relationship between the dependent variable and the covariate(s).
2. Homogeneity of the regression slopes (for one covariate); parallelism of the regression planes for two covariates and for more than 2 covariates homogeneity of the regression hyperplanes.
3. The covariate is measured without error.

Since covariance rests on the same assumptions as ANOVA, any violations that are serious in ANOVA (like dependent observations) are also serious in ANCOVA. Violation of *all 3* of the above regression assumptions can also be serious. For example, if the relationship between the covariate and the dependent variable is curvilinear, then the adjustment of the means will be improper.

There is always measurement error for the variables that are typically used as covariates in social science research. In randomized designs this reduces the power of the ANCOVA, but treatment effects are not biased. For non-randomized designs the treatment effects can be seriously biased.

TABLE 7.2

Syntax Command File for Homogeneity of Slopes Test and
ANCOVA on Myers Data Using SPSS for Windows 8.0

```
TITLE 'MULT. REG ON MYERS DATA - ANCOVA'.
DATA LIST FREE/COVAR DEP DUM1 DUM2 COVDUM1 COVDUM2.
BEGIN DATA.
12 26 1 0 12 0   10 22 1 0 10 0   7 20 1 0 7 0    14 34 1 0 14 0   12 28 1 0 12 0   11 26 1 0 11 0
11 32 0 1 0 11   12 31 0 1 0 12   6 20 0 1 0 6    18 41 0 1 0 18   10 29 0 1 0 10   11 31 0 1 0 11
6 23 0 0 0 0     13 35 0 0 0 0    15 44 0 0 0 0   15 41 0 0 0 0     7 28 0 0 0 0     9 30 0 0 0 0
END DATA.
LIST.
REGRESSION DESCRIPTIVES=DEFAULT/
VARIABLES=COVAR TO COVDUM2/
DEPENDENT=DEP/
①  ENTER COVAR DUM1 DUM2/TEST(COVDUM1 COVDUM2)/.
REGRESSION DESCRIPTIVES=DEFAULT/
VARIABLES=COVAR TO DUM2/
DEPENDENT=DEP/
②  ENTER COVAR/TEST(DUM1 DUM2)/.
```

①This is the statement which yields the homogeneity of slopes test.
②This is testing the main hypothesis in ANCOVA, whether the adjusted population means are equal.

COVAR	DEP	DUM1	DUM2	COVDUM1	COVDUM2
12.00	26.00	1.00	.00	12.00	.00
10.00	22.00	1.00	.00	10.00	.00
7.00	20.00	1.00	.00	7.00	.00
14.00	34.00	1.00	.00	14.00	.00
12.00	28.00	1.00	.00	12.00	.00
11.00	26.00	1.00	.00	11.00	.00
11.00	32.00	.00	1.00	.00	11.00
12.00	31.00	.00	1.00	.00	12.00
6.00	20.00	.00	1.00	.00	6.00
18.00	41.00	.00	1.00	.00	18.00
10.00	29.00	.00	1.00	.00	10.00
11.00	31.00	.00	1.00	.00	11.00
6.00	23.00	.00	.00	.00	.00
13.00	35.00	.00	.00	.00	.00
15.00	44.00	.00	.00	.00	.00
15.00	41.00	.00	.00	.00	.00
7.00	28.00	.00	.00	.00	.00
9.00	30.00	.00	.00	.00	.00

TABLE 7.3
Selected Printout From SPSS for Windows 8.0 for ANCOVA on Myers Data Using Multiple Regression

ANOVA[d]

Model			Sum of Squares	df	Mean Square	F	
1	Regression		793.052	3	264.351	80.644	①
	Residual		45.892	14	3.278		
	Total		838.944	17			
2	Subset Tests	COVDUM1, COVDUM2	2.554	2	1.277	.354	②
	Regression		795.606	5	159.121	44.059	
	Residual		43.338	12	3.612		
	Total		838.944	17			

Variables Entered/Removed[b]

Model	Variables Entered	Variables Removed	Method
1	COVAR[a]	.	Enter
2	DUM1, DUM2	.	Test

a. All requested variables entered.

b. Dependent Variable: DEP

Model Summary

Model	R	R Square	Adjusted R Square	Std. Error of the Estimate
1	.853[a]	.727	.710	3.7808
2	.972[b]	.945	.934	1.8105

a. Predictors: (Constant), COVAR

b. Predictors: (Constant), COVAR, DUM1, DUM2

ANOVA[d]

Model			Sum of Squares	df	Mean Square	F	
1	Regression		610.230	1	610.230	42.689	
	Residual		228.714	16	14.295		
	Total		838.944	17			
2	Subset Tests	DUM1, DUM2	182.822	2	91.411	27.886	③
	Regression		793.052	3	264.351	80.644	
	Residual		45.892	14	3.278		
	Total		838.944	17			

①This is the test for a significant regression on *y* on the covariate.

②This is the test for homogeneity of the regression slopes.

③This is the main test in covariance; whether the adjusted population means are equal.

A violation of the homogeneity of regression slopes can also yield quite misleading results. To illustrate this, we present in Figure 7.3 the situation where the assumption is met and two situations where the slopes are unequal. Notice that with equal slopes the estimated superiority of group 1 at the grand mean is a totally accurate estimate of group 1's superiority for *all* levels of the covariate, since the lines are parallel. For Case 1 of unequal slopes there is a *covariate by treatment interaction*. That is, how much better group 1 is depends on which value of the covariate we specify. This is analogous to the concept of interaction in a factorial design. For Case 2 of heterogeneous slopes the use of covariance would be totally misleading. Covariance estimates no difference between the groups, while for $x = c$, group 2 is quite superior, and for $x = d$, group 1 is quite superior. Later in the chapter we show how to test the assumption of equal slopes on SPSS and on SAS.

Therefore, in examining printout from the statistical packages it is important to *first* make two checks to determine whether analysis of covariance is appropriate:

1. Check to see whether there is a linear relationship between the dependent variable and the covariate.
2. Check to determine whether the homogeneity of the regression slopes is tenable.

If the above assumptions are met, then there is not any debate about the appropriateness of ANCOVA in randomized studies in which the subjects have been randomly assigned to groups. For intact groups, there is a debate, and we discuss that in the next section.

If either of the above assumptions is not satisfied, then covariance is not appropriate. In particular, if (2) is not met, then one should consider using the Johnson–Neyman (1936) technique. For extended discussion on the Johnson–Neyman technique see Rogosa (1977, 1980).

7.8   USE OF ANCOVA WITH INTACT GROUPS

It should be noted that some researchers (Anderson, 1963; Lord, 1969) have argued strongly against using analysis of covariance with intact groups. Although we do not take this position, it is important that the reader be aware of the several limitations and/or possible dangers when using ANCOVA with intact groups. First, even the use of several covariates will *not* equate intact groups, and one should never be deluded into thinking it can. The groups may still differ on some unknown important variable(s). Also, note that equating groups on one variable may result in accentuating their differences on other variables.

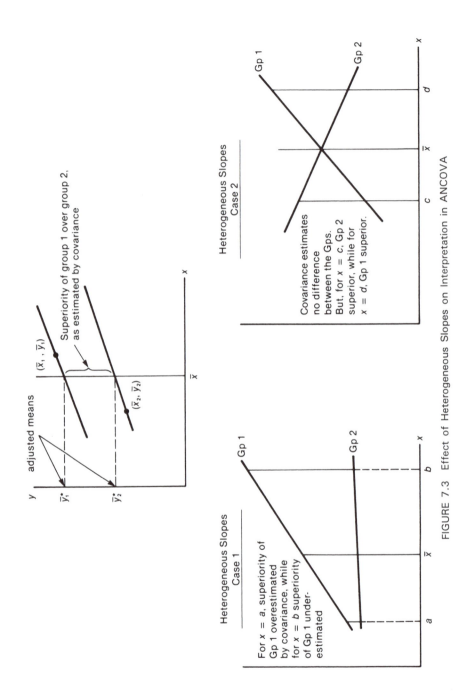

FIGURE 7.3 Effect of Heterogeneous Slopes on Interpretation in ANCOVA

Second, recall that ANCOVA adjusts the posttest means to what they would be if all the groups had started out equal on the covariate(s). You then need to consider whether groups that are equal on the covariate would ever exist in the real world. Elashoff (1969) gives the following example. Teaching methods A and B are being compared. The class using A is composed of high ability students, whereas the class using B is composed of low ability students. A covariance analysis can be done on the posttest achievement scores holding ability constant, as if A and B had been used on classes of equal and average ability. But, as Elashoff notes, "It may make no sense to think about comparing methods A and B for students of average ability, perhaps each has been designed specifically for the ability level it was used with, or neither method will, in the future, be used for students of average ability" (p. 387).

Third, the assumptions of linearity and homogeneity of regression slopes need to be satisfied for ANCOVA to be appropriate.

A fourth issue that can confound the interpretation of results is differential growth of subjects in intact or self selected groups on some dependent variable. If the natural growth is much greater in one group (treatment) than for the control group and covariance finds a significance difference, after adjusting for any pretest differences, then it isn't clear whether the difference is due to treatment, differential growth, or part of each. Bryk and Weisberg (1977) discuss this issue in detail and propose an alternative approach for such growth models.

A fifth problem is that of measurement error. Of course this same problem is present in randomized studies. But there the effect is merely to attenuate power. In non-randomized studies measurement error can seriously bias the treatment effect. Reichardt (1979), in an extended discussion on measurement error in ANCOVA, states,

> Measurement error in the pretest can therefore produce spurious treatment effects when none exist. But it can also result in a finding of no intercept difference when a true treatment effect exists, or it can produce an estimate of the treatment effect which is in the opposite direction of the true effect. (p. 164)

It is no wonder then that Pedhadzur (1982, p. 524), in discussing the effect of measurement error when comparing intact groups, says,

> The purpose of the discussion here was only to alert you to the problem in the hope that you will reach two obvious conclusions: (1) that efforts should be directed to construct measures of the covariates that have very high reliabilities and (2) that ignoring the problem, as is unfortunately done in most applications of ANCOVA, will not make it disappear. (p. 524)

Porter (1967) has developed a procedure to correct ANCOVA for measurement error, and an example illustrating that procedure is given in Huitema (1980, pp. 315–316). This is beyond the scope of the present text.

Given all of the above problems, the reader may well wonder whether we should abandon the use of covariance when comparing intact groups. But other statistical methods for analyzing this kind of data (such as matched samples, gain score ANOVA) suffer from many of the same problems, such as seriously biased treatment effects. The fact is that inferring cause–effect from intact groups is treacherous, regardless of the type of statistical analysis. Therefore, the task is to do the best we can and exercise considerable caution, or as Pedhazur (1982) put it: "But the conduct of such research, indeed all scientific research, requires sound theoretical thinking, constant vigilance, and a thorough understanding of the potential and limitations of the methods being used" (p. 525).

7.9   COMPUTER EXAMPLE FOR ANCOVA

To illustrate how to run an ANCOVA, while at the same time checking the critical assumptions of linearity and homogeneity of slopes, we consider part of a Sesame Street data set from Glasnapp and Poggio (1985), who present data on many variables, including 12 background variables and 8 achievement variables for 240 subjects. Sesame Street was developed as a television series aimed mainly at teaching preschool skills to 3- to 5-year-old children. Data was collected at 5 different sites on many achievement variables both before (pretest) and after (posttest) viewing of the series. We consider here only the achievement variable of knowledge of numbers. The maximum possible score is 54 and the content of the items included recognizing numbers, naming numbers, counting, addition, and subtraction. We use ANCOVA to determine whether the posttest knowledge of numbers for the children at the first 3 sites differed after adjustments are made for any pretest differences.

In Table 7.4 we give the complete control lines for running the ANCOVA on SPSS MANOVA. Table 7.5 gives selected annotated output from that run. We indicate *which* of the *F* tests are checking the assumptions of linearity and homogeneity of slopes, and which *F* addresses the main question in covariance (whether the adjusted population means are equal).

7.10   ALTERNATIVE ANALYSES

When comparing two or more groups with pretest and posttest data, the following other modes of analysis have been used by many researchers:

1. An ANOVA is done on the difference or gain scores (posttest–pretest).
2. A two way repeated measures (this is covered in Chapter 5) ANOVA is done. This is also called a one between (the grouping variable) and one within (pretest–posttest part) factor ANOVA.

TABLE 7.4
SPSS MANOVA Control Lines for Analysis
of Covariance on Sesame Street Data

```
TITLE 'ANALYSIS OF COVARIANCE ON SESAME DATA'.
DATA LIST FREE/SITE PRENUMB POSTNUMB.
BEGIN DATA.

   DATA (IN APPENDIX)
END DATA.
MANOVA PRENUMB POSTNUMB BY SITE(1,3)/
① ANALYSIS POSTNUMB WITH PRENUMB/
② PRINT=PMEANS/
   DESIGN/
③ ANALYSIS=POSTNUMB/
   DESIGN=PRENUMB,SITE,PRENUMB BY SITE/
④ ANALYSIS=PRENUMB.
```

①The covariate(s) follow the keyword WITH.
②This PRINT subcommand is needed to obtain the adjusted means, which is what we are testing for significance.
③This ANALYSIS subcommand and the following DESIGN subcommand are needed to test the homogeneity of the regression slopes assumption.
④This ANALYSIS subcommand is used to test whether the sites differed significantly on the pretest.

Huck and McLean (1975) and Jennings (1988) have compared the above two modes of analysis along with the use of ANCOVA for the pretest–posttest control group design, and conclude that ANCOVA is the preferred method of analysis. Several comments from the Huck and McLean article are worth mentioning. First, they note that with the repeated measures approach it is the *interaction F* that is indicating whether the treatments had a differential effect, and not the treatment main effect. We consider two patterns of means below to illustrate.

	Situation 1				Situation 2	
	Pretest	Posttest			Pretest	Posttest
Treat.	70	80	Treat		65	80
Control	60	70	Control		60	68

In situation 1 the treatment main effect would probably be significant, because there is a difference of 10 in the row means. However, the difference of 10 on the posttest just transferred from an initial difference of 10 on the pretest. There is not a differential change in the treatment and control groups here. On the other hand, in situation 2 even though the treatment group scored higher on the pretest, it increased 15 points from pre to post while the control group increased just 8 points. That is, there was a *differential* change in performance in the two groups. But, recall from Chapter 4 that one way of thinking of an interaction effect is as a "difference in the differences." This is exactly what we have in situation 2, hence a significant interaction effect.

TABLE 7.5
Selected Printout from SPSS MANOVA for ANCOVA on Sesame Street Data

---

TESTS OF SIGNIFICANCE FOR POSTNUMB USING UNIQUE SUMS OF SQUARES

SOURCE OF VARIATION	SS	DF	MS	F	SIG OF F
WITHIN CELLS	15698.73	175	89.71		
REGRESSION	8688.51	1	8688.51	96.85 ①	.000
SITE	1466.39	2	733.20	8.17 ③	.000

ADJUSTED AND ESTIMATED MEANS
VARIABLE . . POSTNUMB

FACTOR	CODE	OBS. MEAN	ADJ. MEAN
SITE	1	30.08333	29.57986
SITE	2	38.72727	④ 35.72853
SITE	3	25.43750	28.93971

TESTS OF SIGNIFICANCE FOR POSTNUMB USING UNIQUE SUMS OF SQUARES

SOURCE OF VARIATION	SS	DF	MS	F	SIG OF F
WITHIN+RESIDUAL	15608.37	173	90.22		
PRENUMB	7669.49	1	7669.49	85.01	.000
SITE	205.97	2	102.98	1.14	.322
PRENUMB BY SITE	90.37	2	45.18	.50 ②	.607

TESTS OF SIGNIFICANCE FOR PRENUMB USING UNIQUE SUMS OF SQUARES

SOURCE OF VARIATION	SS	DF	MS	F	SIG OF F
WITHIN CELLS	18452.08	176	104.84		
SITE	2739.80	2	1369.90	13.07 ⑤	.000

ADJUSTED AND ESTIMATED MEANS
VARIABLE . . POSTNUMB

FACTOR	CODE	OBS. MEAN	ADJ. MEAN
SITE	1	22.40000	22.40000
SITE	2	26.03636	26.03636
SITE	3	16.56250	16.56250

①This indicates there is a significant correlation between the dependent variable and the covariate(PRENUMB), or equivalently a significant regression of POSTNUMB on PRENUMB.

②This test indicates that homogeneity of regression slopes is tenable at the .05 level, since the p value is .607.

③This F is testing the main result in ANCOVA; whether the adjusted population means are equal. This is rejected at the .05 level, indicating SITE differences.

④These are the adjusted means. Since the estimated common regression slope is .686 (given on the printout but not presented here), the adjusted mean for SITE 1 is

$$\bar{y}_1{}^* = 30.083 - .686 (22.4 - 21.67) = 29.58$$

⑤This test indicates the subjects at the 3 sites differ significantly on the pretest, i.e., on PRENUMB.

Second, Huck and McLean (1975) note that the interaction F from the repeated measures ANOVA is *identical* to the F ratio one would obtain from an ANOVA on the gain (difference) scores. Finally, whenever the regression coefficient is not equal to 1 (generally the case), the error term for ANCOVA will be smaller than for the gain score analysis and hence the ANCOVA will be a more sensitive or powerful analysis.

Although not discussed in the Huck and McLean paper, we would like to add a measurement caution against the use of gain scores. It is a fairly well known measurement fact that the reliability of gain (difference) scores is generally not good. To be more specific, *as the correlation between the pretest and posttest scores approaches the reliability of the test, the reliability of the difference scores goes to 0.* The following table from Thorndike and Hagen (1977) quantifies things:

	Average reliability of two tests					
	.50	.60	.70	.80	.90	.95
Correlation between tests						
.00	.50	.60	.70	.80	.90	.95
.40	.17	.33	.50	.67	.83	.92
.50	.00	.20	.40	.60	.80	.90
.60		.00	.25	.50	.75	.88
.70			.00	.33	.67	.83
.80				.00	.50	.75
.90					.00	.50
95						.00

If our dependent variable is some noncognitive measure, or a variable derived from a nonstandardized test (which could well be of questionable reliability), then a reliability of about .60 or so is a definite possibility. In this case, if the correlation between pretest and posttest is .50 (a realistic possibility), the reliability of the difference scores is only .20! On the other hand, the above table also shows that if our measure is quite reliable (say .90), then the difference scores will be reliable for moderate pre-post correlations. For example, for reliability = .90 and pre–post correlation = .50, the reliability of the differences scores is .80.

7.11   BRYANT–PAULSON POST HOC PROCEDURE

Since the covariate(s) used in social science research are essentially always random, it is important that this be incorporated into any post hoc procedure following an analysis of covariance. This is *not* the case for the Tukey procedure. The Bryant–Paulson (1976) procedure was derived under the assumption that the covariate is a random variable. It is a generalization of the Tukey technique. Which particular Bryant–Paulson (BP) statistic we use to determine if a pair of adjusted means is significantly different depends on whether the study is a randomized (subjects randomly assigned to the groups) or a non-randomized design, and on how many covariates are present.

Below we present the appropriate statistics for one covariate for both a randomized and non-randomized design. The statistics for the multiple covariate case are given in Stevens (1986). Note that if the group sizes are unequal, then the harmonic mean is used.

Randomized Design	*Non-Randomized Design*
$$\dfrac{\bar{y}_i{}^* - \bar{y}_j{}^*}{\sqrt{MS_w{}^*[1 + MS_{b_x}/MS_{w_x}]/n}}$$	$$\dfrac{\bar{y}_i{}^* - \bar{y}_j{}^*}{\sqrt{MS_w{}^*[2/n + (\bar{x}_i - \bar{x}_j)^2/SS_{wx}]/2}}$$

where n is common group size, $MS_w{}^*$ is the error term for covariance, and MS_{b_x} and MS_{w_x} are the mean between and within sums of squares from an analysis of variance on *only* the covariate.

To illustrate use of the Bryant–Paulson technique, let us apply it to the Sesame Street data analyzed in Table 7.3 to determine which pairs of sites are significantly different. Since this is a non-randomized design, the appropriate test statistic is

$$\frac{\bar{y}_i{}^* - \bar{y}_j{}^*}{\sqrt{MS_w{}^*[2/n + (\bar{x}_i - \bar{x}_j)^2/SS_{wx}]/2}}$$

Note that the denominator of this statistic must be computed *separately* for each paired comparison. In computing any of the Bryant–Paulson test statistics one also needs the results from an analysis on the groups using just the covariate(s). However, this was done in the previous Sesame Street analysis. Now, using the appropriate values from the selected SPSS MANOVA printout in Table 7.5, we show the calculations for each pair of groups. The number of subjects in sites 1 through 3 respectively are 60, 55, and 64. Since the groups sizes are approximately equal, we use the simple mean of 59.67, because it will not differ much from the harmonic and it simplifies calculations somewhat.

Sites 1 and 2

$$BP = \frac{29.58 - 35.73}{\sqrt{89.71[2/59.67 + (22.40 - 26.036)^2/18452.08]/2}} = -4.96$$

Sites 1 and 3

$$BP = \frac{29.58 - 28.94}{\sqrt{89.71[2/59.67 + (22.4 - 16.56)^2/18452.08]/2}} = .51$$

Sites 2 and 3

$$BP = \frac{35.73 - 28.94}{\sqrt{89.71[2/59.67 + (26.036 - 16.563)^2/18452.08]/2}} = 5.18$$

Now, referring to Table B.5 for the critical value of the .05 level of significance with one covariate, three groups, and 178 degrees of freedom, we find it is 3.37. Thus, we conclude that site 2 differs from sites 1 and 3, but sites 1 and 3 are not significantly different.

7.12   AN ALTERNATIVE TO THE JOHNSON–NEYMAN TECHNIQUE

We consider hypothetical data from Huitema (1980, p. 272). The effects of two types of therapy are being compared on an aggressiveness score. The covariate (x) are scores on a sociability scale. Since the Johnson–Neyman technique is still (10 years after the first edition of this text) not available on SAS or SPSS, we consider an alternative analysis that does shed some light. Recall that a violation of the homogeneity of regression slopes assumption meant there was a covariate by group interaction. Thus, one way of investigating the nature of this interaction would be to set up a factorial design, with groups being one of the factors and two or more levels for the covariate (other factor), and run a regular two way ANOVA. This procedure is not as desirable as the Johnson–Neyman technique for two reasons: (1) the Johnson–Neyman technique is more powerful, and (2) the Johnson–Neyman technique enables us to determine where the group differences are for *all* levels of the covariate, whereas the factorial approach can only check for differences for the levels of the covariate included in the design. Nevertheless, at least most researchers can easily do a factorial design, and this does yield useful information.

For the Huitema data, although there is a strong linear relationship in each group, the assumption of equality of slopes is not tenable (Figure 7.4 shows why). Therefore, covariance is not appropriate, and we split the subjects into three levels for sociability: low (1–4), medium (4.5–7.5) and high (8–11), and set up the following 2 × 3 ANOVA on aggressiveness:

	SOCIABILITY		
	LOW	MEDIUM	HIGH
THERAPY 1			
THERAPY 2			

Results from the resulting run on SPSS for Windows 8.0 are presented in Table 7.6. They show, as expected, that there is a significant sociability by therapy interaction ($F = 19.735$). The nature of this interaction can be gauged by examining the means for the SOCIAL*THERAPY table. These show that for low sociability therapy group 1 is more aggressive, whereas for high sociability therapy group 2 is more aggressive. The results from the Johnson–Neyman analysis for this data, presented in the first edition of this text (p. 179), show

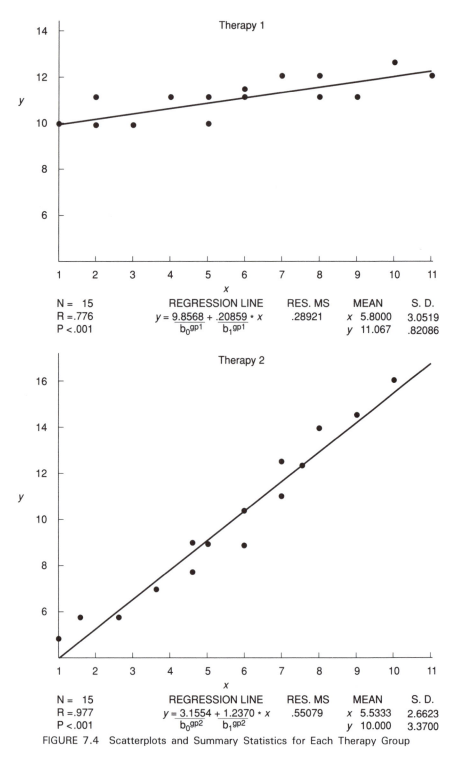

FIGURE 7.4 Scatterplots and Summary Statistics for Each Therapy Group

Tests of Between-Subjects Effects

Dependent Variable: AGGRESS

Source	Type III Sum of Squares	df	Mean Square	F	Sig.
Corrected Model	146.392[a]	5	29.278	22.982	.000
Intercept	3399.116	1	3399.116	2668.153	.000
SOCIAL	97.273	2	48.637	38.178	.000
THERAPY	.484	1	.484	.380	.543
SOCIAL * THERAPY	50.284	2	25.142	19.735	.000
Error	30.575	24	1.274		
Total	3505.500	30			
Corrected Total	176.967	29			

a. R Squared = .827 (Adjusted R Squared = .791)

Estimated Marginal Means

1. SOCIAL

Dependent Variable: AGGRESS

SOCIAL	Mean	Std. Error	95% Confidence Interval Lower Bound	Upper Bound
1.00	8.617	.342	7.911	9.322
2.00	10.925	.342	10.220	11.630
3.00	13.267	.412	12.416	14.117

2. THERAPY

Dependent Variable: AGGRESS

THERAPY	Mean	Std. Error	95% Confidence Interval Lower Bound	Upper Bound
1.00	11.067	.291	10.465	11.668
2.00	10.806	.307	10.172	11.440

3. SOCIAL * THERAPY

Dependent Variable: AGGRESS

SOCIAL	THERAPY	Mean	Std. Error	95% Confidence Interval Lower Bound	Upper Bound
1.00	1.00	10.400	.505	9.358	11.442
	2.00	6.833	.461	5.882	7.784
2.00	1.00	11.100	.505	10.058	12.142
	2.00	10.750	.461	9.799	11.701
3.00	1.00	11.700	.505	10.658	12.742
	2.00	14.833	.652	13.488	16.178

that more precisely there is *no* significant difference in aggressiveness for sociability scores between 6.04 and 7.06.

7.13 USE OF SEVERAL COVARIATES

What is the rationale for using several covariates? First, the use of several covariates will result in greater error reduction than can be obtained with just one covariate. The error reduction will be substantially greater if there are low intercorrelations among the covariates. In this case each of the covariates will be removing a somewhat different part of the error variance from the dependent variable. Also, with several covariates we can make a better adjustment for initial differences among groups.

Recall that with one covariate simple linear regression was involved. With several covariates (predicators), multiple regression is needed. In multiple regression the linear combination of the predictors that is *maximally correlated* with the dependent variable is found. The multiple correlation (R) is a maximized Pearson correlation between the observed scores on y and their predicted scores, $R = r_{yy}$. Although R is more complex it is a correlation and hence R^2 can be interpreted as "proportion of variance accounted for." Also, we will have regression coefficients for each of the covariates (predictors). Below we present a table comparing the single and multiple covariate cases:

	One Covariate	Multiple Covariates
Error Reduction	primarily determined by simple correlation	determined by the multiple correlation
	r_{yx}^2 – within variance on y accounted for by x	R^2 – within variance on y accounted for by the set of covariates
Adjustment of Means:	$y_i^* = y_i - b(\bar{x}_i - \bar{x})$,	$y_j^* = y_j - b_1(\bar{x}_{1j} - \bar{x}_1) - b_2(\bar{x}_{2j} - \bar{x}_2)$
	b is assumed common slope	$- \cdots - b_k(\bar{x}_{kj} - \bar{x}_k)$

where the b_i are the regression coefficients, $\bar{x}_{1j}$ is the mean for covariate 1 in group j, $\bar{x}_{2j}$ is the mean for covariate 2 in group j, etc., and the $\bar{x}_i$ are the grand means for the covariates.

7.14 COMPUTER EXAMPLE WITH TWO COVARIATES

To illustrate running an ANCOVA with more than one covariate, we reconsider the Sesame Street data set used in Section 7.9. Again we shall be interested in site differences on POSTNUMB, but now we use *two* covariates: PRENUMB and PRERELAT (pretest on knowledge of relational terms—amount, size, and position relationship—maximum score of 17). Before we give the control lines for running the analysis, we need to discuss in more detail how to set up the lines for testing the homogeneity assumption. For one covariate this is equality of regression slopes. For two covariates it is parallelism of the regression planes, and for more than two covariates it involves equality of regression hyperplanes.

It is important to recall that a violation of the assumption means there is a covariate by treatment (group) interaction. If the assumption is tenable this means the interaction will *not* be significant. Therefore, what one does in SPSS MANOVA is to set up an effect involving the interaction (for one covariate), and then test whether this effect is significant. If the effect is significant, it means the assumption is not tenable.

For more than one covariate, as in the present case, there is an interaction term for each covariate. The effects are lumped together and then we test whether the combined interactions are significant. Before we give a few examples, note that BY is the keyword used by SPSS to denote an interaction, and + is used to lump effects together.

We show the control lines for testing the homogeneity assumption for two covariates and for three covariates. Denote the dependent variable by y, the covariates by x_1 and x_2 and the grouping variable by gp. The control lines are

```
ANALYSIS = Y/
DESIGN = X1+X2,GP,X1 BY GP+X2 BY GP/
```

Now, suppose there were three covariates. Then the control lines will be:

```
ANALYSIS = Y/
DESIGN = X1+X2+X3,GP,X1 BY GP+X2 BY GP+X3 BY GP/
```

The control lines for running the ANCOVA on the Sesame Street data with the covariates of PRENUMB and PRERELAT are given in Table 7.7. In Table 7.8 we present selected output from the SPSS analysis of covariance.

TABLE 7.7
SPSS MANOVA Control Lines for ANCOVA
on Sesame Street Data With Two Covariates

```
TITLE 'SESAME ST. DATA-2 COVARIATES'.
DATA LIST FREE/ SITE PRENUMB PRERELAT POSTNUMB.
BEGIN DATA.

    DATA LINES

END DATA.
MANOVA PRENUMB PRERELAT POSTNUMB BY SITE (1,3)/
 ANALYSIS POSTNUMB WITH PRENUMB PRERELAT/
 PRINT=PMEANS/
 DESIGN/
 ANALYSIS=POSTNUMB/
 DESIGN=PRENUMB+PRERELAT, SITE, PRENUMB BY SITE+
 PRERELAT BY SITE/
 ANALYSIS=PRENUMB PRERELAT/.
```

TESTS OF SIGNIFICANCE FOR POSTNUMB USING UNIQUE SUMS OF SQUARES

SOURCE OF VARIATION	SS	DF	MS	F	SIG OF F
WITHIN CELLS	15393.38	174	88.47		
REGRESSION	8993.87	2	4496.93	50.83	.000
SITE	1247.08	2	623.54	7.05 ①	.001

DEPENDENT VARIABLE . . . POSTNUMB

COVARIATE		B	BETA	STD. ERR.	T-VALUE	SIG. OF T
PRENUMB	②	.56383249	.49044621	.00556	5.90001	.000
PRERELAT		.62232290	.15443617	.33497	1.85785	.065

ADJUSTED AND ESTIMATED MEANS
VARIABLE . . . POSTNUMB

FACTOR	CODE	OBS. MEAN		ADJ. MEAN	EST. MEAN
SITE	1	30.08333		29.51100	30.08333
SITE	2	38.72727		35.43705	38.72727
SITE	3	25.43750	③	29.30905	25.43750

TESTS OF SIGNIFICANCE FOR POSTNUMB USING UNIQUE SUMS OF SQUARES

SOURCE OF VARIATION	SS	DF	MS	F	SIG. OF F	
WITHIN+RESIDUAL	15229.04	170	89.58			
PRENUMB+PRERELAT	7776.99	2	3888.49	43.41	.000	
SITE	46.41	2	23.21	.26	.772	
PRENUMB BY SITE +	164.33	4	41.08	.46	.766	④
PRERELAT BY SITE						

ADJUSTED AND ESTIMATED MEANS
VARIABLE . . . PRENUMB

FACTOR	CODE	OBS. MEAN
SITE	1	22.40000
SITE	2	26.03636
SITE	3	16.56250

ADJUSTED AND ESTIMATED MEANS
VARIABLE . . . PRERELAT

FACTOR	CODE	OBS. MEAN
SITE	1	10.40000
SITE	2	11.47273
SITE	3	8.56250

①This test indicates significant SITE differences at .05 level.
②These are the regression coefficients
③These are the adjusted means, which would be obtained as follows:

$$\bar{y}_3^* = \bar{y}_3 - b_1(\bar{x}_{13} - \bar{x}_1) - b_2(\bar{x}_{23} - \bar{x}_2)$$
$$= 25.437 - .564(16.563 - 21.67) - .622(8.563 - 10.14)$$
$$= 29.30$$

④This test indicates parallelism of the regression planes is tenable at the .05 level.

7.15 SUMMARY

1. In analysis of covariance a linear relationship is assumed between the dependent variable and the covariate(s).

2. ANCOVA is directly related to the two basic objectives in experimental design of (a) eliminating systematic bias and (b) reduction of error variance. While ANCOVA does not eliminate bias, it can reduce bias. The use of several covariates with low intercorrelations will substantially reduce error variance.

3. Limit the number of covariates (C) so that

$$\frac{C + (J - 1)}{N} < .10$$

where J is the number of groups and N is total sample size.

4. A numerical example is given to show the intimate relationship between ANCOVA and the results for ANOVA on the same data.

5. Measurement error on the covariate causes loss of power in randomized designs, and can lead to seriously biased treatment effects in non-randomized designs.

6. In examining printout from the statistical packages, first make two checks to determine whether covariance is appropriate: (1) check that there is a linear relationship between the covariate and the dependent variable and (2) check that the regression slopes are equal. If *either* of these is not true, then covariance is not appropriate. In particular, if (2) is not true then the Johnson–Neyman technique should be considered.

7. Several cautions are given concerning the use of analysis of covariance with intact groups.

8. The Bryant–Paulson post hoc procedure is presented and illustrated on a computer example. It is a generalization of the Tukey procedure.

9. Three ways of analyzing a k group pretest-posttest design are: ANOVA on the difference scores, analysis of covariance, and a two way repeated measures ANOVA. Articles by Huck and McLean (1975) and by Jennings (1988) show that ANCOVA is generally the preferred method of analysis.

10. Although the Johnson–Neyman technique is preferred when the slopes are not equal, it is still not available on SAS or SPSS. *A violation of the equal slopes assumption means there is a group by covariate interaction effect.* Because of this, we illustrated, in Section 7.12, use of a two way ANOVA to get at the nature of this interaction.

11. We showed how ANCOVA can be done using multiple regression. By dummy coding group membership and appropriate multiplication we obtained both the test for homogeneity of regression slopes and the ANCOVA.

EXERCISES

1. A social psychological study by Novince (1977) examined the effect of behavioral rehearsal, and behavioral rehearsal plus cognitive restructuring (combination treatment) on reducing anxiety and facilitating social skills for female college freshmen. The 33 subjects were randomly assigned (11 each) to either BH, a control group (group 2), or BH + CR. The subjects were pretested and posttested on several variables. The scores for the avoidance variable are given below:

BEHAVIORAL REHEARSAL		CONTROL		BEHAVIORAL REHEARSAL + COGNITIVE RESTRUCTURING	
Avoid	Preavoid	Avoid	Preavoid	Avoid	Preavoid
91	70	107	115	121	96
107	121	76	77	140	120
121	89	116	111	148	130
86	80	126	121	147	145
137	123	104	105	139	122
138	112	96	97	121	119
133	126	127	132	141	104
127	121	99	98	143	121
114	80	94	85	120	80
118	101	92	82	140	121
114	112	128	112	95	92

Table 7.9 shows selected printout from an ANCOVA on SPSS for Windows 7.5 (top two thirds of printout).
(a) Is ANCOVA appropriate for this data? Explain.
(b) If ANCOVA is appropriate, then do we reject the null hypothesis of equal adjusted population means at the .05 level?
(c) The bottom portion of the printout shows the results from an ANOVA on just avoidance. Note that the error term is 280.07. The error term for the ANCOVA is 111.36. How are the two error terms fundamentally related?

2. Forty subjects were randomly assigned to one of 4 teaching methods. Performance on a final examination served as the dependent variable and I.Q. was the covariate. The ANCOVA was significant at the .05 level (F = 16.24, p < .001), and the adjusted means were as follows:

GROUP 1	30.762	GROUP 3	53.129
GROUP 2	61.254	GROUP 4	40.754

TABLE 7.9

```
Tests of Significance for AVOID using UNIQUE sums of squares
Source of Variation            SS     DF        MS        F     Sig of F

WITHIN CELLS              3229.39     29     111.36
REGRESSION                5172.61      1    5172.61     46.45      .000
GP                        1915.45      2     957.72      8.60      .001

(Model)                   9030.24      3    3010.08     27.03      .000
(Total)                  12259.64     32     383.11

R-Squared .=                 .737
Adjusted R-Squared =         .709
```

```
Regression analysis for WITHIN CELLS error term
---Individual Univariate .9500 confidence intervals
Dependent variable .. AVOID

COVARIATE              B        Beta    Std. Err.   t-Value   Sig. of t

PREAVOID            .70028    .67378       .103      6.815       .000

COVARIATE     Lower -95%   CL- Upper

PREAVOID           .490        .910
```

```
Adjusted and Estimated Means
Variable .. AVOID                             Variable .. PREAVOID
 CELL    Obs. Mean    Adj. Mean    Est. Mean    CELL    Obs. Mean
  1      116.909      119.349      116.909       1      103.182
  2      105.909      108.349      105.909       2      103.182
  3      132.273      127.392      132.273       3      113.636
```

```
Tests of Significance for AVOID using UNIQUE sums of squares
Source of Variation            SS     DF        MS        F     Sig of F

WITHIN+RESIDUAL          3077.09     27     113.97
PREAVOID                 5298.80      1    5298.80     46.49      .000
GP                        345.20      2     172.60      1.51      .238
PREAVOID BY GP            152.31      2      76.15       .67      .521

(Model)                   9182.55      5    1836.51     16.11      .000
(Total)                  12259.64     32     383.11

R-Squared .=                 .749
Adjusted R-Squared =         .703
```

```
Tests of Significance for AVOID using UNIQUE sums of squares
Source of Variation            SS     DF        MS        F     Sig of F

WITHIN CELLS             8402.00     30     280.07
GP                       3857.64      2    1928.82      6.89      .003

(Model)                   3857.64      2    1928.82      6.89      .003
(Total)                  12259.64     32     383.11

R-Squared .=                 .315
Adjusted R-Squared =         .269
```

An ANOVA on I.Q. yielded $F = 10.758/115.13 = .09$. Apply the Bryant-Paulson procedure at the .05 level to determine which pairs of means are significantly different.

3. (a) Run an ANOVA on the difference scores for the data in exercise 1.
   (b) Compare the error term for that analysis vs the error term for the ANCOVA on the same data. Relate these results to the discussion in Section 7.10.

4. This question relates the use of a pretest as covariate to experimental design considerations. Suppose in a counseling study eight subjects were randomly assigned to each of three groups. The subjects were pretested and posttested on client satisfaction, which served as the dependent variable.
   (a) What is the main reason for using the pretest here as a covariate?
   (b) In what other way might the covariate be useful?
   (c) What effect would the possibility of pretest sensitization have on your decision to use a pretest in this study?

5. An analysis of variance is run on three intact groups and a significant difference is found at the .05 level. The pattern of means is

	GP 1	GP 2	GP 3
COVARIATE	120	100	110
DEP. VAR.	70	60	65

A few days later the investigator, after talking to a colleague, runs an ANCOVA on this data and no longer finds significance at the .05 level. The correlation between the dependent variable and the covariate is .61 and the homogeneity of regression slopes assumption is found to be tenable. Explain what has happened here, and relate this to the discussion in section 7.3.

6. A study by Huck and Bounds (1972) examined whether the grade assigned an essay test is influenced by handwriting neatness. They hypothesized that an interaction effect would occur, with graders who have neat handwriting lowering the essay grade while graders with messy handwriting will not lower the grade. Students in an Educational Measurement class at the University of Tennessee served as subjects. Sixteen were classified as having neat handwriting and 18 were classified as messy handwriters. Each of these 34 subjects received two one page essays. A person with average handwriting neatness copied the first (better) essay. The second essay was copied by two people, one having neat handwriting and one having messy handwriting. Each subject was to grade each of the two essays on a scale from 0 to 20. Within the neat handwriters, half of them were randomly assigned to receive a neatly written essay to grade and the other half a messy essay. The same was done for the messy handwriters who

were acting as graders. The grade assigned to essay 1 served as the covariate in this study. Means and adjusted means are given below for groups:

		Neat Essay				Messy Essay	
	Essay 1	$\bar{x} =$	14.75		Essay 1	$\bar{x} =$	15.00
Neat	Essay 2	$\bar{x} =$	13.00		Essay 2	$\bar{x} =$	9.75
Writer		$sd =$	2.51			$sd =$	3.62
	Adj. Mean	$=$	13.35		Adj. Mean	$=$	9.98
	Essay 1	$\bar{x} =$	16.33		Essay 1	$\bar{x} =$	15.78
Messy	Essay 2	$\bar{x} =$	12.11		Essay 2	$\bar{x} =$	12.44
Writer		$sd =$	3.14			$sd =$	2.07
	Adj. Mean	$=$	11.70		Adj. Mean	$=$	12.30

The following is from their RESULTS section (Huck & Bounds, 1972):

> Prior to using analysis of covariance, the researchers tested the assumption of homogeneous within-group regression coefficients, Since this preliminary test proved to be nonsignificant ($F = 1.76$, $p > .10$), it was appropriate to use the conventional covariance analysis.
>
> Results of the 2×2 analysis of covariance revealed that neither main effect was significant. However, an interaction between the legibility of the essay and the handwriting neatness of the graders was found to be significant ($F = 4.49$, $p < .05$). To locate the precise nature of this interaction, tests of simple main effects (Kirk, 1968, p. 481) were used to compare the two treatment conditions, first for graders with neat handwriting and then a second time for graders with messy handwriting. Results indicated that neat writers gave higher grades to the neat essay than to the messy essay ($F = 6.13$, $p < .05$), but that messy handwriters did not differentiate significantly between the two essays. (pp. 281–82)

(a) From what is mentioned in the above RESULTS section, can we be confident that analysis of covariance is appropriate? Explain.

(b) What is the main reason for using analysis of covariance in this study?

(c) Should the investigators have been concerned about the homogeneity of cell population variances in this study? Why, or why not?

(d) Estimate the effect size for the interaction effect (see Section 4.6). Is it large or fairly large? Relate this to the sample size in the study and the significance that was found for the interaction effect.

Appendix A
Data Sets

CLINICAL DATA

The data for this study was drawn from the archives of Children's Hospital Medical Center's Department of Psychology in Cincinnati, Ohio. Thirty seven subjects were eventually selected from each of three diagnostic groups:

1. Encopretic children: These children have problems with fecal soiling. Clinically, parents report that the child "forgets," is too engrossed in other activities, or delays in going to the toilet. Problems that have been found to be associated with encopresis include anxiousness, social withdrawal, motor integration, and attention deficit.
2. Hyperactive children.
3. General clinic group: adjustment disorder, disturbed.

The selection criteria for the subjects were: male, 7–14 years of age, Full Scale WISC-R score above 85, and an absence of any concurrent disability or condition that could account for bowel control or attention problems.

Factor scores on the WISC-R were used to assess cognitive development and attention/information intake processes. The factor scores are for verbal comprehension (VERBCOMP), perceptual organization (PERCORG), and freedom from distractability (FREEDIST).

CLINICAL DATA

GPID	VERBCOMP	PERCORG	FREEDIST	GPID	VERBCOMP	PERCORG	FREEDIST
1	7.25	11.00	9.00	2	7.75	11.50	8.33
1	13.50	13.75	9.67	2	9.00	8.75	8.67
1	8.00	8.25	6.67	2	7.50	9.00	7.33
1	8.50	11.75	9.00	2	8.00	9.75	5.33
1	6.25	12.75	7.67	2	14.00	10.25	11.00
1	12.50	14.00	10.33	2	10.00	11.50	8.00
1	11.00	13.25	8.67	2	11.75	6.50	8.33
1	11.25	10.75	9.67	2	9.75	9.25	8.67
1	11.75	13.75	14.67	2	10.00	8.75	7.67
1	7.50	12.50	6.33	2	10.50	13.50	12.00
1	8.00	11.00	7.67	2	9.25	8.25	8.33
1	10.25	11.50	7.00	2	9.75	10.25	6.00
1	9.75	13.25	8.00	2	11.50	9.00	11.33
1	9.00	11.00	7.33	2	12.50	12.50	9.67
1	10.00	10.50	10.00	2	13.75	12.50	11.00
1	12.00	15.25	12.67	2	11.00	11.25	9.33

(Continued)

CLINICAL DATA   (*Continued*)

GPID	VERBCOMP	PERCORG	FREEDIST	GPID	VERBCOMP	PERCORG	FREEDIST
1	9.50	8.50	6.00	2	11.00	8.25	10.00
1	13.25	10.75	8.67	2	9.00	11.25	9.67
1	10.50	11.50	5.33	3	8.50	8.00	9.00
1	10.50	9.25	8.67	3	9.50	10.50	6.67
1	10.50	11.75	7.67	3	8.00	10.25	9.67
1	8.25	11.00	5.67	3	9.25	11.50	5.33
1	7.75	9.25	8.00	3	9.25	9.75	5.33
1	12.75	13.75	12.00	3	15.50	12.50	14.00
1	8.75	9.75	9.00	3	9.25	11.00	10.00
1	7.75	8.75	5.00	3	8.25	10.50	7.00
1	9.50	12.00	7.00	3	11.50	13.00	8.00
1	10.50	11.50	5.33	3	9.25	10.75	8.67
1	15.50	14.00	8.00	3	10.00	10.50	9.33
1	9.75	9.75	6.33	3	12.50	12.00	8.33
1	9.50	12.50	9.33	3	10.00	13.25	9.67
1	8.00	7.50	5.00	3	10.75	12.50	9.00
1	14.75	12.25	8.33	3	11.25	13.50	8.00
1	9.25	9.50	9.00	3	12.25	10.75	9.00
1	9.25	11.75	7.33	3	16.00	13.25	12.67
1	8.50	9.50	8.00	3	12.25	13.75	14.00
1	12.25	10.75	9.00	3	11.00	11.00	9.67
2	9.75	10.25	11.00	3	12.25	12.00	10.33
2	9.50	11.75	11.33	3	6.50	8.25	10.33
2	10.75	12.00	9.67	3	8.75	9.75	10.33
2	9.00	11.50	7.67	3	14.25	16.00	16.33
2	11.25	13.75	12.33	3	6.00	10.00	7.67
2	12.25	11.75	12.00	3	14.00	13.50	9.00
2	12.00	8.75	5.67	3	12.00	9.25	8.00
2	11.00	10.25	7.00	3	10.00	9.50	10.33
2	10.25	8.75	6.33	3	12.50	12.75	9.67
2	12.50	13.75	9.00	3	11.50	12.75	10.33
2	10.25	13.25	8.00	3	10.75	10.75	8.33
2	12.75	13.25	11.67	3	9.00	10.75	11.33
2	6.75	9.50	7.33	3	11.50	13.00	8.00
2	9.00	10.00	8.00	3	11.25	14.25	11.33
2	9.25	9.75	10.00	3	10.00	10.50	9.33
2	13.75	13.25	7.33	3	11.25	12.50	13.00
2	9.00	8.50	11.33	3	8.00	10.25	9.67
2	9.75	7.25	8.67	3	9.75	10.50	9.67
2	8.25	10.25	7.33				

DESCRIPTION OF ALCOHOLICS DATA SET

This is data from a study into the causes of relapse among alcoholics conducted at an Addiction Research Unit in London, England. The 251 subjects are those who presented themselves for treatment of alcoholism at several hospitals and related agencies. The subjects were divided into three groups;

Group 1: those never having previously experienced relapse after trying to give up heavy drinking.

Group 2: those who claimed to have relapsed, but no more than two or three times.

Group 3: those who had a longer history of relapse of four or more times.

The dependent variables for the study came from a Relapse Inventory Precipitants Inventory, which the subjects were asked to fill out at the point of admission into treatment. This inventory was developed from work on a previous survey that had identified three areas of vulnerability to relapse, the measurement of which yielded the following dependent variables:

UNPLMOOD—unpleasant mood states; for example, depression.

EUPHORIC—euphoric states and related situations; for example, celebrations and parties.

LESSVIGL—an area designated as lessened vigilance, for example, a temptation to believe that one or more drinks would cause no problem.

The grouping variable is given first for each subject, with UNPLMOOD, EUPHORIC, and LESSVIGL in that order.

ALCOHOLICS DATA

Grp	UM	ES	LV		Grp	UM	ES	LV
2	27	0	3		2	12	14	4
1	37	19	6		1	31	13	9
2	2	2	6		2	2	3	3
3	24	15	3		3	3	4	0
1	34	13	4		1	26	9	9
1	37	10	7		1	33	14	9
1	34	23	9		1	18	7	6
3	7	9	7		1	16	8	9
3	10	0	0		2	13	9	7
3	6	7	6		1	15	12	3
2	30	16	9		1	25	18	6
3	24	21	8		1	23	11	4
1	22	6	8		1	26	6	9
1	24	7	7		1	18	0	2

(*Continued*)

(*Continued*)

Grp	UM	ES	LV	Grp	UM	ES	LV
1	21	18	6	2	6	6	4
1	0	4	3	1	19	13	6
1	14	7	2	1	34	23	9
2	14	13	0	1	26	21	7
1	10	13	7	2	28	22	7
1	13	18	9	2	36	21	9
3	41	16	9	1	19	16	9
1	24	15	3	1	32	18	8
2	1	6	3	2	3	5	4
2	15	16	7	1	9	16	9
2	6	2	0	2	0	6	7
1	34	16	6	1	8	4	5
1	37	19	9	1	42	22	9
2	2	4	0	1	41	21	8
1	28	6	9	2	16	10	2
2	21	15	8	2	7	12	4
3	13	3	3	2	36	11	7
1	32	9	8	3	18	10	9
2	25	2	9	1	24	9	8
3	0	0	0	1	37	19	9
2	27	13	4	2	3	2	0
1	12	10	4	1	16	12	8
2	11	11	7	2	14	5	7
1	30	13	6	1	35	16	6
2	32	19	5	1	35	15	7
1	9	7	1	1	34	21	9
1	32	24	9	1	34	23	7
2	31	18	5	2	31	7	9
3	26	16	3	1	35	10	5
3	0	2	1	1	24	7	6
1	5	3	4	1	29	16	9
1	15	5	3	1	17	3	9
1	29	18	4	1	11	12	6
1	28	21	9	2	39	23	9
2	16	14	9	1	21	10	9
3	15	5	8	1	11	3	4
1	27	15	7	2	33	17	9
2	21	12	5	2	0	0	0
1	42	23	9	2	31	14	7
2	21	12	9	1	18	14	2
1	16	0	3	3	41	12	9
1	26	0	9	1	5	10	9
1	20	2	5	3	30	12	6
1	1	1	1	2	3	9	6
3	15	23	9	2	9	8	2
1	16	13	3	1	17	20	7

(*Continued*)

(*Continued*)

Grp	UM	ES	LV		Grp	UM	ES	LV
3	0	10	3		2	15	3	6
2	22	10	5		1	28	21	6
3	20	6	1		1	14	10	2
3	14	3	4		2	13	14	7
1	7	7	3		2	0	0	0
3	14	12	4		2	0	6	2
2	14	1	4		1	6	1	2
2	40	5	4		1	35	16	9
1	24	9	7		1	23	3	8
2	15	5	5		3	10	5	6
1	8	17	6		1	29	20	9
2	5	4	3		1	23	12	6
1	25	1	9		2	4	0	2
2	17	2	9		1	11	13	8
1	17	18	8		2	34	16	7
1	26	18	8		3	0	0	0
1	29	10	6		1	26	5	8
1	26	15	9		3	15	15	5
					1	3	5	2
2	20	14	9		3	34	11	7
1	10	17	9		2	6	19	6
3	31	20	6		1	18	12	5
1	18	7	3		1	3	5	7
1	22	13	4		1	35	15	9
2	21	9	6		2	17	5	5
2	3	7	4		2	29	16	7
2	16	1	0		2	32	20	8
1	15	12	7		1	13	5	3
3	7	5	1		2	37	22	9
2	18	12	4		1	26	13	6
1	27	11	9		1	17	9	4
1	18	9	8		1	28	10	5
2	0	0	0		3	28	8	6
1	8	14	6		3	5	3	0
2	7	7	6		2	25	19	8
1	7	4	5		3	19	23	3
2	19	21	8		2	33	14	5
2	30	16	8		2	7	17	4
3	6	16	8		1	19	13	6
1	28	13	9		1	32	13	9
1	17	8	3		3	0	3	0
2	17	13	6					
1	4	4	3		2	16	18	2
2	12	16	6		1	39	18	9
1	2	1	3		1	28	20	3

(*Continued*)

(*Continued*)

Grp	UM	ES	LV	Grp	UM	ES	LV
2	40	4	3	1	24	16	8
1	18	9	8	2	24	14	6
2	11	11	6	2	19	5	7
1	11	21	9	3	33	19	3
				1	15	10	7
2	23	12	7	1	24	16	7
1	32	20	9	2	33	14	7
2	14	3	3	1	26	3	5
2	10	6	4	2	26	12	8
3	32	7	4	1	26	16	6
				2	40	20	9
2	22	19	5	3	33	17	7
1	0	0	0	2	30	13	8
2	29	16	6	2	22	20	7
1	0	10	8	1	21	15	6
1	23	9	7	2	17	9	6
1	37	22	9	1	28	23	9
2	25	17	6	1	15	17	9
1	17	10	3	3	11	5	6
2	18	3	2	3	39	15	6
2	19	22	8	2	30	17	9
1	16	4	5	2	22	11	3
2	0	2	2				

DESCRIPTION OF SESAME STREET DATA BASE

This data is part of a large data set that evaluated the impact of the first year of the Sesame Street television series. Sesame Street was concerned mainly with teaching preschool related skills to children in the 3–5 year age range, with special emphasis on reaching 4 year old disadvantaged children. The format of the show was designed to hold young children's attention through action oriented, short duration presentations teaching specific preschool cognitive skills and some social skills. Each show was one hour and involved much repetition of concepts within and across shows.

A main concern for the evaluation, which was carried out at Educational Testing Service, was that it would permit generalization to the populations of children of most interest to the producers of the program (the Children's Television Workshop). Five populations were of interest:

1. Three to five year old disadvantaged children from inner city areas in various parts of the country.
2. Four year old advantaged suburban children.
3. Advantaged rural children.
4. Disadvantaged rural children.
5. Disadvantaged Spanish speaking children.

Children representative of these populations were sampled from five different sites in the United States.

Both before and after viewing the series the children were tested on a variety of cognitive variables (variables 8 through 19 in the data set), including knowledge of body parts, knowledge about letters, knowledge about numbers, etc. The variables are arranged on the file as follows:

Variable No.	Variable Name	Description
1	ID	Subject identification number
2	SITE	Five different sampling sites coded as 1,2,3,4 or 5.
3	SEX	Male - 1, Female - 2
4	AGE	in months
5	VIEWCAT	Viewing categories coded as a 1 if children rarely watched the show to a 4 if the children watched the show on average of more than 5 times a week

(Continued)

Variable No.	Variable Name	Description
6	SETTING	Setting in which Sesame Street was viewed, coded as 1 for home and coded as 2 for school
7	VIEWENC	A treatment condition in which some children were encouraged to view Sesame St (code - 1) and others were not (code - 2)
8	PREBODY	pretest on knowledge about body parts (maximum score - 32)—naming and functions of body parts
9	PRELET	pretest on knowledge about letters (maximum score - 58)—including recognizing letters, naming capital letters, matching letters in words
10	PREFORM	pretest on knowledge about forms (maximum score - 20)—recognizing and naming forms
11	PRENUMB	pretest on knowledge about numbers (maximum score - 54)—recognizing and naming numbers, counting, addition and subtraction
12	PRERELAT	pretest on knowledge of relational terms (maximum score - 17)—amount, size and position relationship
13	PRECLASF	pretest on knowledge of classification skills (maximum score - 24)—classifying by size, form, number and function
14	POSTBODY	posttest knowledge on body parts
15	POSTLET	posttest knowledge of letters
16	POSTFORM	posttest knowledge of forms
17	POSTNUMB	posttest knowledge of numbers
18	POSTREL	posttest knowledge of relations
19	POSTCLAS	posttest knowledge of classification skills
20	PEABODY	Mental age scores obtained from administration of the Peabody Picture Vocabulary Test as a pretest measure of vocabulary maturity

SESAME STREET DATA

ID	SITE	SEX	AGE	VIEWCAT	SETTING	VIEWENC	PREBODY	PRELET	PREFORM	PRENUMB	PRERELAT	PRECLASF	POSTBODY	POSTLET	POSTFORM	POSTNUMB	POSTREL	POSTCLAS	PEABODY
1	1	1	66	1	2	1	16	23	12	40	14	20	18	30	14	44	14	23	62
2	1	2	67	3	2	1	30	26	9	39	16	22	30	37	17	39	14	22	80
3	1	1	56	3	2	2	22	14	9	9	9	8	21	46	15	40	9	19	32
4	1	1	49	1	2	2	23	11	10	14	9	13	21	14	13	19	8	15	27
5	1	1	69	4	2	2	32	47	15	51	17	22	32	53	18	54	14	21	71
6	1	2	54	3	2	2	29	26	10	33	14	14	27	36	14	39	16	24	32
7	1	2	47	3	2	2	23	12	11	13	11	12	22	45	12	44	12	15	28
8	1	1	51	2	2	1	32	48	19	52	15	23	31	47	18	51	17	23	38
9	1	1	69	4	2	1	27	44	18	42	15	20	32	50	17	48	14	24	49
10	1	2	53	3	2	1	30	38	17	31	10	17	32	52	19	52	17	24	32
11	1	2	58	2	2	2	25	48	14	38	16	18	26	52	15	42	10	17	43
12	1	2	58	4	2	2	21	25	13	29	16	21	17	29	15	40	10	19	58
13	1	2	49	1	2	2	28	8	9	13	8	12	20	16	9	18	10	13	39
14	1	1	64	2	2	1	26	11	15	21	10	15	26	28	15	35	16	14	43
15	1	2	58	2	2	1	23	15	9	16	9	11	28	21	10	22	10	17	56
16	1	1	49	3	2	1	25	12	17	24	12	18	28	45	14	45	13	21	37
17	1	1	57	2	2	1	25	15	13	16	10	18	25	24	16	28	8	18	43
18	1	1	45	4	2	1	16	12	8	11	6	3	25	16	11	17	9	9	29
19	1	1	45	3	2	1	25	16	12	23	10	13	32	46	18	35	14	19	45
20	1	1	60	3	2	2	19	19	8	23	14	10	28	50	12	38	12	13	51
21	1	2	65	4	2	1	29	24	14	41	10	23	29	48	20	51	15	24	55
22	1	1	44	4	1	1	25	15	17	22	11	16	32	42	19	45	15	19	49
23	1	2	38	3	1	1	20	9	2	7	8	9	22	23	17	19	15	14	31
24	1	1	35	4	1	1	11	6	8	16	8	9	22	27	16	20	14	15	40
25	1	2	42	2	1	1	15	7	8	11	12	7	14	13	7	21	12	10	48
26	1	2	50	2	1	1	26	14	10	36	13	17	25	18	14	42	13	18	35
27	1	1	61	4	2	2	28	42	16	40	16	11	24	27	15	20	14	14	62
28	1	2	34	4	1	1	17	13	7	10	5	11	21	17	13	13	10	15	42
29	1	1	60	3	1	2	23	13	9	23	11	14	28	20	18	45	14	21	58
30	1	2	39	2	1	1	11	5	5	5	5	1	27	15	13	9	8	12	29
31	1	1	39	3	1	1	24	4	11	25	11	17	21	11	12	13	9	10	49
32	1	2	41	2	1	1	24	8	3	14	8	8	21	17	10	18	9	14	30
33	1	2	55	3	1	1	31	15	17	45	16	24	32	43	18	46	13	21	62
34	1	2	42	3	1	1	23	11	7	15	6	7	29	27	14	33	9	19	58
35	1	1	50	4	1	1	18	17	12	28	12	17	29	41	15	48	12	22	55
36	1	1	58	2	1	1	13	12	6	10	6	11	29	23	11	27	8	10	33
37	1	2	59	3	1	2	27	7	13	23	12	10	32	39	18	49	16	19	55
38	1	2	36	1	1	2	11	12	9	5	5	3	12	12	6	13	9	6	27
39	1	1	51	2	1	1	32	16	16	34	15	17	21	17	6	21	8	12	62
40	1	1	51	2	1	1	31	18	13	33	15	14	21	16	11	7	9	11	58
41	1	1	48	3	1	1	13	14	8	8	10	11	21	22	10	28	8	19	34
42	1	1	43	2	1	1	17	13	14	13	11	14	24	19	12	22	11	20	32
43	1	2	35	3	1	2	23	12	8	9	5	5	29	11	8	9	11	11	32
44	1	2	36	1	1	2	11	2	6	5	2	4	21	6	11	6	6	7	28

(Continued)

SESAME STREET DATA   (*Continued*)

ID	SITE	SEX	AGE	VIEWCAT	SETTING	VIEWENC	PREBODY	PRELET	PREFORM	PRENUMB	PRERELAT	PRECLASF	POSTBODY	POSTLET	POSTFORM	POSTNUMB	POSTREL	POSTCLAS	PEABODY
45	1	2	39	2	1	2	20	18	6	4	4	6	19	8	11	22	10	10	29
46	1	1	45	4	1	2	14	13	9	16	9	12	29	48	17	48	14	19	35
47	1	1	58	3	1	2	30	38	15	45	14	18	32	48	19	46	14	23	67
48	1	2	38	3	1	1	13	10	7	8	5	7	26	36	14	20	10	16	29
49	1	2	57	4	1	1	26	15	11	22	10	15	24	20	18	28	12	18	35
50	1	1	49	3	1	2	26	35	10	47	13	17	26	13	7	12	11	14	67
51	1	1	55	1	2	2	24	11	10	18	8	10	20	10	14	23	10	10	39
52	1	2	44	4	2	2	25	39	18	41	9	21	30	47	20	50	11	23	90
53	1	1	56	1	2	2	13	11	6	15	10	11	15	13	9	13	10	6	46
54	1	2	48	2	2	2	17	11	9	14	8	9	26	32	15	27	11	11	39
55	1	1	50	2	2	2	16	10	8	9	7	6	21	15	17	17	12	15	34
56	1	1	52	1	2	2	16	15	6	13	11	13	19	14	14	18	7	16	38
57	1	2	51	2	2	1	24	14	10	20	10	17	28	21	17	36	19	17	34
58	1	2	58	1	2	2	25	17	17	23	14	15	25	16	19	28	4	20	37
59	1	2	48	3	2	2	13	10	10	13	9	7	27	15	14	23	11	12	33
60	1	1	54	4	2	2	16	13	10	10	9	7	19	20	14	19	12	11	36
61	2	1	52	4	2	2	20	35	15	21	8	20	27	48	19	47	15	22	49
62	2	2	48	1	2	2	20	12	11	13	7	11	28	19	17	17	11	17	53
63	2	1	55	4	2	2	28	13	10	29	11	12	30	31	19	45	15	22	65
64	2	1	55	2	2	2	23	16	5	32	10	13	28	28	15	46	13	17	55
65	2	2	55	2	1	2	30	27	11	39	12	17	32	40	19	52	17	23	85
66	2	2	56	1	1	1	26	18	10	30	12	9	29	46	13	44	13	17	43
67	2	2	50	3	2	1	31	15	10	24	11	20	31	43	18	52	14	23	65
68	2	1	51	3	2	1	28	19	14	37	13	15	32	47	19	48	15	22	75
69	2	1	58	3	2	2	30	14	17	37	13	20	28	38	15	36	16	18	85
70	2	2	55	4	2	2	27	10	10	12	14	16	31	42	16	31	13	20	40
71	2	2	41	4	1	2	24	22	14	42	14	21	30	49	19	50	14	22	58
72	2	2	51	4	1	2	20	13	11	22	11	15	27	17	11	20	14	14	42
73	2	1	52	4	2	1	29	13	9	18	10	10	30	23	17	28	12	17	69
74	2	2	54	3	2	1	30	26	13	23	10	17	32	42	12	37	12	19	58
75	2	1	47	4	1	1	19	12	11	16	11	12	28	43	18	38	14	17	37
76	2	1	50	4	1	1	31	30	15	47	15	19	23	48	19	49	13	20	62
77	2	2	55	4	1	1	31	13	18	39	15	24	31	51	19	50	14	23	99
78	2	1	50	3	2	1	32	27	13	29	13	12	31	45	19	53	16	23	75
79	2	2	57	2	2	1	31	19	14	36	13	11	32	50	17	47	15	22	82
80	2	2	55	4	1	2	20	12	9	16	11	18	30	30	14	18	12	16	47
81	2	2	55	4	1	2	26	14	8	24	13	12	30	45	19	43	15	24	62
82	2	1	50	3	2	1	30	44	15	45	12	11	32	53	19	52	15	23	67
83	2	1	52	3	2	1	26	13	11	34	12	12	30	45	17	43	13	21	40
84	2	2	45	2	2	1	28	12	9	16	7	8	28	21	14	32	9	17	41
85	2	2	52	3	2	1	24	14	8	18	8	7	28	43	12	41	13	15	56
86	2	1	53	4	1	1	26	17	15	32	13	16	27	37	15	31	14	23	73
87	2	2	53	4	2	2	29	10	17	23	13	15	32	51	19	48	16	21	85
88	2	2	53	2	2	2	23	12	12	15	11	17	28	20	15	19	8	19	59

(*Continued*)

SESAME STREET DATA (Continued)

ID	SITE	SEX	AGE	VIEWCAT	SETTING	VIEWENC	PREBODY	PRELET	PREFORM	PRENUMB	PRERELAT	PRECLASF	POSTBODY	POSTLET	POSTFORM	POSTNUMB	POSTREL	POSTCLAS	PEABODY
89	2	2	56	3	1	2	28	29	11	43	13	22	31	32	15	40	15	21	58
90	2	2	54	4	2	2	32	46	15	48	13	21	32	51	19	50	16	23	92
91	2	1	50	2	2	1	22	17	8	18	12	14	25	16	14	32	14	17	69
92	2	1	50	3	1	1	29	25	14	35	15	20	26	36	16	31	8	15	56
93	2	2	53	4	1	1	25	17	12	30	13	17	29	40	17	40	13	22	78
94	2	1	45	4	1	1	21	16	12	15	11	17	29	36	19	29	10	16	58
95	2	2	56	4	1	1	32	22	15	32	11	13	31	46	20	51	14	24	78
96	2	1	53	3	1	1	31	14	16	29	11	17	32	43	19	42	13	22	67
97	2	2	46	4	1	1	22	28	14	20	5	15	32	42	13	29	15	18	69
98	2	2	46	2	1	2	30	18	14	23	11	11	29	33	13	36	8	16	53
99	2	1	50	3	1	2	18	13	8	14	11	12	19	23	11	31	12	17	55
100	2	2	47	1	1	2	17	10	5	11	8	7	18	19	9	8	10	13	53
101	2	1	56	2	2	1	27	11	15	22	13	14	30	47	20	45	15	24	67
102	2	2	46	3	1	1	27	13	13	22	12	13	28	36	17	46	11	20	62
103	2	2	45	4	1	1	21	23	14	27	13	20	31	48	19	44	11	24	59
104	2	2	46	4	1	1	19	17	4	19	10	13	28	36	16	29	10	15	46
105	2	2	47	3	1	1	31	9	14	24	11	16	32	42	17	42	11	20	58
106	2	1	52	2	2	1	26	16	12	30	14	16	27	29	20	41	15	21	92
107	2	2	52	4	2	1	24	15	12	30	14	14	31	45	18	49	13	23	48
108	2	1	56	2	1	1	21	22	12	25	12	15	29	37	14	46	14	18	65
109	2	1	48	4	1	1	28	22	13	19	11	8	32	48	18	43	15	19	67
110	2	1	49	3	1	1	25	16	13	18	15	15	27	48	13	45	15	18	59
111	2	2	55	4	2	1	32	8	13	23	11	17	29	35	18	36	11	19	39
112	2	2	45	3	1	1	22	15	12	20	9	14	25	21	15	21	9	16	47
113	2	1	45	3	1	1	32	16	14	30	11	17	25	26	17	39	13	19	51
114	2	2	48	4	1	1	31	6	8	13	7	13	29	32	15	23	7	16	43
115	2	1	58	1	1	2	19	14	12	23	11	10	28	15	10	34	11	7	65
116	3	1	55	2	1	1	20	16	7	14	9	9	21	11	13	20	13	13	39
117	3	2	48	1	1	2	20	15	5	13	8	7	21	14	3	17	10	7	33
118	3	2	52	3	1	1	14	6	3	9	4	8	18	19	20	18	12	20	34
119	3	2	58	1	1	1	20	11	5	25	9	7	26	16	10	23	12	12	35
120	3	1	50	3	2	2	13	12	5	11	10	9	21	18	10	19	10	9	32
121	3	1	58	3	2	2	22	19	11	35	10	17	23	44	18	46	13	19	44
122	3	2	49	4	2	2	14	13	7	5	5	7	17	16	12	19	12	15	31
123	3	1	56	4	2	2	24	17	9	16	11	10	29	35	17	40	14	19	44
124	3	1	50	1	1	2	7	14	4	10	5	5	19	15	13	14	13	17	27
125	3	2	49	1	1	1	20	18	3	14	6	6	11	12	6	8	9	5	29
126	3	1	46	2	1	1	15	14	8	23	14	12	25	18	14	30	12	16	47
127	3	1	57	2	1	1	26	14	9	23	15	9	28	15	14	24	12	9	35
128	3	1	44	1	2	2	12	9	7	14	9	14	13	13	7	17	9	7	32
129	3	2	41	2	2	2	16	14	9	10	11	9	22	17	9	23	8	13	36
130	3	2	58	4	2	1	17	9	11	28	8	13	29	13	12	29	12	15	38
131	3	2	60	4	2	1	31	19	11	27	11	16	31	31	17	38	13	22	42

(Continued)

SESAME STREET DATA   (Continued)

ID	SITE	SEX	AGE	VIEWCAT	SETTING	VIEWENC	PREBODY	PRELET	PREFORM	PRENUMB	PRERELAT	PRECLASF	POSTBODY	POSTLET	POSTFORM	POSTNUMB	POSTREL	POSTCLAS	PEABODY
132	3	2	40	2	1	1	12	14	3	17	6	6	16	13	6	17	10	9	27
133	3	2	37	2	1	1	7	4	6	4	5	4	13	13	6	14	9	11	60
134	3	1	45	1	1	1	12	5	5	9	7	7	15	13	12	20	12	11	28
135	3	1	60	3	1	1	17	18	9	14	7	6	32	36	13	32	13	12	33
136	3	1	52	2	1	2	18	13	9	24	10	16	25	15	12	26	11	10	55
137	3	2	46	4	1	1	20	12	4	17	8	8	28	22	17	38	14	20	29
138	3	2	60	4	1	1	23	16	9	25	11	14	29	26	17	38	16	22	46
139	3	1	60	3	1	1	17	11	10	15	10	14	11	13	7	16	9	13	33
140	3	1	59	3	1	1	7	16	11	10	6	10	15	14	9	14	8	10	32
141	3	2	52	3	1	1	29	20	8	37	13	13	28	46	12	42	13	15	47
142	3	1	60	3	1	1	29	13	12	17	12	16	29	25	17	32	13	19	90
143	3	2	56	2	1	1	21	12	12	17	9	14	23	26	16	34	10	20	61
144	3	2	54	2	2	2	18	28	9	14	12	16	27	42	18	37	11	15	36
145	3	2	61	3	1	1	13	12	8	16	7	11	28	15	15	18	7	15	35
146	3	2	61	3	1	1	29	18	12	22	11	14	30	25	17	39	13	19	48
147	3	2	51	3	1	1	17	15	5	11	10	11	32	43	14	44	15	21	35
148	3	1	49	4	2	1	19	17	7	16	3	6	27	27	18	43	15	20	35
149	3	1	52	2	1	1	22	13	10	20	11	14	22	14	9	21	9	7	35
150	3	2	55	3	2	1	25	13	12	16	10	14	26	17	6	31	13	9	35
151	3	2	60	4	2	1	28	10	10	22	12	15	28	15	15	30	11	17	45
152	3	2	43	1	2	2	14	9	5	15	5	6	16	16	12	14	10	14	33
153	3	1	55	3	2	1	14	7	9	15	9	12	18	15	16	22	11	16	42
154	3	2	52	4	2	1	18	11	9	15	8	12	23	23	15	40	13	18	32
155	3	2	56	1	2	1	26	24	13	25	9	10	17	7	3	13	6	5	40
156	3	1	56	4	1	1	24	11	11	28	14	17	27	14	15	40	12	21	42
157	3	2	47	2	1	1	20	19	9	25	12	8	26	24	13	35	11	17	46
158	3	2	56	2	1	1	17	18	8	17	5	9	24	17	10	19	10	15	39
159	3	2	52	3	1	1	28	15	13	27	9	15	31	16	16	22	12	18	69
160	3	2	51	4	1	1	23	14	11	23	8	11	31	37	17	42	14	18	36
161	3	1	51	1	1	1	7	13	6	11	7	6	12	8	14	22	10	16	35
162	3	2	53	3	1	1	15	15	8	18	8	11	29	32	12	28	10	14	34
163	3	1	50	4	1	1	26	11	14	23	10	11	39	22	16	40	14	17	32
164	3	2	59	4	1	1	16	10	8	21	9	12	25	22	14	31	10	18	38
165	3	1	53	3	1	1	14	12	7	9	9	5	22	28	9	30	9	10	32
166	3	1	55	3	1	1	15	10	7	9	6	11	24	20	14	27	9	9	34
167	3	1	57	1	1	1	6	13	2	8	7	7	18	6	4	0	1	4	35
168	3	1	58	2	1	1	16	5	5	8	6	9	13	14	11	11	9	16	34
169	3	1	44	3	1	1	10	12	4	9	10	11	13	15	3	8	3	5	28
170	3	1	39	1	1	2	14	12	4	5	7	5	13	11	8	19	10	8	29
171	3	1	53	4	2	1	21	17	12	16	10	13	27	20	14	29	15	16	37
172	3	2	52	4	1	1	23	10	9	9	7	6	21	16	11	20	9	9	32
173	3	1	57	3	1	2	25	11	10	19	11	13	28	29	20	25	16	19	35
174	3	2	40	3	1	1	11	10	7	14	4	8	16	22	11	21	9	9	35

(Continued)

SESAME STREET DATA (*Continued*)

ID	SITE	SEX	AGE	VIEWCAT	SETTING	VIEWENC	PREBODY	PRELET	PREFORM	PRENUMB	PRERELAT	PRECLASF	POSTBODY	POSTLET	POSTFORM	POSTNUMB	POSTREL	POSTCLAS	PEABODY
175	3	2	47	2	1	1	16	13	7	7	6	9	22	13	4	18	11	9	32
176	3	1	51	2	1	1	25	19	11	24	12	8	26	20	15	24	11	13	47
177	3	1	48	2	1	1	11	7	4	14	3	13	11	12	8	27	11	10	35
178	3	2	49	1	1	2	15	16	6	9	4	7	20	16	7	17	10	5	35
179	3	1	50	2	1	1	12	8	5	17	8	10	18	19	12	13	12	17	30
180	4	2	53	1	2	2	10	13	4	13	7	8	19	16	9	16	7	11	35
181	4	2	52	1	2	2	13	15	8	19	8	9	21	11	8	16	7	11	39
182	4	1	51	1	2	2	19	12	9	17	8	12	27	16	12	27	11	16	39
183	4	1	52	1	2	2	20	16	12	22	11	17	25	19	14	26	11	15	36
184	4	1	46	1	2	2	13	3	3	1	4	4	24	11	10	13	11	13	27
185	4	2	51	1	2	2	21	19	12	25	13	14	24	15	11	25	8	14	45
186	4	2	47	1	2	2	19	12	13	27	8	11	24	14	15	21	7	13	28
187	4	2	51	3	2	1	25	13	12	21	12	16	31	16	15	25	11	18	40
188	4	2	54	1	2	1	8	20	5	8	7	6	14	13	11	11	8	10	47
189	4	2	54	2	2	1	12	4	9	4	7	6	17	13	10	12	9	8	36
190	4	1	57	2	2	1	24	11	10	28	12	11	30	24	18	26	14	16	39
191	4	1	53	2	2	1	17	12	8	9	5	11	26	13	11	20	10	15	39
192	4	2	50	2	2	1	20	16	8	18	9	13	28	25	15	15	9	12	43
193	4	2	57	1	2	2	28	23	16	33	14	11	26	25	16	42	14	11	69
194	4	2	58	1	2	2	31	30	12	44	14	17	32	43	16	44	11	13	69
195	4	2	58	1	2	2	28	29	9	33	14	8	29	44	9	44	15	10	38
196	4	2	53	1	2	2	19	19	14	24	11	16	21	13	9	31	10	16	39
197	4	2	49	1	2	2	20	17	7	13	9	10	30	15	6	21	10	9	30
198	4	2	51	1	2	2	10	1	2	2	4	0	13	0	0	0	0	0	34
199	4	1	58	1	2	2	22	13	9	13	10	9	18	18	11	13	11	8	36
200	4	2	51	1	2	2	18	12	4	10	5	9	17	10	8	14	5	10	48
201	4	2	53	1	2	2	21	17	9	18	9	11	28	15	9	19	12	9	49
202	4	2	56	3	2	1	29	17	17	32	10	20	30	33	17	38	12	20	49
203	4	2	51	3	1	1	19	11	10	19	8	7	22	19	11	39	11	21	37
204	4	1	47	1	1	1	23	12	11	14	11	13	29	15	13	22	14	16	45
205	4	2	54	4	1	1	23	14	12	23	8	15	28	41	16	35	16	22	46
206	4	1	54	4	1	1	17	15	6	15	4	11	24	30	13	42	17	20	32
207	4	2	46	1	1	1	22	14	7	15	3	14	29	24	18	36	13	23	30
208	4	2	52	2	1	1	20	15	14	19	5	13	27	45	16	38	17	22	35
209	4	2	48	1	1	1	24	18	5	21	9	11	23	17	10	16	15	9	36
210	4	1	49	2	1	2	17	21	7	23	9	4	13	14	13	35	15	13	45
211	4	1	58	1	1	2	14	7	3	17	13	6	22	15	11	23	13	9	59
212	4	1	46	3	1	2	18	13	10	11	7	9	22	14	13	23	10	13	42
213	4	1	57	1	1	2	27	19	11	20	10	15	27	19	8	29	23	11	41
214	4	1	48	4	1	2	27	12	15	23	11	16	27	17	13	27	13	10	39
215	4	2	52	2	1	2	23	8	9	16	12	8	20	16	13	23	10	12	94
216	4	1	57	2	1	1	29	17	12	24	12	16	31	32	12	17	9	10	55
217	4	1	46	3	1	1	18	9	10	12	9	14	24	18	11	13	8	10	28

(*Continued*)

SESAME STREET DATA   (Continued)

ID	SITE	SEX	AGE	VIEWCAT	SETTING	VIEWENC	PREBODY	PRELET	PREFORM	PRENUMB	PRERELAT	PRECLASF	POSTBODY	POSTLET	POSTFORM	POSTNUMB	POSTREL	POSTCLAS	PEABODY
218	4	1	55	2	1	1	14	12	8	14	11	11	27	40	18	35	16	21	32
219	4	1	44	3	1	1	8	11	6	10	6	9	31	23	15	18	10	13	28
220	4	1	56	1	2	2	26	15	12	29	11	12	25	23	13	40	12	16	59
221	4	2	44	2	1	1	14	14	12	10	10	12	25	23	16	26	13	12	27
222	4	1	59	4	1	1	28	17	12	27	10	11	31	46	19	29	16	20	61
223	5	1	48	2	1	1	16	8	8	9	8	8	24	11	9	11	8	7	35
224	5	1	56	2	1	1	22	17	11	23	14	13	30	20	17	38	13	21	58
225	5	2	58	2	1	1	20	18	8	26	11	10	30	44	12	40	13	21	59
226	5	2	53	1	1	1	15	11	2	8	10	5	18	19	10	14	6	8	34
227	5	2	53	1	1	1	26	16	8	14	10	9	28	13	12	18	10	11	41
228	5	2	65	1	1	2	15	16	5	24	12	12	22	15	12	26	11	19	44
229	5	1	46	1	1	2	15	5	5	4	9	4	15	13	10	10	8	11	41
230	5	1	49	1	1	2	19	12	12	16	13	15	28	16	14	36	14	16	59
231	5	1	55	1	1	2	21	40	8	36	9	10	27	49	13	47	9	17	53
232	5	2	46	2	1	1	20	9	6	17	10	11	29	13	12	23	12	8	31
233	5	2	58	4	1	1	30	55	19	52	15	23	31	54	19	54	15	23	78
234	5	1	47	4	1	1	18	13	9	20	8	11	28	34	17	33	11	18	43
235	5	1	53	4	1	1	26	25	14	36	13	13	30	44	19	43	15	23	90
236	5	2	51	2	1	1	30	15	8	12	10	10	30	33	12	45	12	20	49
237	5	1	49	4	1	1	17	16	12	15	8	15	25	26	15	20	12	11	41
238	5	1	43	2	1	1	16	13	6	11	8	9	22	19	10	10	9	7	30
239	5	2	60	3	1	1	23	16	9	33	14	16	29	35	18	50	13	23	69
240	5	1	51	4	1	1	21	11	10	27	10	12	25	32	17	47	11	19	65

DESCRIPTION OF HEADACHE DATA SET

This study investigated the effectiveness of different kinds of psychological treatment on the sensitivity of headache sufferers to noise. Each subject was exposed to the following sequence of operations: (1) measurement of initial sensitivity scores, (2) relaxation training, (3) treatment, and (4) measurement of final sensitivity scores.

The sensitivity scores were obtained by having subjects listen to a tone that gradually increased in volume and asking them to rate the levels at which the tone became (1) uncomfortable and (2) definitely unpleasant. These levels, denoted by U and DU, are the dependent variables, with pretest scores on these variables useful for possible covariance analysis.

Relaxation training was applied to all subjects and comprised two stages: (1) The subjects were asked to listen to the tone at their definitely unpleasant level for up to two minutes (with the option to terminate the exposure if they chose). (2) The subjects were then given instruction on breathing techniques and the use of visual imagery to act as a controlled distraction.

There were two types of headache sufferers in the study: (a) migrane and (b) tension. Within each of these groups subjects were randomly assigned to one of the following four treatment groups:

T1—subjects in this group listened to the tone again at their definitely unpleasant (DU) level for the length of time that they were able to stand it in (a) above.

T2—as T1 but with one extra minute's exposure to the tone.

T3—as T2 but having been instructed to use the relaxaton techniques of breathing and imagery.

T4—this was a control group, in that the subjects experienced no exposure to the tone between (a) in the relaxation training and the final sensitivity measures.

Some missing data reduced an intended balanced design to the following 2 × 4 factorial design, with cell sizes indicated:

	T1	T2	T3	T4
MIGRANE	11	11	12	11
TENSION	14	11	16	12

HEADACHE DATA

HEADACHE TYPE	TREAT. GP	PREUNCOMF	PREDFUNPL	UNCOMF	DFUNPL	HEADACHE TYPE	TREAT. GP	PREUNCOMF	PREDFUNPL	UNCOMF	DFUNPL
1	3	2.34	5.30	5.80	8.52	1	1	2.73	6.85	4.68	6.68
2	1	0.37	0.53	0.55	0.84	1	3	7.50	9.12	5.70	7.88
1	3	4.63	7.21	5.63	6.75	1	3	3.60	7.30	4.83	7.32
1	2	2.45	3.75	2.50	3.18	1	1	2.31	3.25	2.00	3.30
1	1	1.38	2.33	2.23	3.98	2	3	0.85	1.42	1.37	1.89
1	3	1.85	3.25	3.40	4.80	1	2	1.90	8.68	2.25	6.70
2	1	6.00	9.90	8.25	10.7	1	2	1.56	2.92	2.00	2.84
2	1	2.95	4.98	3.85	4.75	2	1	2.95	3.45	1.75	2.30
2	2	6.68	9.90	8.52	12.8	1	4	1.72	2.75	2.20	3.95
2	3	3.90	6.50	3.27	7.80	1	3	0.40	0.90	1.40	2.30
1	1	2.19	2.60	2.50	3.50	2	4	1.40	1.82	2.10	3.90
2	3	3.22	5.65	2.70	4.80	2	3	3.50	6.60	4.65	8.00
2	2	3.15	5.25	5.30	7.60	1	4	1.96	3.18	1.20	3.15
2	2	2.55	4.05	4.00	5.45	2	1	1.85	3.30	1.80	3.15
2	4	1.85	3.20	1.42	2.62	2	1	1.50	1.75	1.35	3.40
2	4	4.32	6.15	4.98	6.45	2	1	2.43	7.95	4.08	6.83
1	3	3.42	5.59	4.50	7.18	2	3	3.70	5.88	3.13	4.00
2	3	2.57	4.40	3.27	8.64	1	3	1.62	3.40	4.03	5.70
2	2	4.66	6.82	3.45	6.24	1	2	1.12	1.39	1.06	1.78
2	4	4.10	7.65	3.36	6.58	1	4	2.65	4.88	1.20	3.50
1	4	0.66	1.00	0.43	0.60	2	4	2.08	3.30	2.44	3.47
2	2	3.38	8.27	7.07	0.90	2	4	3.86	5.94	3.20	4.81
2	2	2.39	4.60	2.93	5.42	2	3	3.62	8.83	5.12	7.71
1	4	1.86	4.06	1.78	2.44	2	3	2.19	3.94	2.31	3.48
2	4	2.08	2.64	1.71	2.99	2	4	1.51	2.80	1.24	2.63
1	2	1.60	2.83	1.87	3.00	1	3	0.75	0.94	0.88	1.45
1	1	0.87	1.16	0.59	0.95	1	3	1.92	2.44	2.00	2.54
2	4	1.42	6.47	2.00	3.48	1	4	1.82	2.57	0.64	1.07
2	1	1.86	2.74	0.89	1.41	1	4	1.24	2.69	0.95	1.76
1	3	0.90	1.41	1.56	2.11	2	3	1.24	3.23	1.36	2.86
1	4	1.51	2.79	0.83	1.64	1	1	1.56	8.69	2.35	7.51
2	3	1.44	3.06	1.11	2.58	2	2	0.46	1.12	0.93	1.36
1	2	2.20	5.25	1.04	3.19	2	2	1.29	2.32	1.75	5.30
2	2	2.34	4.25	2.16	4.10	1	1	0.86	1.55	0.88	2.14
1	2	5.91	8.56	2.62	6.08	2	2	1.43	3.94	3.61	7.57
2	3	15.1	16.3	15.5	16.4	2	1	0.55	1.10	1.80	3.92
2	3	7.42	14.5	8.15	13.3	1	4	3.40	5.10	2.80	4.40
2	3	1.52	2.35	1.20	2.55	2	1	1.85	5.68	7.75	16.1
1	1	2.25	4.40	1.75	4.93	1	2	4.22	13.3	12.2	14.1
2	3	3.30	4.55	5.25	5.83	2	3	4.30	11.3	8.78	12.38

(Continued)

HEADACHE DATA

HEADACHE TYPE	TREAT. GP	PREUNCOMF	PREDFUNPL	UNCOMF	DFUNPL	HEADACHE TYPE	TREAT. GP	PREUNCOMF	PREDFUNPL	UNCOMF	DFUNPL
1	3	3.58	5.60	6.94	9.16	2	3	6.17	15.5	7.54	16.24
2	1	0.43	0.64	0.22	0.39	1	1	1.33	10.3	1.67	3.79
2	1	0.87	1.30	1.10	1.45	1	2	5.05	10.05	3.02	10.1
2	1	1.88	4.19	1.79	4.26	1	1	8.94	15.46	3.64	9.00
1	1	2.50	4.64	2.23	3.60	2	1	13.3	17.00	11.87	16.6
2	4	3.25	5.09	1.24	2.11	1	4	10.36	17.0	11.50	15.56
1	2	1.08	1.49	1.09	1.82	2	4	3.01	12.35	4.01	7.51
1	4	0.71	1.13	0.58	0.86	2	2	2.00	8.37	10.08	5.49
1	3	12.72	16.5	15.2	16.8	2	4	11.3	16.8	6.75	16.87

DESCRIPTION OF THE CARTOON DATA SET

This is a data set on 179 subjects from the *Minitab Handbook* (2nd ed., 1985), and is used with permission of the publisher. A short instructional slide presentation was developed, which dealt with the behavior of people in a group situation, and in particular the various roles or character types that group members often assume. The presentation consisted of a 5 minute lecture on tape, accompanied by 18 slides. Each role was identified by an animal. Each animal was shown on two slides: once in a cartoon sketch and once in a realistic picture. All 179 subjects saw all 18 slides, but a randomly selected half of them saw the slides in black and white while the other half saw the slides in color.

After seeing the slides, the subjects took a test on the material. The slides were presented in random order, and the subjects wrote down the character type represented by that slide. They received two scores: one for the number of cartoon characters correctly identified and one for the number of realistic characters correctly identified. Each score could range from 0 to 9, since there were 9 characters. Four weeks later the subjects were retested. Some subjects did not show up for the retest and that is indicated by a blank.

There are three groups of subjects in this study: (1) preprofessional personnel at three hospitals in Pennsylvania involved in an in-service training program, (2) professional personnel involved in the same training program, and (3) a group of Penn State undergraduate students. All these subjects were given the Otis Mental Ability Test, which yields a rough estimate of their natural ability.

The order in which the variables are arranged on the file is as follows:

Variable No.	Variable Name	Description
1	ID	Identification number
2	COLOR	0 = black and white, 1 = color (no participant saw both)
3	ED	Education: 0 = preprofessional, 1 = professional, 2 = college student
4	LOCATION	Location: 1 = hospital A, 2 = hospital B, 3 = hospital C, 4 = Penn State student
5	OTIS	OTIS score: from about 70 to about 130
6	CARTOON1	Score on cartoon test given immediately after presentation (possible scores are 0,1,2,. . .,9)
7	REAL1	Score on realistic test given immediately after presentation (possible scores are 0,1,2,. . .,9)
8	CARTOON2	Score on cartoon test given four weeks (delayed) after presentation (possible scores are 0,1,2,. . .,9; a blank is used for a missing observation)
9	REAL2	Score on realistic test given four weeks (delayed) after presentation (possible scores are 0,1,2,. . .,9; a blank is used for a missing observation)

CARTOON DATA

ID	COLOR	EDUC	LOC	OTIS	CARTOON1	REAL1	CARTOON2	REAL2
1	0	0	1	107	4	4		
2	0	0	2	106	9	9	6	5
3	0	0	2	94	4	2	3	0
4	0	0	2	121	8	8	6	8
5	0	0	3	86	5	5		
6	0	0	3	99	7	8	7	5
7	0	0	3	114	8	9	5	4
8	0	0	3	100	2	1		
9	0	0	3	85	3	2		
10	0	0	3	115	8	7	8	5
11	0	0	3	101	7	6		
12	0	0	3	84	7	5		
13	0	0	3	94	4	3		
14	0	0	3	87	1	3	2	0
15	0	0	3	104	9	9	5	6
16	0	0	3	104	5	6		
17	0	0	3	97	6	5		
18	0	0	3	91	1	0		
19	0	0	3	83	4	4		
20	0	0	3	93	0	0		
21	0	0	3	92	2	2		
22	0	0	3	91	5	2	3	1
23	0	0	3	88	2	1		
24	0	0	3	90	5	4	4	3
25	0	0	3	103	6	2		
26	0	0	3	93	9	9	8	4
27	0	0	3	106	2	0	6	3
28	1	0	1	98	3	3		
29	1	0	1	103	6	5	2	2
30	1	0	2	109	5	4	1	2
31	1	0	2	107	8	8		
32	1	0	2	108	8	8	7	6
33	1	0	2	107	3	2		
34	1	0	3	87	6	4	2	2
35	1	0	3	113	5	4	4	4
36	1	0	3	80	0	3	1	1
37	1	0	3	91	5	6		
38	1	0	3	102	8	9	5	5
39	1	0	3	83	4	1	2	1
40	1	0	3	108	9	9		
41	1	0	3	86	4	4		
42	1	0	3	96	6	3		
43	1	0	3	101	5	3		
44	1	0	3	97	6	3	4	4
45	1	0	3	88	3	1	2	0
46	1	0	3	104	4	2	2	0
47	1	0	3	87	7	3		
48	1	0	3	86	1	1		
49	1	0	3	90	6	5	4	1
50	1	0	3	102	6	2		
51	1	0	3	105	2	2		
52	1	0	3	115	7	8		
53	1	0	3	88	4	3		
54	1	0	3	111	8	8		
55	1	0	3	95	5	4		
56	1	0	3	104	5	5		
57	0	1	1	79	7	4	6	4
58	0	1	1	82	3	2		
59	0	1	1	123	8	8	7	5
60	0	1	1	106	9	7	8	6
61	0	1	1	125	9	9	4	3
62	0	1	1	98	7	6		
63	0	1	1	95	7	7	4	4
64	0	1	2	129	9	9	7	7
65	0	1	2	90	7	6	3	5
66	0	1	2	111	6	2	3	1
67	0	1	2	99	4	5	3	1
68	0	1	2	116	9	7	7	7
69	0	1	2	106	8	7	6	4
70	0	1	2	107	8	5		
71	0	1	2	100	7	6	2	1
72	0	1	2	124	8	9	3	5
73	0	1	3	98	6	7	1	1
74	0	1	3	124	9	6	6	5
75	0	1	3	84	1	4		
76	0	1	3	91	8	3		
77	0	1	3	118	6	6	3	4
78	0	1	3	102	6	4		
79	0	1	3	95	7	4		
80	0	1	3	90	4	3		
81	0	1	3	86	1	0		
82	0	1	3	104	6	4		
83	1	1	1	111	9	9	6	3
84	1	1	1	105	1	0		
85	1	1	1	110	1	0	0	0
86	1	1	1	80	0	0	0	0
87	1	1	1	78	4	1	1	1
88	1	1	2	120	9	9		
89	1	1	2	110	9	6	6	5
90	1	1	2	107	8	6		

(Continued)

CARTOON DATA   (*Continued*)

ID	COLOR	EDUC	LOC	OTIS	CARTOON1	REAL1	CARTOON2	REAL2
91	1	1	2	125	7	8		
92	1	1	2	117	9	9		
93	1	1	2	126	8	8	5	5
94	1	1	2	98	4	5		
95	1	1	2	111	8	6		
96	1	1	2	110	8	7		
97	1	1	2	120	9	7		
98	1	1	2	114	8	7	6	4
99	1	1	2	117	6	7		
100	1	1	3	105	7	6		
101	1	1	3	97	6	6		
102	1	1	3	86	1	1		
103	1	1	3	111	7	5		
104	1	1	3	93	1	0		
105	1	1	3	115	8	7		
106	1	1	3	102	2	3	5	2
107	1	1	3	111	7	3	4	4
108	1	1	3	82	1	1		
109	1	1	3	117	8	5	4	3
110	0	2	4	132	9	9		
111	0	2	4	113	7	8		
112	0	2	4	130	9	7	1	4
113	0	2	4	122	9	9	6	4
114	0	2	4	103	7	5	3	0
115	0	2	4	103	7	5	3	0
116	0	2	4	118	9	9		
117	0	2	4	119	9	9	7	8
118	0	2	4	97	8	8	6	4
119	0	2	4	123	9	9	7	4
120	0	2	4	113	8	7	6	6
121	0	2	4	110	8	7	3	5
122	0	2	4	119	8	7	6	6
123	0	2	4	116	5	7		
124	0	2	4	113	8	6	5	5
125	0	2	4	128	9	9		
126	0	2	4	113	8	5	4	2
126	0	2	4	113	8	5	4	2
127	0	2	4	110	5	7		
128	0	2	4	114	7	6	5	5
129	0	2	4	132	9	8	4	6
130	0	2	4	110	7	8	2	5
131	0	2	4	122	7	7	4	2
132	0	2	4	123	9	9	6	7
133	0	2	4	131	9	9	7	7
134	0	2	4	131	9	9	8	8
135	0	2	4	121	9	8	7	8
136	0	2	4	125	9	8		
137	0	2	4	101	6	6	4	6
138	0	2	4	120	8	9	6	7
139	0	2	4	99	9	6		
140	0	2	4	128	8	9	8	7
141	0	2	4	129	8	6	5	2
142	0	2	4	125	8	6	7	4
143	0	2	4	107	8	8	8	5
144	0	2	4	102	8	7	6	4
145	0	2	4	125	9	8		
146	1	2	4	129	8	8		
147	1	2	4	122	3	0	2	3
148	1	2	4	124	7	6	6	7
149	1	2	4	115	8	8		
150	1	2	4	117	8	6	5	2
151	1	2	4	132	7	6	5	7
152	1	2	4	109	8	5	5	5
153	1	2	4	107	9	5	9	2
154	1	2	4	116	8	7	6	5
155	1	2	4	118	8	5	6	5
156	1	2	4	124	9	9	6	7
157	1	2	4	102	9	5	5	2
158	1	2	4	110	9	7	7	7
159	1	2	4	119	7	5	2	4
160	1	2	4	99	3	2	4	0
161	1	2	4	102	7	8	5	6
162	1	2	4	115	7	7		
163	1	2	4	105	8	6	3	0
164	1	2	4	104	7	6		
165	1	2	4	112	7	7		
166	1	2	4	117	9	9	6	5
167	1	2	4	108	9	9		
168	1	2	4	135	8	8	8	8
169	1	2	4	133	8	8	7	7
170	1	2	4	105	6	4	5	3
171	1	2	4	124	7	7	9	8
172	1	2	4	112	9	9	9	8
173	1	2	4	128	9	9	9	9
174	1	2	4	96	8	8	7	6
175	1	2	4	110	8	8	4	5
176	1	2	4	108	8	8	6	8
177	1	2	4	125	7	6	8	8
178	1	2	4	111	4	3	4	1
179	1	2	4	103	4	3	2	1

DESCRIPTION OF ATTITUDE DATA SET

Data was collected on 189 third through sixth graders from a suburban midwestern public school. The children were measured on preference toward the following subjects: mathematics, language arts, science, reading, and social studies. An intervention was then employed with the teachers (five) to change these preferences (attitudes) in a positive way, and then the children were measured again on subject preference four months later.

The intervention consisted of a three hour lecture and discussion (in-service work) by a professor in September with the teachers on what shapes attitudes and how they could go about changing the attitudes of their students. There was a particular emphasis in this school on changing the mathematics attitude. The professor met again with the teachers in December to discuss whether they had implemented some of the changes he had suggested.

ATTITUDE DATA

SEX	GRADE	TEACHER	PREMATH	PRELANG	PRESCIE	PREREAD	PRESOCS	POSTMATH	POSTLANG	POSTSCIE	POSTREAD	POSTSOCS	SEX	GRADE	TEACHER	PREMATH	PRELANG	PRESCIE	PREREAD	PRESOCS	POSTMATH	POSTLANG	POSTSCIE	POSTREAD	POSTSOCS
1	3	5	1	4	2	5	4	0	5	1	4	2	1	3	4	6	4	3	4	2	6	3	3	2	1
2	3	5	4	7	3	4	5	1	7	4	4	5	1	3	4	7	4	3	5	1	5	2	3	4	3
1	3	5	8	6	5	3	7	8	5	4	3	5	1	3	4	3	0	6	4	1	2	0	6	4	2
2	3	5	1	7	2	4	3	4	6	1	5	2	1	3	4	1	1	7	4	5	2	2	6	3	1
2	3	5	7	3	1	7	5	5	2	5	4	6	2	3	4	4	2	1	5	2	3	2	4	2	4
2	3	5	3	6	3	7	4	1	5	4	2	4	2	3	4	6	4	1	4	2	6	2	6	3	4
1	3	5	5	3	1	6	2	5	2	2	7	4	1	3	4	6	6	5	4	3	6	1	8	5	7
1	3	5	6	1	5	7	3	7	2	5	3	6	1	3	4	2	1	3	6	3	4	5	2	7	2
2	3	5	7	4	3	5	1	5	2	4	6	3	2	3	4	3	2	3	6	1	4	2	3	4	3
2	3	4	3	1	2	4	3	5	2	1	2	3	1	3	4	5	3	3	2	2	7	2	6	2	5
2	3	4	7	2	4	4	3	5	5	2	6	1	2	6	2	5	1	5	7	5	3	2	5	7	0
2	3	4	6	1	3	4	2	3	1	5	7	2	1	6	2	2	1	6	0	7	3	0	7	1	7
1	3	4	7	1	6	5	1	6	1	6	5	2	2	6	2	5	4	2	2	7	4	3	4	5	4
1	3	4	7	2	3	4	2	7	0	4	6	3	1	6	2	4	0	4	1	7	7	2	4	3	6
1	3	4	6	3	1	3	5	6	1	7	2	5	2	6	2	4	3	2	4	3	4	1	5	1	2
2	3	4	4	4	1	4	2	5	2	2	7	3	1	6	2	3	1	2	4	7	8	2	1	3	5
2	3	4	6	2	3	4	1	7	1	4	4	0	1	6	2	6	1	3	2	5	7	3	5	6	2
2	3	4	5	1	4	5	5	4	4	3	6	1	2	6	3	3	6	8	4	7	3	8	4	4	5
2	3	4	6	5	1	7	3	4	5	1	3	3	1	6	2	6	3	5	4	7	8	4	5	1	6
2	3	4	4	2	1	6	0	4	2	1	7	0	1	6	2	6	1	5	3	8	8	3	5	4	6
1	3	4	5	6	2	5	4	7	4	2	6	5	2	6	2	1	5	4	3	5	2	6	3	5	2
2	3	4	6	2	1	6	4	6	1	4	5	2	1	6	2	7	4	8	2	6	0	1	3	4	5
1	3	4	5	2	2	4	2	7	2	1	7	2	1	6	2	2	0	4	4	5	8	4	7	0	5
2	3	4	4	2	6	6	0	4	3	4	6	3	1	6	2	8	3	5	5	7	6	2	4	5	1

(Continued)

ATTITUDE DATA (*Continued*)

SEX	GRADE	TEACHER	PREMATH	PRELANG	PRESCIE	PREREAD	PRESOCS	POSTMATH	POSTLANG	POSTSCIE	POSTREAD	POSTSOCS
2	6	2	0	6	3	5	4	0	2	3	4	5
1	6	2	0	3	7	1	5	0	1	5	2	3
2	6	2	6	2	8	5	4	7	2	8	5	3
2	6	2	5	3	6	3	7	3	5	7	0	6
2	6	2	4	6	2	8	1	3	6	4	8	2
1	6	2	4	2	5	7	7	1	3	4	7	8
2	6	2	2	5	8	5	5	5	4	7	2	6
2	6	2	8	1	3	1	2	7	4	2	5	0
1	6	2	6	0	8	4	4	8	2	7	3	4
2	6	2	7	5	7	1	7	6	4	8	1	7
2	6	2	6	2	3	5	3	6	3	1	5	2
1	6	2	3	4	7	2	5	6	3	8	4	7
2	6	2	4	1	6	2	7	4	0	7	6	1
2	6	2	7	6	5	2	3	5	6	7	3	3
1	6	2	8	4	5	6	2	8	7	1	4	2
2	6	2	7	4	4	1	4	5	3	1	3	5
1	6	2	7	2	4	0	8	8	0	3	2	3
2	6	2	2	7	4	1	4	3	5	5	4	1
2	6	2	4	3	8	3	4	5	6	6	2	1
2	6	2	7	8	3	2	5	8	6	2	2	2
1	6	2	6	0	8	3	7	4	3	8	5	7
1	6	2	5	5	6	4	2	6	6	4	1	3
2	6	2	2	8	7	6	1	2	8	6	7	4
2	6	2	0	1	5	4	7	1	0	3	6	7
2	6	2	7	5	2	4	6	3	5	3	3	6
2	6	2	7	6	2	5	3	6	2	2	3	1
1	6	2	7	0	6	5	3	8	0	5	4	1
1	6	2	7	0	5	2	3	5	5	4	1	0
2	6	2	2	5	6	7	8	4	3	1	8	5
1	6	2	5	4	6	1	8	1	2	5	3	6
1	6	2	7	1	5	4	7	3	5	6	1	8
2	6	2	6	2	3	2	3	6	3	6	1	3
2	6	2	8	5	6	3	2	8	4	7	3	3
1	6	2	6	7	2	5	1	5	6	2	3	3
2	6	2	7	2	0	6	1	7	4	1	6	0
2	6	2	4	5	1	7	2	8	5	4	6	3
2	6	2	7	1	1	3	6	8	1	3	2	5
1	6	2	5	0	2	3	6	3	1	6	2	6
2	6	2	6	4	1	1	5	8	5	6	1	2
1	6	2	5	3	5	2	7	6	5	4	1	2
1	6	2	6	3	6	3	3	7	3	7	0	4
1	6	2	7	1	2	8	0	7	1	3	5	3
2	6	2	8	1	5	6	3	8	4	6	3	5

SEX	GRADE	TEACHER	PREMATH	PRELANG	PRESCIE	PREREAD	PRESOCS	POSTMATH	POSTLANG	POSTSCIE	POSTREAD	POSTSOCS
1	6	2	6	2	5	4	4	4	4	7	4	7
2	6	2	5	7	3	2	5	4	5	1	2	3
2	6	2	4	2	7	1	6	5	2	8	0	5
2	4	1	7	2	6	4	0	6	2	7	2	1
2	4	1	8	6	1	5	0	6	5	1	3	0
1	4	1	6	0	5	1	2	6	2	8	0	3
2	4	1	4	5	2	6	2	4	3	4	5	0
2	4	1	7	4	3	7	2	7	4	2	7	0
2	4	1	7	5	1	7	2	5	2	2	5	0
1	4	1	7	1	5	5	8	4	2	5	6	6
1	4	1	7	4	4	5	2	7	5	1	6	3
2	4	1	6	5	3	8	1	5	3	5	8	0
2	4	1	8	4	1	7	0	8	6	5	7	3
1	4	1	6	2	6	6	3	5	1	8	2	4
2	4	1	7	1	4	1	4	6	0	5	4	3
1	5	1	8	7	1	5	3	8	4	1	4	3
2	5	1	7	3	1	8	3	7	3	2	7	1
2	4	1	3	8	4	7	1	6	6	5	8	1
2	5	1	8	0	2	5	2	8	0	4	6	4
1	5	1	5	5	2	7	3	5	4	1	6	0
2	5	1	8	4	1	4	1	8	6	5	3	4
1	4	1	7	2	7	0	3	7	5	6	0	4
1	5	1	6	3	1	5	0	7	2	0	3	0
2	4	1	6	2	5	6	5	8	3	0	6	1
1	5	1	5	1	7	3	4	4	3	6	7	1
2	5	1	8	3	3	4	0	7	4	2	2	1
1	5	1	7	7	3	3	2	6	8	1	4	3
2	5	1	4	6	8	2	5	6	4	7	3	8
1	5	1	7	4	0	1	2	7	2	2	4	2
1	5	1	8	6	4	2	5	8	7	1	3	4
1	5	1	7	0	6	5	3	5	0	7	2	3
2	4	1	7	2	5	3	1	6	2	5	5	0
2	4	1	8	3	3	4	2	8	5	2	3	4
1	4	1	3	5	7	3	3	6	4	4	1	2
2	4	1	6	3	2	7	1	3	3	3	7	0
1	5	1	5	1	3	6	3	6	3	1	4	0
1	5	1	8	1	5	5	2	7	3	8	2	5
2	4	1	5	1	4	6	0	4	3	4	1	1
2	4	1	5	2	1	7	1	5	2	4	8	0
1	5	1	7	3	1	4	0	6	2	5	2	3
2	5	1	0	4	2	6	4	0	4	2	6	5
2	5	1	7	6	1	5	0	8	4	0	6	1
1	4	1	7	0	6	3	2	8	1	6	0	4

(*Continued*)

ATTITUDE DATA (*Continued*)

SEX	GRADE	TEACHER	PREMATH	PRELANG	PRESCIE	PREREAD	PRESOCS	POSTMATH	POSTLANG	POSTSCIE	POSTREAD	POSTSOCS
2	4	1	7	2	0	6	1	8	3	2	5	3
2	4	1	8	0	2	4	1	8	3	1	6	0
1	4	1	8	0	7	1	5	8	1	2	3	0
2	4	1	7	3	2	6	2	7	4	1	7	3
2	4	1	8	7	1	6	0	7	3	2	6	1
2	4	1	7	7	1	5	0	6	7	1	0	4
1	4	1	6	6	3	7	1	8	5	4	3	2
1	4	1	4	0	4	3	6	2	0	7	1	6
2	4	1	6	3	1	7	0	0	3	4	7	4
2	4	1	7	4	2	6	3	7	5	1	6	0
1	5	1	6	4	4	5	4	7	2	5	4	5
2	5	1	5	5	0	6	3	5	5	0	6	1
1	5	1	6	1	3	1	1	6	5	3	1	0
2	5	1	8	4	2	6	3	8	2	4	6	6
1	5	1	6	2	5	3	3	8	3	4	1	5
2	5	1	7	4	2	5	0	7	4	1	7	2
2	5	1	7	4	0	6	1	8	3	0	7	0
2	4	1	4	1	7	1	5	4	2	8	2	7
1	4	1	6	0	7	5	4	5	1	4	7	5
2	5	1	7	4	3	6	5	7	3	1	6	4
2	4	1	6	0	6	1	5	8	2	4	3	4
2	4	1	8	5	2	4	0	8	5	3	5	0
2	4	1	6	7	3	3	6	7	2	4	6	2
2	4	1	7	6	2	4	0	8	4	1	5	0
1	4	1	3	4	2	4	0	6	3	3	3	3
1	4	1	8	4	5	0	3	8	4	0	5	2
2	4	1	8	0	4	1	4	8	6	4	1	3
2	4	1	7	6	5	2	3	7	5	2	3	1

SEX	GRADE	TEACHER	PREMATH	PRELANG	PRESCIE	PREREAD	PRESOCS	POSTMATH	POSTLANG	POSTSCIE	POSTREAD	POSTSOCS
1	4	1	7	1	4	5	2	8	0	6	2	5
2	5	1	7	0	5	6	1	5	2	1	6	0
2	5	1	6	3	6	8	3	3	2	1	6	6
2	5	1	8	5	5	6	4	8	4	7	6	5
2	5	1	7	6	1	3	3	8	7	1	5	3
1	5	1	7	1	5	6	3	7	4	1	5	0
2	5	1	8	5	3	5	2	8	5	1	6	0
1	5	1	3	6	5	1	2	6	4	3	0	2
2	5	1	7	4	0	4	2	7	4	1	6	0
1	5	1	4	0	6	7	6	1	0	5	8	7
1	5	1	7	4	5	1	4	8	5	2	4	2
1	5	1	7	4	3	8	2	6	2	3	7	4
2	5	1	7	5	2	6	2	7	6	0	6	2
2	5	1	6	3	3	7	5	4	4	0	7	6
2	5	1	4	2	5	5	4	7	4	3	7	0
2	5	1	6	3	4	6	3	5	4	7	6	5
1	4	1	6	1	4	8	1	1	2	3	7	1
2	5	1	8	4	2	4	3	8	4	0	3	3
2	5	1	7	5	0	8	3	7	6	1	8	5
1	4	1	7	1	5	6	0	7	5	5	4	3
1	4	1	5	3	6	0	3	8	3	6	0	5
2	4	1	8	2	0	7	4	4	4	0	8	5
2	5	1	4	4	2	6	1	7	3	4	7	5
1	5	1	7	2	7	3	1	7	4	5	0	1
2	4	1	7	4	2	6	5	6	3	2	5	4
2	6	2	3	2	0	2	3	3	3	0	2	3
2	4	1	6	4	4	7	2	6	5	5	4	1

DESCRIPTION OF NATIONAL ACADEMY OF SCIENCES DATA

The following data is from a 1982 National Academy of Sciences published report rating the "scholary quality" of research programs in the humanities, physical sciences and social sciences. The ratings were based on the rankings of quality and reputation made by senior faculty in the field who taught at institutions other than the one being rated.

The data to be presented are the quality ratings of 46 research doctorate programs in psychology, as well as six potential correlates of the quality ratings. Here is a description of the variables: QUALITY Mean rating of scholarly quality of program faculty NFACULTY Number of falculty members in program as of December 1980 NGRADS Number of program graduates from 1975 through 1980 PCTSUPP Percentage of program graduates from 1975-1979 that received fellowships or training grant support during their graduate education PCTGRANT Percent of faculty members holding research grants from the Alcohol, Drug Abuse and Mental Health Administration, the National Institute of Health or the National Science Foundation at any time during 1978-1980 NARTICLE Number of published articles attributed to program faculty members 1978-1980 PCTPUB Percent of faculty with one or more published articles from 1978-1980

OBS	NAME	QUALITY	NFACULTY	NGRADS	PCTSUPP	PCTGRANT	NARTICLE	PCTPUB
1	ADELPHI	12	13	19	16	8	14	39
2	ARIZONA–TUSCON	23	29	72	67	3	61	66
3	BOSTON UNIV	29	38	111	66	13	68	68
4	BROWN	36	16	28	52	63	49	75
5	U C BERKELEY	44	40	104	64	53	130	83
6	U C RIVERSIDE	21	14	28	59	29	65	79
7	CARNEGIE MELLON	40	44	16	81	35	79	82
8	UNIV OF CHICAGO	42	60	57	65	40	187	82
9	CLARK UNIV	24	16	18	87	19	32	75
10	COLUMBIA TEACHERS	30	37	41	43	8	50	54
11	DELAWARE, UNIV OF	20	20	45	26	25	49	50
12	DETROIT, UNIV OF	8	11	27	7	0	9	27
13	FLORIDA ST–TALAH	28	29	112	64	35	65	69
14	FULLER THEOL SEMIN	14	14	57	10	0	11	43
15	UNIV OF GEORGIA	27	38	167	28	13	196	84
16	HARVARD	46	27	113	62	52	173	85
17	HOUSTON, UNIV OF	29	32	122	51	119	79	69
18	UNIV ILLINOIS-CHAMP	42	56	116	56	32	208	73
19	IOWA, UNIV OF	33	32	54	49	10	120	69
20	KANSAS, UNIV OF	31	42	79	41	14	114	71
21	KENT STATE UNIV	23	30	76	22	20	87	67
22	LOUISIANA STATE	18	18	62	39	6	10	39
23	UNIV OF MARYLAND	29	41	98	41	12	101	66
24	MIAMI UNIV	21	23	52	33	4	59	78
25	U MICH–ANN ARB	45	111	222	64	32	274	70
26	U MISSOURI	25	26	63	39	23	160	89
27	U NEW HAMPSHIRE	18	16	24	4	31	39	63
28	NEW YORK UNIV	33	38	154	55	34	84	63
29	U NC–GREENSBORO	21	19	40	7	5	60	84
30	NORTHEASTERN	24	16	18	25	63	31	63
31	NOTRE DAME	15	13	29	23	15	62	85
32	OKLA ST–STILLWATER	15	23	41	51	4	24	57
33	PENN STATE	36	32	69	65	16	122	75
34	PRINCETON	38	21	38	28	48	92	91
35	UNIV OF ROCHESTER	32	28	90	70	36	117	61
36	SUNY ALBANY	27	22	52	10	27	114	86
37	ST LOUIS UNIVERSITY	16	20	80	46	10	19	40
38	UNIV SOUTH FLORIDA	26	32	41	13	6	64	56
39	STANFORD	48	26	81	70	58	155	100
40	TEMPLE	26	40	81	42	10	70	68
41	TEXAS TECH LUBBOCK	14	19	87	15	5	72	79
42	UNIV OF TOLEDO	12	17	26	9	6	15	59
43	UNIV OF UTAH, SALT L	29	29	71	74	17	85	76
44	VIRGINIA POLYTECH	34	27	20	0	29	79	57
45	WASHINGTON UNIV-ST. L	28	26	70	68	27	84	73
46	UNIV WISC–MADISON	39	36	59	57	67	172	83

Jones, L. V., Lindzey, G., & Coggeshall, P. (Eds.) (1982). *An Assessment of Research-Doctorate Programs in the United States: Social and Behavioral Sciences,* (Washington, DC: National Academy Press).

AGRESTI HOME SALES DATA

	price	size	nobed	nobath	new
1	48.50	1.10	3.00	1.00	.00
2	55.00	1.01	3.00	2.00	.00
3	68.00	1.45	3.00	2.00	.00
4	137.00	2.40	3.00	3.00	.00
5	309.40	3.30	4.00	3.00	1.00
6	17.50	.40	1.00	1.00	.00
7	19.60	1.28	3.00	1.00	.00
8	24.50	.74	3.00	1.00	.00
9	34.80	.78	2.00	1.00	.00
10	32.00	.97	3.00	1.00	.00
11	28.00	.84	3.00	1.00	.00
12	49.90	1.08	2.00	2.00	.00
13	59.90	.99	2.00	1.00	.00
14	61.50	1.01	3.00	2.00	.00
15	60.00	1.34	3.00	2.00	.00
16	65.90	1.22	3.00	1.00	.00
17	67.90	1.28	3.00	2.00	.00
18	68.90	1.29	3.00	2.00	.00
19	69.90	1.52	3.00	2.00	.00
20	70.50	1.25	3.00	2.00	.00
21	72.90	1.28	3.00	2.00	.00
22	72.50	1.28	3.00	1.00	.00
23	72.00	1.36	3.00	2.00	.00
24	71.00	1.20	3.00	2.00	.00
25	76.00	1.46	3.00	2.00	.00
26	72.90	1.56	4.00	2.00	.00
27	73.00	1.22	3.00	2.00	.00
28	70.00	1.40	2.00	2.00	.00

	price	size	nobed	nobath	new
29	76.00	1.15	2.00	2.00	.00
30	69.00	1.74	3.00	2.00	.00
31	75.50	1.62	3.00	2.00	.00
32	76.00	1.66	3.00	2.00	.00
33	81.80	1.33	3.00	2.00	.00
34	84.50	1.34	3.00	2.00	.00
35	83.50	1.40	3.00	2.00	.00
36	86.00	1.15	2.00	2.00	1.00
37	86.90	1.58	3.00	2.00	1.00
38	86.90	1.58	3.00	2.00	1.00
39	86.90	1.58	3.00	2.00	1.00
40	87.90	1.71	3.00	2.00	.00
41	88.10	2.10	3.00	2.00	.00
42	85.90	1.27	3.00	2.00	.00
43	89.50	1.34	3.00	2.00	.00
44	87.40	1.25	3.00	2.00	.00
45	87.90	1.68	3.00	2.00	.00
46	88.00	1.55	3.00	2.00	.00
47	90.00	1.55	3.00	2.00	.00
48	96.00	1.36	3.00	2.00	1.00
49	99.90	1.51	3.00	2.00	1.00
50	95.50	1.54	3.00	2.00	1.00
51	98.50	1.51	3.00	2.00	.00
52	100.10	1.85	3.00	2.00	.00
53	99.90	1.62	4.00	2.00	1.00
54	101.90	1.40	3.00	2.00	1.00
55	101.90	1.92	4.00	2.00	.00
56	102.30	1.42	3.00	2.00	1.00

	price	size	nobed	nobath	new
57	110.80	1.56	3.00	2.00	1.00
58	105.00	1.43	3.00	2.00	1.00
59	97.90	2.00	3.00	2.00	.00
60	106.30	1.45	3.00	2.00	1.00
61	106.50	1.65	3.00	2.00	.00
62	116.00	1.72	4.00	2.00	1.00
63	108.00	1.79	4.00	2.00	1.00
64	107.50	1.85	3.00	2.00	.00
65	109.90	2.06	4.00	2.00	1.00
66	110.00	1.76	4.00	2.00	.00
67	120.00	1.62	3.00	2.00	1.00
68	115.00	1.80	4.00	2.00	1.00
69	113.40	1.98	3.00	2.00	.00
70	114.90	1.57	3.00	2.00	.00
71	115.00	2.19	3.00	2.00	.00
72	115.00	2.07	4.00	2.00	.00
73	117.90	1.99	4.00	2.00	.00
74	110.00	1.55	3.00	2.00	.00
75	115.00	1.67	3.00	2.00	.00
76	124.00	2.40	4.00	2.00	.00
77	129.90	1.79	4.00	2.00	1.00
78	124.00	1.89	3.00	2.00	.00
79	128.00	1.88	3.00	2.00	1.00
80	132.40	2.00	4.00	2.00	1.00
81	139.30	2.05	4.00	2.00	1.00
82	139.30	2.00	4.00	2.00	1.00
83	139.70	2.03	3.00	2.00	1.00
84	142.00	2.12	3.00	3.00	.00

	price	size	nobed	nobath	new
85	141.30	2.08	4.00	2.00	1.00
86	147.50	2.19	4.00	2.00	.00
87	142.50	2.40	4.00	2.00	.00
88	148.00	2.40	5.00	2.00	.00
89	149.00	3.05	4.00	2.00	.00
90	150.00	2.04	3.00	3.00	.00
91	172.90	2.25	4.00	2.00	1.00
92	190.00	2.57	4.00	3.00	1.00
93	280.00	3.85	4.00	3.00	.00

Appendix B
Statistical Tables

Table B.1 Critical Values for F
Table B.2 Percentile Points of Studentized Range Statistic (+-test)
Table B.3 Critical Values for Dunnett's Test
Table B.4 Critical Values for F (max) Statistic
Table B.5 Critical Values for Bryant-Paulson Procedure

TABLE B.1
Critical Values for F

df error	α	df for Numerator							
		1	2	3	4	5	6	8	12
1	.01	4052	4999	5403	5625	5764	5859	5981	6106
	.05	161.45	199.50	215.71	224.58	230.16	233.99	238.88	243.91
	.10	39.86	49.50	53.59	55.83	57.24	58.20	59.44	60.70
	.20	9.47	12.00	13.06	13.73	14.01	14.26	14.59	14.90
2	.01	98.49	99.00	99.17	99.25	99.30	99.33	99.36	99.42
	.05	18.51	19.00	19.16	19.25	19.30	19.33	19.37	19.41
	.10	8.53	9.00	9.16	9.24	9.29	9.33	9.37	9.41
	.20	3.56	4.00	4.16	4.24	4.28	4.32	4.36	4.40
3	.001	167.5	148.5	141.1	137.1	134.6	132.8	130.6	128.3
	.01	34.12	30.81	29.46	28.71	28.24	27.91	27.49	27.05
	.05	10.13	9.55	9.28	9.12	9.01	8.94	8.84	8.74
	.10	5.54	5.46	5.39	5.34	5.31	5.28	5.25	5.22
	.20	2.68	2.89	2.94	2.96	2.97	2.97	2.98	2.98
4	.001	74.14	61.25	56.18	53.44	51.71	50.53	49.00	47.41
	.01	21.20	18.00	16.69	15.98	15.52	15.21	14.80	14.37
	.05	7.71	6.94	6.59	6.39	6.26	6.16	6.04	5.91
	.10	4.54	4.32	4.19	4.11	4.05	4.01	3.95	3.90
	.20	2.35	2.47	2.48	2.48	2.48	2.47	2.47	2.46
5	.001	47.04	36.61	33.20	31.09	29.75	28.84	27.64	26.42
	.01	16.26	13.27	12.06	11.39	10.97	10.67	10.29	9.89
	.05	6.61	5.79	5.41	5.19	5.05	4.95	4.82	4.68
	.10	4.06	3.78	3.62	3.52	3.45	3.40	3.34	3.27
	.20	2.18	2.26	2.25	2.24	2.23	2.22	2.20	2.18
6	.001	35.51	27.00	23.70	21.90	20.81	20.03	19.03	17.99
	.01	13.74	10.92	9.78	9.15	8.75	8.47	8.10	7.72
	.05	5.99	5.14	4.76	4.53	4.39	4.28	4.15	4.00
	.10	3.78	3.46	3.29	3.18	3.11	3.05	2.98	2.90
	.20	2.07	2.13	2.11	2.09	2.08	2.06	2.04	2.02
7	.001	29.22	21.69	18.77	17.19	16.21	15.52	14.63	13.71
	.01	12.25	9.55	8.45	7.85	7.46	7.19	6.84	6.47
	.05	5.59	4.74	4.35	4.12	3.97	3.87	3.73	3.57
	.10	3.59	3.26	3.07	2.96	2.88	2.83	2.75	2.67
	.20	2.00	2.04	2.02	1.99	1.97	1.96	1.93	1.91
8	.001	25.42	18.49	15.83	14.39	13.49	12.86	12.04	11.19
	.01	11.26	8.65	7.59	7.01	6.63	6.37	6.03	5.67
	.05	5.32	4.46	4.07	3.84	3.69	3.58	3.44	3.28
	.10	3.46	3.11	2.92	2.81	2.73	2.67	2.59	2.50
	.20	1.95	1.98	1.95	1.92	1.90	1.88	1.86	1.83
9	.001	22.86	16.39	13.90	12.56	11.71	11.13	10.37	9.57
	.01	10.56	8.02	6.99	6.42	6.06	5.80	5.47	5.11
	.05	5.12	4.26	3.86	3.63	3.48	3.37	3.23	3.07
	.10	3.36	3.01	2.81	2.69	2.61	2.55	2.47	2.38
	.20	1.91	1.94	1.90	1.87	1.85	1.83	1.80	1.76

(*cont.*)

TABLE B.1 (Continued)

| df error | α | \multicolumn{8}{c}{df for Numerator} |
		1	2	3	4	5	6	8	12
10	.001	21.04	14.91	12.55	11.28	10.48	9.92	9.20	8.45
	.01	10.04	7.56	6.55	5.99	5.64	5.39	5.06	4.71
	.05	4.96	4.10	3.71	3.48	3.33	3.22	3.07	2.91
	.10	3.28	2.92	2.73	2.61	2.52	2.46	2.38	2.28
	.20	1.88	1.90	1.86	1.83	1.80	1.78	1.75	1.72
11	.001	19.69	13.81	11.56	10.35	9.58	9.05	8.35	7.63
	.01	9.65	7.20	6.22	5.67	5.32	5.07	4.74	4.40
	.05	4.84	3.98	3.59	3.36	3.20	3.09	2.95	2.79
	.10	3.23	2.86	2.66	2.54	2.45	2.39	2.30	2.21
	.20	1.86	1.87	1.83	1.80	1.77	1.75	1.72	1.68
12	.001	18.64	12.97	10.80	9.63	8.89	8.38	7.71	7.00
	.01	9.33	6.93	5.95	5.41	5.06	4.82	4.50	4.16
	.05	4.75	3.88	3.49	3.26	3.11	3.00	2.85	2.69
	.10	3.18	2.81	2.61	2.48	2.39	2.33	2.24	2.15
	.20	1.84	1.85	1.80	1.77	1.74	1.72	1.69	1.65
13	.001	17.81	12.31	10.21	9.07	8.35	7.86	7.21	6.52
	.01	9.07	6.70	5.74	5.20	4.86	4.62	4.30	3.96
	.05	4.67	3.80	3.41	3.18	3.02	2.92	2.77	2.60
	.10	3.14	2.76	2.56	2.43	2.35	2.28	2.20	2.10
	.20	1.82	1.83	1.78	1.75	1.72	1.69	1.66	1.62
14	.001	17.14	11.78	9.73	8.62	7.92	7.43	6.80	6.13
	.01	8.86	6.51	5.56	5.03	4.69	4.46	4.14	3.80
	.05	4.60	3.74	3.34	3.11	2.96	2.85	2.70	2.53
	.10	3.10	2.73	2.52	2.39	2.31	2.24	2.15	2.05
	.20	1.81	1.81	1.76	1.73	1.70	1.67	1.64	1.60
15	.001	16.59	11.34	9.34	8.25	7.57	7.09	6.47	5.81
	.01	8.68	6.36	5.42	4.89	4.56	4.32	4.00	3.67
	.05	4.54	3.68	3.29	3.06	2.90	2.79	2.64	2.48
	.10	3.07	2.70	2.49	2.36	2.27	2.21	2.12	2.02
	.20	1.80	1.79	1.75	1.71	1.68	1.66	1.62	1.58
16	.001	16.12	10.97	9.00	7.94	7.27	6.81	6.19	5.55
	.01	8.53	6.23	5.29	4.77	4.44	4.20	3.89	3.55
	.05	4.49	3.63	3.24	3.01	2.85	2.74	2.59	2.42
	.10	3.05	2.67	2.46	2.33	2.24	2.18	2.09	1.99
	.20	1.79	1.78	1.74	1.70	1.67	1.64	1.61	1.56
17	.001	15.72	10.66	8.73	7.68	7.02	6.56	5.96	5.32
	.01	8.40	6.11	5.18	4.67	4.34	4.10	3.79	3.45
	.05	4.45	3.59	3.20	2.96	2.81	2.70	2.55	2.38
	.10	3.03	2.64	2.44	2.31	2.22	2.15	2.06	1.96
	.20	1.78	1.77	1.72	1.68	1.65	1.63	1.59	1.55
18	.001	15.38	10.39	8.49	7.46	6.81	6.35	5.76	5.13
	.01	8.28	6.01	5.09	4.58	4.25	4.01	3.71	3.37
	.05	4.41	3.55	3.16	2.93	2.77	2.66	2.51	2.34
	.10	3.01	2.62	2.42	2.29	2.20	2.13	2.04	1.93
	.20	1.77	1.76	1.71	1.67	1.64	1.62	1.58	1.53

(cont.)

TABLE B.1 (*Continued*)

				df *for Numerator*					
df *error*	α	*1*	*2*	*3*	*4*	*5*	*6*	*8*	*12*
19	.001	15.08	10.16	8.28	7.26	6.61	6.18	5.59	4.97
	.01	8.18	5.93	5.01	4.50	4.17	3.94	3.63	3.30
	.05	4.38	3.52	3.13	2.90	2.74	2.63	2.48	2.31
	.10	2.99	2.61	2.40	2.27	2.18	2.11	2.02	1.91
	.20	1.76	1.75	1.70	1.66	1.63	1.61	1.57	1.52
20	.001	14.82	9.95	8.10	7.10	6.46	6.02	5.44	4.82
	.01	8.10	5.85	4.94	4.43	4.10	3.87	3.56	3.23
	.05	4.35	3.49	3.10	2.87	2.71	2.60	2.45	2.28
	.10	2.97	2.59	2.38	2.25	2.16	2.09	2.00	1.89
	.20	1.76	1.75	1.70	1.65	1.62	1.60	1.56	1.51
21	.001	14.59	9.77	7.94	6.95	6.32	5.88	5.31	4.70
	.01	8.02	5.78	4.87	4.37	4.04	3.81	3.51	3.17
	.05	4.32	3.47	3.07	2.84	2.68	2.57	2.42	2.25
	.10	2.96	2.57	2.36	2.23	2.14	2.08	1.98	1.88
	.20	1.75	1.74	1.69	1.65	1.61	1.59	1.55	1.50
22	.001	14.38	9.61	7.80	6.81	6.19	5.76	5.19	4.58
	.01	7.94	5.72	4.82	4.31	3.99	3.76	3.45	3.12
	.05	4.30	3.44	3.05	2.82	2.66	2.55	2.40	2.23
	.10	2.95	2.56	2.35	2.22	2.13	2.06	1.97	1.86
	.20	1.75	1.73	1.68	1.64	1.61	1.58	1.54	1.49
23	.001	14.19	9.47	7.67	6.69	6.08	5.65	5.09	4.48
	.01	7.88	5.66	4.76	4.26	3.94	3.71	3.41	3.07
	.05	4.28	3.42	3.03	2.80	2.64	2.53	2.38	2.20
	.10	2.94	2.55	2.34	2.21	2.11	2.05	1.95	1.84
	.20	1.74	1.73	1.68	1.63	1.60	1.57	1.53	1.49
24	.001	14.03	9.34	7.55	6.59	5.98	5.55	4.99	4.39
	.01	7.82	5.61	4.72	4.22	3.90	3.67	3.36	3.03
	.05	4.26	3.40	3.01	2.78	2.62	2.51	2.36	2.18
	.10	2.93	2.54	2.33	2.19	2.10	2.04	1.94	1.83
	.20	1.74	1.72	1.67	1.63	1.59	1.57	1.53	1.48
25	.001	13.88	9.22	7.45	6.49	5.88	5.46	4.91	4.31
	.01	7.77	5.57	4.68	4.18	3.86	3.63	3.32	2.99
	.05	4.24	3.38	2.99	2.76	2.60	2.49	2.34	2.16
	.10	2.92	2.53	2.32	2.18	2.09	2.02	1.93	1.82
	.20	1.73	1.72	1.66	1.62	1.59	1.56	1.52	1.47
26	.001	13.74	9.12	7.36	6.41	5.80	5.38	4.83	4.24
	.01	7.72	5.53	4.64	4.14	3.82	3.59	3.29	2.96
	.05	4.22	3.37	2.98	2.74	2.59	2.47	2.32	2.15
	.10	2.91	2.52	2.31	2.17	2.08	2.01	1.92	1.81
	.20	1.73	1.71	1.66	1.62	1.58	1.56	1.52	1.47
27	.001	13.61	9.02	7.27	6.33	5.73	5.31	4.76	4.17
	.01	7.68	5.49	4.60	4.11	3.78	3.56	3.26	2.93
	.05	4.21	3.35	2.96	2.73	2.57	2.46	2.30	2.13
	.10	2.90	2.51	2.30	2.17	2.07	2.00	1.91	1.80
	.20	1.73	1.71	1.66	1.61	1.58	1.55	1.51	1.46

(*cont.*)

TABLE B.1   (*Continued*)

df *error*	α	1	2	3	4	5	6	8	12
				df *for Numerator*					
28	.001	13.50	8.93	7.19	6.25	5.66	5.24	4.69	4.11
	.01	7.64	5.45	4.57	4.07	3.75	3.53	3.23	2.90
	.05	4.20	3.34	2.95	2.71	2.56	2.44	2.29	2.12
	.10	2.89	2.50	2.29	2.16	2.06	2.00	1.90	1.79
	.20	1.72	1.71	1.65	1.61	1.57	1.55	1.51	1.46
29	.001	13.39	8.85	7.12	6.19	5.59	5.18	4.64	4.05
	.01	7.60	5.42	4.54	4.04	3.73	3.50	3.20	2.87
	.05	4.18	3.33	2.93	2.70	2.54	2.43	2.28	2.10
	.10	2.89	2.50	2.28	2.15	2.06	1.99	1.89	1.78
	.20	1.72	1.70	1.65	1.60	1.57	1.54	1.50	1.45
30	.001	13.29	8.77	7.05	6.12	5.53	5.12	4.58	4.00
	.01	7.56	5.39	4.51	4.02	3.70	3.47	3.17	2.84
	.05	4.17	3.32	2.92	2.69	2.53	2.42	2.27	2.09
	.10	2.88	2.49	2.28	2.14	2.05	1.98	1.88	1.77
	.20	1.72	1.70	1.64	1.60	1.57	1.54	1.50	1.45
40	.001	12.61	8.25	6.60	5.70	5.13	4.73	4.21	3.64
	.01	7.31	5.18	4.31	3.83	3.51	3.29	2.99	2.66
	.05	4.08	3.23	2.84	2.61	2.45	2.34	2.18	2.00
	.10	2.84	2.44	2.23	2.09	2.00	1.93	1.83	1.71
	.20	1.70	1.68	1.62	1.57	1.54	1.51	1.47	1.41
60	.001	11.97	7.76	6.17	5.31	4.76	4.37	3.87	3.31
	.01	7.08	4.98	4.13	3.65	3.34	3.12	2.82	2.50
	.05	4.00	3.15	2.76	2.52	2.37	2.25	2.10	1.92
	.10	2.79	2.39	2.18	2.04	1.95	1.87	1.77	1.66
	.20	1.68	1.65	1.59	1.55	1.51	1.48	1.44	1.38
120	.001	11.38	7.31	5.79	4.95	4.42	4.04	3.55	3.02
	.01	6.85	4.79	3.95	3.48	3.17	2.96	2.66	2.34
	.05	3.92	3.07	2.68	2.45	2.29	2.17	2.02	1.83
	.10	2.75	2.35	2.13	1.99	1.90	1.82	1.72	1.60
	.20	1.66	1.63	1.57	1.52	1.48	1.45	1.41	1.35
∞	.001	10.83	6.91	5.42	4.62	4.10	3.74	3.27	2.74
	.01	6.64	4.60	3.78	3.32	3.02	2.80	2.51	2.18
	.05	3.84	2.99	2.60	2.37	2.21	2.09	1.94	1.75
	.10	2.71	2.30	2.08	1.94	1.85	1.77	1.67	1.55
	.20	1.64	1.61	1.55	1.50	1.46	1.43	1.38	1.32

Source: Reproduced from E. F. Lindquist, *Design and Analysis of Experiments in Psychology and Education,* Houghton Mifflin, Boston, 1953, pp. 41–44, with the permission of the publisher.

t-test

TABLE B.2
Percentile Points of Studentized Range Statistic

90th Percentiles

number of groups

df error	2	3	4	5	6	7	8	9	10
1	8.929	13.44	16.36	18.49	20.15	21.51	22.64	23.62	24.48
2	4.130	5.733	6.773	7.538	8.139	8.633	9.049	9.409	9.725
3	3.328	4.467	5.199	5.738	6.162	6.511	6.806	7.062	7.287
4	3.015	3.976	4.586	5.035	5.388	5.679	5.926	6.139	6.327
5	2.850	3.717	4.264	4.664	4.979	5.238	5.458	5.648	5.816
6	2.748	3.559	4.065	4.435	4.726	4.966	5.168	5.344	5.499
7	2.680	3.451	3.931	4.280	4.555	4.780	4.972	5.137	5.283
8	2.630	3.374	3.834	4.169	4.431	4.646	4.829	4.987	5.126
9	2.592	3.316	3.761	4.084	4.337	4.545	4.721	4.873	5.007
10	2.563	3.270	3.704	4.018	4.264	4.465	4.636	4.783	4.913
11	2.540	3.234	3.658	3.965	4.205	4.401	4.568	4.711	4.838
12	2.521	3.204	3.621	3.922	4.156	4.349	4.511	4.652	4.776
13	2.505	3.179	3.589	3.885	4.116	4.305	4.464	4.602	4.724
14	2.491	3.158	3.563	3.854	4.081	4.267	4.424	4.560	4.680
15	2.479	3.140	3.540	3.828	4.052	4.235	4.390	4.524	4.641
16	2.469	3.124	3.520	3.804	4.026	4.207	4.360	4.492	4.608
17	2.460	3.110	3.503	3.784	4.004	4.183	4.334	4.464	4.579
18	2.452	3.098	3.488	3.767	3.984	4.161	4.311	4.440	4.554
19	2.445	3.087	3.474	3.751	3.966	4.142	4.290	4.418	4.531
20	2.439	3.078	3.462	3.736	3.950	4.124	4.271	4.398	4.510
24	2.420	3.047	3.423	3.692	3.900	4.070	4.213	4.336	4.445
30	2.400	3.017	3.386	3.648	3.851	4.016	4.155	4.275	4.381
40	2.381	2.988	3.349	3.605	3.803	3.963	4.099	4.215	4.317
60	2.363	2.959	3.312	3.562	3.755	3.911	4.042	4.155	4.254
120	2.344	2.930	3.276	3.520	3.707	3.859	3.987	4.096	4.191
∞	2.326	2.902	3.240	3.478	3.661	3.808	3.931	4.037	4.129

TABLE B.2 (*Continued*)

95th Percentiles

number of groups

df error	2	3	4	5	6	7	8	9	10
1	17.97	26.98	32.82	37.08	40.41	43.12	45.40	47.36	49.07
2	6.085	8.331	9.798	10.88	11.74	12.44	13.03	13.54	13.99
3	4.501	5.910	6.825	7.502	8.037	8.478	8.853	9.177	9.462
4	3.927	5.040	5.757	6.287	6.707	7.053	7.347	7.602	7.826
5	3.635	4.602	5.218	5.673	6.033	6.330	6.582	6.802	6.995
6	3.461	4.339	4.896	5.305	5.628	5.895	6.122	6.319	6.493
7	3.344	4.165	4.681	5.060	5.359	5.606	5.815	5.998	6.158
8	3.261	4.041	4.529	4.886	5.167	5.399	5.597	5.767	5.918
9	3.199	3.949	4.415	4.756	5.024	5.244	5.432	5.595	5.739
10	3.151	3.877	4.327	4.654	4.912	5.124	5.305	5.461	5.599
11	3.113	3.820	4.256	4.574	4.823	5.028	5.202	5.353	5.487
12	3.082	3.773	4.199	4.508	4.751	4.950	5.119	5.265	5.395
13	3.055	3.735	4.151	4.453	4.690	4.885	5.049	5.192	5.318
14	3.033	3.702	4.111	4.407	4.639	4.829	4.990	5.131	5.254
15	3.014	3.674	4.076	4.367	4.595	4.782	4.940	5.077	5.198
16	2.998	3.649	4.046	4.333	4.557	4.741	4.897	5.031	5.150
17	2.984	3.628	4.020	4.303	4.524	4.705	4.858	4.991	5.108
18	2.971	3.609	3.997	4.277	4.495	4.673	4.824	4.956	5.071
19	2.960	3.593	3.977	4.253	4.469	4.645	4.794	4.924	5.038
20	2.950	3.578	3.958	4.232	4.445	4.620	4.768	4.896	5.008
24	2.919	3.532	3.901	4.166	4.373	4.541	4.684	4.807	4.915
30	2.888	3.486	3.845	4.102	4.302	4.464	4.602	4.720	4.824
40	2.858	3.442	3.791	4.039	4.232	4.389	4.521	4.635	4.735
60	2.829	3.399	3.737	3.977	4.163	4.314	4.441	4.550	4.646
120	2.800	3.356	3.685	3.917	4.096	4.241	4.363	4.468	4.560
∞	2.772	3.314	3.633	3.858	4.030	4.170	4.286	4.387	4.474

(*cont.*)

TABLE B.3
Critical Values for Dunnett's Test

Error df	α	Two-Tailed Comparisons k = number of treatment means, including control								
		2	3	4	5	6	7	8	9	10
5	0.05	2.57	3.03	3.29	3.48	3.62	3.73	3.82	3.90	3.97
	0.01	4.03	4.63	4.98	5.22	5.41	5.56	5.69	5.80	5.89
6	0.05	2.45	2.86	3.10	3.26	3.39	3.49	3.57	3.64	3.71
	0.01	3.71	4.21	4.51	4.71	4.87	5.00	5.10	5.20	5.28
7	0.05	2.36	2.75	2.97	3.12	3.24	3.33	3.41	3.47	3.53
	0.01	3.50	3.95	4.21	4.39	4.53	4.64	4.74	4.82	4.89
8	0.05	2.31	2.67	2.88	3.02	3.13	3.22	3.29	3.35	3.41
	0.01	3.36	3.77	4.00	4.17	4.29	4.40	4.48	4.56	4.62
9	0.05	2.26	2.61	2.81	2.95	3.05	3.14	3.20	3.26	3.32
	0.01	3.25	3.63	3.85	4.01	4.12	4.22	4.30	4.37	4.43
10	0.05	2.23	2.57	2.76	2.89	2.99	3.07	3.14	3.19	3.24
	0.01	3.17	3.53	3.74	3.88	3.99	4.08	4.16	4.22	4.28
11	0.05	2.20	2.53	2.72	2.84	2.94	3.02	3.08	3.14	3.19
	0.01	3.11	3.45	3.65	3.79	3.89	3.98	4.05	4.11	4.16
12	0.05	2.18	2.50	2.68	2.81	2.90	2.98	3.04	3.09	3.14
	0.01	3.05	3.39	3.58	3.71	3.81	3.89	3.96	4.02	4.07
13	0.05	2.16	2.48	2.65	2.78	2.87	2.94	3.00	3.06	3.10
	0.01	3.01	3.33	3.52	3.65	3.74	3.82	3.89	3.94	3.99
14	0.05	2.14	2.46	2.63	2.75	2.84	2.91	2.97	3.02	3.07
	0.01	2.98	3.29	3.47	3.59	3.69	3.76	3.83	3.88	3.93
15	0.05	2.13	2.44	2.61	2.73	2.82	2.89	2.95	3.00	3.04
	0.01	2.95	3.25	3.43	3.55	3.64	3.71	3.78	3.83	3.88
16	0.05	2.12	2.42	2.59	2.71	2.80	2.87	2.92	2.97	3.02
	0.01	2.92	3.22	3.39	3.51	3.60	3.67	3.73	3.78	3.83
17	0.05	2.11	2.41	2.58	2.69	2.78	2.85	2.90	2.95	3.00
	0.01	2.90	3.19	3.36	3.47	3.56	3.63	3.69	3.74	3.79
18	0.05	2.10	2.40	2.56	2.68	2.76	2.83	2.89	2.94	2.98
	0.01	2.88	3.17	3.33	3.44	3.53	3.60	3.66	3.71	3.75
19	0.05	2.09	2.39	2.55	2.66	2.75	2.81	2.87	2.92	2.96
	0.01	2.86	3.15	3.31	3.42	3.50	3.57	3.63	3.68	3.72
20	0.05	2.09	2.38	2.54	2.65	2.72	2.80	2.86	2.90	2.95
	0.01	2.85	3.13	3.29	3.40	3.48	3.55	3.60	3.65	3.69
24	0.05	2.06	2.35	2.51	2.61	2.70	2.76	2.81	2.86	2.90
	0.01	2.80	3.07	3.22	3.32	3.40	3.47	3.52	3.57	3.61
30	0.05	2.04	2.32	2.47	2.58	2.66	2.72	2.77	2.82	2.86
	0.01	2.75	3.01	3.15	3.25	3.33	3.39	3.44	3.49	3.52
40	0.05	2.02	2.29	2.44	2.54	2.62	2.68	2.73	2.77	2.81
	0.01	2.70	2.95	3.09	3.19	3.26	3.32	3.37	3.41	3.44
60	0.05	2.00	2.27	2.41	2.51	2.58	2.64	2.69	2.73	2.77
	0.01	2.66	2.90	3.03	3.12	3.19	3.25	3.29	3.33	3.37
120	0.05	1.98	2.24	2.38	2.47	2.55	2.60	2.65	2.69	2.73
	0.01	2.62	2.85	2.97	3.06	3.12	3.18	3.22	3.26	3.29
∞	0.05	1.96	2.21	2.35	2.44	2.51	2.57	2.61	2.65	2.69
	0.01	2.58	2.79	2.92	3.00	3.06	3.11	3.15	3.19	3.22

Reproduced from: C. W. Dunnett (1964). New tables for multiple comparisons with a control, *Biometrics* **20**:482–491. With permission of The Biometric Society.

Number of Variances

df for each variance	$1 - \alpha$	2	3	4	5	6	7	8	9	10	11	12
2	.95	39.0	87.5	142	202	266	333	403	475	550	626	704
	.99	199	448	729	1036	1362	1705	2063	2432	2813	3204	3605
3	.95	154	27.8	39.2	50.7	62.0	72.9	83.5	93.9	104	114	124
	.99	47.5	85	120	151	184	216	249	281	310	337	361
4	.95	9.60	15.5	20.6	25.2	29.5	33.6	37.5	41.4	44.6	48.0	51.4
	.99	23.2	37.	49.	59.	69.	79.	89.	97.	106.	113.	120
5	.95	7.15	10.8	13.7	16.3	18.7	20.8	22.9	24.7	26.5	28.2	29.9
	.99	14.9	22.	28.	33.	38.	42.	46.	50.	54.	57	60
6	.95	5.82	8.38	10.4	12.1	13.7	15.0	16.3	17.5	18.6	19.7	20.7
	.99	11.1	15.5	19.1	22.	25.	27.	30.	32.	34.	36	37
7	.95	4.99	6.94	8.44	9.70	10.8	11.8	12.7	13.5	14.3	15.1	15.8
	.99	8.89	12.1	14.5	16.5	18.4	20.	22.	23.	24.	26	27
8	.95	4.43	6.00	7.18	8.12	9.03	9.78	10.5	11.1	11.7	12.2	12.7
	.99	7.50	9.9	11.7	13.2	14.5	15.8	16.9	17.9	18.9	19.8	21
9	.95	4.03	5.34	6.31	7.11	7.80	8.41	8.95	9.45	9.91	10.3	10.7
	.99	6.54	8.5	9.9	11.1	12.1	13.1	13.9	14.7	15.3	16.0	16.6
10	.95	3.72	4.85	5.67	6.34	6.92	7.42	7.87	8.28	8.66	9.01	9.34
	.99	5.85	7.4	8.6	9.6	10.4	11.1	11.8	12.4	12.9	13.4	13.9
12	.95	3.28	4.16	4.79	5.30	5.72	6.09	6.42	6.72	7.00	7.25	7.48
	.99	4.91	6.1	6.9	7.6	8.2	8.7	9.1	9.5	9.9	10.2	10.6
15	.95	2.86	3.54	4.01	4.37	4.68	4.95	5.19	5.40	5.59	5.77	5.93
	.99	4.07	4.9	5.5	6.0	6.4	6.7	7.1	7.3	7.5	7.8	8.0
20	.95	2.46	2.95	3.29	3.54	3.76	3.94	4.10	4.24	4.37	4.49	4.59
	.99	3.32	3.8	4.3	4.6	4.9	5.1	5.3	5.5	5.6	5.8	5.9
30	.95	2.07	2.40	2.61	2.78	2.91	3.02	3.12	3.21	3.29	3.36	3.39
	.99	2.63	3.0	3.3	3.4	3.6	3.7	3.8	3.9	4.0	4.1	4.2
60	.95	1.67	1.85	1.96	2.04	2.11	2.17	2.22	2.26	2.30	2.33	2.36
	.99	1.96	2.2	2.3	2.4	2.4	2.5	2.5	2.6	2.6	2.7	2.7

[a]Reproduced with permission of the trustees of *Biometrika*.

*Equal group size (n) is assumed in the table; hence $df = n - 1$. If group sizes are not equal, then use the average group size (rounding off to the nearest integer) as the n.

379

TABLE B.5
Critical Values for Bryant-Paulson Procedure

Error df	Number of Covariates (C)	α	|	2	3	4	5	6	7	8	10
						Number of Groups					
3	1	.05		5.42	7.18	8.32	9.17	9.84	10.39	10.86	11.62
		.01		10.28	13.32	15.32	16.80	17.98	18.95	19.77	21.12
	2	.05		6.21	8.27	9.60	10.59	11.37	12.01	12.56	13.44
		.01		11.97	15.56	17.91	19.66	21.05	22.19	23.16	24.75
	3	.05		6.92	9.23	10.73	11.84	12.72	13.44	14.06	15.05
		.01		13.45	17.51	20.17	22.15	23.72	25.01	26.11	27.90
4	1	.05		4.51	5.84	6.69	7.32	7.82	8.23	8.58	9.15
		.01		7.68	9.64	10.93	11.89	12.65	13.28	13.82	14.70
	2	.05		5.04	6.54	7.51	8.23	8.80	9.26	9.66	10.31
		.01		8.69	10.95	12.43	13.54	14.41	15.14	15.76	16.77
	3	.05		5.51	7.18	8.25	9.05	9.67	10.19	10.63	11.35
		.01		9.59	12.11	13.77	15.00	15.98	16.79	17.47	18.60
5	1	.05		4.06	5.17	5.88	6.40	6.82	7.16	7.45	7.93
		.01		6.49	7.99	8.97	9.70	10.28	10.76	11.17	11.84
	2	.05		4.45	5.68	6.48	7.06	7.52	7.90	8.23	8.76
		.01		7.20	8.89	9.99	10.81	11.47	12.01	12.47	13.23
	3	.05		4.81	6.16	7.02	7.66	8.17	8.58	8.94	9.52
		.01		7.83	9.70	10.92	11.82	12.54	13.14	13.65	14.48
6	1	.05		3.79	4.78	5.40	5.86	6.23	6.53	6.78	7.20
		.01		5.83	7.08	7.88	8.48	8.96	9.36	9.70	10.25
	2	.05		4.10	5.18	5.87	6.37	6.77	7.10	7.38	7.84
		.01		6.36	7.75	8.64	9.31	9.85	10.29	10.66	11.28
	3	.05		4.38	5.55	6.30	6.84	7.28	7.64	7.94	8.44
		.01		6.85	8.36	9.34	10.07	10.65	11.13	11.54	12.22
7	1	.05		3.62	4.52	5.09	5.51	5.84	6.11	6.34	6.72
		.01		5.41	6.50	7.20	7.72	8.14	8.48	8.77	9.26
	2	.05		3.87	4.85	5.47	5.92	6.28	6.58	6.83	7.24
		.01		5.84	7.03	7.80	8.37	8.83	9.21	9.53	10.06
	3	.05		4.11	5.16	5.82	6.31	6.70	7.01	7.29	7.73
		.01		6.23	7.52	8.36	8.98	9.47	9.88	10.23	10.80
8	1	.05		3.49	4.34	4.87	5.26	5.57	5.82	6.03	6.39
		.01		5.12	6.11	6.74	7.20	7.58	7.88	8.15	8.58
	2	.05		3.70	4.61	5.19	5.61	5.94	6.21	6.44	6.82
		.01		5.48	6.54	7.23	7.74	8.14	8.48	8.76	9.23
	3	.05		3.91	4.88	5.49	5.93	6.29	6.58	6.83	7.23
		.01		5.81	6.95	7.69	8.23	8.67	9.03	9.33	9.84
10	1	.05		3.32	4.10	4.58	4.93	5.21	5.43	5.63	5.94
		.01		4.76	5.61	6.15	6.55	6.86	7.13	7.35	7.72
	2	.05		3.49	4.31	4.82	5.19	5.49	5.73	5.93	6.27
		.01		5.02	5.93	6.51	6.93	7.27	7.55	7.79	8.19
	3	.05		3.65	4.51	5.05	5.44	5.75	6.01	6.22	6.58
		.01		5.27	6.23	6.84	7.30	7.66	7.96	8.21	8.63

Error df	Number of Covariates (C)	α	2	3	4	5	6	7	8	10
						Number of Groups				
12	1	.05	3.22	3.95	4.40	4.73	4.98	5.19	5.37	5.67
		.01	4.54	5.31	5.79	6.15	6.43	6.67	6.87	7.20
	2	.05	3.35	4.12	4.59	4.93	5.20	5.43	5.62	5.92
		.01	4.74	5.56	6.07	6.45	6.75	7.00	7.21	7.56
	3	.05	3.48	4.28	4.78	5.14	5.42	5.65	5.85	6.17
		.01	4.94	5.80	6.34	6.74	7.05	7.31	7.54	7.90
14	1	.05	3.15	3.85	4.28	4.59	4.83	5.03	5.20	5.48
		.01	4.39	5.11	5.56	5.89	6.15	6.36	6.55	6.85
	2	.05	3.26	3.99	4.44	4.76	5.01	5.22	5.40	5.69
		.01	4.56	5.31	5.78	6.13	6.40	6.63	6.82	7.14
	3	.05	3.37	4.13	4.59	4.93	5.19	5.41	5.59	5.89
		.01	4.72	5.51	6.00	6.36	6.65	6.89	7.09	7.42
16	1	.05	3.10	3.77	4.19	4.49	4.72	4.91	5.07	5.34
		.01	4.28	4.96	5.39	5.70	5.95	6.15	6.32	6.60
	2	.05	3.19	3.90	4.32	4.63	4.88	5.07	5.24	5.52
		.01	4.42	5.14	5.58	5.90	6.16	6.37	6.55	6.85
	3	.05	3.29	4.01	4.46	4.78	5.03	5.23	5.41	5.69
		.01	4.56	5.30	5.76	6.10	6.37	6.59	6.77	7.08
18	1	.05	3.06	3.72	4.12	4.41	4.63	4.82	4.98	5.23
		.01	4.20	4.86	5.26	5.56	5.79	5.99	6.15	6.42
	2	.05	3.14	3.82	4.24	4.54	4.77	4.96	5.13	5.39
		.01	4.32	5.00	5.43	5.73	5.98	6.18	6.35	6.63
	3	.05	3.23	3.93	4.35	4.66	4.90	5.10	5.27	5.54
		.01	4.44	5.15	5.59	5.90	6.16	6.36	6.54	6.83
20	1	.05	3.03	3.67	4.07	4.35	4.57	4.75	4.90	5.15
		.01	4.14	4.77	5.17	5.45	5.68	5.86	6.02	6.27
	2	.05	3.10	3.77	4.17	4.46	4.69	4.88	5.03	5.29
		.01	4.25	4.90	5.31	5.60	5.84	6.03	6.19	6.46
	3	.05	3.18	3.86	4.28	4.57	4.81	5.00	5.16	5.42
		.01	4.35	5.03	5.45	5.75	5.99	6.19	6.36	6.63
24	1	.05	2.98	3.61	3.99	4.26	4.47	4.65	4.79	5.03
		.01	4.05	4.65	5.02	5.29	5.50	5.68	5.83	6.07
	2	.05	3.04	3.69	4.08	4.35	4.57	4.75	4.90	5.14
		.01	4.14	4.76	5.14	5.42	5.63	5.81	5.96	6.21
	3	.05	3.11	3.76	4.16	4.44	4.67	4.85	5.00	5.25
		.01	4.22	4.86	5.25	5.54	5.76	5.94	6.10	6.35
30	1	.05	2.94	3.55	3.91	4.18	4.38	4.54	4.69	4.91
		.01	3.96	4.54	4.89	5.14	5.34	5.50	5.64	5.87
	2	.05	2.99	3.61	3.98	4.25	4.46	4.62	4.77	5.00
		.01	4.03	4.62	4.98	5.24	5.44	5.61	5.75	5.98
	3	.05	3.04	3.67	4.05	4.32	4.53	4.70	4.85	5.08
		.01	4.10	4.70	5.06	5.33	5.54	5.71	5.85	6.08

TABLE B.5   (*Continued*)

Error df	Number of Covariates (C)	α	2	3	4	5	6	7	8	10
						Number of Groups				
40	1	.05	2.89	3.49	3.84	4.09	4.29	4.45	4.58	4.80
		.01	3.88	4.43	4.76	5.00	5.19	5.34	5.47	5.68
	2	.05	2.93	3.53	3.89	4.15	4.34	4.50	4.64	4.86
		.01	3.93	4.48	4.82	5.07	5.26	5.41	5.54	5.76
	3	.05	2.97	3.57	3.94	4.20	4.40	4.56	4.70	4.92
		.01	3.98	4.54	4.88	5.13	5.32	5.48	5.61	5.83
60	1	.05	2.85	3.43	3.77	4.01	4.20	4.35	4.48	4.69
		.01	3.79	4.32	4.64	4.86	5.04	5.18	5.30	5.50
	2	.05	2.88	3.46	3.80	4.05	4.24	4.39	4.52	4.73
		.01	3.83	4.36	4.68	4.90	5.08	5.22	5.35	5.54
	3	.05	2.90	3.49	3.83	4.08	4.27	4.43	4.56	4.77
		.01	3.86	4.39	4.72	4.95	5.12	5.27	5.39	5.59
120	1	.05	2.81	3.37	3.70	3.93	4.11	4.26	4.38	4.58
		.01	3.72	4.22	4.52	4.73	4.89	5.03	5.14	5.32
	2	.05	2.82	3.38	3.72	3.95	4.13	4.28	4.40	4.60
		.01	3.73	4.24	4.54	4.75	4.91	5.05	5.16	5.35
	3	.05	2.84	3.40	3.73	3.97	4.15	4.30	4.42	4.62
		.01	3.75	4.25	4.55	4.77	4.94	5.07	5.18	5.37

Appendix C
Power Tables

NOTES

The quantity u refers to the degrees of freedom for the effect being tested. For a one way ANOVA with a levels we have $u = a-1$. For a two way ANOVA with a levels for A and b levels for B, then $u = (a-1)$ for the A main effect, $u = (b-1)$ for the B main effect, and $u = (a-1)(b-1)$ for the interaction effect.

Group size is the assumed common number of subjects in each group. For two groups with unequal group sizes n_1 and n_2, use the harmonic mean $2n_1n_2/(n_1+n_2)$ to enter the table. For more than two groups, use the average group size to enter the table.

TABLE C.1
Power of F Test at $\alpha = .05$, $u = 1$

Group Size n	f (effect size)											
	.05	.10	.15	.20	.25	.30	.35	.40	.50	.60	.70	..80
4	05	06	06	07	09	11	13	16	23	30	39	48
5	05	06	07	08	11	13	16	20	29	39	50	61
6	05	06	07	09	12	15	20	24	35	47	60	71
7	05	06	08	10	14	18	23	28	41	55	68	79
8	05	06	08	11	15	20	26	32	47	62	75	85
9	05	07	09	12	17	22	29	36	52	68	80	89
10	05	07	09	13	18	25	32	40	57	73	85	93
11	05	07	10	14	20	27	35	44	62	77	88	95
12	05	07	10	15	22	29	38	47	65	81	91	97
13	05	07	11	16	23	32	41	51	70	84	93	98
14	05	08	11	17	25	34	44	54	73	87	95	98
15	06	08	12	18	26	36	47	57	76	89	96	99
16	06	08	12	19	28	38	49	60	79	91	97	99
17	06	08	13	20	30	40	52	63	82	93	98	*
18	06	08	14	21	31	42	54	66	84	94	98	
19	06	09	14	22	33	44	57	68	86	95	99	
20	06	09	15	23	34	46	59	70	88	96	99	
22	06	09	16	26	37	50	63	75	91	97		
24	06	10	17	28	40	54	67	78	93	98		
26	06	10	18	30	43	58	71	82	95	99		
28	06	11	19	32	46	61	74	84	96	99		
30	06	11	21	34	49	66	77	87	97			
32	06	12	22	36	51	67	80	89	98			
34	07	12	23	38	54	69	82	91	98			
36	07	13	24	40	56	72	84	92	99			
38	07	13	25	41	59	74	86	94	99			
40	07	14	27	43	61	77	88	95	99			
44	07	15	29	47	65	80	91	96				
48	07	16	31	50	69	84	93	97				
52	08	17	33	53	73	87	95	98				
56	08	18	36	57	75	89	96	99				
60	08	19	38	60	79	91	97	99				
64	08	20	40	62	81	93	98	*				
68	08	21	42	65	83	94	98					
72	09	22	44	68	85	95	99					
76	09	23	46	70	87	96	99					
80	09	24	48	72	89	97	99					
100	10	29	57	81	94	99						
140	13	39	72	92	99							
200	16	52	86	98								

TABLE C.2
Power of F Test at $\alpha = .05$, $u = 2$

Group Size n	.05	.10	.15	.20	.25	.30	.35	.40	.50	.60	.70	.80
4	05	06	06	08	09	11	14	17	24	33	44	54
5	05	06	07	09	11	14	17	22	32	44	56	69
6	05	06	07	10	13	16	21	26	39	53	67	79
7	05	06	08	11	14	19	25	31	46	62	76	87
8	05	06	08	12	16	22	28	36	53	69	83	92
9	05	07	09	13	18	24	32	40	59	75	88	95
10	05	07	10	14	20	27	35	45	64	81	91	97
11	05	07	10	15	21	30	39	49	69	85	94	98
12	06	07	11	16	23	32	42	53	74	88	96	98
13	06	08	11	17	25	35	46	57	77	91	97	99
14	06	08	12	18	27	38	49	61	81	93	98	*
15	06	08	13	20	29	40	52	64	84	95	99	
16	06	08	13	21	31	43	55	67	86	96	99	
17	06	09	14	22	33	45	58	70	89	97	99	
18	06	09	14	23	34	48	61	73	90	98	*	
19	06	09	15	24	36	50	64	76	92	99		
20	06	00	16	26	38	52	66	78	93	99		
22	06	10	17	28	42	57	71	82	96	99		
24	06	10	18	30	45	61	75	86	97			
26	06	11	20	33	48	65	79	89	98			
28	06	11	21	35	52	68	82	91	99			
30	06	12	22	37	55	71	85	93	99			
32	07	12	24	40	58	75	87	94	99			
34	07	13	25	42	61	77	89	96				
36	07	13	26	44	63	80	91	97				
38	07	14	28	46	66	82	92	97				
40	07	15	29	48	68	84	94	98				
44	07	16	32	53	73	88	96	99				
48	08	17	34	57	77	90	97	99				
52	08	18	37	60	80	93	98					
56	08	19	40	64	83	94	99					
60	08	21	42	67	86	96	99					
64	08	22	45	70	88	97	99					
68	09	23	47	73	90	98	*					
72	09	24	49	75	92	98						
76	09	25	52	78	93	99						
80	09	27	54	80	94	99						
100	11	32	64	88	98							
140	14	44	79	97								
200	18	59	92									

TABLE C.3
Power of F Test at $\alpha = .05$, $u = 3$

Group Size						f (effect size)						
n	.05	.10	.15	.20	.25	.30	.35	.40	.50	.60	.70	.80
4	05	06	07	08	10	12	15	18	27	38	50	62
5	05	06	07	09	12	15	19	24	36	50	64	76
6	05	06	08	10	13	18	23	29	44	60	75	86
7	05	06	08	11	15	21	27	35	52	69	83	92
8	05	07	09	12	17	24	31	40	59	77	89	96
9	05	07	09	14	19	27	36	46	66	82	93	98
10	05	07	10	15	21	30	40	51	71	87	96	99
11	06	07	11	16	24	33	44	55	76	91	97	99
12	06	08	11	17	26	36	48	60	81	93	98	*
13	06	08	12	19	28	39	52	64	84	95	99	
14	06	08	13	20	30	42	55	68	87	97	99	
15	06	08	13	21	32	45	59	71	90	98	*	
16	06	09	14	23	34	48	62	75	92	98		
17	06	09	15	24	37	51	65	78	94	99		
18	06	09	16	26	39	53	68	80	95	99		
19	06	09	16	27	41	56	71	83	96	99		
20	06	10	17	28	43	59	73	85	97			
22	06	10	18	31	47	63	78	88	98			
24	06	11	20	34	51	68	82	91	99			
26	06	11	22	37	54	72	85	94	99			
28	07	12	23	39	58	75	88	95				
30	07	13	25	42	61	79	90	96				
32	07	13	26	45	65	81	92	97				
34	07	14	28	47	68	84	94	98				
36	07	14	29	50	70	86	95	99				
38	07	15	31	52	73	88	96	99				
40	07	16	32	54	76	90	97	99				
44	08	17	35	59	80	93	98					
48	08	18	39	63	84	95	99					
52	08	20	42	67	87	96	99					
56	08	21	45	71	89	97						
60	09	22	47	74	91	98						
64	09	24	50	77	93	99						
68	09	25	53	80	95	99						
72	09	27	56	82	96	99						
76	10	28	58	84	97	*						
80	10	29	61	86	97							
100	11	36	71	93	99							
140	14	49	86	99								
200	19	66	96									

TABLE C.4
Power of F Test at $\alpha = .05$, $u = 4$

Group Size	f (effect size)											
n	.05	.10	.15	.20	.25	.30	.35	.40	.50	.60	.70	.80
4	05	06	07	08	10	13	16	20	30	42	56	69
5	05	06	07	09	12	16	21	26	40	55	70	83
6	05	06	08	10	14	19	25	32	49	66	81	91
7	05	06	09	12	16	22	30	39	58	76	88	96
8	05	07	09	13	19	26	35	45	65	83	93	98
9	05	07	10	14	21	29	40	51	72	88	96	99
10	06	07	10	16	23	33	44	56	78	92	98	*
11	06	08	11	17	26	37	49	61	82	94	99	
12	06	08	12	19	28	40	53	66	86	96	99	
13	06	08	13	20	31	43	57	70	89	98	*	
14	06	08	13	22	33	47	61	74	92	98		
15	06	09	14	23	36	50	65	78	94	99		
16	06	09	15	25	38	53	68	81	95	99		
17	06	09	16	26	40	56	71	83	96	*		
18	06	09	17	28	43	59	74	86	97			
19	06	10	17	30	45	62	77	88	98			
20	06	10	18	31	47	65	79	90	99			
22	06	11	20	34	52	69	84	93	99			
24	06	11	22	37	56	74	87	95				
26	07	12	23	40	60	78	90	96				
28	07	13	25	43	64	81	92	98				
30	07	13	27	46	67	84	94	99				
32	07	14	29	49	71	87	96	99				
34	07	15	30	52	74	89	97					
36	07	15	32	55	76	91	97					
38	07	16	34	57	79	92	98					
40	07	17	36	60	81	94	99					
44	08	18	39	65	85	96	99					
48	08	20	43	69	91	97	*					
52	08	21	46	73	93	98						
56	09	23	49	77	95	99						
60	09	24	52	80	96	99						
64	09	26	55	83	97	*						
68	09	28	58	85	98							
72	10	29	61	87	98							
76	10	31	64	89	99							
80	10	32	66	91								
100	12	40	77	96								
140	15	54	91	99								
200	20	72	98									

TABLE C.5
Power of F Test at $\alpha = .10$, $u = 1$

Group Size n	.05	.10	.15	.20	.25	.30	.35	.40	.50	.60	.70	.80
					f (effect size)							
4	10	11	13	14	17	20	23	27	36	45	55	64
5	10	11	13	16	19	23	27	32	43	55	66	76
6	10	12	14	17	21	26	31	37	50	63	74	83
7	10	12	15	19	23	29	35	42	56	69	80	89
8	10	12	15	20	25	32	39	47	62	75	85	92
9	10	13	16	21	28	35	43	51	66	80	89	95
10	10	13	17	23	30	37	46	55	71	83	92	97
11	11	13	18	24	32	40	49	58	75	87	94	98
12	11	14	19	25	34	43	52	62	78	89	96	99
13	11	14	19	27	36	45	55	65	81	91	97	99
14	11	14	20	28	37	48	58	68	83	93	98	99
15	11	15	21	29	39	50	60	70	86	95	98	*
16	11	15	22	31	41	52	63	73	88	96	99	
17	11	15	23	32	43	54	65	75	89	97	99	
18	11	16	23	33	45	56	68	77	91	97	99	
19	11	16	24	34	46	58	70	79	92	98	*	
20	11	16	25	36	48	60	72	81	93	98		
22	11	17	26	38	51	64	75	84	95	99		
24	12	18	28	40	54	67	78	87	96	99		
26	12	19	29	43	57	70	81	89	97	*		
28	12	19	31	45	60	73	84	91	98			
30	12	20	32	47	62	76	86	93	99			
32	12	21	34	49	65	78	89	94	99			
34	12	21	35	51	67	80	90	95	99			
36	13	22	36	53	69	82	91	96	*			
38	13	23	38	55	71	84	92	97				
40	13	24	39	57	73	85	93	97	*			
44	13	25	42	60	77	88	95	98				
48	14	26	44	63	80	91	96	99				
52	14	28	47	66	82	92	97	99				
56	14	29	49	69	85	94	98	*				
60	15	30	51	72	87	95	99					
64	15	31	53	74	89	96	99					
68	16	33	56	76	90	97	99					
72	16	34	58	78	92	98	99					
76	16	35	59	80	93	98	*					
80	17	36	61	82	94	99						
100	18	42	70	89	97							
140	22	53	82	96	99							
200	27	65	92	99								

TABLE C.6
Power of F Test at $\alpha = .10$, $u = 2$

Group Size	f (effect size)											
n	.05	.10	.15	.20	.25	.30	.35	.40	.50	.60	.70	.80
4	10	11	13	15	17	20	24	28	38	48	59	70
5	10	12	13	16	20	24	29	34	46	59	71	81
6	10	12	14	18	22	27	33	40	54	68	80	89
7	10	12	15	19	24	30	37	45	61	75	86	93
8	11	13	16	21	27	34	41	50	67	81	90	96
9	11	13	17	22	29	37	45	55	72	85	94	98
10	11	13	18	24	31	40	49	59	76	89	96	99
11	11	14	18	25	33	43	53	63	80	92	97	99
12	11	14	19	27	36	46	56	67	84	94	98	*
13	11	14	20	28	38	49	60	70	86	95	99	
14	11	15	21	30	40	51	63	73	89	97	99	
15	11	15	22	31	42	54	66	76	91	97	*	
16	11	16	23	32	44	56	68	79	92	98		
17	11	16	24	34	46	59	71	81	94	99		
18	11	16	24	35	48	61	73	83	95	99		
19	11	17	25	37	50	63	75	85	96	99		
20	12	17	26	38	52	65	77	87	97	*		
22	12	18	28	41	55	69	81	90	98			
24	12	19	29	43	59	73	84	92	99			
26	12	19	31	46	62	76	87	94	99			
28	12	20	33	48	65	79	89	95	99			
30	12	21	34	51	68	82	91	96				
32	13	22	36	53	70	84	93	97				
34	13	22	37	55	73	86	94	98				
36	13	23	39	57	75	88	95	98				
38	13	24	40	60	77	89	96	99				
40	13	25	42	62	79	91	97	99	*			
44	14	26	45	65	82	93	98					
48	14	28	48	69	85	95	99					
52	15	29	50	72	88	96	99					
56	15	31	53	75	90	97	99					
60	15	32	55	78	92	98						
64	16	33	58	80	93	98						
68	16	35	60	82	95	99						
72	17	36	62	84	96	99						
76	17	38	65	86	96	99						
80	17	39	67	88	97	*						
100	19	45	75	93	99							
140	23	57	87	98								
200	29	71	96									

TABLE C.7
Power of F Test at $\alpha = .10$, $u = 3$

Group Size n	f (effect size)											
	.05	.10	.15	.20	.25	.30	.35	.40	.50	.60	.70	.80
4	10	11	13	15	18	21	25	30	41	53	65	76
5	10	12	14	17	20	25	30	37	50	64	77	87
6	10	12	15	18	23	29	35	43	59	73	85	93
7	11	12	15	20	26	32	40	49	66	81	91	96
8	11	13	16	22	28	36	45	54	72	86	94	98
9	11	13	17	23	31	40	49	59	78	90	97	99
10	11	14	18	25	33	43	54	64	82	93	98	*
11	11	14	19	27	36	46	58	68	86	95	99	
12	11	14	20	28	38	50	61	72	89	97	99	
13	11	15	21	30	41	53	65	76	91	98	*	
14	11	15	22	31	43	56	68	79	93	98		
15	11	16	23	33	45	59	71	82	95	99		
16	11	16	24	35	48	61	74	84	96	99		
17	11	16	25	36	50	64	77	86	97	*		
18	11	17	26	38	52	66	79	88	98			
19	12	17	27	39	54	69	81	90	98			
20	12	18	28	41	56	71	83	91	99			
22	12	18	29	44	60	75	86	94	99			
24	12	19	31	47	64	79	89	95	*			
26	12	20	33	50	67	82	91	97				
28	12	21	35	53	70	84	93	98				
30	13	22	37	55	73	87	95	98				
32	13	23	39	58	76	89	96	99				
34	13	23	40	60	78	91	97	99				
36	13	24	42	63	81	92	98	99				
38	14	25	44	65	83	93	98	*				
40	14	26	45	67	84	94	99					
44	14	28	49	71	88	96	99					
48	15	29	52	75	90	97	*					
52	15	31	55	78	92	98						
56	15	33	58	81	94	99						
60	16	34	60	83	95	99						
64	16	36	63	85	96	99						
68	17	37	66	88	97	*						
72	17	39	68	89	98							
76	17	41	70	91	98							
80	18	42	72	92	99							
100	20	49	81	96								
140	24	62	92	99								
200	30	77	98									

TABLE C.8
Power of F Test at $\alpha = .10$, $u = 4$

Group Size n	\textit{f} (effect size)											
	.05	.10	.15	.20	.25	.30	.35	.40	.50	.60	.70	.80
4	10	11	13	15	18	22	27	32	44	57	70	81
5	10	12	14	17	21	26	32	39	54	69	82	91
6	10	12	15	19	24	31	38	45	63	79	89	96
7	11	13	16	21	27	35	43	53	71	85	94	98
8	11	13	17	23	30	39	48	59	77	90	97	99
9	11	13	18	24	33	43	53	64	82	94	98	*
10	11	14	19	26	36	47	58	69	87	96	99	
11	11	14	20	28	38	50	62	73	90	97	*	
12	11	15	21	30	41	54	66	77	92	98		
13	11	15	22	32	44	57	70	81	94	99		
14	11	16	23	34	46	60	73	84	96	99		
15	11	16	24	35	49	63	76	86	97	*		
16	11	16	25	37	51	66	79	88	98			
17	11	17	26	39	54	69	81	90	98			
18	12	17	27	41	56	71	84	92	99			
19	12	18	28	42	58	74	86	93	99			
20	12	18	29	44	61	76	87	94	99			
22	12	19	31	47	65	80	90	96				
24	12	20	33	51	69	83	93	97				
26	12	21	35	54	72	86	95	98				
28	13	22	37	57	75	89	96	99				
30	13	23	39	60	78	91	97	99				
32	13	24	41	62	81	92	98	*				
34	13	25	43	65	83	94	98					
36	14	26	45	67	85	95	99					
38	14	26	47	70	87	96	99					
40	14	27	49	72	89	97	99	*				
44	14	29	52	76	91	98						
48	15	31	56	79	94	99						
52	15	33	59	83	95	99						
56	16	35	62	85	96	*						
60	16	37	65	88	97							
64	17	38	68	90	98							
68	17	40	70	91	99							
72	18	42	73	93	99							
76	18	44	75	94	99							
80	19	45	77	95	*							
100	21	53	86	98								
140	25	67	95									
200	32	82	99									

References

Agresti, A. (1990). *Statistical methods for social science*. Englewood Cliffs, NJ: Prentice Hall.

Anderson, N. H. (1963). Comparison of different populations: Resistance to extinction and transfer. *Psychological Bulletin, 70*, 162–179.

Anscombe, F. (1973). Graphs in statistical analysis. *American Statistician, 27*, 11–21.

Barcikowski, R. (1981). Statistical power with group mean as the unit of analysis. *Journal of Educational Statistics, 6*, 267–285.

Barcikowski, R., & Robey, R. (1984). Decisions in a single group repeated measures analysis: Statistical tests and three computer packages. *American Statistician, 38*, 248–250.

Becker, B. (1987). Applying tests of combined significance in meta-analysis. *Psychological Bulletin, 102*, 164–171.

Bloom, B. (1984). The 2-sigma problem: The search for methods of group instruction as effective as one-to-one. *Educational Researcher, 13*, 4–16.

Bock, R. D. (1975). *Multivariate statistical methods in behavioral research*. New York: McGraw-Hill.

Box, G. P. (1954). Some theorems on quadratic forms applied in the study of analysis of variance problems: II. Effect of inequality of variance and of correlations between errors in the two way classification. *Annals of Mathematical Statistics, 25*, 484–498.

Brown, M. B., & Forsythe, A. B. (1974). Robust tests for the equality of variances. *Journal of the American Statistical Association, 69*, 364–367.

Bryan, T. (1974). Peer popularity of learning disabled children. *Journal of Learning Disabilites, 7*, 31–35.

Bryant, J. L., & Paulson, A. S. (1976). An extension of Tukey's method of multiple comparisons to experimental designs with random concomitant variables. *Biometrika, 63*, 631–638.

Bryk, A. S. (1977). Evaluating program impact: A time to cast away stones, a time to gather stones together. *New Directions for Program Evaluation, 1*, 31–58.

Bryk, A. S., & Weisberg, H. I. (1977). Use of the nonequivalent control group design when subjects are growing. *Psychological Bulletin, 85*, 950–962.

Carlson, J., & Timm, N. (1974). Analysis of non-orthogonal fixed effects designs. *Psychological Bulletin, 81*, 563–570.

Chase, C. (1986). Essay test scoring: Interaction of relevant variables. *Journal of Educational Measurement, 23*, 33–41.

Cobb, G. (1987). Introductory textbooks: A framework for evaluation. *Journal of the American Statistical Association, 82,* 321–339.

Cochran, W. G. (1957). Analysis of covariance: Its nature and uses. *Biometrics, 13,* 261–281.

Cohen, J. (1968). Multiple regression as a general data-analytic system. *Psychological Bulletin, 70,* 426–443.

Cohen, J. (1969). *Statistical power analysis for the behavioral sciences.* New York: Academic Press.

Cohen, J. (1973). Eta squared and partial eta squared in fixed factor designs. *Educational and Psychological Measurement, 33,* 107–112.

Cohen, J. (1977). *Statistical power analysis for the behavioral sciences.* New York: Academic Press.

Cohen, J. (1990). Things I have learned (so far). *American Psychologist, 15,* 1304–1312.

Cohen, J., & Cohen, P. (1983). *Applied multiple regression/correlation analysis for the behavioral sciences.* Hillsdale, NJ: Lawrence Erlbaum Associates.

Collier, R., Baker, F., Mandeville, C. K., & Hayes, T. (1967). Estimates of test size for several test procedures on conventional variance ratios in the repeated measures design. *Psychometrika, 32,* 339–353.

Cook, R. D. (1977). Detection of influential observations in linear regression. *Technometrics, 19,* 15–18.

Cook, R. D., & Weisberg, S. (1982). *Residuals and influence in regression.* New York: Chapman and Hall.

Cradler, J., & Goodwin, D. (1971). Conditioning of verbal behavior as a function of age, social class and type of reinforcement. *Journal of Educational Psychology, 62,* 279–284.

Cronbach, L. (1975). Beyond the two disciplines of scientific psychology. *American Psychologist, 30,* 116–127.

Cronbach, L., & Snow, R. (1969). *Individual differences in learning ability as a function of instructional variables.* Unpublished report, School of Education, Stanford University, Stanford, CA.

Cronbach, L., & Snow, R. (1977). *Aptitudes and instructional methods.* New York: Irvington Press.

Crowder, R. (1975). An investigation of the relationship between social I. Q. and vocational evaluation ratings with an adult trainable mental retardate work activity center population. Unpublished doctoral dissertation, University of Cincinnati, OH.

Crystal, G. (1988). The wacky, wacky world of CEO pay. *Fortune, 117,* 68–78.

Dance, K., & Neufeld, R. (1988). Aptitude treatment interaction research in the clinical setting: A review of attempts to dispel the "Patient Uniformity" myth. *Psychological Bulletin, 104,* 192–213.

Daniels, R., & Stevens, J. (1976). The interaction between the internal-external locus of control and two methods of college instruction. *American Educational Research Journal, 13,* 103–113.

Davidson, M. L. (1972). Univariate versus multivariate tests in repeated measures experiments. *Psychological Bulletin, 77,* 446.

Dizney, H., & Gromen, L. (1967). Predictive validity and differential achievement on three MLA Comparative Foreign Language tests. *Educational and Psychological Measurement, 27,* 1127–1130.

Draper, N., & Smith, H. (1981). *Applied regression analysis.* New York: Wiley.

Dunnett, C. W. (1955). A multiple comparison procedure for comparing several treatments with a control. *Journal of the American Statistical Association, 50,* 1096–1121.

Dunnet, C. W. (1980). Pairwise multiple comparisons in the homogeneous variance, unequal sample size cases. *Journal of the American Statistical Association, 75,* 789–795.

Elashoff, J. (1969). Analysis of covariance: A delicate instrument. *American Educational Research Journal, 6,* 383–401.

Elashoff, J. (1981). Data for the panel session in software for repeated measures analysis of variance. *Proceedings of the Statistical Computing Section,* American Statistical Association.

Feshback, S., Adelman, H., & Williamson, F. (1977). Prediction of reading and related academic problems. *Journal of Educational Psychology, 69,* 299–308.

Frane, J. (1976). Some simple procedures for handling missing data in multivariate analysis. *Psychometrika, 41,* 409–415.

Games, P., & Howell, J. K. (1976). Pairwise multiple comparison procedures with unequal n's and/or variances: A Monte Carlo study. *Journal of Educational Statistics, 1,* 113–125.

Glass, G., & Hopkins, K. (1984). *Statistical methods in education and psychology.* Englewood Cliffs, NJ: Prentice Hall.

Glass, G., Peckham, P., & Sanders, J. (1972). Consequences of failure to meet assumptions underlying the fixed effects analyses of variance and covariance. *Review of Educational Research, 42,* 237–288.

Glassnapp, D., & Poggio, J. (1985). *Essentials of statistical analysis for the behavioral sciences.* Columbus, OH: Charles Merrill.

Greenhouse, S., & Geisser, S. (1959). On methods in the analysis of profile data. *Psychometrika, 24,* 95–112.

Hand, D. J., & Taylor, C. C. (1987). *Multivariate analysis of variance and repeated measures.* London: Chapman and Hall.

Harrington, S. (1968). *Sequencing organizers in meaningful verbal learning* (Research Paper No. 10). Boulder: University of Colorado, Laboratory of Educational Research.

Hays, W. (1963). *Statistics for psychologists.* New York: Holt, Rinehart and Winston.

Hays, W. (1981). *Statistics* (3rd ed.). New York: Holt, Rinehart and Winston.

Hayter, A. (1984). A proof of the conjecture that the Tukey-Kramer multiple comparison procedure is conservative. *Annals of Statistics, 12,* 61–75.

Herzberg, P. A. (1969). The parameters of cross validation. *Psychometrika* (Monogr. Suppl., No. 16).

Hintze, J. (1996). *PASS 6.0 User's Guide.* Kaysville, Utah.

Hoaglin, D., & Welsch, R. (1978). The hat matrix in regression and ANOVA. *American Statistician, 32,* 17–22.

Holland, B. S., & Copenhaver, M. D. (1988). Improved Bonferroni type multiple testing procdures. *Psychological Bulletin, 104,* 145–149.

Holm, S. (1979). A simple sequentially rejective multiple test procedure. *Scandinavian Journal of Statistics, 6,* 65–70.

Huberty, C. (1987). On statistical testing. *Educational Researcher, 16,* 4–9.

Huberty, C. J. (1989). Problems with stepwise methods—Better alternatives. In B. Thompson (Ed.), *Advances in social science methodology* (Vol. 1, pp. 43–70), Greenwich, CT: JAI Press.

Huck, S., & Bounds, W. (1972). Essay grades: An interaction between graders handwriting clarity and the neatness of examination papers. *American Educational Research Journal, 9,* 279–283.

Huck, S., Cormier, W., & Bounds, W. (1974). *Reading statistics and research.* New York: Harper and Row.

Huck, S., & McLean, R. A. (1975). Using a repeated measures ANOVA to analyze the data from a pretest-posttest design: A potentially confusing task. *Psychological Bulletin, 82,* 511–518.

Huitema, B. (1980). *The analysis of covariance and alternatives.* New York: Wiley.

Huynh, H., & Feldt, L. (1970). Conditions under which mean square ratios in repeated measures designs have exact distributions. *Journal of the American Statisitcal Association, 65,* 1582–1589.

Huynh, H., & Feldt, L. (1976). Estimation of the Box correction for degrees of freedom from sample data in the randomized block and split plot designs. *Journal of Educational Statistics, 1,* 69–82.

Jennings, E. (1988). Models for pretest-posttest data: Repeated measures ANOVA revisited. *Journal of Educational Statistics, 13,* 273–280.

Johnson, P. O., & Neyman, J. (1936). Tests of certain linear hypotheses and their application to some educational problems. *Statistical Research Memoirs, 1,* 57–93.

Johnson, R., & Wichern, D. (1988). *Applied multivariate statistical analysis* (2nd ed.). Englewood Cliffs, NJ: Prentice Hall.

Jones, L. V., Lindzey, G., & Coggeshall, P. (Eds.) (1982). *An Assessment of Research-Doctorate Programs in the United States: Social and Behavioral Sciences,* (Washington, DC: National Academy Press).

Kenny, D., & Judd, C. (1986). Consequences of violating the independence assumption in analysis of variance. *Psychological Bulletin, 99,* 422–431.

Keppel, G. (1983). *Design and analysis: A researcher's handbook.* Englewood Cliffs, NJ: Prentice Hall.

Kerlinger, F., & Pedhazur, E. (1973). *Multiple regression in behavioral research.* New York: Holt, Rinehart & Winston.

Keselman, H. J. & Keselman, J. C. (1988). Repeated measures multiple comparison procedures: Effects of violating multisample sphericity in unbalanced designs. *Journal of Educational Statistics, 13,* 215–226.

Keselman, H. J., Murray, R., & Rogan, J. (1976). *Effect of very unequal group sizes on Tukey's multiple comparison test.* Paper presented at the annual meeting of the American Educational Research Association, 1975, Washington, DC.

Keselman, H. J., Rogan, J., Mendoza, J., & Breen, L. (1980). Testing the validity conditions of repeated measures F tests. *Psychological Bulletin, 87,* 479–481.

Kirk, R. (1982). *Experimental design: Procedures for the behavioral sciences.* Belmont, CA: Brooks-Cole.

Levin, J., McCormick, C., Miller, G., Berry, J., & Presley, M. (1982). Mnemonic versus nonmnemonic vocabulary learning strategies for children. *American Educational Research Journal, 19,* 121–136.

Light, R., & Pillemer, D. (1984). *Summing up: The science of reviewing research.* Cambridge, MA: Harvard University Press.

Lord, F. M. (1969). Statistical adjustments when comparing pre-existing groups. *Psychological Bulletin, 70,* 162–179.

Lord, F., & Novick, M. (1968). *Statistical theories of mental test scores.* Reading, MA: Addison-Wesley.

Mallows, C. L. (1973). Some comments on C_p. *Technometrics, 15,* 661–676.

Marwit, S., & Neumann, G. (1974). Black and white children's comprehension of standard and nonstandard English passages. *Journal of Educational Psychology, 66,* 324–332.

Maxwell, S. (1980). Pairwise multiple comparison procedures in repeated measures designs. *Journal of Educational Statistics, 5,* 269–287.

Moore, D., & McCabe, G. (1989). *Introduction to the practice of statistics.* New York: Freeman.

Morrison, D. (1976). *Multivariate statistical methods.* New York: McGraw-Hill.

Morrison, D. F. (1983). *Applied linear statistical methods.* Englewood Cliffs, NJ: Prentice Hall.

Myers, J. (1979). *Fundamentals of experimental design.* Boston: Allyn and Bacon.

Myers, R. (1990). *Classical and modern regression with applications* (2nd ed.). Boston, MA: Duxbury Press.

Myers, J., & Well, A. (1991). *Research design and statistical analysis.* Hillsdale, NJ: Lawrence Erlbaum Associates.

Novince, L. (1977). *The contribution of cognitive restructuring to the effectiveness of behavior rehearsal in modifying social inhibition in females.* Unpublished doctoral dissertation, University of Cincinnati.

Nunnally, J. (1978). *Psychometric theory.* New York: McGraw-Hill.

O'Brien, R., & Kaiser, M. (1985). MANOVA method for analyzing repeated measures designs: An extensive primer. *Psychological Bulletin, 97,* 316–333.

O'Grady, K. (1982). Measures of explained variance: Cautions and limitations. *Psychological Bulletin, 92,* 766–777.

Overall, J., & Spiegel, D. (1969). Concerning the least squares analysis of experimental data. *Psychological Bulletin, 72,* 311–322.

Park, C., & Duddycha, A. (1974). A cross validation approach to sample size determination for regression models. *Journal of the American Statistical Association, 69,* 214–218.

Pedhazur, E. (1982). *Multiple regression in behavioral research.* New York: Holt, Rinehart and Winston.

Porter, A. (1967). *The effects of using fallible variables in the analysis of covariance.* Unpublished doctoral dissertation, University of Wisconsin, Madison.

Pukulski, J. (1970). Effects of reinforcement on word recognition. *The Reading Teacher, 23,* 516–522.

Raudenbush, S., & Byrk, A. S. (1987). Examining correlates of diversity. *Journal of Educational Statistics, 12,* 241–269.

Reichardt, C. S. (1979). The statistical analysis of data from nonequivalent group designs. In T. Cook & D. Campbell (Eds.), *Quasi-experimentation: Design and analysis issues for field settings* (pp. 147–205). Chicago: Rand McNally.

Rogosa, D. (1977). *Some results for the Johnson-Neyman technique.* Doctoral dissertation, Stanford University, Stanford, CA.

Rogosa, D. (1980). Comparing non-parallel regression lines. *Psychological Bulletin.*

Rosenthal, R., & Rosnow, R. (1984). *Essentials of behavioral research.* New York: McGraw-Hill.

Rounet, H., & Lepine, D. (1970). Comparison between treatments in a repeated measures design: ANOVA and multivariate methods. *British Journal of Mathematical and Statistical Psychology, 213,* 147–163.

Sarachan-Diely, A. (1985). Written narrative of deaf and hearing students: Story recall and inference. *Journal of Speech and Hearing Research, 28,* 151–159.

SAS Institute Inc. (1990). *SAS/STAT User's Guide,* Version 6, Fourth Edition, Volume 2, Cary, NC.

Scariano, S., & Davenport, J. (1987). The effects of violations of independence assumptions in the one-way ANOVA. *American Statistician, 41,* 123–129.

Schutz, W. (1977). *Leaders of schools: FIRO theory applied to administrators.* LaJolla, CA: University Associates.

Shiffler, R. (1988). Maximum *z* scores and outliers. *American Statistician, 42,* 79–80.

Singer, J., & Willett, J. (1988). *Opening up the black box of recipe statistics: Putting the data back into data analysis.* Paper presented at the annual meeting of the American Educational Research Association, April, New Orleans, LA.

Smith, S., Jones, L. & Waugh, M. (1986). Production and evaluation of interactive videodisc lessons in laboratory instruction. *Journal of Computer-Based Instruction, 13,* 117–121.

SPSS Inc. (1993). *SPSS for Windows Base System User's Guide: Release 6.0.* Chicago.

SPSS Inc. (1997). *SPSS Base 7.5 User's Guide.* Chicago.

SPSS Inc. (1998). *SPSS Base 8.0 User's Guide.* Chicago.

Stein, C. (1960). Multiple regression. In I. Olkin (Ed.), *Contributions to probability and statistics, essays in honor of Harold Hotelling.* Stanford, CA: Stanford University Press.

Stevens, J. P. (1996). *Applied multivariate statistics for the social sciences* (3rd ed.). Mahwah, NJ: Lawrence Erlbaum Associates.

Stoloff, P. H. (1967). *An empirical evaluation of the effects of violating the assumption of homogeneity of covariance for the repeated measures design of the analysis of variance* (Tech. Rep.). College Park: University of Maryland.

Thorndike, R. L., & Hagen, E. (1977). *Measurement and evaluation in psychology and education.* New York: Wiley.

Tomarken, J. J., & Serlin, R. (1986). Comparison of ANOVA alternatives under variance heterogeneity and specific noncentrality structures. *Psychological Bulletin, 99,* 90–99.

Tuckman, B., Steber, J., & Hyman, R. (1979). Judging the effectiveness of teaching styles: The perceptions of principals. *Educational Administration Quarterly, 15,* 104–115.

Weisberg, S. (1985). *Applied linear regression.* New York: Wiley.

Welch, B. L. (1951). On the comparison of several mean values: An alternative approach. *Biometrika, 38,* 330–336.

Wilkinson, L. (1979). Tests of significance in stepwise regression. *Psychological Bulletin, 86,* 168–174.

Answers to
Selected Exercises

CHAPTER 1

1. (a) The $22,000 figure was misleading because of the extreme salaries of $70,000 and $250,000. Recall that the mean is very sensitive to extreme values.

(b) The median should have been used. It is essentially unaffected by extreme values. The median for this set of data is $15,000, and indicates where most of the salaries are concentrated.

3. She should not be concerned, since considerable research has shown that a violation of the normality assumption has little effect on the Type I error rate.

5. (a) $\Sigma cx_i = \Sigma 3x_i = 3 \Sigma x_i = 3 (5 + 8 + 1 + 7) = 63$

(b) First, note that the mean for the scores $cx_1, cx_2, \ldots, cx_n$ is given by

$$\bar{x}_{cx} = \frac{cx_1 + cx_2 + \ldots + cx_n}{n} = \frac{c(x_1 + x_2 + \ldots + x_n)}{n} = c\bar{x}$$

where $\bar{x}$ is the mean for $x_1, x_2, \ldots, x_n$.

Now, using the definitional formula for variance, we have

$$s^2_{cx} = \frac{\Sigma(cx_i - c\bar{x})^2}{n-1} = \frac{\Sigma[c(x_i - \bar{x})]^2}{n-1} = \frac{\Sigma c^2(x_i - \bar{x})^2}{n-1} = \frac{c^2 \Sigma(x_i - \bar{x})^2}{n-1}$$

$$= c^2 s^2_x, \text{ as was to be proved.}$$

(c) The grand mean for the groups is 6.3. Therefore,

$$\Sigma\, 10(\bar{x}_i - \bar{x})^2 = \Sigma\, 10(\bar{x}_i - 6.3)^2$$
$$= 10\, [(4.1 - 6.3)^2 + (8.5 - 6.3)^2] = 96.8$$

7. (a) The correlation for all 14 data points is .587, indicating a moderate relationship between height and weight.
(b) The outlier is subject 10, whose weight of only 115 lbs is very unusual for someone over 6 ft tall.
(c) The correlation without subject 10 is now .867, indicating that there is indeed a strong relationship between height and weight.

9. (a) The 95% confidence interval for the first study is given by $4 \pm 2.101(.57)$, or $(2.8, 5.2)$, while the 95% confidence interval for the second study is given by $4 \pm 1.96(1.74)$, or $(.59, 7.41)$. The null hypothesis of equal population means is rejected in both cases, since 0 is *not* in either interval.
(b) We can be confident of clinical significance in the first study since the interval is indicating that the difference in the population means is at least 2.8, that is, greater than 2. We cannot be confident of clinical significance in the second study since the interval indicates the population mean difference could be as small as .59.

CHAPTER 2

1. overall $\alpha = 1 - (1 - .05)^{21} = 1 - .34 = .66$

3. (a) $df_b = 2$, $df_w = 27$. Therefore, the critical value at the .05 level is 3.35.
(b) $df_b = 3$, $df_w = 76$. Therefore, the critical value at the .10 level is 2.17.
(c) $df_b = 4$, $df_w = 35$. Therefore, the critical value at the .01 level is 3.9.

5. Using a calculator, we obtain first the means and variances for each group:

	GROUP 1	GROUP 2	GROUP 3	GROUP 4
$\bar{x}_i$	4	9	4.8	6.5
s_i^2	3.33	4	3.7	3

Now, sum of squares within is given by

$$SS_w = (n_1 - 1)s_1^2 + (n_2 - 1)s_2^2 + \ldots + (n_k - 1)s_k^2$$
$$= 3(3.33) + 2(4) + 4(3.7) + 3(3) = 41.79$$
$$MS_w = SS_w/(N - k) = 41.79/12 = 3.48$$

$SS_b = 4(4 - 5.81)^2 + 3(9 - 5.81)^2 + 5(4.8 - 5.81)^2 + 4(6.5 - 5.81)^2$
$= 50.64$
$MS_b = SS_b/(k - 1) = 50.64/3 = 16.88$

Therefore, $F = MS_b/MS_W = 16.88/3.48 = 4.85$
The critical value at the .05 level is 3.49. Thus, we reject and conclude there is an overall difference among the groups.

7. Recall that the formula for obtaining the intervals is

$$(\bar{x}_i - \bar{x}_j) \pm q_{\alpha;k;N-k} \sqrt{MS_w/n},$$

where q is studentized range statistic (Table D), MS_w is the error term from the ANOVA, and n is the common number of subjects per group.

$$q \sqrt{MS_w/n} = 3.312 \sqrt{22.35/15} = 4.043$$

Now, we obtain the confidence intervals:

GROUPS	CRITICAL VALUE	CONFIDENCE INTERVALS
$\bar{x}_1 - \bar{x}_2 = -1.7$	4.043	(–5.743, 2.343)
$\bar{x}_1 - \bar{x}_3 = 1.5$	4.043	(–2.543, 5.543)
$\bar{x}_1 - \bar{x}_4 = -3.1$	4.043	(–7.143, .943)
$\bar{x}_2 - \bar{x}_3 = 3.2$	4.043	(–.843, 7.243)
$\bar{x}_2 - \bar{x}_4 = -1.4$	4.043	(–5.433, 2.643)
$\bar{x}_3 - \bar{x}_4 = -4.6$	4.043	(–8.643, –.557)

Since the intervals for the first 5 paired comparisons all cover 0, none of these are significant. Only the last paired comparison is significant, since that interval does not cover 0, that is, 0 is not a likely value for $\mu_3 - \mu_4$.

9. The estimate of the contrast is

$$L_2 = (5.6 + 7.3)/2 - (8.1 + 4.2)/2 = .30$$
$$\Sigma c_i^2/n_i = (.5)^2/10 + (.5)^2/8 + (-.5)^2/11 + (-.5)^2/13$$
$$= .098$$
$$F = \frac{(.30)^2/.098}{8.7} < 1$$

Since we have more error variation than effect variation, the contrast is clearly not significant.

11. O'Grady's statement relates to the restriction of range phenomenon you encountered when studying the Pearson correlation in your introductory statistics course. In this case there would undoubtedly be the least amount of variance in heart efficiency to account for in a population of runners (more homogeneous), while a random sample of the American adult population is much more heterogeneous and therefore the potential of accounting for more variance.

13. The form of the control lines for running the analysis is identical to that presented in the chapter. To obtain both the Scheffe and Tukey intervals in one run simply insert in the MEANS statement:

MEANS REGION/SCHEFFE TUKEY;

where REGION is the name I have given to the grouping variable.
(a) There is a significant overall difference at the .05 level, since from the printout we have $F = 3.38$, $p = .0285$.
(b) There are no significant pairwise differences found with the Scheffé procedure, while a significant pairwise difference, between Groups 1 and 4, is found with the Tukey procedure.
c) The Scheffé is a more conservative procedure than Tukey, and is not as powerful for detecting pairwise differences.

15. (a) The 5 comparisons are given schematically:

	KEYWORD	EXPERIENTAL	PICTURE	CONTROL
$L1$	1	0	0	−1
$L2$	1	0	−1	0
$L3$	1	−1	0	0
$L4$	0	0	1	−1
$L5$	0	1	0	−1

(b) First of all, note that the set of 5 comparisons must have dependencies since there are only 3 degrees of freedom between, and hence at most 3 independent comparisons. If we compute the sum of products for $L1$ and $L2$ we find

$$1(1) + 0(0) + 0(-1) + (-1)(0) = 1$$

Therefore, there is a dependency for $L1$ and $L2$.
(c) Since the group sizes are equal ($n = 16$), the error term (MS_w) for each contrast is simply the average of the group variances. Therefore,

$$MS_w = \frac{(22.9)^2 + (27)^2 + (23.1)^2 + (25.6)^2}{4} = 610.6$$

Recall from page 68 that if the group sizes are equal, then the F statistic for testing a contrast for significance is

$$F = \frac{n\hat{L}^2/\Sigma c_i^2}{MS_w}$$

Keyword Versus Control

$$F = \frac{16(72.3 - 48.7)^2/2}{610.6} = 7.2972 \implies t = 2.701$$

Keyword Versus Picture

$$F = \frac{16(72.3 - 42.4)^2/2}{610.6} = 11.713 \implies t = 3.42$$

Keyword Versus Experiental

$$F = \frac{16(72.3 - 36.2)^2/2}{610.6} = 17.074 \implies T = 4.132$$

17. (a) The null hypothesis is $\mu_1 = \mu_2 = \mu_3$. It is rejected at the .10 level since $F = 3.115$ and $p = .053$.
(b) The Levene test is not significant at the .05 level, since $p = .766$.
(c) For the Tukey procedure at the .10 level, only Groups 1 and 3 are significantly different.

SELECTED PRINTOUT FROM SPSS FOR WINDOWS 8.0

Oneway

Descriptives

		N	Mean	Std. Deviation	Std. Error	95% Confidence Interval for Mean	
						Lower Bound	Upper Bound
FREEDIST GP	1.00	21	8.3019	2.0796	.4538	7.3553	9.2485
	2.00	17	8.8624	1.9765	.4794	7.8461	9.8786
	3.00	13	10.2300	2.6396	.7321	8.6349	11.8251
	Total	51	8.9802	2.2927	.3210	8.3354	9.6250

Test of Homogeneity of Variances

	Levene Statistic	df1	df2	Sig.
FREEDIST	.267	2	48	.766

ANOVA

		Sum of Squares	df	Mean Square	F	Sig.
FREEDIST	Between Groups	30.204	2	15.102	3.116	.053
	Within Groups	232.612	48	4.846		
	Total	262.816	50			

Post Hoc Tests

Multiple Comparisons

Dependent Variable: FREEDIST
Tukey HSD

(I) GP	(J) GP	Mean Difference (I-J)	Std. Error	Sig.	90% Confidence Interval	
					Lower Bound	Upper Bound
1.00	2.00	-.5604	.718	.717	-2.0704	.9496
	3.00	-1.9281*	.777	.043	-3.5614	-.2948
2.00	1.00	.5604	.718	.717	-.9496	2.0704
	3.00	-1.3676	.811	.221	-3.0729	.3376
3.00	1.00	1.9281*	.777	.043	.2948	3.5614
	2.00	1.3676	.811	.221	-.3376	3.0729

*. The mean difference is significant at the .10 level.

19. (a) $1 - (1 - \alpha')^3 = 1 - (1 - 3\alpha' + 3\alpha'^2 - \alpha'^3) = 3\alpha' - 3\alpha'^2 + \alpha'^3$
    (b) $3\alpha' = 3(.01) = .03$
         $3\alpha' - 3\alpha'^2 + \alpha'^3 = 3(.01) - 3(.01)^2 + (.01)^3 = .0297$

What we have shown is that the two quantities are approximately the same for small α.

CHAPTER 3

1.

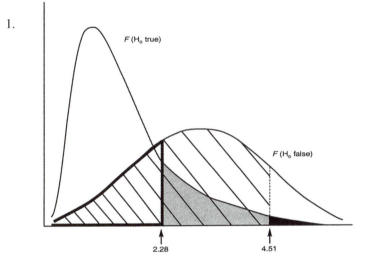

We have shown that as Type I error decreases (from light shaded area to dark shaded), Type II error increases (from boldfaced lined area to the total lined area).

3. In doing a two-tail test, say at .05, the alpha level is divided into two equal portions of .025. Thus, in effect we are working at a more severe alpha level, and therefore we will have less power for the two tailed test.

5. Using the formula for effect size, $\hat{d} = t\sqrt{(1/n_1 + 1/n_2)}$, we obtain

(a) Study	$\hat{d}_i$
1	.69
2	.72
3	.56
4	.37
5	.89
6	.67
8	.48
9	.93

(b) The vast majority of the studies (8 of 10) show medium to large effect sizes, which would undoubtedly be of practical significance. Yet in 7 of the 8 cases, significance was not found because of a power problem (small to very small group sizes). There is systematic evidence to document the superiority of the combined treatment.

7. To estimate power we first find the estimated effect size $\hat{f}$, from $\hat{f} = \sqrt{(k-1)F/N} = \sqrt{4(2.03)/125} = .255$

Now, using Table C.4, with $f = .25$ and $n = 25$, we find that power = .58. To obtain power at $\alpha = .10$, we use Table C.8 and find that power = .71.

9. (a) $\hat{f} = \sqrt{3(5.61)/800} = .145$. Now, using Table C.3 with $f = .15$ and an average group size of 200 we find that power = .96.

(b) These results do not appear to have any practical significance. First, the effect size is small. Secondly, look at the size of the mean differences (for a scale which has a range from 10 to 50). The mean differences for all pairs of groups, except Jewish and Protestant 2, are about 2 or less. These are trivial differences on a scale with a range of 40.

11. Below is the PASS 6.0 printout.

Power does not become adequate for any of the sample sizes. Note that at the .05 level the power is only .34 even with 120 subjects per group! Also, even at the .10 level, the power is just .4626 with 120 subjects per group.

SELECTED PRINTOUT FROM PASS 6.0

Numeric Results for Two-Sample T-Test
Null Hypothesis: Mean1=Mean2   Alternative Hypothesis: Mean1<>Mean2
The sigmas were assumed to be known and equal. The N's were forced to be equal.

Power	N1	N2	Alpha	Beta	Mean1	Mean2	Sigma1	Sigma2
0.02665	20	20	0.01000	0.97335	0.00	0.20	1.00	1.00
0.04660	40	40	0.01000	0.95340	0.00	0.20	1.00	1.00
0.09500	80	80	0.01000	0.90500	0.00	0.20	1.00	1.00
0.15231	120	120	0.01000	0.84769	0.00	0.20	1.00	1.00
0.09694	20	20	0.05000	0.90306	0.00	0.20	1.00	1.00
0.14547	40	40	0.05000	0.85453	0.00	0.20	1.00	1.00
0.24414	80	80	0.05000	0.75586	0.00	0.20	1.00	1.00
0.34085	120	120	0.05000	0.65915	0.00	0.20	1.00	1.00
0.16706	20	20	0.10000	0.83294	0.00	0.20	1.00	1.00
0.23205	40	40	0.10000	0.76795	0.00	0.20	1.00	1.00
0.35380	80	80	0.10000	0.64620	0.00	0.20	1.00	1.00
0.46260	120	120	0.10000	0.53740	0.00	0.20	1.00	1.00

CHAPTER 4

1. A fourth advantage of a factorial design is that it can help to increase the generalizability of results. For example, suppose we had compared 3 treatments in a one way ANOVA and found a significant difference. Someone then says to us

that the relative efficacy of treatments might depend on the sex of the subjects, and we run a factorial ANOVA (sex by treatments) to check this out. If we had adequate power and the interaction effect is not significant, we can generalize our results.

3. The control lines for running Problem 2 are as follows:

```
DATA TWOWAY;
INPUT AGE TREAT DEP @@;
CARDS;
1 1 21   1 1 27   1 1 23   1 1 28   1 1 20
1 2 24   1 2 32   1 2 30   1 2 35   1 2 32
1 3 19   1 3 30   1 3 27   1 3 20   1 3 21
2 1 18   2 1 25   2 1 27   2 1 20   2 1 23
2 2 24   2 2 16   2 2 18   2 2 19   2 2 20
2 3 34   2 3 28   2 3 21   2 3 30   2 3 29
PROC PRINT;
PROC GLM;
CLASS AGE TREAT;
MODEL DEP=AGE TREAT AGE*TREAT;
MEANS AGE TREAT AGE*TREAT;
```

Selected printout from the above run is given below:

SOURCE	DF	TYPE I SS	F VALUE	PR > F	TYPE III SS
AGE	1	45.63333	2.82	.1063	45.63333
TREAT	2	37.80000	1.17	.3284	37.80000
AGE*TREAT	2	334.06667	10.31	.0006	334.06667

Notice that the Type I and Type III sums of squares are the same, as they always will be for equal cell size factorial ANOVA. The F values will also be the same, and are not repeated twice here. If we had decided to test each effect at the .05 level, then only the interaction effect is significant, since only that p value is less than .05.

5. (a) $f_B = \sqrt{2 \cdot 5.57/24} = .681$

The n needed to enter the table is

$$n_B = [(N - rc)/c] + 1 = [(24 - 6)/3] + 1 = 7$$

Now, using Table C.6 and $f = .70$ (since our estimated effect size is very close to this value), we find that power is .86. Actually, if we had interpolated power would be slightly less, but the main point here is that power for detecting the reinforcement main effect was quite good.

(b) $\hat{f}_{AB} = \sqrt{2 \cdot 1.87/24} = .395$

The n needed to enter the table is

$$n_{AB} = \frac{(N - rc)}{(r - 1)(c - 1) + 1} + 1 = \frac{(24 - 6)}{(2 - 1)(3 - 1) + 1} + 1 = 7$$

(c) Given that Pukulski had less than a 50% chance of detecting a large interaction effect, the study should be replicated with larger sample size for more adequate power. Using Table C.6, we see that for $f = .40$, power is only .45.

7. (a) For each dependent variable in a two-way design, there are 3 statistical tests (2 main effects and interaction effects). Since 5 two-way ANOVAs were done, this means $5(3) = 15$ statistical tests were done.
(b) Upper bound on overall α is $1 - (1 - .05)^{15} = 1 - .463 = .537$.
(c) The investigator should be quite cautious, since the probability of at least a few spurious rejections is very high.

9. (a) We present below the rearranged means from the printout on p. 132, along with the row, column, and grand means, and the estimated interaction effects:

		TREATMENT		ROW MEANS
	6.5	7.8333	8.3333	7.5556
	(−.1667)	(.5)	(−.3333)	
AGE				
	8.8333	8.8333	11	9.5556
	(.1667)	(−.5)	(.3333)	
COLUMN MEANS	7.6667	8.3333	9.6667	8.5556 (GRAND MEAN)

$$SS = 6[2(.0278) + 2(.25) + 2(.1111)] = 6(.7778) = 4.6668$$

(b) We follow the same process as above for calculating the sex by age sum of squares:

	AGE		ROW MEANS
	7.5556	9.6667	8.6112
	(−.0556)	(.0556)	
SEX			
	7.5556	9.4444	8.5000
	(.0556)	(−.0556)	
COLUMN MEANS	7.5556	9.5556	8.5556 (GRAND MEAN)

$$SS = 9[4(.00309)] = .1112$$

(c) $SS_{age} = 18 [(7.5556 - 8.5556)^2 + (9.5556 - 8.5556)^2] = 36$

11. The n to enter Cohen's tables for the treatment main effect is given by $n = [(90 - 9)/3] + 1 = 28$. The power at .05 is .52 and power at .10 is .65 (here $u = 2$, since there are 2 df for treatment). Thus, power is still not quite adequate, even at the .10 level of significance. For the interaction effect, the n to enter the table is $n = [(90 - 9)/(4 + 1)] + 1 = 17$ (approx.). The degrees of freedom for interaction here is $(3 - 1)(3 - 1) = 4$, which recall is u in Cohen's tables. Thus, power = .40 at .05 and .54 at .10. Assuming power would increase roughly by the same amount (.14), in going from $\alpha = .10$ to $\alpha = .15$, we estimate that power would be about .68 at $\alpha = .15$.

13. (a) The significant dynamism and warmth and acceptance interaction effects indicate that the principals rate more versus less effective teachers differentially on each of this traits, depending on the level of schooling.
    (b) The cell means for dynamism and warmth and acceptance are

	DYNAMISM		WARMTH & ACCEPT.	
	MORE EFF	LESS EFF	MORE EFF	LESS EFF
ELEM	25.7	28.9	39.3	23.9
INTERM	27.9	22.8	35.6	26.5
SENIOR	28.2	17.6	31.7	26.7

Note that the means for dynamism increased (for the more effective teachers) as the school level of the principal increases, and decreased for the less effective teachers, as the authors hypothesized. Recall that an interaction can be thought of as a difference in the differences, and here those differences are −3.2, 5.1, and 10.6.

Regarding warmth and acceptance, the difference in means for more and less effective teachers is sharpest for the elementary principals and decreases in size as the level of the principal increases (as the authors had hypothesized). The differences are 15.4, 9.1, and 5.

(c) Basically half of their hypotheses were confirmed, that is, that warmth and acceptance and dynamism would be important in distinguishing more versus less effective teachers. However, they also hypothesized that creativity would discriminate for elementary school principals, while organized demeanor would be important for intermediate and high school principals, and neither of these was confirmed. As a matter of fact, the discrepancy between more versus less effective teachers on creativity is sharpest for the senior-level principals. On organized demeanor the means for elementary, intermediate, and high school principals are 34.8, 36.8, and 36.3.

(d) To check which pairs of means on organized demeanor are significantly different one should use the Tukey procedure. You will find that there are no significant differences.

15. (a) From the printout the following effects are significant at the .01 level: SEX ($F = 22.067$, $p = .000$), TREAT ($F = 8.685$, $p = .001$) and SEX*TREAT ($F = 6.034$, $p = .005$)

(b) From the marginal means, it is clear that males (if males are coded as 1) did better than females, and that Treatment 2 was the best (assuming higher is better). However, the interaction tells us that things are more complicated, and an examination of the SEX*TREAT means reveals that males do particularly well with Treatment 2.

Tests of Between-Subjects Effects

Dependent Variable: DEP

Source	Type III Sum of Squares	df	Mean Square	F	Sig.
Corrected Model	655.729[a]	11	59.612	5.125	.000
Intercept	17518.521	1	17518.521	1506.070	.000
AGE	11.021	1	11.021	.947	.337
SEX	256.688	1	256.688	22.067	.000
TREAT	202.042	2	101.021	8.685	.001
AGE * SEX	28.521	1	28.521	2.452	.126
AGE * TREAT	10.042	2	5.021	.432	.653
SEX * TREAT	140.375	2	70.188	6.034	.005
AGE * SEX * TREAT	7.042	2	3.521	.303	.741
Error	418.750	36	11.632		
Total	18593.000	48			
Corrected Total	1074.479	47			

a. R Squared = .610 (Adjusted R Squared = .491)

Estimated Marginal Means

1. AGE

Dependent Variable: DEP

AGE	Mean	Std. Error	95% Confidence Interval	
			Lower Bound	Upper Bound
1.00	18.625	.696	17.213	20.037
2.00	19.583	.696	18.171	20.995

2. SEX

Dependent Variable: DEP

SEX	Mean	Std. Error	95% Confidence Interval	
			Lower Bound	Upper Bound
1.00	21.417	.696	20.005	22.829
2.00	16.792	.696	15.380	18.204

3. TREAT

Dependent Variable: DEP

TREAT	Mean	Std. Error	95% Confidence Interval	
			Lower Bound	Upper Bound
1.00	17.812	.853	16.083	19.542
2.00	22.000	.853	20.271	23.729
3.00	17.500	.853	15.771	19.229

4. AGE * SEX

Dependent Variable: DEP

AGE	SEX	Mean	Std. Error	95% Confidence Interval Lower Bound	95% Confidence Interval Upper Bound
1.00	1.00	20.167	.985	18.170	22.163
	2.00	17.083	.985	15.087	19.080
2.00	1.00	22.667	.985	20.670	24.663
	2.00	16.500	.985	14.503	18.497

5. AGE * TREAT

Dependent Variable: DEP

AGE	TREAT	Mean	Std. Error	95% Confidence Interval Lower Bound	95% Confidence Interval Upper Bound
1.00	1.00	17.625	1.206	15.179	20.071
	2.00	21.875	1.206	19.429	24.321
	3.00	16.375	1.206	13.929	18.821
2.00	1.00	18.000	1.206	15.554	20.446
	2.00	22.125	1.206	19.679	24.571
	3.00	18.625	1.206	16.179	21.071

6. SEX * TREAT

Dependent Variable: DEP

SEX	TREAT	Mean	Std. Error	95% Confidence Interval Lower Bound	95% Confidence Interval Upper Bound
1.00	1.00	18.000	1.206	15.554	20.446
	2.00	26.375	1.206	23.929	28.821
	3.00	19.875	1.206	17.429	22.321
2.00	1.00	17.625	1.206	15.179	20.071
	2.00	17.625	1.206	15.179	20.071
	3.00	15.125	1.206	12.679	17.571

7. AGE * SEX * TREAT

Dependent Variable: DEP

AGE	SEX	TREAT	Mean	Std. Error	95% Confidence Interval Lower Bound	95% Confidence Interval Upper Bound
1.00	1.00	1.00	17.500	1.705	14.042	20.958
		2.00	25.000	1.705	21.542	28.458
		3.00	18.000	1.705	14.542	21.458
	2.00	1.00	17.750	1.705	14.292	21.208
		2.00	18.750	1.705	15.292	22.208
		3.00	14.750	1.705	11.292	18.208
2.00	1.00	1.00	18.500	1.705	15.042	21.958
		2.00	27.750	1.705	24.292	31.208
		3.00	21.750	1.705	18.292	25.208
	2.00	1.00	17.500	1.705	14.042	20.958
		2.00	16.500	1.705	13.042	19.958
		3.00	15.500	1.705	12.042	18.958

17. Below is selected printout from SPSS for Windows 8.0. From the table we can see that none of the effects are significant at the .05 level.

General Linear Model

Descriptive Statistics

	SEX	GRADE	Mean	Std. Deviation	N
CHGMATH	1.00	3.00	.7500	1.3887	8
		4.00	-.3750	2.7223	8
		5.00	.0000	1.1547	4
		6.00	.5556	1.9437	9
		Total	.2759	1.9438	29
	2.00	3.00	-.4545	1.8635	11
		4.00	-.3750	1.4079	8
		5.00	-.3333	.5000	9
		6.00	.0000	2.0548	10
		Total	-.2895	1.5580	38
	Total	3.00	5.263E-02	1.7472	19
		4.00	-.3750	2.0936	16
		5.00	-.2308	.7250	13
		6.00	.2632	1.9676	19
		Total	-4.5E-02	1.7445	67

Levene's Test of Equality of Error Variances[a]

	F	df1	df2	Sig.
CHGMATH	1.368	7	59	.236

Tests the null hypothesis that the error variance of the dependent variable is equal across groups.

a. Design: Intercept+SEX+GRADE+SEX * GRADE

Tests of Between-Subjects Effects

Dependent Variable: CHGMATH

Source	Type III Sum of Squares	df	Mean Square	F	Sig.	Noncent. Parameter	Observed Power[a]
Corrected Model	12.666[b]	7	1.809	.567	.779	3.971	.224
Intercept	5.199E-02	1	5.199E-02	.016	.899	.016	.052
SEX	4.221	1	4.221	1.323	.255	1.323	.205
GRADE	4.424	3	1.475	.462	.710	1.387	.138
SEX * GRADE	3.320	3	1.107	.347	.791	1.041	.114
Error	188.199	59	3.190				
Total	201.000	67					
Corrected Total	200.866	66					

a. Computed using alpha = .05

b. R Squared = .063 (Adjusted R Squared = -.048)

CHAPTER 5

1. UNIVARIATE REPEATED MEASURES ANALYSIS

		TREATMENTS				ROW
		1	2	3	4	MEANS
	1	5	6	2	5	4.5
	2	3	4	1	6	3.5
	3	3	7	4	10	6.0
$S's$	4	6	8	3	3	5.0
	5	4	9	7	8	7.0
	6	5	7	4	9	6.25
	7	2	10	1	2	3.75
	8	4	3	2	5	3.50
		4	6.75	3	6	4.9375 (GRAND MEAN)

$$SS_b = 8[(4 - 4.9375)^2 + (6.75 - 4.9375)^2 + (3 - 4.9375)^2 + (6 - 4.9375)^2]$$
$$= 72.374$$
$$MS_b = 72.374/3 = 24.125$$

$$SS_w = \quad 12 \quad + \quad 39.5 \quad + \quad 28 \quad + \quad 56$$
$$\text{sum of squares for} \quad \text{Treat 1} \quad \text{Treat 2} \quad \text{Treat 3} \quad \text{Treat 4}$$
$$SS_w = 135.5$$

SUM OF SQUARES FOR BLOCKS

$$SS_{bl} = 4[(4.5 - 4.9375)^2 + (3.5 - 4.9375)^2 + \ldots + (3.5 - 4.9375)^2]$$
$$= 51.375$$
$$SS_{res} = 135.5 - 51.375 = 84.125$$
$$MS_{res} = 84.125/21 = 4.006$$
$$F = 24.125/4.006 = 6.022$$

(a) The critical value at the .05 level, on 3 and 21 degrees of freedom, is 3.07. Therefore, we have a significant overall difference.

(b) Tukey post hoc procedure—The critical value against which each mean difference is to be compared is

$$q_{.05;4,21} \sqrt{MS_{res}/n} = 3.95\sqrt{4.006/8} = 2.795$$

The only mean differences that exceed 2.795 in absolute value are for Groups 2 and 3, and Groups 3 and 4. Thus, these are the only pairs of groups that are significantly different at the .05 level with the Tukey procedure.

3. (a) First, we compute the basic quantities that are to be plugged into the formula:

$$\bar{s}_{ii} = (76.8 + 42.8 + 64)/3 = 61.2$$

This is the average of the diagonal elements.

$$\bar{s} = (76.8 + 53.2 + 69 + 53.2 + \ldots + 47 + 64)/9 = 58$$

This is the average of all the elements in the covariance matrix.

$$\Sigma s_{ij}^2 = 76.8^2 + 53.2^2 + 69^2 + \ldots + 47^2 + 64^2 = 31426.56$$

This is just the sum of all the squared elements in the matrix.
(b) $\bar{s}_i =$ these are the row averages
$\bar{s}_1 = (76.8 + 53.2 + 69)/3 = 66.333$
$\bar{s}_2 = (53.2 + 42.8 + 47)/3 = 47.667$
$\bar{s}_3 = (69 + 47 + 64)/3 = 60$

$$\hat{\varepsilon} = \frac{9(61.2 - 58)^2}{2[31426.56 - 6(10272.21) + 9(3364)]} = .6649$$

(c) Recall that the min $\varepsilon = 1/(k - 1)$, where k is the number of levels for the repeated measures factor. Since $k = 3$ here, it follows that min $\varepsilon = 1/(3 - 1) = .50$.
(d) For the design, there were two groups, with eight subjects per group, and five repeated measures. Thus we have $g = 2$, $n = 8$ and $k = 5$. Therefore,

$$\tilde{\varepsilon} = \frac{8(2)(4)(.44629) - 2}{4[2(7) - 4(.44629)]} = \frac{26.56256}{48.85936} = .54365$$

5. Below we present selected printout which gives the F tests for the contrasts and the associated p values:

VARIABLE	HYPOTH. MS	ERROR MS	F	SIG OF F
HELMERT1	24.29999	2.76889	8.77608	.016
HELMERT2	16.53750	1.08639	15.22245	.004
HELMERT3	.00050	.18272	.00274	.959

If overall α is set at .10, then each contrast is being tested at the .10/3 = .0333 level of significance. Thus, the first two Helmert contrasts are significant.

The first Helmert contrast is testing whether the control group differs from the remaining 3 groups (the three treatment or drug groups here), while the second Helmert contrast is testing whether the effect of Drug Type I differs from that of the two remaining drugs (which were similar in composition).

CHAPTER 6

1. (a) There definitely does appear to be a linear relationship.

(c) There is not a pattern in the residuals, which indicates a linear model is appropriate (see Fig. A.3).

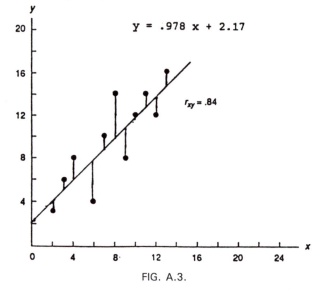

FIG. A.3.

3. (a) If x_1 enters the equation first, it will account for $(.60)^2 \times 100$, or 36% of the variance on y.

(b) To determine how much variance on y predictor x_1 will account for if entered second we need to partial out x_2. Hence we compute the following semi partial correlation:

$$r_{y1.2(s)} = \frac{r_{y1} - r_{y2}\, r_{12}}{\sqrt{1 - r_{12}^2}}$$

$$= \frac{.60 - .50(.80)}{\sqrt{1 - (.8)^2}} = .33$$

$$r_{y1.2(s)}^2 = (.33)^2 = .1089$$

Thus, x_1 accounts for about 11% of the variance if entered second.

(c) Since x_1 and x_2 are strongly correlated (multicollinearity), when a predictor enters the equation influences greatly how much variance it will account for. Here when x_1 entered first it accounted for 36% of variance, while it only accounted for 11% when entered second.

5. (a) For STEPWISE regression the model selected has SIZE, NEW and NO-BATH as predictors.

(b) For BACKWARD elimination the same model is selected.

7.

```
TITLE 'USING FIXED FORMAT AND TESTING SET OF PREDICTORS'.
DATA LIST FIXED/X1 1 X2 2 X3 3-4 X4 5-6 X5 7-8 X6 9-11(2) X7 12-14
   X8 15-16.
BEGIN DATA.
DATA LINES
END DATA.
LIST.
REGRESSION VARIABLES=X1 TO X8/
  DEPENDENT=X8/
  ENTER X1 X2/TEST(X3 X4 X5)/.
```

CHAPTER 7

1. (a) ANCOVA is appropriate since there is a significant linear relationship ($p = .000$) and the homogeneity of regression slopes assumption is tenable ($p = .521$).

(b) We do reject the hypothesis of equal adjusted means since $F = 8.61$ with $p = .001$.

(c) The error terms are related by the equation:

$$MS_w \; MS_w \, (1 - r_{xy}^2)$$

3. The error term for the ANCOVA is considerably smaller: 111.72 versus 139.98 for the ANOVA on the difference scores. The regression coefficient from the ANCOVA is .69876. In 5.10 it was stated that, ". . . whenever, the regression coefficient is not equal to 1, the error term for ANCOVA will be smaller than that for the gain score analysis and hence the ANCOVA will be a more sensitive or powerful analysis of variance assumption since the cell sizes were approximately equal, and ANOVA is known to be robust in this situation.

From 4.6, the relationship between the interaction effect size and the test statistic is given by

$$\hat{f} = \sqrt{(r-1)(c-1)\ F/N}$$

Therefore, $\hat{f} = \sqrt{(2-1)(2-1)\ 4.49/34} = .3634$

The effect size is fairly large. The n that we would use to enter Cohen's power tables is

$$n = [(N - rc)/(r-1)(c-1) + 1] + 1$$
$$n = [(34 - 4)/(2-1)(2-1) + 1] + 1 = 16$$

Since the degrees of freedom for interaction here is 1, we use Table C.1 and find that power is around .50. Thus, although power was not good in this study, nevertheless significance was found.

5. The fact that the correlation is .61 and that the homogeneity of slopes assumption is tenable means that ANCOVA is appropriate. The grand mean for the study (assuming equal n per group) is 110. Therefore, when the means on the dependent variable are adjusted they will be drawn much closer together, causing a much smaller mean sum of squares between and the loss of significance. The mean of 70 for Group 1 will be adjusted downward (perhaps to a value of 67) while the mean for Group 2 will be adjusted upward (perhaps to a value of 63). Thus, the adjusted means for the 3 groups would be 67, 63, and 65.

Author Index

A

Agresti, A. 250
Anderson, N. 321
Anscombe, F. 247

B

Barcikowski, R. 79, 211
Becker, B. 126
Bloom, B. 77
Bock, R. D. 75, 204, 233
Box, G. P. 210
Brown, M. B. 91
Bryan, J. L. 200
Bryant, J. 327
Bryk, A. 77, 323

C

Carlson, J. 165
Chase, C. 181, 182
Cochran, W. 307
Cohen, J. 91, 95, 124, 125, 137, 139, 188, 255, 279, 289
Collier, R. 211
Cook, R. 246, 282
Cradler, J. 168
Cronbach, L. 127, 146, 171

Crowder, R. 276
Crystal, G. 250

D

Dance, K. A. 146
Daniels, R. 147, 166
Davidson, M. 211
Dizney, R. 254
Draper, N. 251, 270
Dunnett, C. 86, 87

E, F

Elashoff, J. 225, 307, 323
Fishbach, N. 248
Fisher, R. 66
Frane, J. 186

G

Games, P. 91
Glass, G. 75, 78, 97, 204
Glassnapp, D. 242, 324
Greenhouse, S. 210

H

Hand, D. J. 163

Subject Index

421